THE CAPTAIN'S KEYS

THE FOUR PEOPLE EVERY SUCCESSFUL LEADER NEEDS

JEFF MAINS

Author: Jeff Mains
Title: The Captain's Keys
ISBN: 978-1-953313-01-0
Category: Business and Economics/Leadership

Publisher: Champion Books LLC
2300 McDermott Rd, Ste 200-322
Plano, TX 75025
ChampionBooks.com

DEDICATION

To my Anchor, Crew, Navigator,
and so many Champions over the years—
you made this voyage possible.

CONTENTS

HOW TO NAVIGATE THIS BOOK

Welcome aboard, Captain! Unlike traditional leadership books, "The Captain's Keys" puts you at the helm of your learning expedition. As you'll discover, great leadership isn't about having all the answers – it's about making deliberate choices with the information available.

This book mirrors that reality.
At the end of each chapter, you'll face a navigation decision:

SAIL THE STORY – Follow the narrative journey of Captain Jimmy *Beyond the Storm* and witness leadership principles in action through story. These sections reveal the human dynamics of leadership through an engaging tale that will resonate with your own experiences.

STUDY THE MAPS – Dive directly into frameworks, research, and practical applications. These sections provide clear, actionable guidance you can implement immediately for yourself and with your team.

FULL JOURNEY – Experience both the narrative and the frameworks in parallel together for the most comprehensive understanding.

The beauty of this approach?
Just as in leadership, there's no single "right" path.

Some people love novels, adventure and inspiration through story.
Others prefer "just the facts" practical tools and examples to implement quickly.

Right Brain.
Left Brain.
Both.

This is for you. The book adapts to your preferences and needs in the moment while ensuring you ultimately discover all four keys to transformative leadership.

The choice is yours - what kind of journey will you choose?

☸ NAVIGATE

Study the Maps / Full Journey - Continue on to the next page

To Start the Story - Sail on to page 31

Someday

INTRODUCTION

The Captain's Dilemma

The alarm blared at 4:30 a.m., jolting Sarah from a fitful sleep. She reached for her phone, squinting at the screen. Three missed calls, seventeen unread emails, and a calendar that looked like a game of Tetris gone wrong. She sighed, swinging her legs over the side of the bed. Another day at the helm of her startup, a new day of navigating the unpredictable waves of entrepreneurship.

As she shuffled to the kitchen for her first cup of coffee. Black. No time for cream. Sarah couldn't shake the feeling that she was drowning.

This is leadership's dirty little secret. The part nobody talks about at conferences.

She stares out the window. The city sleeps. But, captains, they don't get that luxury.

The weight settles on her shoulders. Every decision. Every failure. Every success.

All hers to bear.

Alone.

Sarah's eyes drift to a family photo on the fridge. Her daughter's recital is tonight. She promised she'd be there. But that investors' meeting . . . She sighs, a familiar guilt gnawing at her insides. When did success start to feel like failure?

As she rushes out the door, already late, Sarah wonders: How much longer can she keep this up?

The mounting pressures and expectations Sarah faces aren't unique. Across town, three other leaders face their own battles.

Jay stares at his computer screen, frustration etched on his face. His software is brilliant. Game-changing, even. But sales? Barely a trickle. Some days it feels like he can't even give it away.

He's exhausted every contact, every lead. Cold calls. Emails. Social media blasts.

Nothing.

We're the world's best-kept secret, he thinks bitterly. This is light years ahead of any competitor, but what good is the best product if no one knows about it?

Jay feels the walls closing in. It's not really his fault. What did he expect anyway? He's a tech genius, not a sales guy. But who else can tell his story? Who else can open those doors?

He glances at the photo of his team, all bright smiles and optimism from their launch day. They believed in him, in his vision. Now, their futures hang in the balance, weighing on his shoulders.

Jay's hand hovers over his phone. Another day of rejection ahead. He swallows hard, fighting the urge to just . . . give up. To admit that maybe, just maybe, he's not cut out for this. But giving up means letting everyone down. It means the dream dies, and a little piece of him with it. OK, a big piece.

So he picks up the phone. One more call. One more rejection. One step closer to . . . what? Success or failure? He's not sure anymore. It's a grind, no doubt about it, but he's determined not to give up.

Seven blocks over on the 32nd floor of an artistically beautiful green glass tower, Renee paces her office. Whiteboards covered in flowcharts and projections surround her.

Her company is growing. Scaling up. Rapidly. New markets. New products. New challenges.

It should feel like winning. Instead, it feels like wading through an alligator-filled swamp.

Every decision seems to spawn ten more. Each choice, every step forward, reveals hidden dangers lurking beneath.

She's navigated her company this far. But this? This is uncharted territory.

Renee stares at the decisions before her. Each path, a leap of faith.

She's never felt so alone.

Her eyes land on the latest financial projections. The numbers are good. Great, even. But with growth comes complexity. More employees look to her for direction. More stakeholders demand results. More competitors eye her market share.

Renee's mind races with questions. Should they expand internationally now or wait? Is it time to pivot their product line for a new market? How can they maintain their culture as they scale?

She closes her eyes and takes a deep breath. The weight of every decision, every potential consequence, presses down on her. The right next step will propel growth, but one wrong move could undo years of hard work. She's come so far, but now . . . now she feels more lost than ever.

In a suburban home office, Will winces as he shifts in his chair. The pain is getting worse.

His doctor's words echo in his head. "You've got to slow down. Delegate more. Your condition is progressing. It's treatable now, but this level of stress is killing you."

Will almost laughs. Slow down? In this economy? With the board breathing down his neck?

"Not a chance," he thinks, trying to smother the advice under layers of self-assurance.

He pops another painkiller. Washes it down with cold coffee.

No one can know. They'd see it as weakness. A chink in the armor.

Someday, he thinks, this'll make a great story of perseverance.

If he survives to tell it.

Will glances at a text from his wife. "Don't forget dinner with the kids tonight. You promised."

He closes his eyes, guilt and frustration warring inside him. He wants to be there. He should be there. But the quarterly report is due, investors are getting antsy, and he's pretty sure his CFO is eyeing his job.

The pain in his back flares again, a stark reminder of the toll this life is taking. But what choice does he have? Leaders push through. They don't show weakness. They don't let people down.

Will opens his eyes and stares at his reflection in the computer screen. The man looking back seems older and tired. A stranger. When did that happen?

He picks up his phone to cancel dinner. Again. The kids will understand. They have to.

Right?

Different titles. Different industries. Same crushing weight.

Sound familiar?

This is the Captain's Dilemma – the brutal paradox at the heart of leadership that nobody talks about at conferences:

The higher you rise, the more you need clarity, yet the less likely you are to get it. The more responsibility you carry, the more support you require, yet the fewer people you can turn to. The greater your impact, the more perspective becomes critical, yet the more isolated your view becomes.

It's not just loneliness at the top. It's a structural trap. A design flaw in how we've built the very concept of leadership.

Most captains don't sink because of external storms. They capsize under the weight of this dilemma–trying to navigate complex waters while simultaneously bearing the full weight of command alone.

In offices and home studies across the globe, leaders wake up to this reality every day. They step into the arena, expected to have all the answers, make all the right moves.

The seas of business are choppy. Market shifts. Tech disruptions. Global crises.

And there you are. At the top of the org chart. Expected to navigate it all with unwavering confidence and clarity.

Solo.

When was the last time you felt that weight?

Was it this morning when you stared at the ceiling before your alarm went off?

Was it yesterday when you smiled confidently through the board meeting while your stomach churned with doubt?

Was it last week when you made that decision that affected fifty families, with no one to truly talk it through with?

I see you, Captain. I've been where you are.

The question isn't whether you face this dilemma. The question is what you're going to do about it.

The siren song beckons. Irresistible. Deadly.

Each note draws another founder closer to the whirlpool's vortex. Not because they're naive. Because the song is masterfully composed . . . and we've seen it work.

Who doesn't want to be the lone visionary? The singular genius whose brilliance outshines all others? The captain whose name alone commands respect? LEGENDS!

We don't just hear this song. We hunt for it. We play it on repeat. We build entire mythologies around its melody.

And the vortex spins. Faster. Hungrier. More seductive with each passing ship it claims.

We've all heard the stories - Steve Jobs revolutionizing personal computing from his garage, Elon Musk working 120-hour weeks to keep Tesla afloat, Jeff Bezos sketching out the idea for Amazon on a cross-country drive.

Tales about captains of industry conquering the business world have become modern mythology. They feed into our cultural obsession with rugged individualism, the idea that true success comes from solitary brilliance and sheer willpower.

But here's the kicker:

It's a myth.

A dangerous one.

The reality? Leadership is messy. Nuanced. And managed well, WAY less lonely than those stories would have you believe.

Behind every outfront leader is a team, a squad, a band. A supporting cast of characters playing absolutely crucial roles. Unsung heroes who never make the headlines.

But we don't talk about them. It doesn't fit the narrative.

So we perpetuate the myth. And leaders like Sarah, Jay, Renee, and Will? They internalize it.

Asking for help? Weakness.
Not having all the answers? Failure.
Admitting vulnerability? Career suicide.

The cost?

Staggering.

A study by the National Institute of Mental Health found that 72% of entrepreneurs are directly or indirectly affected by mental health issues, compared to just 48% of non-entrepreneurs. According to Gallup, 45% of entrepreneurs report feeling highly stressed.

The struggles of Sarah, Jay, Renee, and Will aren't just isolated stories. They're manifestations of the same structural flaw in how we've designed leadership itself.

When you look closer, you see these leaders aren't failing because of their personal shortcomings. They're struggling against a leadership model that was built to break them.

A model that expects captains to navigate, steer, maintain, and command all at once. A model that isolates them precisely when they need connection most. A model that tells them to be all things to all people at all times.

But what if there was a different way?

What if the answer isn't trying harder within a broken system? What if the solution is redesigning the system itself?

The toll isn't just personal - it ripples out to affect entire organizations. CEO turnover hit historic highs in 2024, driven by burnout, rising performance pressures, and the disruptive effects of technology and economic uncertainty. Burnout and isolation are pervasive among CEOs, with most reporting significant loneliness and a lack of support, which in turn can hinder performance and increase the risk of leadership exits.

According to Russell Reynolds Associates, CEO exits are at an all-time high. Average CEO tenure plummeted from 8.2 years in 2016 to 6.8 years in early 2025, with some sectors seeing tenures under 3 years. Breakdown, burnout, flame out with nice PR spin.

These aren't just numbers - they represent careers derailed, visions unfulfilled, and companies left adrift. Behind each statistic is a human story. A father, mother, spouse, friend. A person. A leader who tried to do it all. Someone who bought into the myth, and paid the price.

Sarah knows these stats all too well. She's lived them. There was the night she almost quit, sitting alone in her office at 2 AM, staring at a financial report that seemed to spell certain doom for her company. There was the panic attack in the middle of a board meeting, when the weight of expectations felt like it would crush her. There was the missed recital, the forgotten anniversary, the strained relationships that came with prioritizing the business above all else. Not her fault. That's just the current phase. She'll make it up later. Right?

But what if . . .

What if there was a better way?
What if there was another way where leadership didn't feel like drowning?

What if there were a system, a structure, a way of approaching leadership that could transform the experience of being at the helm? What if you could navigate the treacherous waters of business with confidence, knowing you had the right support in place?

This isn't about passing the buck, offloading responsibility, or diminishing your role as a leader. Far from it. It's about maximizing your impact, amplifying your vision, and creating a sustainable model of leadership that doesn't come at the cost of your health, your relationships, or your sanity. Sound good?

Imagine:
Waking up energized, not drained.
Facing challenges with confidence, not dread.
Leading with clarity and purpose, not confusion and burnout.

Sound like fantasy? It's not.

It's achievable but requires a shift. A fundamental rethinking of what leadership means.

That's what this book is about.

We're going to uncover a system. One that's been hiding in plain sight. Used by history's most effective leaders.

A system that, when understood and implemented, doesn't just change how you lead.

It changes how you live.

The secret lies in four specific relationships that create a stability matrix around you - not to diminish your authority, but to enhance it. Not to reduce your control, but to expand your influence. Not to make you less of a leader, but to make you more effective than you ever thought possible.

Ready to rethink everything you know about leadership?

Prepared to challenge the myth of the solo genius?

Willing to embrace a more powerful, more sustainable way of captaining your ship?

Then it's time to set sail.

The journey ahead will challenge you. It'll make you question long-held beliefs. It'll ask you to look at leadership - and yourself - in a whole new light.

But I promise you this:

By the time we reach our destination, you'll never see leadership the same way again.

Here's a map of the voyage ahead:

First, we'll dismantle the lone genius myth. We'll explore how even the most celebrated leaders throughout history and in today's business landscape rely on key support roles to achieve their success.

Next, we'll dive deep into the four key roles that form this revolutionary leadership system. You'll learn to identify these roles in your own life and business. You'll discover how to cultivate relationships that transcend traditional networking.

We'll explore how this system provides stability in our chaotic business world. You'll get strategies for work-life integration that actually work. Techniques for stress management that go beyond "just breathe."

But this isn't just about assembling a team.

It's about fundamentally shifting how you view leadership.

We'll challenge common misconceptions. We'll explore how this new paradigm leads to both professional success and personal fulfillment.

YES! We can have both TODAY.
It's such a waste to wait until "Someday when I [*reach the magic goal*]
... then I'll be happy."
... then I'll work on my health."
... then I'll prioritize my relationships."

Start NOW, not then.
Someday is today.

You'll learn to be not just a recipient of support, but a crucial pillar in others' success stories. We'll discuss the power of reciprocity in leadership. How giving support can be just as transformative as receiving it. Sometimes even more.

Throughout our voyage, you'll hear stories of leaders who've implemented these principles. You'll see the extraordinary impact on their businesses and lives. You'll discover how this system adapts to any industry, any company size, any leadership style.

In fact, once you see it . . . you can't unsee it.

You'll probably start seeing this leadership support system and framework all around you, even in your favorite books and movies.

By journey's end, you'll have a comprehensive roadmap for implementing this system in your own leadership practice. You'll be equipped with practical tools, strategies, and insights to transform your approach.

The seas of business are rough.
But you don't have to navigate them alone.

It's time to assemble your crew.
Chart your course.
Discover the true power of leadership.

Are you ready, Captain?

Your voyage begins now.

Turn the page. Let's set sail towards a new horizon of leadership. One where success doesn't demand your sanity, your relationships, or your soul as payment.

The challenges won't disappear. But armed with what you'll learn in the coming chapters, you'll be better equipped than ever to face them.

That's what we're here to explore.

Welcome aboard, Captain.

Your transformation starts here.

The myth ends now.

Real leadership begins.

Are you ready?

Let's go.

⚙ NAVIGATE

Study the Maps / Full Journey - Continue on to the next page
To Sail the Story - Ride a wave to page 31

LEADERSHIP

KNOW YOUR VESSEL
WHY SOME SHIPS SINK AND OTHERS SAIL

"You can't change the direction of the wind, but you can adjust your sails"
— H. JACKSON BROWN JR

Water has always pulled at the human soul. Whether it's a tranquil pond, a rushing river, a vast lake, or the endless ocean, something about being near water speaks to us at a primal level.

For me, it's the ocean. On it, in it, or underneath, exploring a beautiful alien world that far too few see except on the Discovery Channel. It's my happy place. The ocean seems to call those seeking something more. Maybe that's because, like business, the ocean represents both opportunity and challenge - a delicate balance of power and possibility.

Just as water can be both nurturing and destructive, business leadership requires us to navigate similar dualities. Some days, the waters are calm, everything flows smoothly. Other days, we face storms that test every skill we possess.

Life has a way of serving up perfect moments on these waters. You know the kind - when everything seems to align just right. Like that golden hour just before sunset, when the light makes everything look magical. Business is humming along, the team is performing well, and you find yourself thinking, "This is it. I've made it. Can life get any better than this?"

I remember sitting in my office on a Friday afternoon, wrapping up our best quarter ever. The phone had finally stopped ringing, and the final meeting of the day was done. The last employee had left for the day. The gentle hum of the air conditioning was the only sound as I leaned back in my chair, feet up on the desk, exhausted but taking a few moments to savor a sense of accomplishment.

And at the same time, fighting back the weird question of "Why?"

After all, Monday would just start the mad scramble all over again for a new quarter.

It's in those quiet moments, when the day's chaos subsides, there's often a whisper. A gentle but persistent voice asking, "What if?" What if there's more?

And not just the "more" of beating the last quarterly number or hitting a new milestone. More to business. More to life. More than the pursuit of "more."

What if I'm capable of greater impact?

Am I living out the purpose I was created for? Is there a better way?

What is beyond the horizon that I just can't see from here?

It's the same voice that nudged great explorers out of safe European ports. The voice that pushes leaders to leave cushy corporate jobs and start something new.

A call to the unknown, to adventure, to destiny. The voice that keeps asking:

Is this all there is?

Think of your business as a ship.

Not in some cute, motivational poster way, but in the most practical sense.

It has mass and momentum. It requires constant maintenance. It houses precious cargo - your dreams, your team's livelihoods, your customers' trust, your net worth, your family. And like any ship, it's either moving purposefully toward a destination, drifting with the currents, or stuck in port.

Types of Ships

Walk down any marina and you'll see vessels of every shape and size. Each is designed with a specific purpose in mind.

Speedboats are built for agility and quick maneuvers.
Fishing boats are equipped for hauling in the day's catch.
Cruise ships are designed to carry thousands in comfort.
Container ships move cargo across vast distances.

Each has its strengths. Each has its limitations.

Your business is no different.

Maybe you're like Sarah, running a startup - quick and nimble like a speedboat, able to change direction instantly when you spot an opportunity. You might not have the resources of larger vessels, but you can navigate waters they wouldn't dare enter.

Or perhaps you're more like Jay at the helm of a mid-sized company - like a commercial fishing boat, sturdy and reliable, with established routes and proven methods. You've got the systems in place to weather storms, but you're still agile enough to chase new opportunities when they appear.

Then there are leaders like Renee, steering enterprise-level organizations - the massive container ships of the business world. They can carry incredible loads and weather serious storms, but every course change requires careful planning and precise execution. Try to turn too quickly and you risk capsizing from your own momentum.

Here's the key: No type of ship is inherently better than another.

A speedboat isn't "worse" than a cruise ship – it's just built for a different purpose.

The problems arise when we try to operate our vessel in ways it wasn't designed for. Like when we try to maneuver a cargo ship like a speedboat, or pile a small craft with loads it was never built to carry.

I've seen too many businesses sink because their captains didn't understand what type of ship they were really commanding.

The startup that tried to scale like an enterprise before building proper systems. The established company that tried to pivot like a startup without considering the human cost. The enterprise that tried to maintain startup-style control as it grew, creating bottlenecks that nearly sank it.

At the Helm

Every ship needs a Captain. That's you. And oh boy, does that title carry weight. Not the kind that shows up on business cards or LinkedIn profiles. I'm talking about the real weight - the kind that sits heavy on your shoulders at 3 AM when decisions need to be made and lives depend on getting it right.

I remember my first day as CEO. Walking into that corner office with "Chief Executive Officer" freshly painted on the window. Man, did I feel ready. I had the credentials, the experience, the vision. I was going to change the world, or at least our little corner of it.

Funny how life has a way of humbling those grand ambitions, isn't it?

Here's what they don't tell you in business school: The higher you rise in an organization, the harder it becomes to see what's really happening.

You've got the best view of the horizon, but you're often the last to know about the leak in the engine room. It's like being in a glass tower - spectacular view, but surprisingly isolated.

This creates what I call the "Captain's Dilemma" - three challenges that every leader faces:

First, there's the **Visibility Paradox**. Everything you do is visible - every decision, every mood, every subtle shift in demeanor gets noticed and interpreted by your crew. Yet paradoxically, you see less and less of what's really happening. Like a captain on the bridge, you have the best vantage point for spotting opportunities on the horizon, but you might be the last to hear about problems below deck.

I learned this lesson the hard way when our biggest client was about to jump ship. Everyone in the company knew there were issues - everyone except me. My team had been trying to protect me from "unnecessary worry." By the time I found out, we were nearly too late to save the relationship. Nearly.

Second, there's the **Decision Weight**. It's not just about making choices – it's about understanding how those choices ripple through your entire organization. Every decision you make carries exponential impact. When you're at the center, your choices affect not just operations, but culture, morale, and future direction.

I remember agonizing over whether to expand into a new market. On paper, it was a clear "yes." The numbers worked, the opportunity was there, and the timing seemed right. But something felt off. My team was eager to move forward. Investors were pushing for growth. Yet I kept thinking about what it would mean for our culture, our core customers, our people's families.

Another time, I was evaluating an acquisition offer. It was a lucrative all-cash deal, an obvious strategic fit, and the acquirer was saying all the right things. A week before closing, it inadvertently came out that the plan was to split the business into two units. They would keep one part and release most of the staff. Then resell the second and remaining employees along with it. Big weighty decision - exit rich and hope for the best, or walk away?

That's the thing about sitting in the Captain's Chair - sometimes the hardest decisions aren't about strategy or finances, but about the human cost of our choices.

This weight can be paralyzing. I've seen capable leaders freeze up, stuck between analysis and action. Others swing the opposite way, making impulsive decisions just to keep moving. Both reactions come from the same place - the crushing awareness that people's livelihoods depend on getting it right.

Then there's the **Leadership Bubble** - possibly the trickiest challenge of all. The higher you rise, the more you need honest feedback, yet the harder it becomes to get it. People naturally filter what they tell the boss. Bad news gets softened. Concerns get sugarcoated. Pretty soon, you're living in an echo chamber of your own making.

I once had an executive tell me everything was "great" in his department for six straight months. Meanwhile, his team was quietly updating their resumes. He wasn't lying - he just didn't want to be the bearer of bad news. By the time I discovered the truth, we'd lost some of our best talent.

This is where most leadership books get it wrong. They talk about strategy and skills, about making tough decisions and casting bold visions. All important stuff. But they miss the fundamental truth about leadership: It's not about being the smartest or strongest or most decisive person in the room. It's about building the right support system that lets you access the wisdom, strength, and clarity you need when you need it.

Living in the Leadership Bubble

It starts subtly. Almost imperceptibly. Like a fog rolling in so gradually you don't notice until you can barely see the bow of your ship.

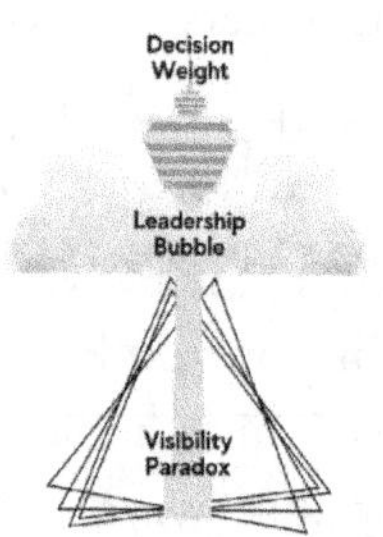

First, the casual conversations stop. People tense up when you enter the room. Meetings become more formal. Laughter fades when you join the group. You tell yourself it's natural – you're the boss after all. They can't treat you like just another colleague.

Then the information starts getting filtered. Bad news arrives late, if at all. Problems are downplayed. Concerns are muffled. You hear about issues only after they're "handled." Again, you rationalize. They're just trying to be efficient, right? Only bringing you the important stuff.

Before you know it, you're living in what I call the Leadership Bubble - a distorted reality where everything seems fine until suddenly it isn't. It is a magical place where you have access to more information than ever, but less true understanding. A bizarre world where you're surrounded by people but increasingly alone.

I've lived in this bubble. Most leaders have. The strange thing is that many of them don't know it. Bubbles are clear. You think you can see just fine - maybe a little blurry now and then, but it's "no big deal." It's seductive because it feels like what leadership should be - calm, controlled, above the fray. But it's actually a form of slow-motion isolation that kills effectiveness and breeds disaster.

The cruel irony? The higher you rise, the more you need real connection and honest feedback. Yet the higher you rise, the harder these become to maintain. A study by Harvard Business Review found that 72% of executives feel lonely in their roles. Not just alone - lonely. There's a difference.

Think about the great captains throughout maritime history. None of them sailed alone. They had navigators to chart the course, crews to work the ship, and trusted advisors to offer counsel. Yet somewhere along the way, we bought into this myth of the trailblazing solitary leader - the visionary CEO who single-handedly steers their company to treasure island.

It's a dangerous myth. One that's costing us dearly in burned-out leaders, failed businesses, and broken relationships.

The Control Paradox

Here's a truth every captain learns eventually: You control far less than you think.

I saw this lesson play out during the 2008 financial crisis. Despite perfect planning, stellar execution, and a strong team, revenue evaporated overnight. What took ten years to build was cut in half in six months. No amount of control could have prevented it.

The same thing happened to thousands of companies in 2020. A global pandemic forced the closure of countless businesses. Some pivoted and went remote. Some tried to ride it out. Some industries excelled. Others closed shop. The ocean of business doesn't care about your five-year plan.

Stay tuned . . . there will be another major business/life/financial crisis - or maybe all three wrapped in one. Could be this year, next year, five years from now, who knows when? Candidly, "when" doesn't really matter. The sure thing is that *crisis is coming*. It's a natural part of every cycle, from seasons and rainstorms to market collapses and family emergencies. *When it does, how will we handle it?*

Our instinct as leaders is to grip the wheel tighter. To try to control everything. I caught myself doing this after losing a major contract - micromanaging every decision, demanding updates every hour, trying to will success through sheer force. You know what happened? My best people started leaving. Turns out nobody enjoys working for Captain Ahab. Or the other "A word" some of them preferred . . . And between you and me, they weren't wrong about it.

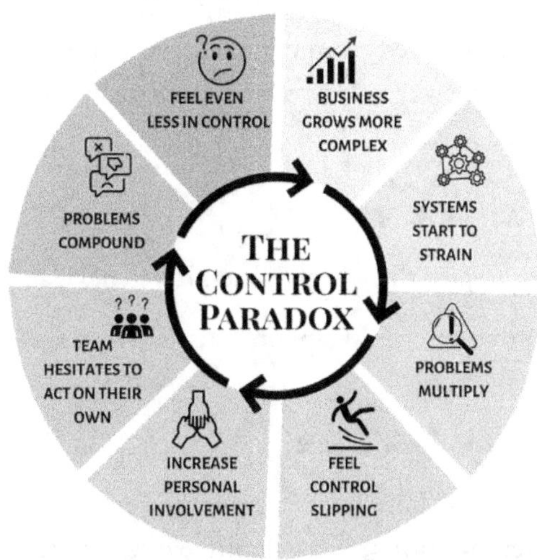

The Control Paradox shows up in three critical areas:

Market Forces: Like ocean currents, market forces operate whether we acknowledge them or not. Smart captains study these currents and use them to their advantage rather than exhausting resources fighting them. Netflix didn't fight the streaming current - they rode it. Blockbuster tried to fight it and sank.

Team Dynamics: The tighter you grip your crew, the more likely they are to jump ship. I worked with a founder who insisted on maintaining control as they grew past $50 million in revenue. He still approved every hire, reviewed every proposal, and second-guessed every decision. His best people didn't leave for more money - they left for more autonomy.

Innovation and Growth: The most dangerous aspect of over-control is what it does to innovation. Like a ship so firmly anchored it can't move with the tide, companies that control too tightly become brittle. They mistake process for progress. Security for strength.

But here's the thing - letting go of control doesn't mean giving up leadership. Just the opposite. There's a way to navigate these waters that doesn't require superhuman strength or solitary sacrifice. A way to lead that actually lets you sleep at night, see your family, and build something lasting.

I learned this the hard way, but you don't have to. The solution isn't more control – it's better support. The right kind of support. The kind that turns isolation into strength, chaos into clarity, and overwhelming responsibility into shared purpose.

But before we get to that, we need to understand the difference between known and unknown waters. Because the way you navigate familiar channels is very different from how you handle uncharted seas . . .

Known and Unknown Waters

Your job as Captain isn't to grip the wheel tighter. It's to navigate better.

This brings us to the question every Captain must answer, the one that separates the remembered from the forgotten:

Are you sailing to win, or sailing not to lose?

Every harbor has its regulars - those boats that never venture far from the breakwater. Their captains know every mooring, every depth, every current. They're successful, in their way. Safe. Predictable.

Visit any marina and you'll see them - beautiful boats, meticulously maintained, that rarely leave their slips. Their owners have a thousand reasons why today isn't a good day to sail. Too windy. Not windy enough. Might rain. Might be sunny.

But *ships aren't built for harbors.*

The real opportunities - the ones that transform businesses and lives - lie beyond the familiar channels. Out where the water gets deeper, where the maps get less detailed, where experience matters more than routine.

Consider Amazon's journey from online bookstore to cloud computing giant. If Jeff Bezos had stayed in the known waters of bookselling, or even ecommerce, AWS - now their most profitable division - would never have existed. Every major innovation in history came from someone willing to sail into unknown waters.

Every business operates in both known and unknown waters. Known waters are your established markets, proven products, and reliable processes. Unknown waters represent new opportunities, untested strategies, and emerging markets. The art of leadership lies in navigating both.

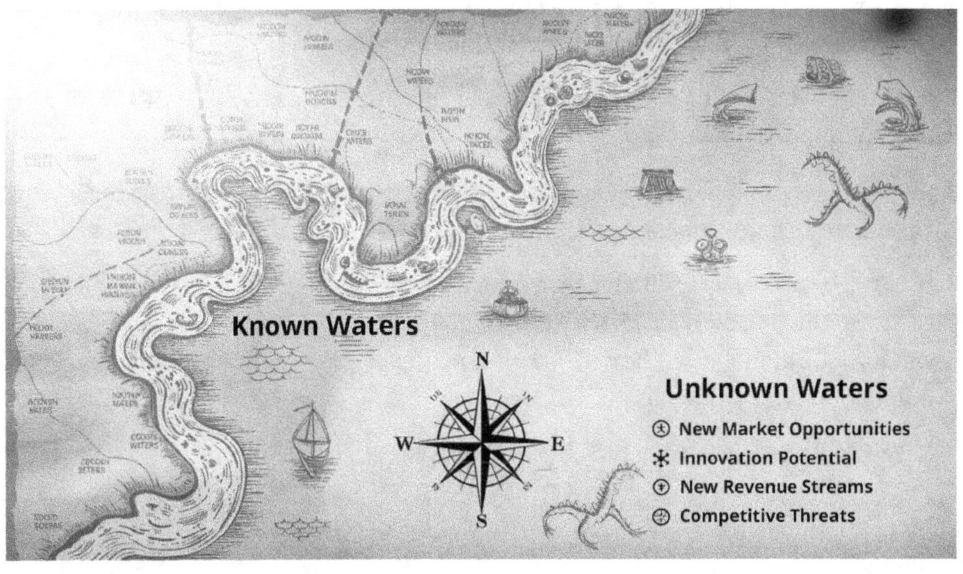

Known Waters: The Familiar Channels

Like well-charted shipping lanes, known waters offer predictability and established patterns:

- Clear metrics for success

- Predictable outcomes
- Understand the competitive landscape
- Proven customer base
- Tested operational processes

That isn't to say that known waters are without danger.

Remember the cruise ship *Costa Concordia*? It was the pride of the cruise line. Ran aground, rolled on its side, and sank in 2012 on a very familiar route the Captain had successfully navigated hundreds of times previously.

One of the biggest dangers lurking beneath familiar waters is a relaxed attitude. *Complacency kills companies. Vigilance is a must.* Competition congregates in familiar channels. Margins tend to shrink as routes become commoditized. *Ignored hazards sink ships.*

Unknown Waters: The Open Sea

Unknown waters hold both greater risk and greater potential. It's where breakthroughs happen, where markets are created rather than merely served. But it's also where the monsters live - those challenges that can swallow companies whole.

I remember when we decided to enter a new adjacent market. At least that is how we viewed it in the beginning. In reality, it was an entirely new market.

Everything we thought we knew about our business had to be relearned. Our assumptions that it would be "pretty much the same" were completely off base.

Customer behaviors were different.
Reasons for buying didn't align with our marketing.
Our playbook didn't cover the detailed questions being asked.
Competition came from unexpected directions.

Even our proven processes had to be completely rethought.

It was terrifying. Exhilarating. Essential.

Simple choice.

Adapt and innovate, or give up and go home.

Navigation Principles

Smart captains follow certain principles when deciding between known and unknown waters. Think of it like planning a voyage - you need to understand your resources, your capabilities, and the conditions you're sailing into.

Just like going on an actual trip, one of the first things we do is make sure we have what we need, a **Resource Review**. Before venturing into unknown waters, you need to take honest stock of what you've got:

- Do you have the right crew? How experienced are they?
- How much fuel (capital) do you have?
- Are your systems and equipment up to the challenge?
- Do you have reliable intelligence about where you're heading?

I learned this lesson the expensive way when we tried to expand too quickly with too little. We had the vision, the enthusiasm, and about half the resources we actually needed. Like a ship running out of fuel mid-ocean, we found ourselves stuck between where we'd been and where we wanted to go. Hard lesson learned. The smarter choice would have been to sail back to known waters, but we plowed on, cutting costs and resources from everywhere possible to make it work. My biggest regret was burning out team members, which slowed the next growth phase.

Once we're confident in the resources we do and don't have, it's time to make a plan. Next up is **Market Mapping** - like studying weather patterns before a long voyage. You need to understand:

- Which way are the currents (trends) moving?
- Where are your competitors positioning themselves?
- What storms (disruptions) are brewing?
- Where are the safe harbors if things get rough?

But here's the tricky part - timing matters as much as direction. I've seen brilliant strategies fail simply because the market wasn't ready. Or because the company wasn't ready. Or because the timing was perfect, but the execution flopped.

You know what separates successful captains from the ones who end up on the rocks? It's not just their skill at the helm. It's their ability to read the signs, to understand when to push forward and when to pull back.

The best part is that choosing between known and unknown waters is not an "either/or" decision. It's a question of allocation and focus. The most successful companies maintain operations in both. They're like those captains who keep one eye on the horizon while still watching the depth gauge. They understand that today's unknown waters become tomorrow's known channels, and today's safe harbors might be tomorrow's dead ends.

I remember asking a seasoned captain how he knew when to venture out beyond the familiar routes or choose to weather a hurricane at sea. His answer stuck with me: "When staying in the harbor becomes riskier than leaving it."

That's the entrepreneurial tightrope: balancing the known and unknown. Too much time in safe harbors leads to stagnation. Too much time in unknown seas risks capsizing. The art is knowing when to push beyond the familiar and when to return to port for repairs and reflection.

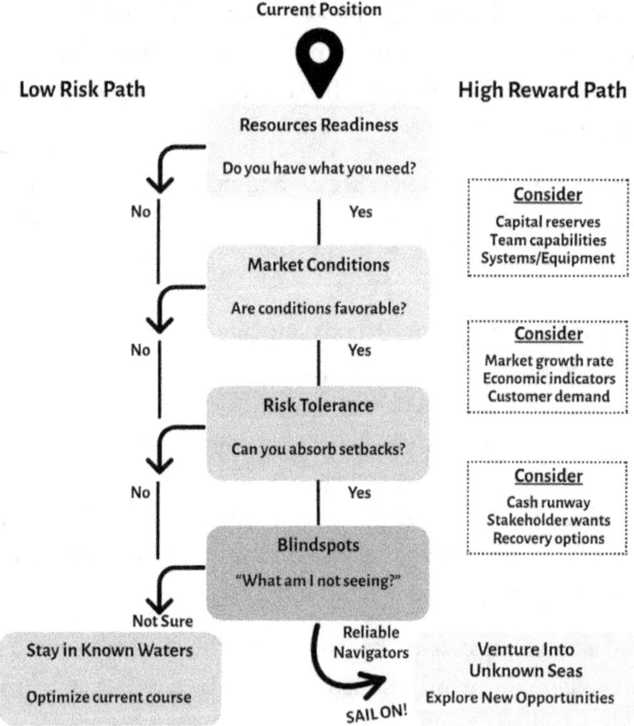

Ask yourself: Is your ship in harbor because it needs to be, or because you're afraid to sail? Are you settling for known waters because they're comfortable, or because they're truly your best option?

The sea of business forgives many mistakes, but it never forgives the sin of playing too safe for too long. Markets change. Technologies evolve. Customer needs shift. Opportunities break like waves. The harbor that feels safe today might be obsolete tomorrow.

Your ship was built to sail. Not recklessly, but purposefully.
Not without preparation, but with courage.
Not without rest, but also not without adventure.

The truth is, you probably already know the areas where you're pushing boundaries, and a few of the areas where you're settling.

You feel it in those quiet moments when the whisper comes.

Maybe it's when you're looking at a competitor's bold move.
Maybe it's when you're explaining to your team why "now isn't the right time" for that exciting new initiative.
Maybe it's when you're making another promise to yourself (or your family) about "later" or "someday."

Maybe someday is today?

The Sea Ahead

Every great journey begins with a decision - not just to leave port, but to embrace the full purpose of your vessel. Your business, like any ship, was built for more than safe harbor. It was built to navigate both familiar channels and open seas, to weather storms and seize opportunities, to carry precious cargo toward meaningful destinations.

The question isn't whether your ship was built to sail. The question is whether you were built to captain alone.

Most captains answer wrong.

They mistake isolation for leadership. Exhaustion for dedication. Control for competence.

They stand alone at the helm, day after grueling day, scanning horizons, plotting courses, making every decision. They call it responsibility. They call it excellence.

I call it limitation.

Look at the most successful voyages throughout history. The ones that discovered new worlds. The ones that established trade routes that lasted centuries. The ones that weathered storms that sank lesser vessels.

What do they have in common?

Not the strength of their captains. But the strength of their command structures.

The captains who changed history didn't just master themselves. They mastered the art of creating support systems that amplified their vision, extended their reach, and compensated for their inevitable blind spots.

They understood that leadership isn't a solo performance. It's a carefully orchestrated symphony where each role plays a crucial part in navigating the seas ahead.

So here's the real choice you face, Captain:

Will you continue to navigate alone, carrying the full weight of command on your shoulders? Making yourself the single point of both success and failure? Becoming the constraint on your own business?

Or will you build a command structure that transforms how you lead?

The decision point isn't about skill. It's about courage.

What happens when your success no longer depends entirely on you? What happens when your limitations are no longer the ceiling? What happens when you're not the hero of every story?

There's a system that makes this possible - one that's been hiding in plain sight, used by history's most effective captains. It doesn't diminish your authority. It amplifies it. It doesn't reduce your control. It extends your reach.

The captains who master this system don't just survive the journey. They transform it.

They turn isolated command into orchestrated impact. They convert white-knuckled survival into sustainable progress. They build vessels that can sail beyond their own limitations.

The seas ahead don't care about your competence. They don't respect your credentials. They won't yield to your determination.

But they do respond to something more powerful: A captain who understands that true command isn't measured by control, but by capacity. Not by doing more, but by enabling more. Not by knowing everything, but by creating systems that harness collective wisdom.

Are you ready to expand your definition of leadership? Are you willing to build beyond your own capabilities? Are you brave enough to become the kind of captain who creates a legacy instead of limitation?

To answer that, let me tell you a story about a different kind of Captain . . .

NAVIGATING UNKNOWN WATERS

Adobe's Transition to Cloud

Adobe shifted from years of delivering packaged software to cloud subscriptions. It seems obvious now, but the new sales and delivery model wasn't without risk. I personally hated the idea of having to be online to use the software (they fixed that), and instead of upgrading every 2 or 3 versions, now I had to pay for every one and stay current.

They recognized the approaching storm of cloud computing and made a bold move despite the short-term financial impact. It was a well-executed and masterful navigation into unknown waters.

Their approach exemplifies key navigation principles:

- Maintained strong revenue in known waters while building cloud capabilities
- Invested heavily in new systems, training, and end-user education
- Communicated clearly with stakeholders about the journey ahead
- Adjusted course based on early customer feedback.

The result? Adobe's revenue grew from $4.2 billion in 2011 to over $21.5 billion in 2024. A clear win by any measure. I'm still a user, and have been since 2000. Even with free alternatives today, Adobe Creative Suite is still the gold standard.

Microsoft's Gaming Strategy

Microsoft's core business was operating systems and productivity software. Windows, Office, SQL Server, Exchange Server, and similar tech marketed primarily to businesses. The least logical product expansion I can think of is consumer gaming. Not only far outside their core business, but also one dominated by two major players - Sony and Nintendo. Yet the success of the XBOX and entry into gaming shows how to leverage known waters (operating systems) to explore unknown seas (console gaming, then later expanding into cloud gaming). Their XBOX journey demonstrates:

- Using core strengths (software, distribution) in new markets
- Making strategic acquisitions (Bethesda, Activision) to gain expertise and content
- Maintaining flexibility in strategy (shifting focus to Game Pass)
- Being patient with long-term investments.

Their willingness to venture into unknown waters transformed them from a potential gaming industry footnote to a major player. It was far from easy. From a strong launch to a $4B loss due to cost overruns is the definition of stormy seas! Patience and persistence paid off big and continue to. In the 2024 calendar year, revenue was $21.5 billion - a clear win. With their continued innovation into cloud gaming and acquisitions, revenue growth was strong even as hardware sales decreased.

Netflix's Multiple Transformations

Netflix has repeatedly navigated unknown waters - from DVD rental to streaming to content creation. Each transition required:

- Careful timing of resource allocation
- Maintaining service in known waters while exploring new ones
- Clear communication with stakeholders
- Willingness to cannibalize existing business for future growth

Their success came not from avoiding risks but from methodically exploring new waters while maintaining enough stability in known areas. This is an extremely difficult and delicate balance. The fear of cannibalizing a current revenue stream would drive most companies to inaction. Unknown waters require calculated risks and bold moves.

Innovation never ends.

REFLECT: What type of vessel are you really commanding?
Are you sailing a nimble speedboat but longing for the stability of a cargo ship?
Or have you built a massive vessel that you're trying to maneuver like a pleasure craft?
The mismatch capsizes more businesses than any market storm ever could.

ACT: Draw your ship. Seriously. Sketch it on paper.
Is it a speedboat? A fishing trawler? A container ship? Sportfishing boat? A yacht?
Now ask: Am I trying to operate it like something it's not?

This simple exercise reveals misalignments between your business design and your leadership approach.

Curious about your vessel?

The ship metaphor resonates with leaders at every stage—from solo captains in speedboats to admirals commanding fleets.

I've created resources to help you identify your vessel type and connect with fellow captains facing similar waters. It might just save you from some unnecessary storms.

It's free, my gift to you.

https://TheCaptainsKeys.com/bonus

"Realizing I was trying to captain a container ship with speedboat strategies was my breakthrough moment. These tools helped me adapt my leadership to what my business actually needed."

— TAYLOR M., FOUNDER

☸ NAVIGATE

To Sail the Story / Full Journey - Continue on to the next page
Study the Maps - Jump ahead to page 51

CAPTAIN'S LOG

Chart your course forward

29

Reflections

Action Items

REEL DREAM
Floridian-Keos

BEYOND THE STORM
Part 1

"Aye-Aye, Cap'n!!! We gonna get this thing in the water or what?"

Jimmy Meyer forced a smile as he scanned his quartet of passengers sprawled across the cushioned seats he typically reserved for women and children. Three investment bankers and their female companion, already working on their second round before ten. His smile didn't reach his eyes.

Every tourist from New York or Chicago seemed to fancy themselves sailors about ninety seconds after boarding his charter. Make that forty-five seconds if they'd already knocked back a few Coronas. And this crew - showing up nearly an hour late - was definitely feeling no pain.

Jimmy adjusted the throttle with practiced ease, one hand on the wheel, the other checking his bait supply. Multi-tasking had become as natural as breathing after eighteen years on the water. On a boat this size, being a one-man crew just made sense.

"We're heading for the yellowtail grounds first," he called over his shoulder. "Unless you gentlemen want to try for something bigger right off the bat?"

"Marlin!" shouted the loudest of the three bankers, a red-faced man named Doug whose Rolex probably cost more than Jimmy's monthly take. "We didn't come all this way to catch baitfish!"

Jimmy nodded without committing. He'd seen this movie before. Fortunately he was sitting in the director's chair.

Ten minutes later the big city anglers had lines in the water accompanied by constant smack talk about which one of them would score the first fish of the day.

A flash of silver cut through the water near the port side - a barracuda eyeing their catch as Doug reeled in a big yellowtail. Before the tourists even noticed the predator trailing the hooked fish, Jimmy had already shifted position. He grabbed the gaff hook with practiced efficiency, his casual demeanor vanishing in an instant.

"Easy now," he murmured, not to the fish but to himself.

With a swift, precise movement, he hauled the yellowtail aboard just as the barracuda lunged. The water churned where their catch had been a split second earlier. The tourists barely even noticed the near miss, but for a moment, Jimmy's easygoing mask had slipped, revealing something sharper, more focused - a glimpse of the captain he could be if the stakes were ever truly high.

The moment passed. The barracuda moved on, disappointed. Jimmy slipped back into his role of affable guide, but the brief intensity lingered somewhere behind his eyes.

The morning air clung to his skin, thick with salt and promise. A brown pelican swooped low over their wake, its wings nearly skimming the jade-green swells. Jimmy checked the weather radar on his phone. The marine forecast had mentioned a low-pressure system forming in the Caribbean, but nothing serious for at least three days. The sky stretched above them, a perfect postcard blue. Tourist weather, he called it.

Paradise. At least that's what they all thought.

Jimmy knew better. Paradise had teeth.

A distant rumble of thunder proved his point, though the tourists were too busy with their beers to notice. Nothing serious yet, but worth keeping an eye on. Summer storms could build fast down here, turning placid waters treacherous in minutes.

"Hey Captain Gorgeous," called the woman, adjusting her bikini top with practiced precision. "Got anything stronger than these wine coolers below deck?"

Jimmy met her eyes briefly before returning his attention to the controls. She was the main reason they'd been late – a last-minute addition who clearly thought heeled boots and a miniskirt made perfect sense for six hours at sea. She'd made eyes at him twice in twenty minutes, first when he mentioned the guest cabin below, then again when he'd handed her the Seagram's she was nursing.

Ten years ago, he might have shown her his private stash of the good stuff below. Might have given her that private tour she was fishing for. But he'd sworn off those kinds of complications. Word got around fast in the Keys if you were the kind of captain who disappeared below deck with someone's date while they were fighting a monster fish.

"Sorry, ma'am. Coast Guard regulations." A convenient lie, delivered with practiced charm.

He adjusted course, watching a massive luxury yacht glide past in the distance, a flotilla of tenders and support craft buzzing around it like pilot fish.

"Look at that circus," he muttered under his breath. "Give me simple any day."

Everything he needed was within arm's reach. The wheel, the throttle, the radio, the bait. No crew to manage, no personalities to soothe. Just Jimmy, the ocean, and paying customers who'd be gone by sunset.

Doug was already pointing out spots he thought would be "perfect," despite having never fished these waters before. Jimmy just nodded. Let them think what they wanted. He'd get them on fish, take their money, and send them home with photos and stories to impress their friends back in their high-rises.

He'd seen other charter captains bring on mates, splitting the already thin profit margins for what? Having someone to handle lines and clean fish? Jimmy could do that in his sleep. Extra hands just meant extra complications. Besides, he'd seen how other captains spent half their time managing personalities instead of fishing.

No thanks.

The Cabo 31 responded instantly to his touch as he guided them past the harbor markers. This wasn't just his boat - it was an extension of himself. Every creak, every vibration spoke to him in a language as familiar as his own heartbeat.

"You run this whole operation yourself, Captain?" asked the quieter banker, genuinely curious.

Jimmy nodded. "Just me and Bella."

"Bella?"

"My first mate." Jimmy smiled, thinking of the golden retriever waiting at home. "Best crew I ever had. Never argues, always shows up on time, works for treats."

The man laughed, but Jimmy wasn't entirely joking. The days she wasn't on board the boat Bella waited for him on the porch swing. She never complained about long hours, never asked for raises. Simple. Uncomplicated. Just the way he liked it.

"You ever watch that show, Wicked Tuna?" Doug interrupted, clearly wanting to steer the conversation back to himself. "My cousin knows a guy who knows one of those captains."

"Catch it sometimes," Jimmy said noncommittally.

Truth was, he rarely missed an episode. Anything about boats or fishing was irresistible. Something about those wild tuna fishing boats battling waves and chasing 600 lb monsters made for compelling television. Though he always thought those captains made things harder than necessary. All that yelling and drama. Leadership seemed pretty straightforward to him - just tell people what to do, get out of their way, and bring in a fifteen thousand dollar fish.

"Those guys are the real deal," Doug continued, sipping his beer. "Not that this isn't . . . you know . . . nice." He gestured vaguely at the calm turquoise waters surrounding them.

Jimmy didn't take the bait. The Keys had dangers of their own, just different ones. But no point explaining that to someone who thought danger could be summarized in a reality TV highlight reel.

"We're coming up on our next spot," he announced instead, throttling down. "Who wants to be first on the line?"

By day's end, everyone aboard was sunburned and satisfied. Doug had landed a decent sailfish within the first hour and had already inflated its length and weight by twenty-five percent in texts to friends back home. The woman - Melissa, though Doug kept calling her Missy - had spent most of the day sunbathing and checking her phone, occasionally pretending to be impressed by their catches.

Jimmy guided them back toward the marina as the late afternoon sun painted the water copper and gold. His back ached from the day's work, but the weight of the cash in his pocket made it worthwhile. The tourists had tipped well - $150 extra. Not bad for a Thursday.

The harbor came into view, the familiar jumble of masts and antennas silhouetted against the darkening sky. Jimmy spotted Mickey's boat already docked, the captain hosing down the deck. They exchanged distant waves - friendly but not familiar. No point getting tangled up in marina politics when you ran your own show.

"Captain," Melissa said quietly, sidling up next to him at the wheel. "I'm actually staying a few days longer than the boys." She slipped him a business card with her cell number scrawled on the back. "In case you want to take a girl to dinner."

Jimmy pocketed the card with a practiced smile. "I appreciate the offer, but I've already got a special lady I spend my evenings with."

Technically true, though Bella might object to being called a lady.

Docking was a one-man ballet he'd perfected years ago. Just skill and timing. He secured the boat while the tourists gathered their belongings and fish, already planning where they'd eat dinner and how many drinks they'd have.

"Great day, Captain!" Doug called as they disembarked, slightly unsteady after a day of sun and beer. "Maybe we'll see you next year!"

Jimmy knew he'd never see them again. The Keys were full of charter options, and memory faded with distance. But he smiled and waved anyway. "Looking forward to it!"

Then they were gone, and he was alone again with his boat. Just the way he liked it.

The porch swing creaked softly beneath him as Jimmy watched the sun sink into the Gulf, painting the sky in brilliant shades of orange and red. Bella lay across his lap, her golden coat catching the last rays of daylight. He scratched behind her ears, her favorite spot.

"Another day, another dollar, girl," he murmured, feeding her the final shrimp from his plate.

His modest stilted house wasn't much compared to the waterfront mansions that increasingly crowded the Keys, but it was his. Paid for and maintained by his own two hands. Every repair, every improvement done himself. If something broke, Jimmy fixed it. Quick, simple solutions were his specialty. Duct tape, zip ties, and WD-40 handled most problems on his boat and in this house.

From his porch, he could see both sunrise over the Atlantic and sunset over the Gulf. A perfect symmetry that never failed to center him after a long day on the water.

The distant thunder growled again, closer now. Bella's ears perked up, her brown eyes showing concern. Jimmy pulled out his phone to check the weather radar one more time before bed. The low-pressure system had intensified slightly but would probably blow on by and swing south toward Cuba like they usually did.

Probably.

He pushed away a nagging feeling that something bigger was coming. Not just weather, but change itself. The kind of change that reshapes a man's whole world.

"Just you and me, Bella," he said, feeling the weight of the evening settle around him. "That's all we need, right?"

The dog wagged her tail in agreement, but somehow, for the first time in years, Jimmy wasn't entirely convinced.

Sunrise over the Atlantic, and sunset over the Gulf. Life didn't get much better than this.

Or at least, that's what he kept telling himself.

CHAPTER 2

The next morning brought the kind of sticky heat that made even the seagulls look miserable. Jimmy watched a Coast Guard cutter heading out as he prepped his boat for another day of tourist-wrangling. The big ship cut an impressive silhouette against the horizon, stirring something in him he couldn't quite name. Envy? Nostalgia? Or maybe just that nagging itch that had been bothering him lately - the one that whispered there might be more out there than playing tour guide to sunburned stockbrokers.

"Some weather coming," called Marcus, the fuel dock attendant who fancied himself an amateur meteorologist. "System's building faster than they predicted. Might want to keep your trips short today."

Jimmy nodded but didn't respond. He'd heard plenty of Marcus's weather predictions over the years. The guy could find threatening clouds in a desert.

His phone buzzed - his sister Lily. Probably checking up on him again. She'd been doing that more often lately, as if she sensed something was off. He let it go to voicemail. He'd call her back later when he had the energy to convince her everything was fine.

The morning charter was a handful of tourist couples and a family of four from Minnesota - parents and two teenage boys who actually listened to his safety briefing and handled his equipment with respect. The kind of clients that reminded him why he loved this job. The father had been a commercial fisherman on Lake Superior before "getting sensible" and taking a job with an accounting firm.

"Miss it sometimes," the man confided while his sons were busy with their lines. "The challenge, you know? The feeling that what you do matters."

Jimmy knew exactly what he meant, but he just smiled and changed the subject.

By afternoon, the air had turned electric. Dark clouds were building to the south, taller and angrier than usual. Even Marcus had gone quiet, watching the horizon with worried eyes. The radio crackled with increased chatter about wind speeds and pressure drops.

His evening charter cancelled - something about the wife getting seasick before they even left the dock. Jimmy didn't mind. It gave him time to secure everything that might blow around in the storm. Beside him, Bella paced restlessly, picking up on the changing energy in the air.

"Just another summer storm, girl," he told her, but his voice lacked conviction.

That's when his phone buzzed again. This time it wasn't Lily. The caller ID read "Law Office".

No thank you, don't want any, he thought as he sent it off to voicemail he'd never check.

An awkward figure stood on Jimmy's dock.

Suit. Tie. Leather briefcase. Everything about him screamed "wrong place, wrong time." Nobody wore suits in the Keys. Not unless they were getting married or buried.

Jimmy guided his boat into the slip, watching the stranger sweat through his Brooks Brothers armor. The man stood like a statue, radiating discomfort in the morning heat. A walking, breathing reminder of the world Jimmy had worked so hard to escape.

"Nice work everyone," Jimmy called to his departing tourists. "Remember what I always say about tips - if you're not finding enough spots where the fish are biting, maybe you need a better captain!"

The usual chuckles followed. So did the usual theater - wallets appearing, apologies about only having twenties, promises to "get you next time." Tourist code for "never."

Still, eighty bucks in tips for a four-hour morning charter wasn't bad. He'd had worse days.

He kept an eye on the suit still standing there on his pier like a robot waiting for its activation code. The guy was probably a shade past 50, slightly paunchy around the middle, and clearly was not used to standing outside for any great length of time.

Everything about his walk screamed "official business." Each careful step calculated to avoid splinters, fish guts, and the general messiness of dock life.

"James Earl Meyer?"

Jimmy's gut twisted. It's never good when someone uses your full name. Not unless something was seriously wrong.

Government? Legal? Either way, this great day had just gone sideways.

He forced a smile. "That's me. What can I do for you?"

"James Goodall, Goodall & Meltzer Law Firm." The man extended a hand that had never seen a day of real work. "I'm afraid I have some bad news."

Of course you do, Jimmy thought. Men in suits never brought good news to the docks.

"Captain Keith Meyer has passed away."

Jimmy blinked. The name hung in the heavy air between them. "Who?"

"Keith Meyer. Your uncle, if I do have the right James Earl Meyer."

The sound of Jimmy's full name again grated on him.

"People called him Rocky as I understand it. Ring any bells?"

Uncle Rocky.

Just like that, Jimmy was eight years old again. Sitting cross-legged on the living room floor, listening to stories of monster waves and record catches. The uncle who appeared like a mythical figure every few years, bringing exotic gifts and wild tales from the far north.

The same uncle he hadn't seen in over twenty years.

"What happened?" Jimmy's voice sounded distant in his own ears.

"Heart attack. Quick, they tell me. No suffering."

Jimmy nodded, memories crashing over him like waves.

Uncle Rocky was something of a mystery to Jimmy; he had probably only been in the same room with his dad's brother a handful of times, Yet, the man's fishing exploits had fueled his imagination growing up and certainly influenced Jimmy's career choice of making his living on the open water.

Their relationship had never been more than a passing thing, but he was still family. More importantly he was a direct connection to Jimmy's late father, who had himself gone into the ground 23 years ago. Even though he was only nine years old back then, Jimmy could still clearly picture Rocky at his father's funeral. The last living link to a life that seemed more dream than reality now.

"So what's this got to do with me?"

Goodall's expression shifted. The bearers of bad news usually didn't smile. "Your uncle had no children, Mr. Meyer. In his will, he left his entire estate to you."

The words hit Jimmy like a shot of top-shelf tequila. Warm. Dangerous. Full of promise.

And beneath it all, a faint undercurrent of guilt. Uncle Rocky had reached out twice in the past five years. Voicemails Jimmy had meant to return but never did.

Christmas cards with far away postmarks, tucked away in a drawer. Why had Rocky remembered him when Jimmy had practically forgotten Rocky?

He did remember the whispers growing up. Family folklore mostly. Stories that Uncle Rocky had made a fortune up north. The kind of money that turned fishing tales into legends.

"Perhaps we could sit somewhere?" Goodall gestured at his briefcase. "Review the paperwork?"

Jimmy led him to the charter office. A cramped space that smelled of fish and salt air. He swept a stack of receipts onto the floor to clear space. The lawyer's wince was almost audible.

Goodall opened his briefcase like a man defusing a bomb. Everything precise. Everything in its place.

"Your uncle has left you several assets from his estate, which you will need to claim in person at your convenience. What you choose to do with them after taking possession is up to you."

Jimmy leaned forward. "OK, lay it on me. What'd I get?"

"Item one," he began. "A 3,700 square foot home in Spruce Cape Subdivision. Ocean views. Three bedroom, two bath. Appraised at $870,000."

Jimmy's head spun. This wasn't just an inheritance. This was a lottery win.

"Item two: Hisun Strike UTV. Item three: 2019 Chevrolet Silverado 2500, four-wheel drive."

The numbers kept coming. Each one more impressive than the last.

"And finally," Goodall said, shuffling papers, "Item four: the *Bering Steel*. A 110-foot . . ." He frowned. "I apologize. The next page seems to be missing."

"A 110-foot what?" Jimmy leaned forward. "Yacht? Please tell me it's a yacht."

"I'll have my office send the complete details." Goodall was already reaching for his phone. "Email acceptable?"

Jimmy barely heard himself rattling off his email address. His mind was already at sea, standing at the helm of a luxury vessel. Finally, a real ship. Something worthy of a captain.

"Last I heard Rocky was in San Diego," he said. "That where the boat is?"

Goodall checked his perfectly-printed and stapled report (sans the back page) and carefully thumbed through the documents, "No, Mr. Meyer. Your new home and vessel are located at 3960 Spruce Cape Road, Kodiak, 99615."

"Kodiak?" The word felt strange in Jimmy's mouth. "KODIAK? Where is Kodiak?"

"Kodiak Island?", Goodall replied.

"Like the bears? Where's that? Alaska?" Jimmy joked.

Goodall checked a third time.

"Alaska. Yes indeed, Mr. Meyer."

A sudden chill rippled through Jimmy's body, something that should have been theoretically impossible given it was balmy and in the mid 80s today.

"You're telling me my uncle left me a house and a boat in Kodiak freaking Alaska?"

CHAPTER 3

The lawyer, Goodall, nodded to the affirmative.

Jimmy's body felt strangely weightless, as if the dock beneath him had suddenly vanished. He remembered a few stories that painted his uncle as larger than life. The kind of tales that grew with each telling, so you never knew where truth ended and myth began. Given the size of his inheritance there was some truth in the legends.

The old sea dog probably retired to SoCal trading ice floes for sunshine, frozen decks for poolside loungers. Year-round 72 degrees, non-stop bingo, sightseeing trips, casino weekends, and whatever else old people do in retirement. That's what Jimmy had always pictured – chillin' not chilling in retirement. Kick back somewhere warm, somewhere the salt air didn't burn your lungs when you inhaled in January.

Who knows maybe he sailed the yacht back and forth from San Diego on his own version of an Alaskan Cruise? Maybe. That would be a hoot wouldn't it? Jimmy's mind wandered at the possibilities. But as he sat down and waited for the details on his new boat to come across his smartphone, he was already formulating The Plan 2.0.

A grand adventure. Take ownership of the house, the vehicles, and the mega-yacht. Sell the first three. Make his own one-way Alaskan cruise sailing that beauty down the West Coast and back up through the Caribbean.

That was a solid plan.

Since income wouldn't be an issue he would take a few months, maybe even a year off from the charters. Time to really see what the rest of the world had to offer.

He mapped the route in his mind: Pacific Coast, Baja, through the Panama Canal like he'd always dreamed. There would definitely be a lengthy stop in Cancun and maybe even head up to New Orleans before returning to the Keys. A year of truly feeling alive, truly being a captain of a proper vessel. Maybe take on a few crewmembers and see what it felt like to lead a team, to explore the ocean instead of just hitting the same handful of spots over and over again where he was fairly certain that something would be biting.

When tourists asked if he got bored, he always put on his best smile and said how the sea was always changing, that you saw something new everyday, and that thinking you could outsmart the ocean was a fool's errand. Many days he did see something different, if not entirely new, but many days felt like carbon copies of the one before: tourists ready to drink, expecting a 1,000-pound marlin, flapping their arms on the bow making "King of the World" jokes and finding some new way to irritate him or break something.

He told himself he liked his nights quiet and peaceful, just him and Bella on the porch watching the sun go down. That was mostly true. The unspoken part was that most of his old running buddies had moved away or settled down. Scotty, the guy who had given him his first job on a charter boat became a grandfather last fall. Just feeling a little left behind. Passed up. That's all.

The Keys were changing. More and more it was becoming the land of extremes - old people rich enough to retire in style, young folks content to live in beach shacks, tourists blowing a month's salary for a week's luxury, and Jimmy, the easy-going charter boat captain who claimed he'd never have a "real job."

More and more these days, that didn't always sound like something to be proud of.

The 'ping' of his email chime snapped him back to reality.

Time to see his new dream boat. One-hundred and ten feet of sailing bliss just waiting for his command. He held his breath as the images downloaded, savoring these last moments of fantasy about spinning that big wheel and pointing the mega-yacht toward the far horizon.

The first photo loaded.

Jimmy stared. Blinked. Stared again.

This had to be some elaborate prank.

Except he couldn't think of anyone who knew him well enough anymore to pull it off.

There was the *Bering Steel* alright. And she was definitely 110 feet long.

It wasn't a mega-yacht. She was his late uncle's fishing boat.

Jimmy looked at the pictures. Zoomed in, out, down, up.

Some things were familiar.

Some things were completely foreign.

Exactly what kind of fishing boat was this anyway?

CHAPTER 4

Jimmy stared at the photos on his phone, then laughed out loud.

Not the laugh of someone amused. The laugh of a man who just realized the universe had played him for a fool.

The *Bering Steel* was a crab boat. Not just any crab boat - a massive 110-foot commercial fishing vessel straight out of Deadliest Catch. The kind that battled 40-foot waves in the most dangerous waters on Earth. The kind where men died.

His stomach twisted as reality crushed his fantasy. The taste of bitter disappointment coated his tongue, metallic and sharp.

If Jimmy hadn't been so busy conjuring luxury yachts in his mind, he might have guessed the truth from the name alone. The *Bering Steel*. It wasn't subtle.

He zoomed in on the photo again, his finger trembling slightly. The name painted on the hull seemed to mock him now.

"The vessel is in good condition," Goodall continued, oblivious to Jimmy's internal turmoil. "I'm told your uncle maintained it meticulously."

Jimmy barely heard him. His thoughts were already racing north, conjuring images of ice-slicked decks and brutal Arctic storms. Of men in survival suits battling conditions that would make his toughest day in the Keys seem like a kiddie pool at a resort. His throat constricted, the air in the office suddenly insufficient.

"I take it you'll need some time to arrange transport to Alaska?" Goodall prompted.

Jimmy blinked, forcing himself back to the present. The lawyer stood before him, fountain pen extended toward a document requiring his signature. The pen hovered in the air between them, waiting.

"Yes," he managed, his voice sounding distant in his own ears. "Some time."

As he scrawled his name, Jimmy felt as though he was signing something away rather than claiming a legacy. The scratch of the pen on paper sounded like tiny claws against his future.

Now it was his inheritance.

Jimmy left his marina office. Instead of taking the short drive home, he headed south on the Overseas Highway with the Gulf on one side and Atlantic on the other. He needed some time to think. Process. Make sense of it all.

He lowered the window, letting in a blast of humid Florida air. Eighty-seven degrees at 7 PM. The warmth wrapped around him like a familiar blanket. He couldn't remember the last time he'd seen anything below 55 in the Keys. As a matter of principle, he grabbed a hoodie when the temperature dropped into the high 60s.

His chest tightened at the thought of Alaskan cold - the kind that froze eyelashes and turned breath into ice crystals. The kind that killed with quiet efficiency if respected.

He pulled off the road near the top of his favorite bridge. The waters of the Gulf and Atlantic swirled together underneath, turquoise meeting cobalt in an eternal dance. Jimmy had crossed under this bridge thousands of times to access epic fishing spots. This was also where he took charter guests to catch a legendary Keys sunset on the water. He'd facilitated more than a few proposals onboard his boat here.

Now he had a proposal of his own to consider.

As the sun sank low, casting long golden fingers across the water, he closed his eyes, trying to imagine it. Working the deck in those conditions. Ice forming on the rails, not just the occasional morning condensation he battled here, but actual thick, deadly ice. Waves crashing over the bow, not the playful four-footers that sometimes rocked his charter, but monsters that could flatten a man. The constant knowledge that one wrong move meant death.

Captain Jimmy, king crab fisherman?

The thought was unfathomable.

Delusional.

Lunacy on stilts.

A fever dream.

Pure madness.

Yet something stirred in him. A memory surfaced with such clarity it stole his breath: being eight years old, sitting cross-legged on the living room floor while Uncle Rocky spun tales of monster waves and record catches. The man's hands, already weathered and scarred at thirty-five, moving through the air like they were parting actual seas. The smell of the cigar he wasn't supposed to smoke in the house. The gleam in his eye that made Jimmy believe every word.

Jimmy remembered himself in the backyard afterward, a plastic bucket on his head for a captain's hat, battling imaginary storms and sea monsters with a stick for a harpoon. The bathtub had become the storm-tossed ocean. Every game ended with triumph snatched from the jaws of disaster. Giant waves conquered. Sea monsters defeated. Men overboard rescued through impossible heroism. He hadn't thought about this in two decades.

Back then, every adventure had been life-or-death.

Reality had turned out different. His biggest challenges these days? Drunk tourists falling overboard while showing off for girls. Weekend warriors separating shoulders fighting marlins. The occasional choppy surf from a passing storm. He'd once pulled a teenage boy from the water after his jet ski capsized. The moment had made the local paper, Jimmy's single brush with actual danger in eighteen years of running charters.

Safe. Predictable. Familiar.

Easy.

Nothing wrong with that, right?

A dolphin broke the surface below, its sleek body catching last light before disappearing back into the deep. Jimmy watched the ripples spread and fade.

When was the last time he'd felt truly alive out there?

He scrolled through the photos again, each swipe of his finger revealing new details. The massive crane for hauling pots. The reinforced hull built for ice. The high bow designed to punch through waves that would swamp his charter boat ten times over.

This wasn't some pleasure craft for sipping cocktails and watching sunsets.

This was a war machine.

And somewhere in the back of his mind, a voice that sounded suspiciously like his eight-year-old self whispered: *Maybe*.

CHAPTER 5

Jimmy arrived home, poured himself three fingers of bourbon, and carried it to the porch. The liquid caught the last light of day as he swirled it, amber like a fossil containing some ancient truth.

"It's a joke, right?" he said aloud, as if Uncle Rocky might answer from beyond the grave. "You're having a laugh at my expense?"

Bella padded out from the house, nails clicking on the weathered deck boards. She settled at his feet with a sigh, her warm weight against his ankle a silent comfort.

Jimmy drained half the glass, the alcohol burning a path to his stomach. The bourbon's warmth spread through him - so different from the bone-deep cold he'd face in Alaska. Of course it was a fishing boat. What else would Uncle Rocky have been stashing in Alaska all these years?

His phone pinged again. As more photos downloaded, the vessel became both more familiar and more alien - a behemoth machine that seemed to belong to another world entirely. A world of ice and darkness and brutal efficiency.

Jimmy ran a finger over the boat's name in the photo. The *Bering Steel.* He had to admit it was a clever play on words. It took steel resolve to sail the Bering Sea hunting the crustacean equivalent of gold. It took steel everything to survive treacherous Alaskan waters where the temperature hovered just above freezing. Waters filled with hidden hazards that claimed the *Princess Sophia, Islander,* and countless other passenger and commercial vessels, all piloted by captains who thought they'd mastered the sea.

The Florida night pressed against him, heavy with moisture and life. Insects hummed in the darkness. A palm frond scraped against the railing in the gentle breeze. Across the channel, music drifted from a waterfront bar. Familiar sounds. Comfortable sounds.

He tried to imagine their opposites. The crack of ice against the hull. The roar of winds powerful enough to strip the skin from your face if you weren't covered. The banshee howl of a Bering Sea storm. The absolute silence when the engines stopped - a silence that meant danger, not peace.

His hand trembled slightly as he set down the glass. Not from fear, he told himself. From the absurdity of it all.

Yet for a brief, electric moment, he could almost feel the weight of command on his shoulders - not of a thirty-one foot charter but of a vessel that could bend steel and break men. In that flash, the quiet voice of truth whispered that he'd been sleepwalking through his life, that the comfortable predictability he'd built wasn't freedom but a cage of his own making.

Jimmy pushed the thought away. That was nonsense.

He was happy here.

Content.

Wasn't he?

His memory pulled him back to Uncle Rocky's last visit, summer of '01. Fifteen-year-old Jimmy had been mesmerized by the man's stories. How Rocky had once worked three days straight during a record haul. How he'd pulled a man from the freezing water after he'd gone overboard, performing CPR until the crewman coughed back to life. How he'd navigated through a whiteout when the radar failed, using nothing but a compass, instinct and depth finder to bring his crew home.

"That's what it means to be alive, Jimmy-boy," Rocky had told him, the glean in his eye communicating deep wisdom. "Not just existing. Not just getting by. But testing yourself against the worst the world can throw at you, and winning."

How different reality had turned out.

Last week, a tourist had fallen off the bow while trying to impress a bikini-clad college student with his balance. Jimmy had simply circled back, tossed him a line, and cracked a joke about fishing for chum. Another client had separated his shoulder fighting a marlin and spent the rest of the trip moaning about his golf game being ruined.

His biggest challenges? Hangovers and sunburns. Picking which cheesy joke to use when tourists asked if he'd ever seen a shark. Deciding whether he should bother replacing the cushions on his boat or just flip them over again.

When was the last time his pulse had quickened from anything other than annoyance?

"Cold. Really, really, brutally, miserably cold," Jimmy said aloud, draining his glass. The bourbon's fire faded quickly, unlike the Alaskan cold that would seep into his bones and stay there for months.

Bella's ears perked up at his voice, her brown eyes watching him with infinite patience.

The solution was obvious. Sell everything. Or maybe rent it out? Generate some passive income that might let him retire before his skin turned to leather and his joints gave out from hauling lines. No risk, decent reward.

"What do you think, Bella?" he asked, reaching down to scratch behind her ears.

A drowsy Bella opened one eye and gave a few tail wags before drifting back off to dreams of tennis balls and fish scraps. She'd never felt snow, never had ice between her paws. And she never would if Jimmy stayed the course.

"No, definitely sell it. There is no way on earth I am ever going to Alaska."

His laughter echoed off the stilts holding up his house, startling a night heron from its perch below. Bella lifted her head, confused by the sudden outburst.

"Can you imagine?" Jimmy asked her, gesturing wildly with his empty glass. "Me? Us? Alaska? How completely insane would that be?"

The thought of Uncle Rocky's legends - stories that had circulated through family gatherings like treasured heirlooms - always left Jimmy feeling like he'd somehow missed a crucial turn in life's road. Two men of the sea, yet worlds apart. One had made a fortune undertaking the most dangerous work in the world, returning to port with frosted eyebrows and stories carved from ice and courage. The other gave sunburn warnings and mixed drinks between catching snappers and yellowtail, returning home with a farmer's tan and tourist tips.

One wore survival suits and braved ice storms. The other didn't own a single pair of shoes that required socks.

Jimmy chuckled to himself, but the sound fell flat in the humid night. Clothes would be the least of his problems in Alaska. What about his business? Would any of his regular clients remember "Captain Jimmy" after a year away? Or would some younger, hungrier charter captain snap them up, leaving him to start from scratch?

The night deepened around him as he weighed his life in the balance. Very little stress. Total freedom. Enough money to live on, if not extravagantly. A dog who served as best friend, pillow, sounding board, and occasional vacuum cleaner for those nights when his coordination abandoned him after one too many.

His USCG license was technically valid for vessels up to 200 tons thanks to a few years running car ferries in a previous life. He'd kept it current, occasionally captaining larger boats for wealthy tourists who wanted something more impressive than his sport fisher, or filling in for dinner cruises. But there was a vast difference between a luxury cruiser on calm waters and a working vessel in the Bering Sea. One was playing at being a captain. The other was the real thing.

He'd seen how locals responded to outsiders pushing into their fishing territory. It didn't matter if it was crab, tuna, or something else. The old guard saw them as strangers, aliens, intruders. Fresh meat. Prey.

No, no, no . . . much better to stay in the familiar embrace of the Keys, where the worst danger was a sunburn or a hangover. When the charter season slowed, he'd fly to Alaska, get everything appraised, and either lease the property or sell it outright.

Either way, Uncle Rocky was about to make him a significantly richer man - without Jimmy ever having to feel that legendary Alaskan cold bite into his bones. Without him ever having to prove whether he was truly his uncle's successor or just a pale imitation playing at being a sea captain in friendly waters.

He resolved to stop by the store on his way home tomorrow and have the butcher cut two extra-thick ribeyes - one for him, one for Bella. A small celebration of good fortune that required no frost-bitten fingers, sixteen-hour shifts or forty-foot waves trying to swallow him whole.

The reasonable choice. The safe choice.

Jimmy caught his reflection in the window glass - a man haloed by the soft interior light. For a moment, he didn't recognize himself. The image blurred, shifted, and for a moment he could have sworn he saw Uncle Rocky staring back at him.

He blinked, and it was just himself again.

Same face he'd seen for forty years. Same life he'd lived for eighteen.

Life was good in the Keys. Life was about to get even better.

And that was enough.

Wasn't it?

☸ NAVIGATE

Study the Maps / Full Journey - Continue on to the next page
To Sail the Story - Ride a wave to page 67

CAPTAIN'S LOG

Chart your course forward

49

Reflections

____

____

____

____

____

____

Action Items

____

____

____

____

____

____

SURPRISE ADVANTAGE
FINDING GOLD WHERE OTHERS SEE CHAOS

"Life is what happens while you're busy making other plans."
— JOHN LENNON

The knock comes when you least expect it.

Almost never during business hours.
In the middle of a million other things going on.
Often wrapped in unexpected packaging.

No warning. No preparation. No manual to follow.

For Rachel, it came disguised as a last-minute invitation to speak at her industry's flagship conference after the headliner caught laryngitis.

For Devon, it appeared as an email from a dream client who had somehow stumbled across his half-finished portfolio website.

For Mei, it materialized when a competitor's surprise acquisition left their shared market wide open for just 72 hours.

Most leaders call these moments luck.
Some call them accidents.
A few recognize them for what they truly are:
Tests.

Not tests of capability.
Tests of readiness.
Tests of vision.

Because here's what most miss about opportunity:
It doesn't knock to give you something. It knocks to reveal something.

Something about who you are.
Something about what you see.
Something about what you're willing to become.

Watch carefully what happens in that microscopic gap between the unexpected gift and response:
Some freeze in disbelief.
Some grab without direction.
A rare few transform completely.

The moment between an unexpected event and our reaction to it – that's where leadership lives. It's the space between stimulus and response, between surprise and decision, between opportunity and action.

Life throws us curveballs when we least expect it.
The timing is never "right."
The circumstances are never "perfect."

And our first reaction . . . is rarely our best one.

Categories of Surprises

Here's the thing about surprises:
The same event can be perceived completely differently.
Filtered through an individual lens.

Opportunity. Chaos. Opening. Threat.
Same event.
Different perception.
Different response.

Most of us default to threat assessment or focus on the negative. We're conditioned to categorize the unexpected as dangerous. To retreat, resist, or react without thinking.

But that's the amateur move.

Great leaders have developed something rare - the ability to parse surprises in real time. To see opportunity where others see only chaos. To recognize which surprises demand immediate action and which reward patient consideration. To understand that our first interpretation is rarely our best one.

The difference isn't luck or temperament.

It's a deliberate practice of seeing differently.

Surprises generally fall into three categories:

 PERCEIVED POSITIVE	< PERCEIVED NEUTRAL >	PERCEIVED NEGATIVE 
· Unexpected promotion · Win a large client · Acquisition or merger opportunity · Windfall inheritance · Innovative technology breakthrough	· Technology change · Market shift · Regulatory update · Industry evolution	· Loss of key team member · Market downturn · Major regulatory change · Competitor receives $50M in funding · Natural disaster

Notice the word "perceived" in each category. What makes this fascinating is how often these perceptions prove wrong over time.

The "positive" large client win becomes a nightmare.
The "negative" setback opens new opportunities.
The "neutral" market shift becomes transformative.

Why We Resist

Our brains are wired for stability, not opportunity.

Seeking the familiar isn't just a preference – it's hardwired into our neural pathways. Even positive change triggers resistance. Our brains consume about 20% of our body's energy, and familiar patterns are essentially energy-saving shortcuts.

When we encounter something new, our brain's energy consumption spikes as it works to process and categorize the unknown. This biological reality explains why even positive changes can feel exhausting. (Aren't you glad it isn't just you?)

Uncertainty avoidance shows up in fascinating ways across organizations. Teams will often choose a known negative outcome over an unknown possibility of a better result. This isn't irrational – it's our risk-assessment systems operating exactly as they were created to. Avoiding uncertainty protects us from danger.

The challenge is that these same systems designed to protect us from dangers in the wild now protect us from profitable opportunities. Ironic, isn't it?

This makes perfect sense in an environment where we need to avoid predators on the Savannah. It makes less sense in today's business environment where **the biggest risk is often not taking any risks at all.**

THE RESISTANCE CYCLE
Why we resist change

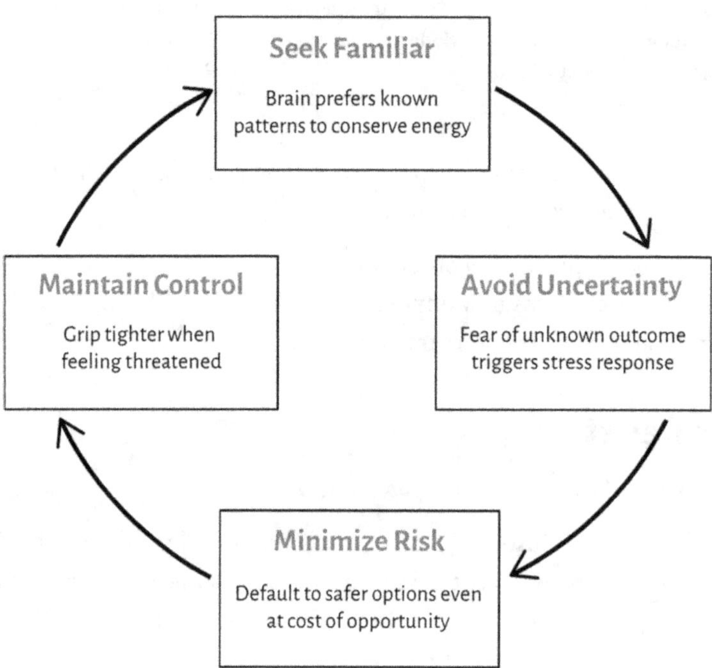

When faced with change, our instinct to minimize risk often becomes counterproductive. In today's rapidly evolving business landscape, playing it safe is paradoxically one of the riskiest strategies. Leaders who reflexively choose the safest path often find themselves falling behind more adaptive competitors. This isn't about reckless risk-taking – it's about recognizing that clinging to outdated safety mechanisms can be more dangerous than carefully chosen risks. The most successful leaders develop a calibrated approach to risk, understanding that some level of uncertainty is not just inevitable but necessary for growth.

Our desire for control runs far deeper than simple preference – it's a fundamental human need that shapes our decision-making in profound ways. When faced with change, we often focus more on what we might lose control of than what we might gain. We fear loss far more than we desire gain. This control bias explains why many leaders resist delegating even when they're overwhelmed, or why successful small business owners often struggle with expansion opportunities. The irony is that by trying to maintain absolute control, we often end up losing it entirely as circumstances evolve beyond our grasp.

The Comfort Trap

We talk about "comfort zones" like they're physical places. They're not, unless you're reading this while getting a massage in a day spa. (If so, that counts.) They're patterns. Habits. Mental models that worked in the past may not serve our future. We rely on them because they have worked for us this far, and we have a reasonable expectation they'll work for the next obstacle too. They're known. Proven. Reliable.

Think about Jimmy's charter business. It's not just comfortable because it's warm and sunny. It's comfortable because it's known, predictable, and manageable. He's mastered its patterns. But mastery can become a cage if we let it.

The Growth Zone

Real growth happens at the edge of our comfort zone - not so far out that we're paralyzed by fear, but far enough that we're stretched by challenge. This edge is different for everyone:

- For some, it's leading larger teams
- For others, it's leaving a job and starting a new business
- For CEO's, it's often entering new markets
- For many, it's facing unfamiliar challenges

The key isn't leaving your comfort zone entirely. It's expanding it strategically.

Understanding your growth zone requires mapping where different challenges fall on the spectrum of support and difficulty. This creates four distinct zones of experience:

STRATEGIC EXPANSION

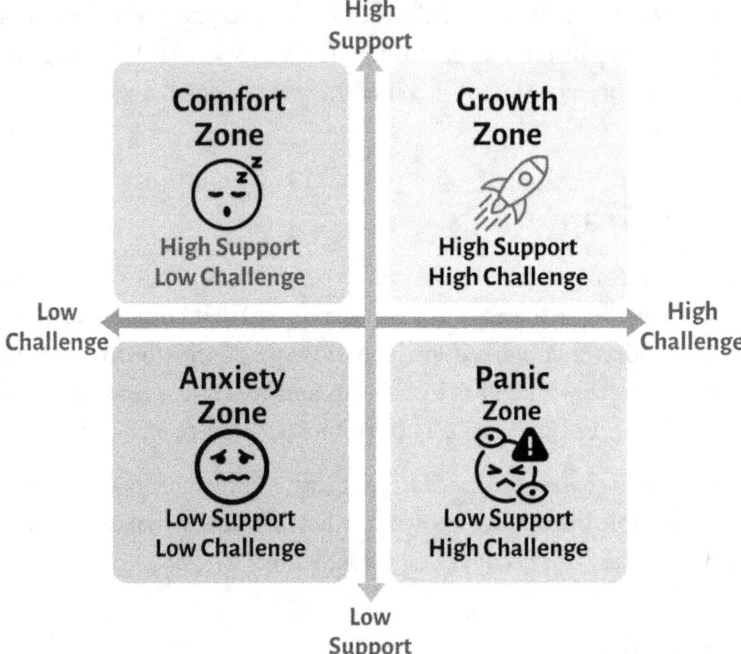

What Strategic Expansion Looks Like in Each Zone:

Comfort Zone (Low Challenge, High Support)
This is where you're competent and confident. It's essential for recovery and building foundations, but staying here too long leads to stagnation. Use this zone to build resources and confidence for your next push forward.

Growth Zone (High Challenge, High Support)
This is your target zone for strategic expansion. Here, you're stretching your capabilities while maintaining enough support to learn from failures. Examples include:

- Taking on a new project with mentor guidance
- Entering new markets with strong partner networks
- Leading larger teams while receiving executive coaching
- Building new skills through structured programs

Anxiety Zone (Low Challenge, Low Support)

This zone often feels deceptively safe because challenges are minimal, but the lack of support means you're not building resilience. Many people get stuck here, feeling neither threatened nor strengthened. It's like treading water - safe for now, but leading nowhere.

Panic Zone (High Challenge, Low Support)

This is where growth opportunities turn into survival situations. While some people thrive here briefly, it's usually unsustainable and can lead to burnout. The key is to recognize when you're here and either increase support or strategically reduce challenge levels.

The Art of Strategic Expansion:

1. Identify where you currently operate most often
2. Map your next challenge to these zones
3. Focus on moving activities from the Panic Zone to the Growth Zone by building support systems
4. Gradually expand your comfort zone by mastering Growth Zone challenges
5. Use the Comfort Zone strategically for recovery and preparation

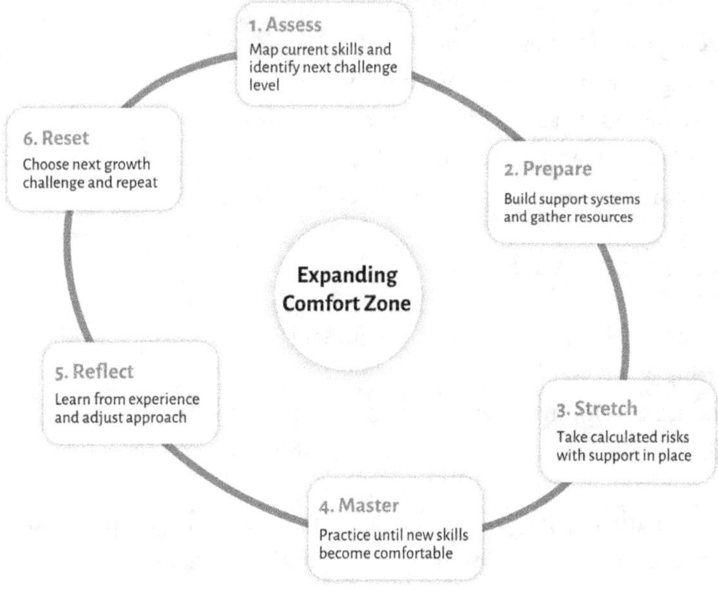

STRATEGIC EXPANSION PATH
Growing Your Comfort Zone

Mastering Growth Zone Challenges:

After understanding the path of strategic expansion, the next step is translating this framework into actionable challenges. The key is selecting challenges that stretch your capabilities while maintaining adequate support systems. These challenges should feel ambitious but not overwhelming - like stepping onto a high wire with a safety net beneath you. Let's look at specific examples at different career/life phases. These can come in any order. Great leadership is not linear. Each is designed to push boundaries while building sustainable growth.

Common growth challenges that stretch leaders are:

Early Leadership:

- Leading project teams with increasing scope and complexity
- Taking ownership of client relationships and revenue targets
- Developing and mentoring team members
- Driving cross-functional initiatives
- Managing department budgets and resources
- Building strategic partnerships

Executive Leadership:

- Scaling organizational capabilities
- Leading through market transitions
- Shaping company vision and strategy
- Managing board and stakeholder relationships
- Driving M&A and growth initiatives
- Transforming organizational culture

Founder/Entrepreneur:

- First hiring decisions with mentor guidance
- Raising capital with accelerator support
- Product development with customer feedback loops
- Market expansion with strategic partnerships

While these growth challenges provide a structured path for expansion, the most powerful accelerator of growth often comes from how we handle the unexpected. Even the best-planned challenges will present unforeseen obstacles and opportunities. This is where developing a Surprise Mindset becomes crucial – it's the difference between being derailed by the unexpected and using it as rocket fuel for growth.

> ## REAL WORLD EXAMPLE:
>
> When Discord launched in 2015, it was specifically designed as a chat platform for gamers. During the pandemic in 2020, while other companies saw remote communication as a temporary crisis to weather, Discord's leadership recognized a larger opportunity.
>
> Instead of doubling down on their gaming niche, they reframed their platform as a solution for any community - from study groups to book clubs to remote workplaces.
>
> By seeing beyond their original market during a market disruption, they transformed from a gaming chat app into a $15 billion communication platform that spans generational divides and is now used for everything from class projects to side hustles.
>
> What started as a pivot to fill a market need became a cultural shift in how younger generations approach online communities and collaboration.

The Surprise Mindset

Leaders who thrive in uncertainty share a common trait – they've developed what we call the Surprise Mindset. This mindset isn't just about surviving uncertainty – it's about harnessing it. When leaders embrace the Surprise Mindset, they transform their relationship with the unknown. Instead of bracing for disruption, they begin actively scanning for it, knowing that within each unexpected turn lies the seed of opportunity.

Common challenges viewed through the lens of a Surprise Mindset might look like this:

Market Shifts → New Customer Needs

- Instead of: "Our traditional market is shrinking."
- Reframe as: "We can now serve emerging needs."

Technology Disruption → Innovation Catalyst

- Instead of: "Our processes are becoming obsolete."
- Reframe as: "We can leapfrog legacy constraints."

Team Changes → Capability Expansion

- Instead of: "We lost key talent."
- Reframe as: "We can rebuild stronger."

This shift in perspective doesn't deny the challenges - it simply places them in a larger context of possibility. The more you practice this mindset, the more natural it becomes *to find the advantage in adversity.*

THE SURPRISE MINDSET

1. Expect the unexpected
2. View disruption as normal
3. See opportunity in uncertainty
4. Transform challenges into advantages

The Surprise Mindset sets the stage for growth, but mindset alone isn't enough. Leaders need a practical way to translate this perspective into action. You may recall the crisis response framework Stop-Breathe-Think-Act I introduced in my first book, which focuses on regaining stability in important or urgent situations - aka crisis. This is valid and works well.

PAFA (Pause-Assess-Frame-Act) follows a similar rhythm but expands each step to capture opportunity rather than just manage risk. Where SBTA helps you regain control, PAFA helps you leverage uncertainty for growth. In first aid terms, think of SBTA as triage - stop the bleeding and get the patient stable. And PAFA is surgery, rehab, and ongoing care to make the patient stronger than before.

Make sense?

Here's how it works . . .

The formula is simple but powerful, creating a systematic approach to handling surprises.

Pause - Create space between the event and your reaction

- Take a deliberate step back from the immediate situation
- Control your initial emotional response
- Give yourself time to think clearly rather than react instinctively
- Use this moment to gather yourself and observe

Assess - Look beyond initial perceptions

- Gather information from multiple perspectives
- Question your assumptions about what's happening
- Consider both immediate and longer-term implications
- Look for patterns and connections others might miss

Frame - Choose how to view the situation

- Actively select the lens through which you view the challenge
- Identify potential opportunities within the disruption
- Consider multiple possible outcomes
- Define what success could look like from here

Act - Move forward purposefully

- Make deliberate choices rather than reactive decisions
- Take clear, decisive steps based on your chosen frame
- Communicate your perspective to build alignment
- Maintain flexibility as new information emerges

This process transforms surprises into strategic advantages regardless of whether our initial reaction is positive, negative, or neutral. By following these steps, leaders can consistently find opportunity in uncertainty and transform unexpected challenges into stepping stones for growth.

But knowing the framework is just the beginning. The real power emerges when you practice it deliberately in daily leadership moments. Let's look at how to apply this in real time.

DEFAULT RESPONSE VS STRATEGIC RESPONSE

Navigating unexpected events with the PAFA framework

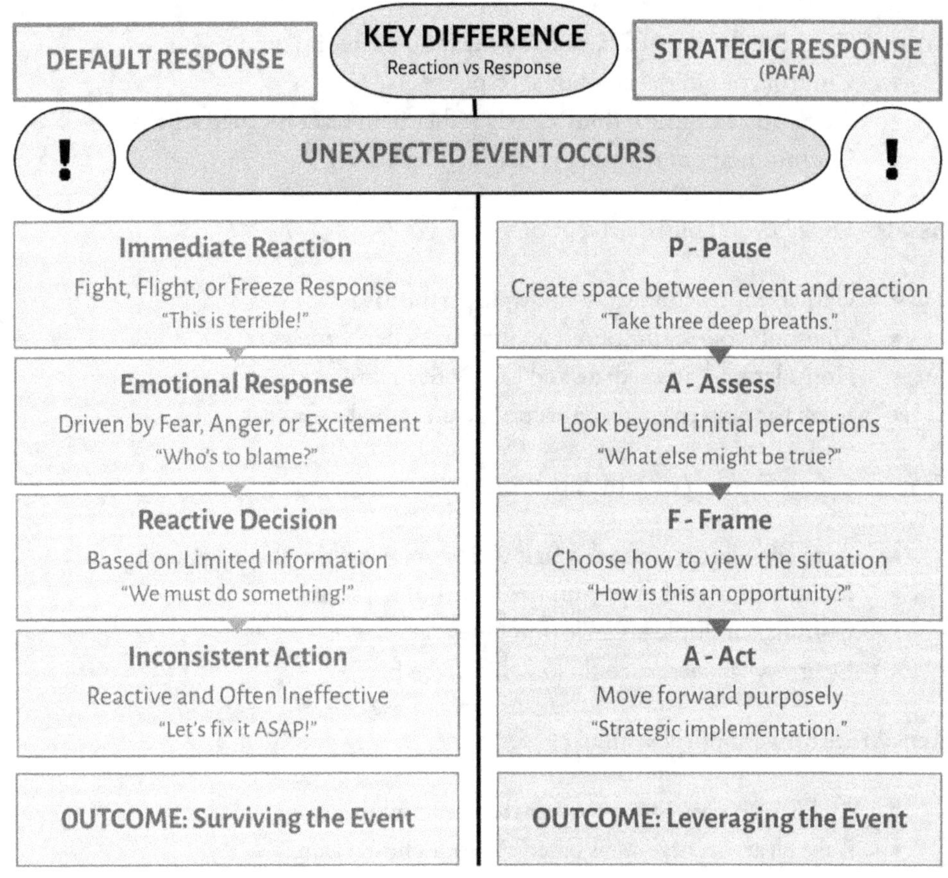

When a trigger event occurs:

1. **PAUSE** - Take three deep breaths before responding. Feel the physical sensation of stopping.

2. **ASSESS** - Ask yourself: "What am I assuming is happening here?

Is it true? Really?
OK, what else might be true?"

3. **FRAME** - Consciously choose a different frame: "How might this be an opportunity rather than a problem?"

4. **ACT** - Respond from this new frame rather than your initial reaction.

Record the difference between your instinctive response and your chosen response.

What possibilities opened up?
What relationships strengthened?
What insights emerged?

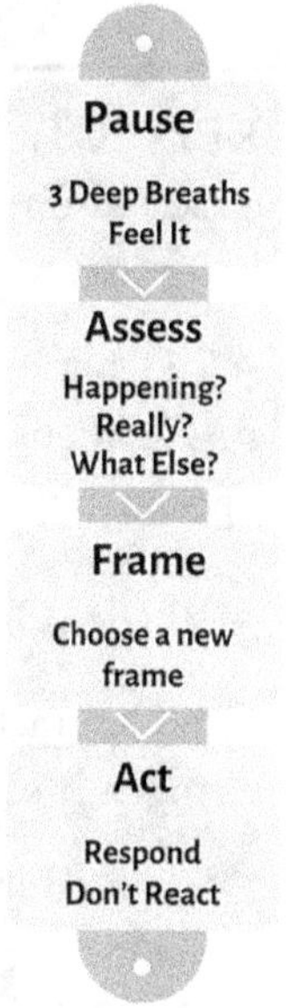

Next time opportunity knocks, don't just answer the door.
Invite it in for coffee.

Remember: The best opportunities often come disguised as impossible situations.

So what happens when opportunity doesn't just knock - it breaks down your door?
When disruption isn't just a possibility, but a certainty?

That's when resilience becomes your most valuable asset.

REFLECT: Think about your last "surprise" - an opportunity or challenge that appeared unexpectedly. Did you pause before reacting? Or did your first response become your only response?

ACT: The next time something unexpected happens this week (and it will), practice PAFA: **Pause** for three breaths, **Assess** what's really happening, **Frame** it as an opportunity, then **Act** deliberately. Don't just react. Respond.

Still thinking about that PAFA framework?

There's something powerful about having a structured way to approach unexpected changes. It's even more powerful when shared with others.

I've created additional tools and resources for mastering the surprise mindset. We can turn the "oh crap!" 💩 moments of life into "oh wow!" 😲 opportunities. Come see for yourself.

It's free, my gift to you.

https://TheCaptainsKeys.com/bonus

*"I used to face unexpected changes alone.
Now I have a crew that helps me see the opportunities
I was missing. Game-changer."*
—CHRIS R., CEO

⚓ NAVIGATE

To Sail the Story / Full Journey - Continue on to the next page
Study the Maps - Jump ahead to page 75

CAPTAIN'S LOG

Chart your course forward

Reflections

Action Items

BEYOND THE STORM
Part 2

Her name was Claudette and she was the biggest, baddest bitch Jimmy had ever seen.

She began as a tropical wave over Western Africa in late August. Within days, she gathered enough strength for weather bugs to take notice. The National Weather Service upgraded her to a tropical depression just after midnight, and six hours later, she transformed into Tropical Storm Claudette, the third named storm of the Atlantic season.

Now, everyone from the Caribbean to New York City was tracking her path. Another rapid-fire intensification came on August 31 when she swirled into a Category 2 hurricane. When the weather service sent a recon aircraft from Barbados into the eye, winds measured 135 miles per hour.

Things only got worse.

Claudette reached Category 5 status in shockingly quick form. She missed San Juan by about 100 miles, but her sheer size and power caused major flooding and decimated the power grid. A week later she made landfall on the eastern tip of Cuba before ramping back up again barreling straight toward the Keys.

Hurricane warnings weren't rare in South Florida, but Claudette was different. Even die-hard residents started evacuating. They boarded up homes and businesses, then crowded onto bridges and causeways back to the mainland. Traffic on I-75 and I-95 north resembled a parking lot for 72 straight hours. Panic brought out the best and worst in people. Many booked last-minute stays at Disney resorts near Orlando, massive hotels specifically built to withstand hurricane-force winds.

Jimmy finally evacuated about 16 hours before landfall. Steve, a buddy from his earlier days on a different charter boat, had a pilot's license and a little Cessna that could seat eight. Jimmy had bumped into him three days earlier at the hardware store where both men had joined throngs buying every spare scrap of lumber to board up their homes and businesses.

"Where you planning to go?" Steve asked.

Jimmy had been caught flat-footed. He had ridden out dozens of hurricanes over the years.

Steve played good Samaritan and found a seat on his manifest for Jimmy. He somehow squeezed Bella onboard too. They'd flown to Houston. Jimmy and Bella snagged a hotel room near the airport despite Steve's frequent offers to let him stay with his family.

Claudette blasted into the Keys as a Category 4 storm with 130 mile-per-hour winds.

Devastation personified.

Houston seemed like a good idea until the storm crossed over South Florida and into the Gulf. The entire coast was on alert. The Florida refugees prepped to flee again until the monster storm veered north into Alabama and finally dissipated over Missouri three days later.

The return flight home was somber and silent. They had all seen the devastation on the news. It was just a matter of getting back to see what was still standing - and afloat.

Jimmy stood in what used to be his living room, though you'd never know it now.

The hurricane had turned his comfortable home into an abstract art installation of broken wood, twisted metal, and scattered memories. His charter business - gone. His boat - vanished. His community - scattered. Even his daily routines of morning coffee on the deck watching the sunrise had been washed away with everything else.

Jimmy looked at his watch - 6:47 AM. Normally he'd be heading out to the marina now, checking weather reports and preparing for the day's charter. Instead, he stood in his ruined living room watching the sunrise through a hole where his east wall used to be.

The light caught the edge of a framed photo, now cracked but still hanging stubbornly on a remaining wall section - his first charter group, all smiles and fresh-caught fish. He carefully took it down and wiped away the debris.

Every house near the lagoon had been flattened. Of the sixteen properties visible in the next neighborhood, twelve were gone. Three had major damage, and one appeared to still be standing, but it was only one wall. The rest of the house was a pile behind it.

Jimmy's car, an aged Toyota Camry, had somehow survived, although it was at least 150 feet farther down the street than he had left it. It even started the first time he put the key in the ignition, earning the Japanese engineers behind this model his infinite respect. It was a good thing too - he and Bella could shelter there until he could find a motel vacancy or temporary place back up toward Miami to rent while he figured out his next move.

His boat was gone. If not for the many photos of it on his social media page and smartphone, you could believe it had never existed. It was difficult to mourn it too severely, though. Everyone's boat was gone. Everyone's house was gone. And those were just the material things.

The loss of life was far worse.

Too many people had been too stubborn to leave. Jimmy could have gone to a funeral a week for the next month if he'd chosen to. He didn't go to any of them. Destruction has a way of dragging you down.

Jimmy retreated to Miami and to a rent-by-the-week hotel that took dogs and understood money would be tight. He did his due diligence with the insurance claims guy and waited patiently on the results, telling himself that it was a once-in-a-lifetime disaster and just a drop in the bucket of all his days on this earth.

Things would get better.

That thought carried him until he got the initial estimate on what his insurance settlement would be. Calling it small would be kindness. The adjuster had not agreed with his estimates of anything he had filed. After paying off the boat and mortgage, the claim check would allow him to buy a new boat to rebuild his business or a new house to live in

It would likely not afford him both.

Considering the devastation the rest of the Keys had suffered, he doubted he would have more than ten customers in the next six months even if he did get the charter started back up. That meant finding work onboard a vessel somewhere else and likely starting at the bottom all over again.

Ugh!

The alternative sounded worse. Heading further north than he had ever traveled.

Double ugh!

He couldn't help feeling like the hand of fate was pressed up against his back as he went over the emails again - one from the insurance agent apologizing for not giving him what he was after, the other from the lawyer, Goodall, letting him know he had seven more months to claim his inheritance before it was dispersed by other means.

For the first time in decades, Jimmy had no idea what to do next. He felt like a kid again, and that feeling of helplessness led him to pick up his phone, punch in the numbers, and smile in spite of himself when his older sister Lily picked up on the other end and said,

"You know the biggest problem with a hurricane? It totally blows."

It was par for the course for her lame Mom joke brand of humor. He laughed way too loudly and said, "Lily, I need your help."

Lily was four years older than Jimmy, which meant she had been half-mom, half-big sister to him for most of his childhood. Now he poured his heart out to her. What road to take? Start over in Florida and hope to build up a clientele and enough savings to buy another boat? But the Keys were home, and the Keys were now shut down for at least six months before they had rebuilt enough to start bringing tourists back. That was six months of nothing.

The other choice seemed to make almost as little sense. Move to the polar opposite point of the country into a miserable environment and start working one of the most dangerous jobs in the world? In a landscape he knew nothing about surrounded by people he did not know, sailing a ship he was barely qualified for?

They sounded like choosing between tuna casserole left in a hot car and anchovy ice cream.

He was dumping a lot of information rather rapidly on Lily, but really trusted her opinion. She knew him as well as anyone. Lily had a remarkable gift to peer right into his mind and help him find clarity. That distillation helped him make solid choices quickly.

So she listened. One of her best qualities. She never seemed urgent to talk. She would listen for long stretches, which is exactly what he needed now. When he had finished unspooling the last crazy three weeks of his life, she said, "Jimmy, I wish I could give you a big hug right now. That must be so tough going through it all alone."

He thanked her and meant it, then went quiet as his sister took her time picking her first words.

"Jimmy, do you remember when Dad died?"

He frowned. He was going through the worst experience of his adult life and she wanted to remind him of the worst experience of his childhood? Maybe he had picked the wrong person to call for advice.

"Of course I do. I was sitting right there when he stopped breathing and they took him off the ventilator. Not exactly the best experience for an 8-year-old boy, was it? Why the hell would you bring that up?"

Her soothing tone came back across the line. "Not the moment he died, Jimmy, but the time frame. When he and Mom realized that the cancer was back, that the tumor had grown again. I know you were young, but I'm sure you remember how much time we all started spending together. They took us out of school for the last few weeks? We went to the beach house and just hung out?"

Jimmy did remember it. He had blocked a lot of that stuff out, of course. When you're young, you can't imagine your parents growing older, let alone dying. Seeing his dad get tired so easily had unsettled him. Seeing him lose his hair and need help standing and walking had made it worse.

But the time at the beach house had seemed like a secret hideout for the family. They watched movies and played board games. Went to the beach and ate ice cream on the boardwalk. In some ways, he realized he had taken that laid-back, beach-town, do-what-I-want mentality and translated it into his day-to-day life in the Keys.

How had he never noticed that before?

He realized he had drifted off deep into the recesses of his mind while Lily had resumed talking.

" . . .Mom had gone to bed, but we stayed up late to watch Star Wars with Dad. It was always his favorite. He could recite it line by line and never got tired of it. There's that part where Luke Skywalker meets Obi-Wan Kenobi in the desert and Obi-Wan wants him to come save the Princess, remember? But Luke says he has chores and his uncle will get mad at him if he's not back on the farm soon. Dad told us that night that his biggest regrets in life were the things he didn't do. The opportunities he had in his grasp that he let slip away for one reason or another."

Jimmy traced a line in the carpet with his toe, suddenly feeling like he was eight years old again.

"I know you never read the diary he left. Mom gave it to me to read years ago when I was struggling on whether to have another baby or go back to work. Dad loved the hell out of us, Jimmy, and he treasured every second we had together. But he also regretted his missed opportunities. So many things he said no to because it was risky, unfamiliar, unknown, even before he had any big responsibilities."

Jimmy thought about the flights he never took, the trips he never made, the chances he never embraced. All while telling himself he was living a life of freedom.

"One specific example was passing up Uncle Rocky's offer for him to come up to Alaska and work a year or two on the boats. It would have been grueling work, and he would have been away from Mom while he was out on the boat when they were first married. But it also would have made him a fortune, and let him experience a real, true adventure. That's what he wrote."

Jimmy's chest tightened. Maybe he and his dad weren't so different after all.

"That last night we watched Star Wars, when he was tucking us in, Dad told us that when he was gone, the only thing he really wanted from us was to go and do. Don't live your lives wondering what might have happened if you had taken the chance, taken the risk, tried the thing that was a little bit scary and a little bit exciting. That's what he always wanted from us, Jimmy. That's what I want most of all for you."

Lily's voice caught on the last words.

"Maybe this is a sign that it's time to leave the easy life behind, brother. Go and do. Go and do."

Go and Do.

The words hung in the air between them, a challenge and a promise all at once.

Have you ever had to start over?

What would you try if you knew you couldn't fail?

What dreams do you have that you haven't attempted? Why?

What resonates with you about this advice?

What would need to happen to make you refuse the status quo and wake up the Adventurer in you?

⚙ NAVIGATE

Study the Maps / Full Journey - Continue on to the next page
To Sail the Story - Ride a wave to page 89

UNSINKABLE
THE HIDDEN RULES OF LEADERSHIP RECOVERY

"It's not about how hard you hit. It's about how hard you can get hit and keep moving forward."
— ROCKY BALBOA

Sometimes life doesn't just throw you a curveball - it throws the whole stadium at you.

Jimmy stood in what used to be his living room, though you'd never know it now. The hurricane had turned his comfortable home into an abstract art installation of broken wood, twisted metal, and scattered memories.
His charter business - gone.
His boat - vanished.
His community - scattered.

Even his daily routines of morning coffee on the deck watching the sunrise had been washed away, with everything else familiar.

When disaster strikes, it reveals truths about leadership that prosperity obscures.

Finding Resilience

The greatest storms don't just test your skill. They reveal your soul. The myth of "bouncing back" echoes hollow when you're staring at the wreckage of everything you've built. In business schools and leadership books, they teach you about crisis management, contingency planning, and risk mitigation. But theory crumbles in the face of total devastation. What they don't teach you is how it feels when everything you've built disappears overnight. They don't prepare you for the gut punch of complete loss or the paralysis that follows.

For some leaders, it's a natural disaster that wipes out everything. For others, it's losing key team members at the worst possible moment. Sometimes it's more personal - health issues, family crises, or the crushing weight of decisions that affect hundreds of lives.

What separates those who emerge stronger from those who never recover isn't talent, resources, or luck. It's understanding that resilience isn't about bouncing back – it's about bouncing forward. The myth of "getting back to normal" after a catastrophic loss can actually hinder recovery. There is no "back" - there is only forward into a new reality.

The Phoenix Principle

Rising from ashes isn't just mythology – it's a fundamental truth about transformation through devastation. But unlike the mythical bird, human renewal isn't automatic or magical. It requires something deeper than just "pushing through" or "staying positive."

Traditional advice tells us to keep a positive attitude, focus on next steps, learn from the experience, and move forward quickly. But when you're standing in ruins – literal or metaphorical – advice like that feels not just inadequate, but almost insulting.

There's a profound difference between a setback and catastrophic failure. A setback is a temporary obstacle, like a flat tire. Catastrophic failure dismantles your entire reality, like your car just melted into a puddle while you were driving down the highway.

Way different.

Real transformation requires three key elements:

1. **Radical Acceptance** - Most leaders' first instinct in a crisis is resistance. We fight reality, bargain with circumstances, or retreat into denial. But true resilience begins with accepting reality exactly as it is - not as we wish it to be. This means:

   - Facing the full scope of loss without minimizing or denying
   - Understanding what can and cannot be recovered
   - Acknowledging the emotional impact without shame

Early in 2025, Mark's Los Angeles manufacturing company lost 80% of its inventory, a casualty of the worst wildfires of the past 70 years. "For weeks, I was consumed with 'if only' thinking," he says. "If only we'd installed better sprinklers. If only we'd spread more inventory across multiple locations. I was so focused on what could have been different, I couldn't see what needed to be done now.

The turning point came when my mentor Jeff asked me a simple question: 'Are you ready to build your next chapter, or do you want to keep editing the last one?' It was exactly what I needed to hear. That's when I realized acceptance isn't giving up – it's choosing to focus your energy where it can actually make a difference."

2. **Strategic Assessment** - Once we accept reality, we can evaluate it objectively, do a damage assessment, and begin formulating next steps. This isn't just about counting losses – it's about seeing the situation with new eyes. While acceptance deals with what was, strategic assessment focuses on what is and what could be. It requires:

    - Taking inventory of remaining resources and capabilities
    - Identifying new opportunities within the crisis
    - Recognizing potential advantages in starting fresh
    - Understanding how relationships and support systems can be leveraged

3. **Purposeful Reconstruction** - The final element is rebuilding with intention. Like a master architect designs with both beauty and strength in mind, rebuilding after devastation requires both vision and practicality. But it isn't about rebuilding an exact replica of what was lost. Instead, it's about creating something that incorporates both the wisdom gained from the loss and the opportunities revealed in the last step.

    - Creating stronger foundations based on lessons learned
    - Implementing systems for future resilience
    - Building deeper connections and support networks
    - Leading with newfound wisdom and perspective

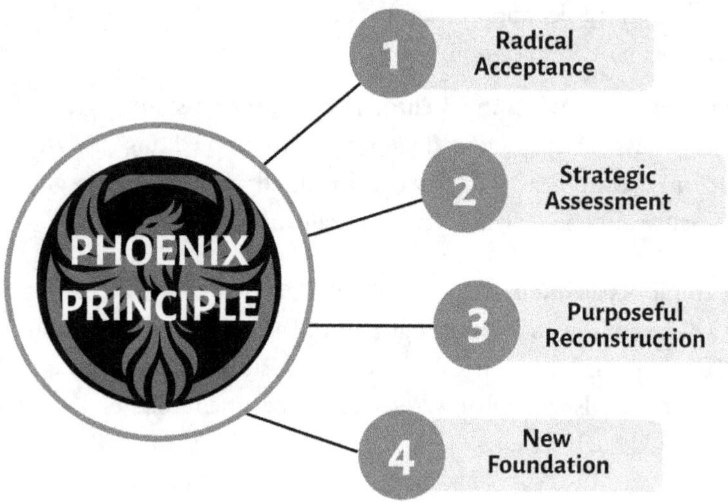

But before we can embrace these elements of transformation, we must first understand the very real physical impact of catastrophic loss. The body doesn't distinguish between different types of devastation - it responds to all major threats with the same fundamental survival mechanisms.

The Physical Toll of Failure

What's rarely discussed in leadership literature is the physical impact of catastrophic loss.

The body keeps score:

- Sleep disruption
- Immune system suppression
- Cognitive fog
- Decision fatigue
- Physical exhaustion

These aren't signs of weakness – they're normal biological responses to extreme stress. The latest research in neuroscience shows that major business losses trigger the same brain regions as physical pain. This isn't metaphorical - your brain literally processes business failure as physical injury. This understanding is crucial because it changes how we approach recovery.

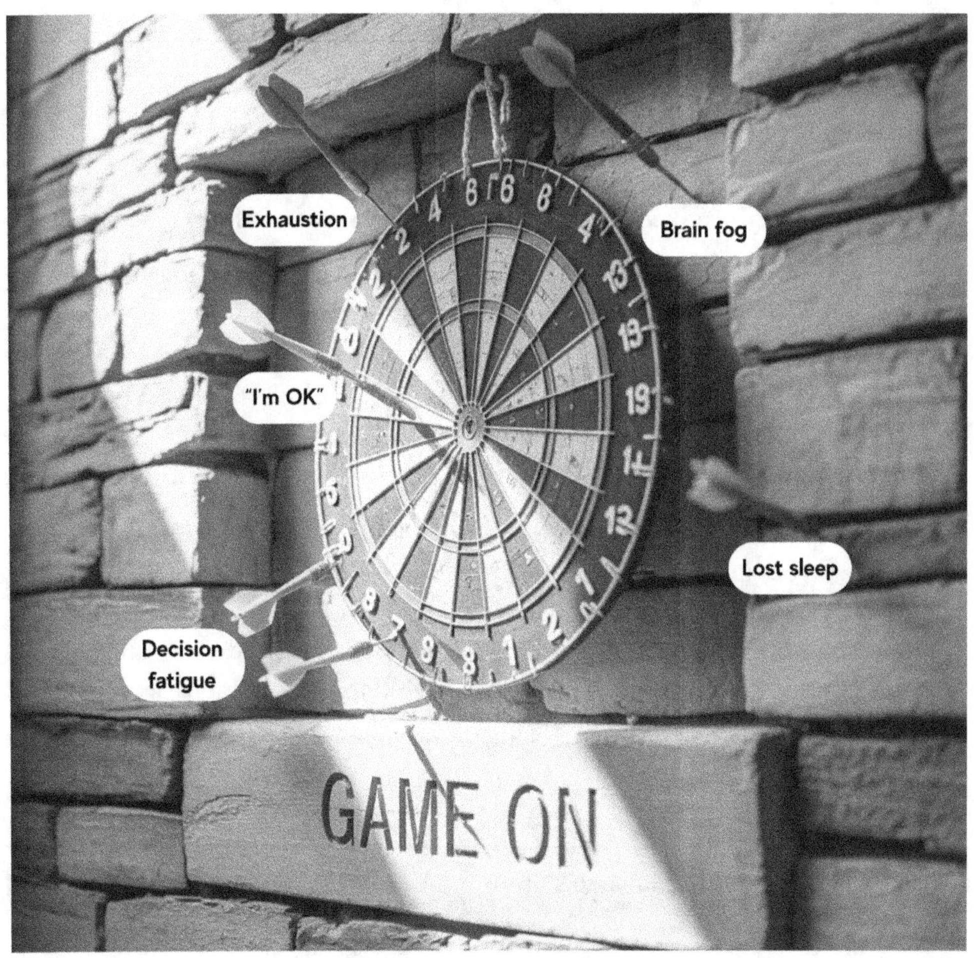

A 2024 study in the Journal of Leadership & Organizational Development found that 72% of executives experiencing a business crisis showed physical symptoms similar to those with chronic stress conditions. More concerning, 81% attempted to hide these symptoms from their teams and families.

My client Monika ran a successful tech consulting firm until a major client's reorganization (aka bankruptcy) nearly destroyed her company. "I kept telling myself I just needed to work harder," she recalls. "I was sleeping maybe three hours a night, living on coffee and adrenaline.

Then one morning, I couldn't remember my daughter's birthday. That's when it hit me - I wasn't just tired, my body was shutting down. It was ridiculous. My doctor said my cortisol levels were higher than some combat veterans. That was my wake-up call. You can't out-hustle biology."

This tendency to conceal our struggles doesn't just mask physical symptoms.
It creates a dangerous spiral into isolation.

Leaders believe they're protecting others by shouldering burdens alone.
That's the lie.

This self-imposed solitude becomes the biggest threat to recovery.
Not the original problem.
The isolation itself.

The Isolation Trap

Leaders often isolate themselves during a crisis, believing they must project strength or shield others from uncertainty. A 2024 Gallup study found that 67% of leaders report feeling "very lonely" during times of crisis, yet only 24% actively seek support. This instinct, while natural, creates a dangerous feedback loop: stress leads to isolation, which increases stress, which impairs decision making. Impaired decisions lead to more setbacks, which lead to further isolation.

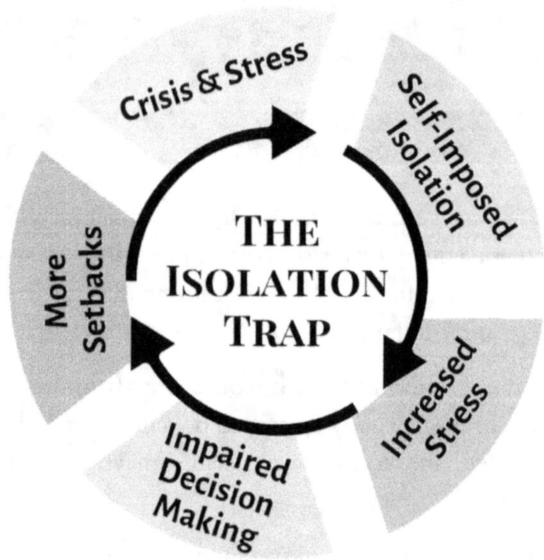

The myth of the self-reliant leader becomes its own prison. While independence is celebrated in success, it becomes toxic in crisis. Research shows that isolated leaders take 60% longer to recover from major setbacks and are three times more likely to make catastrophic secondary mistakes.

Breaking free from isolation might seem straightforward - after all, there are numerous traditional support systems available to leaders. Yet these conventional approaches often prove inadequate during catastrophic loss, not because they lack value, but because they typically operate in isolation from each other and fail to address the full scope of the crisis.

Think of it like trying to solve a complex puzzle while different experts each hold different pieces, but none can see the full picture. Each advisor, friend, or support system views the crisis through their own specialized lens, offering well-meaning but fragmented solutions to what is, in reality, an interconnected challenge.

Why Traditional Support Systems Fail

The core reason support systems fail is that they don't really exist. There may be a couple of people to lean on, or there may be no one at all. Most leaders have not consciously constructed a support system. We weren't taught how. It is assumed that leaders have friends, peers, colleagues, and mentors. Somehow things will work out. *"Suck it up buttercup!"*

Sometimes they do.
Far too often, the storm comes and blows our house down. Then what?

A solid building does not exist by accident. It is engineered, architected, and constructed from the foundation up. Yes, every part is important, but you can't build from the roof down. In the same way, a solid leadership support system doesn't happen by osmosis. It is purposely built.

Elena's story sadly exemplifies the fragmentation of traditional support. When her company faced a cybersecurity breach that exposed customer data, she found herself bouncing between advisors. "My executive coach focused on leadership messaging, my therapist worked on my anxiety, and a few peers shared crisis management tips they probably found on Google.

Everyone was trying to help, but no one saw the whole picture. It was like having specialists treat different symptoms while nobody looked at the whole patient. I was exhausting myself trying to integrate all their advice into a coherent response. What I needed was a comprehensive approach that brought everything together."

How are leaders traditionally supported?
Many aren't. Too busy, too tired, too expensive.
What I hear weekly is "I know I should, but . . ."

The next phrase is irrelevant. No matter what it is, it keeps leaders isolated.

Those who take courageous action to escape the Isolation Trap tend to rely on one or maybe two of these.

Professional Networks: Your usual network often disappears precisely when you need it most. Fair-weather friends and business connections tend to distance themselves from failure or personal loss. Consciously or unconsciously, most seem to perceive it as contagious. They strap on the old pandemic mask and move six feet away. "Well, good luck with that. Hope things work out for you."

Peer Groups: Whether formal roundtables or informal networks, these groups often maintain surface-level discussions. Leaders, still caught in the need to project strength, rarely reveal the true depth of their struggles. The result? Everyone shares sanitized versions of their challenges, reinforcing the illusion that others are coping better. "Everything is awesome! 😀 "

Traditional Executive Coaching: Most executive coaching models focus on performance optimization or specific skill development. While these can be valuable for strategic guidance, most aren't trained to handle the deep emotional and psychological impact of catastrophic loss. They focus on performance when you're barely able to function. "Suck it up, buttercup!"

Therapists: Essential for mental health support, but often lack the business context to fully grasp the complex interplay between personal and professional devastation. They might help you process emotions, but struggle to connect this to concrete business recovery steps. "And how does that make you feel?"

Board Members: While they should be a source of support, the power dynamics and fiduciary responsibilities often create pressure rather than relief. Leaders feel compelled to project confidence and control, perpetuating the isolation cycle. "We understand." publicly [*Start looking for a replacement* privately]

Family and Friends: Their support is genuine but often complicated by their own emotional investment in the situation. Close family may struggle to separate their anxiety about financial security or status from their role as emotional supporters. "Uh . . . how bad is it this time?" *"We aren't going to lose the house, right?"*

Friends want to help, but often don't know how to process problems or a crisis themselves. They can feel very unqualified and hesitant to provide counsel. This is especially true if entrepreneurship or leadership isn't part of their world. *"Get well soon."* *"Call me if you need anything."* Circle back to my comments about peers earlier. It's not their fault. It's what we default to when we don't know what to do.

The fundamental problem isn't that these support systems are flawed. They are all good sources to one degree or another, but each has significant limitations, especially on its own. The problem is that if they are even present at all, they operate in silos. Each addresses only one dimension of a multi-faceted challenge. That challenge could be anything from a weighty decision to a full-blown crisis. Leaders bounce between various people, trying to piece together a complete support structure, but the gaps between these isolated supports often become traps themselves.

The missing element isn't just coordination – it's calibration. When everything falls apart, leaders need a system that can accurately assess both damage and capacity across all dimensions of their reality. They need a framework that can identify not just what's broken, but what's still solid enough to build upon, and the walls that are missing entirely.

This is where traditional approaches consistently fall short. They either focus too narrowly on specific problems or try to apply one-size-fits-all solutions to uniquely complex situations.

It's like trying to rebuild a house without first understanding which walls are still structurally sound. Sometimes "oops" doesn't cut it.

What's needed is a way to make sense of both daily challenges and overwhelming chaos - to see any situation not as an insurmountable wall but as an opportunity for transformation. To get there, we need a framework that can:

- Help leaders see the full picture across personal, professional, and organizational dimensions
- Reveal points of stability in both everyday pressure and apparent chaos
- Offer clear ways to measure where you are and how far you've come
- Be easy for leaders to use, remember, and share

The beauty of such an approach lies in its dual nature - providing both a lifeline in crisis and a compass for daily navigation. When integrated into regular practice, it doesn't just help us survive challenges - it transforms them into catalysts for growth and evolution.

The Need for a New Model

When everything falls apart, the path forward isn't just about strategy or emotional support – it's about comprehensive reconstruction. Traditional approaches treat business devastation like a broken machine that simply needs the right parts replaced. But total loss is more like a shipwreck in stormy seas - you need navigation, repair, and a new course all at once.

The solution isn't finding better ways to "bounce back." It's about building a systematic approach to transformation that addresses every dimension of recovery - professional, personal, and practical. This new model must serve as both compass and blueprint, guiding leaders through immediate crisis while laying the foundation for sustainable growth.

By understanding how to navigate the worst moments, we discover principles that make us more effective in our best moments. The key lies in a framework that's both comprehensive enough to address total devastation and practical enough for daily leadership challenges.

The good news is that a time-tested model exists. In good times, it focuses on ability, strength, and energy to make a leader feel invincible. In tough times, it can transform a journey from devastation to transformation and from an overwhelming maze into a clear, actionable path forward. In the next chapter, we'll explore exactly how it works.

REFLECT: What's the story you tell yourself about why you sail alone?
Is it really about capability? Or is it about control?
About trust? About fear?

ACT: Conduct a simple "support system stress test."

Identify one area of your business that would devastate you if lost, then spend 15 uninterrupted minutes visualizing this loss in detail.

Who would you call first? This reveals your true support network - or lack of one.

Rising from the ashes?

The Phoenix Principle isn't just a concept – it's a lived reality for many of us who've faced devastating setbacks. None of us rises alone - but we can rise!

If you're in that process now (or supporting someone who is), I've gathered resources, stories, and connections that might lighten the journey. It's free, my gift to you.

https://TheCaptainsKeys.com/bonus

"After my first business went down in flames, I needed more than reflection—I needed real connections with people who'd been there. The Challenge gave me exactly that."
—JORDAN L., ENTREPRENEUR/"PHOENIX"

⊛ NAVIGATE

To Sail the Story / Full Journey - Continue on to the next page
Study the Maps - Jump ahead to page 121

CAPTAIN'S LOG

Chart your course forward

Reflections

Action Items

RAVEN'S FORTUNE

BEYOND THE STORM
Part 3

Three weeks later, Jimmy Meyer stood in the doorway of his uncle's Alaskan home, breathing in the dust that had settled over everything like a shroud. The silence was absolute - so different from the constant symphony of waves, wind, and tourist chatter he'd left behind in the Keys. His fingers trembled slightly, though whether from the cold or the enormity of what he'd done, he couldn't say.

"Well, Bella," he whispered to the golden retriever fidgeting beside him, her nose twitching at unfamiliar scents, "we're not in Florida anymore."

The house waited like a time capsule, Uncle Rocky's life suspended in mid-sentence - photos keeping their silent watch, fishing magazines standing at attention by his chair, coffee mugs lined up like artifacts in a museum of a life Jimmy had barely known. His uncle's absence filled these rooms more completely than he ever had, visible in every untouched surface and silent corner.

The first insurance settlement check had cleared, giving Jimmy a little cushion to launch his new life as a crabber - if he could figure out how to start.

When you lose almost everything, moving becomes strangely simple. Jimmy arrived with little more than clothes, memories, and a dog who'd spent most of the flight snoozing on the floor, partially under the seat next to Jimmy like a furry carry-on bag. Not bad for a first time commercial flyer.

Jimmy flipped a switch, and the electricity hummed to life - a small victory in the day's silent battle against inertia. He'd connected utilities before arrival, his Charter Captain efficiency somehow translating to this unfamiliar terrain.

The satellite TV fired up to show a forecast that made him flinch - a gentle snow was falling outside, and the weatherman cheerfully reported it would be "warming up to 20 degrees later this week." Jimmy shivered despite the three layers he'd crammed on himself before venturing outside.

Bella, released from her leash, approached her first encounter with snow like a bomb technician eyeing a suspicious package. Her initial trepidation as white flakes landed on her nose made Jimmy smile for the first time since landing. Soon she was sticking out her tongue to taste it, rolling in patches that had accumulated, suddenly a puppy again.

Jimmy hadn't seen snow since he was 10, spending Christmas with grandparents in Kansas. It had delighted him then, largely because he could retreat inside whenever he wanted, where Gramma Rose waited with steaming cups of hot chocolate and homemade cookies.

No Gramma Rose in Kodiak. No food in the entire house except for Bella's kibble.

His stomach growled in protest. Bella had devoured half the hamburger he gotten at the airport. Jimmy couldn't stomach another bite of fast food – he'd been eating from drive-thrus for nearly a month since Claudette had demolished his life in the Keys.

By the time he layered himself in enough sweaters to prevent immediate frostbite and settled Bella into her crate in the kitchen, the sun was already slipping below the horizon, though his watch insisted it was barely 4:30 PM. He fired up Uncle Rocky's Silverado pickup - instantly the nicest vehicle Jimmy had ever owned - and punched "restaurants" into his phone's GPS.

The search returned a list so short he checked twice to make sure his signal hadn't failed. He'd gone from the Keys - where tourists could sample everything from five-star seafood to beachside taquerias - to what felt like a culinary wasteland. He set the truck toward the main highway, figuring he'd find something, anything, that served hot food not wrapped in paper.

A flickering neon sign reading "Carl's" with a blinking hamburger-and-beer logo caught his attention minutes later. The parking lot was packed with pickup trucks, most of them weather-beaten Fords, Dodges, and Chevys. Men in heavy jackets were streaming inside, their breath forming clouds in the frigid air.

Jimmy found parking down the street and hopped out, immediately shivering despite his layers of Florida winter wear. Tomorrow's priority would be proper clothes, he decided, teeth chattering as he pushed through the front doors.

The blast of warmth hit him first, followed by the smell - wood smoke, beer, fried food, and the unmistakable scent of men who worked with their hands. Carl's was packed with what appeared to be clones: weather-beaten faces beneath wool caps, massive padded jackets on every chairback, and work-roughened hands wrapped around beer mugs.

Conversation faltered as heads turned toward the newcomer. Jimmy felt their eyes catalog him in an instant - sweaters, leather jacket, blue jeans, and boat shoes crammed over multiple pairs of white athletic socks. Someone muttered something, triggering ripples of laughter that spread across the room like a contagion.

Jimmy felt heat rise to his face despite the lingering chill in his bones. He moved away from the crowded tables toward the bar, putting his back to the chuckles. So focused was he on escaping the scrutiny that he barely registered the bartender until halfway through his order.

"Hey buddy, I need a Budweiser and I'd love a look at the menu to see what - " he broke off, startled to realize the bartender's shoulder-length red hair and half-smirk belonged to the only woman visible in the entire establishment. She stood five-foot-nine, maybe five years older than Jimmy, with the easy confidence of someone completely at home in a sea of testosterone.

"Hey yourself," she said, sizing him up with sharp green eyes. "You look like a man who's worked a long day on the open seas and is ready to relax and forget about crabs for a while."

Her assumption threw him. Had she somehow mistaken him for a local fisherman? Maybe it was something about the Meyer look? People said he favored both his dad and his uncle. A surge of confidence straightened his shoulders.

"Actually, no," he replied, trying to sound casual. "I'm just in from the Florida Keys to take over my uncle's business. I'm a sailor myself, but never been on one of these big hulks before."

She made a point of looking him up and down, focusing particularly on his absurd footwear.

"No shit," she said with a smirk, turning away and walking down the length of the bar.

Jimmy felt the flush returning, but she reappeared moments later with his beer and a laminated menu. "It's an effort getting up here from anywhere. But you've got to get yourself up to speed if you want anyone to take you seriously. Sit here and have your dinner." She nodded toward the rowdy tables. "If you try to mingle, those boys will eat you alive."

He thanked her for the beer and menu, irritation flaring at the suggestion he needed protection. He might not spend twelve hours a day fighting storms and hauling crabs, but he'd been on the open ocean for eighteen years. He'd faced massive bull sharks, 2,000-pound swordfish, and a pair of hurricanes that would have sent most of these guys running for their mamas.

The sea was the sea. He wasn't some pier stomper who didn't know port from starboard. He wasn't going to be pushed around.

An hour later, the place had mostly cleared out save for a few older men watching Monday Night Football on the bar's big-screen. Jimmy had demolished a chicken-fried steak, a basket of onion rings, and was working on his third beer. The female bartender – who'd introduced herself as Carly - was wiping down tables as he explained how he'd ended up in Alaska: the charter business, the inheritance, Hurricane Claudette's devastation, and his decision to start fresh.

He conveniently omitted the part where his sister Lily had essentially told him to quit feeling sorry for himself and get his butt to Alaska. The decision to embrace adventure sounded better as his own idea. He wasn't necessarily trying to hit on the redhead, but he wasn't necessarily not trying either. Her occasional smiles and questions kept him talking.

A meaty hand slapped his shoulder, interrupting his story. Three men from the football tables had approached the bar, and one stood uncomfortably close - tall, with a weather-beaten face and bloodshot eyes. His smile seemed friendly, but something predatory lurked behind it.

"Hey buddy, just wanted to welcome you to the island," the man said, swaying slightly. "Name's Derek Pressman, captain of the *Northern Gambit*. I heard you were in town to take over Rocky Meyer's boat?"

How this stranger knew about him was beyond Jimmy, but news clearly traveled faster in Kodiak than storm clouds.

"Yeah, hi, Derek," Jimmy replied, extending his hand. "James Meyer - you can call me Jimmy - I guess that makes me the new captain of the *Bering Steel*. Really good to meet you."

Derek continued grinning while the two men behind him traded a snort of laughter.

"Jimmy, we thought we'd officially welcome you by inviting you to take a shot with us - kind of a tradition when a new captain joins our ranks." He turned toward Carly. "Hey barkeep! Four shots of the Fish Oil Express for my boys and our new friend!"

Had Jimmy been watching Carly, he might have caught the fleeting look of pity crossing her face. But her job wasn't to police the captains, just to keep them from fighting and ensure they left generous tips. She disappeared into the storeroom to fetch Derek's drink of choice.

She returned with four shot glasses containing a viscous greenish-yellow liquid that Jimmy disliked on sight. The smell hit him from ten feet away - briny, pungent, and deeply wrong.

"Uh, you guys drink this stuff?" he asked, eyeing the shot dubiously.

Derek and his companions chortled with laughter. "Jimmy, this is the drink of choice up here! If you're going to be one of us, you've got to drink with us. It's the cardinal rule of Kodiak, now pound one down, you won't regret it!"

Jimmy took the shot glass, figuring one taste would ingratiate him with the locals. Perhaps earn him some respect and entry into their circle where he could get advice on hiring a crew and recommendations for the best fishing grounds. The captains clinked their glasses and tilted their heads back.

Jimmy shrugged, did likewise, and nearly convulsed as the liquid hit his tongue. He'd expected high-octane alcohol, the Alaskan version of moonshine, but this was uniquely horrific - bitter, slimy, and profoundly wrong. His throat closed in protest.

He retched, liquid spattering his boat shoes as the room erupted in laughter, joined by the half-dozen men still watching the game across the room. Carly appeared with a towel, her expression confirming his suspicion that she'd known what was coming.

"What the hell was in that drink?" he rasped when he could finally form words.

"Fish oil," she replied with a resigned sigh. "Weren't you listening?"

Laughter erupted around him, the sound bouncing off Carly's wooden walls.

Jimmy wiped his mouth with the back of his hand. He'd walked right into that one.

Derek and his two fellow pranksters - introduced as Rich Hills, captain of *Red Dawn*, and Johnny Antonelli, captain of *Godfather's Revenge*. The trio bought him a consolation beer and peppered him with questions. When they confirmed he was indeed a Florida deep-sea charter captain, the one-liners flowed as freely as the beer.

"You know the Pacific has a special place for Atlantic captains, Jimmy. We call it the bottom."

"You realize when we say the low temperature is 45 tonight, that means 45 *below* zero, right, Sunshine?"

"Hey Margaritaville, is there any truth to the rumor that you flew all the way from Florida to Alaska searching for your lost shaker of salt?"

The jokes came at his expense, but Jimmy found himself oddly grateful for the human contact. A few more men drifted over as rounds continued, each one telling him Uncle Rocky had been a great man and legendary captain, but he was insane if he thought he could fill those boots.

A mountain of a man detached himself from the shadows in the corner. Unlike the others, he wasn't laughing. His beard was thick and black, shot through with silver - the only hint of age on an otherwise powerful frame. Unlike the others, he didn't bother with superficial friendliness. His eyes never left Jimmy's face as he approached, studying him with the cold calculation of a predator assessing prey.

The bar fell silent. Even the drunken deck hands seemed to straighten up.

"So this is Rocky Meyer's nephew," the bearded man said, his voice a graveled rumble that carried effortlessly across the room. "Thought you'd be . . . more."

Jimmy, determined to kill him with kindness, stuck out his hand. "Hi, James Meyer of Islamorada, but you can call me Jimmy."

The big man pointedly ignored the offered hand. "I'll shake your hand when you've completed your first season, fish. Assuming you're still alive."

Jimmy met his gaze. "And who are you Blackbeard?"

The silence deepened. Someone coughed nervously.

"Burns. Steven Burns." He spoke his name like it should mean something. From the reaction around them, Jimmy realized it did. "Captain of the *Nordic Throne*."

The name triggered a memory - something Uncle Rocky had written in one of his rare letters. Maybe. It had been so long ago. Something about a Captain proudly sitting on the Throne, too stubborn to admit when he was wrong. Cost him more than money could replace.

"Oh yeah? I've heard of you," Jimmy said, surprised to find his voice steady.

"Have you now?" Burns raised an eyebrow. "From who? Your uncle?" He spat the word 'uncle' like it tasted foul.

"Something like that."

Burns leaned in, close enough that Jimmy could smell the whiskey on his breath. "Let me give you some free advice, Florida boy. Go home. That rust bucket you inherited isn't worth the paint it would take to make it look respectable. And you're not half the captain your uncle was."

The insult stung, but Jimmy held his ground. "Thanks for the welcome. But I'm not going anywhere."

Burns' mouth curved into something too cold to be called a smile. "We'll see about that."

He turned his massive back deliberately - the clear dismissal of someone who didn't consider Jimmy worth his time - and returned to his darkened corner, the crowd parting before him like water around the bow of a ship.

"Careful with that one," Carly murmured as she slid another beer across to Jimmy. "Burns and your uncle had a history. Twenty years of bad blood doesn't wash away easy."

Jimmy watched Burns settle back into his corner throne, holding court amid his crew. The man's eyes found Jimmy's across the room, and something unspoken passed between them - a challenge issued and accepted.

Somehow, Jimmy knew this was just the first skirmish in a much longer war.

Jimmy decided he'd made enough "friends" for one night and paid his tab.

As he headed for the door, Burns stepped into his path, leaning down until their faces were inches apart.

"You're wasting your time, and now you're going to waste ours," he growled. "Get your scrawny ass back home before your foolishness gets a good man killed on that wreck you call a ship."

Jimmy bristled at the intimidation but confusion tempered his anger. "A wreck? What are you talking about?"

Burns barked a laugh and turned to his companions. "He doesn't know! He hasn't seen it!" He turned back to Jimmy, eyes gleaming with malice. "That floating garbage pile hasn't even been out to sea in five years, Fish. Enjoy your inheritance, Sunshine!"

CHAPTER 8

Jimmy slept fitfully that night, the bearded captain's words chasing him through restless dreams.

That floating garbage pile hasn't even been out to sea in five years, Fish.

He woke before dawn, Bella's cold nose pressed against his cheek. Through the bedroom window, an alien landscape spread before him - jagged mountains silhouetted against a sky just beginning to lighten, nothing like the flat horizon of the Keys. Everything here seemed designed to remind him he didn't belong.

But the sea - the sea would be the same. Water was water. And if there was one thing Jimmy Meyer knew, it was how to handle a boat on open water.

"Today we see what we've got, girl," he told Bella as he made coffee. "Can't be as bad as dopey Blackbeard says."

His voice sounded unnaturally loud in the quiet house.

"After we check out our boat, I've got to get me some proper clothes. Maybe I'll get you a sweater too. What do you think?"

Bella pranced and wagged her tail in agreement like she understood every word.

Jimmy needed to prove something - to the locals, to himself, to his sister back in Florida who'd told him he could do this. Most of all, to the ghost of Uncle Rocky, whose shadow seemed to fill every corner of this strange new world he'd inherited.

Jimmy broke out the special beans this morning from his favorite Cuban roastery in Miami he missed so much. Some days called for the good stuff, and this was one of them. The familiar aroma filled his kitchen, a splash of Florida sunshine in the northern morning. A taste of home. Coffee in hand and Bella at his side, he headed to the dock to see his ship.

He'd prayed the night before and again that morning that the bearded captain had been exaggerating. The photos from the law office had shown a vessel that, while not new, appeared seaworthy, well maintained, and professional. The boat in those images had gleamed with purpose, ready to slice through northern waters in pursuit of fortune.

Parking at the dock, he thought he must be in the wrong place. Most berths stood empty, their occupants already at sea. Only one contained what appeared to be a floating junkyard - a tangle of rust, frayed cables, and general disarray that sent his stomach plummeting toward his feet.

He pulled out his phone, comparing the vessel before him to the law office photographs. Same shape, same size, same configuration. What had happened? The nameplate in the photo was gleaming, "The *Bering Steel*" painted in bold red letters. The one before him was faded and peeling, barely legible against the rust-streaked hull.

He squinted at a smaller marking in the photo he hadn't noticed before, zooming in with his fingertips. There, painted in smaller letters but the same bright red: "Sarah! Vote McCain-Palin 2008."

Seventeen years ago. The photo of the gleaming boat was *seventeen years old*. Babies born then were now graduating high school. He'd inherited a floating tetanus risk.

Getting aboard wasn't difficult. The gangplank, at least, seemed structurally sound. The more Jimmy looked around, the more his initial dismay battled with cautious hope. The hull integrity hadn't been compromised, and the interior spaces remained largely sound. It was the exterior that had surrendered to the elements.

The crane had seized completely, refusing to budge. Rust devoured every exposed metal surface like acid, and cables hung loosely in places they should have been taut. While Bella contented herself gnawing on a throw rug in the forward compartment, Jimmy checked the mechanicals and threw a few switches.

CHAPTER 9

Jimmy looked at the laminated starting procedure checklist. Brittle and faded, it was surprisingly readable. Not as simple as turning a key, but the process was clear.

Jimmy followed it meticulously. Step by step.

The massive diesel engine turned over with surprising ease, awakening with a deep-throated rumble that Jimmy felt in his bones. The vibration traveled up his legs, through his spine, settling somewhere behind his ribs - familiar yet foreign.

A mix of digital and analog gauges came to life. Jimmy studied them quickly and carefully. All showed in normal range.

Maybe it's not quite as bad as it looks, he thought, running his hands over the wheel. The smooth, worn surface told stories of countless voyages, of Uncle Rocky's calloused hands gripping the same spot through brutal storms and flat seas alike.

Jimmy put on hearing protection earmuffs and opened the door leading down to the engine room. Bella looked at him quizzically. Walking around the massive engine he could feel it's power. While not completely smooth, it actually sounded . . . consistent? Rhythmic? Not bad for something that had been sitting for awhile. Certainly not five years like that jackanape said.

He made is way back upstairs, then around the perimeter of the ship. The water cooling pumps faithfully doing their job of circulating chilly seawater through the system was evident by the telltale holes pushing a steady stream out of the sides of the hull. While not perfect, amazingly everything appeared to be working.

Surprised and satisfied Jimmy made his way back to the wheelhouse. Bella was "standing guard" in the Captain's chair

"You know that's my seat right?", Jimmy said to Bella giving her scruffies behind the ears.

All the gauges remained within normal range. Jimmy grabbed the laminated card again and meticulously followed the engine shutdown procedure.

Quiet.

Nothing but seagulls, and the windblown lap of water on the side of the hull.

A thought bubbled up from the depths of Jimmy's soul. "What if . . . Could I?"

Jimmy knew piloting this beast was possible, even solo.

Between his training on larger vessels, ferry runs, and filling in more than a few dinner cruises in the Keys, the mechanics weren't mystical. Every boat was different, but fundamentally the same principles.

More than a month had passed since he'd felt a deck roll beneath his feet. For weeks he'd been like a cowboy without a horse since Claudette had ransacked his life flipping from comfortable routine to absolute nothing.

The yearning hit him like thirst - primal, undeniable. The seductive siren song of the ocean.

Just a short sprint.

Just a small taste of what had been unfairly stripped away from him.
Reckless? Almost certainly.

Irresistible? Absolutely.

CHAPTER 10

The ocean called, its voice carried on the salt-laden wind whipping through the harbor. Somewhere beneath the anxiety of being in this strange place, something else stirred - pride. The need to prove himself capable, not just to the smirking local captains but to the ghost of his uncle watching from wherever old sea dogs went when they died.

"Driving big boats is just like riding a bike, right?" he said, glancing down at Bella, who tilted her head curiously. "Just like home . . . only bigger. It'll come back pretty quickly."

Her tail wagged once - all the approval he needed.

Jimmy was happy to have Bella in the wheelhouse, away from the danger of the open deck. No chances with his only true friend in a place where the sea killed without remorse.

Jimmy initiated the startup sequence again, a series of valves, levers, and buttons. The *Bering Steel* shuddered awake with a growl that seemed to come from deep within her hull, vibrating through the deck plates, through Jimmy's boots, into his chest. The harbor lay empty - all the real fishermen already at work, battling the sea while he played pretend captain.

If I'm going to join them someday, I need to know what I'm working with.

The rationalization was paper-thin, but he clung to it.

Thirty minutes. That's all he promised himself - fifteen out and fifteen back. A confidence booster. A feel for these waters that looked nothing like the crystal blue Caribbean he knew.

To his surprise, the vessel responded to a gentle touch - not the forceful commands his charter boat had required. She moved with deliberate purpose, her massive weight carrying momentum that demanded respect and foresight.

Away from the dock, the harbor opened before him. Then beyond, to the vast gray expanse of the Bering Sea. Not too far - just paralleling the shoreline, staying within sight of land.

Minutes passed as Jimmy found his rhythm, muscle memory returning with each adjustment. Part skill, part sophisticated controls that made the ferries he'd captained years ago seem prehistoric.

"Hey Bella, I'm getting the hang of this."

Silence answered him.

Jimmy whipped around, scanning the empty wheelhouse. Through the window, he spotted her golden form racing along the deck, barking joyfully at the spray and wind. The sight warmed him - Bella was a water dog at heart, as eager to be back on the ocean as he was.

Fifteen minutes stretched to twenty. Time to turn back.

The distant harbor entrance beckoned, but as Jimmy studied the route home, he noticed something he'd missed on the outbound journey - a channel cutting between a rocky outcropping and the mainland. A shortcut, invisibly positioned from his earlier angle.

He checked the chart. The pass connected directly back to the harbor. Quick and convenient.

Why go around when you can go through?

Jimmy adjusted course. As he entered the mouth of the channel, the *Bering Steel* fought him. Her massive bulk responded sluggishly, like a stubborn animal resisting the bit.

The wind had picked up, driving spray across the wheelhouse windows. Dark clouds massed to the west, turning the afternoon prematurely dim.

He'd almost completed the turn when he heard it.

The engine coughed.

Once.

Twice.

Then devastating silence.

The sudden absence of the diesel's rumble hit Jimmy like a physical blow. The constant vibration that had become background noise vanished, leaving a void that screamed danger.

"No, no, no . . ."

His fingers frantically worked the throttle, panic rising in his throat. Nothing happened. The massive vessel drifted sideways now, caught in a current he hadn't noticed, hadn't respected.

Without power, the *Bering Steel* was just a floating coffin being carried inexorably toward the unfamiliar shoreline.

Through the spray-streaked glass, Jimmy spotted something that turned his blood to ice - a rusted hull, shattered and broken, perched on the very rocks they were drifting toward. A grim monument to some long-ago captain's miscalculation.

He wasn't the first captain to make this mistake. Just the latest.

He tried the starter again. The engine turned over with a grinding screech but wouldn't catch. Each failed attempt drove his heart rate higher. Through the windows, he could see they'd drifted significantly west of the harbor and much farther from shore than he'd intended.

Bella appeared in the wheelhouse doorway, whining softly, sensing his distress.

"It's okay, girl," he said, voice tight with forced calm. "Just a little engine trouble."

A glance at the fuel gauge showed half a tank. Not fuel. Something else. Jimmy wiped cold sweat from his forehead and tried to think. Back in the Keys, engines sometimes vapor-locked in the heat. Could the opposite happen in extreme cold? He'd heard something about condensation in fuel lines freezing up.

The boat lurched as a wave caught her broadside, sending Bella sliding across the deck. She yelped, scrambling for purchase on the smooth surface.

"Stay, Bella! Just stay!"

Jimmy was out of the chair in an instant, dropping to his knees to check the engine compartment access panel in the wheelhouse floor. The smell of diesel and damp metal filled his nostrils as he yanked it open. Beneath him, the complicated heart of the vessel lay exposed - a maze of pipes, wires, and machinery he only partially understood.

Another wave rocked the boat, and something caught his eye through the port window.

In a moment of crystallizing terror, he saw it wasn't a beach at all - not the forgiving sand of the Keys, but a field of rock. Car-sized boulders formed a savage breakwater, with countless more stones lurking just beneath the surface, revealed by each passing wave. And the *Bering Steel* was being driven straight toward them, gaining speed with each passing second.

Jimmy scrambled back to the helm, heart hammering against his ribs. He tried the starter again, but the engine only groaned in protest.

Three minutes. Maybe less. That's all they had before impact.

Jimmy forced himself to stop, breathe, to think. Uncle Rocky's voice seemed to float up from his childhood memories with his mini bike: *"Every engine's got a personality, Jimmy-boy. You gotta sweet-talk 'em sometimes."*

He returned to the engine compartment, this time looking not with panic but with purpose. There - a small glass bowl on the fuel line, cloudy with what looked like water and ice crystals. The sediment separator. It needed to be drained.

Thirty seconds later, he was back at the helm, fingers slick with diesel and trembling with cold. Through the window, the rocks were close enough now that he could see individual barnacles clinging to their surface. The skeletal remains of the wrecked vessel seemed to be watching him, waiting to welcome him to its lonely grave.

He turned the key again.

Nothing.

Again.

A stutter, then silence.

The rocks were maybe a hundred yards away now. Bella had retreated to the corner of the wheelhouse, ears flat against her head.

"Come on, you stubborn piece of . . ." Jimmy slammed his palm against the console in frustration.

One last try.

He turned the key, but this time, instead of gunning the throttle, he eased it forward just a hair, coaxing rather than demanding.

The engine coughed, sputtered - then roared to life.

Relief washed through him like a physical force, but there was no time to celebrate. They were still being pulled toward the rocks, now barely seventy yards away.

His instinct screamed to gun the engines, to blast away from danger at full power. But eighteen years on the water had taught him better. When pushing against a current, overpower was the amateur's mistake. The ocean couldn't be bullied; it had to be negotiated with. Trying to muscle through would only burn out the engine on a vessel this size, one never built for speed.

But there was another danger - one potentially more catastrophic than engine strain. The seabed around these rocks would be littered with smaller boulders, invisible beneath the churning surface. The hull could probably take it, but one solid strike of the propeller and they'd be dead in the water again, this time with no chance of recovery.

Time collapsed into a series of heartbeats. Each decision point a crossroads between life and death.

In the Keys, mistakes meant inconvenience—a tow back to harbor, an embarrassing story at the bar, maybe a bad Yelp review. Here, mistakes made you a cautionary tale. Another wreck for future captains to navigate around.

Or worse—fish food.

Jimmy's world narrowed to the helm beneath his hands. The subtle vibrations speaking a language only captains understood. Read wrong, those signals would be his epitaph.

Through spray-lashed windows, he searched for betrayal in the water's surface - ripple patterns, wave disturbances, anything hinting at lurking danger beneath. This wasn't the crystal Caribbean where you spotted trouble twenty feet down. Alaska's waters kept their secrets until you found them with your hull.

Every adjustment was Russian roulette. Too close to the rocks: certain destruction. Too far out: surrendering to the current again. The margin for error had vanished like morning fog.

Jimmy worked the helm with surgeon's precision, using the current instead of fighting it.

Each correction a silent prayer.

Each successful moment borrowed time.

The distance between them and disaster remained terrifyingly small.

Fifty yards.

Forty.

Thirty-five.

The gap stopped shrinking.

Then, almost imperceptibly, began to widen.

He'd found the sweet spot - just enough power to counter the current without overstraining the engine, and gradually increase it. The rusty wreck on the rocks seemed to recede reluctantly, as if disappointed to be denied fresh company.

Jimmy forced himself to exercise patience, slipping between the swells, inching slowly back toward the harbor's safety. As they finally cleared the danger zone, he noticed details about the wrecked vessel he hadn't seen before - the shattered wheelhouse, the name *Raven's Fortune* still barely visible on her bow, the gaping holes where powerful waves had punched through her hull.

What story lay there? Who was Raven? What fortune? What fatal error or mechanical failure had sealed her fate? Jimmy shivered, knowing how close he'd come to finding out firsthand.

When he finally reached his designated berth, his hands were shaking uncontrollably, sweat pouring down his back despite the freezing temperature.

He shut down the boat and crouched on the deck, fighting back tears of relief and frustration. Bella trotted over and licked his face, then settled onto his feet. Nestled and secure underneath him, yet her warm weight anchoring him to the present.

Dogs know.

They always know when their humans were drowning, even on dry land.

CHAPTER 11

Jimmy was securing the *Bering Steel*'s stern lines when he heard the distinctive rumble of an approaching vessel. The *Nordic Throne* – Burns' boat - backed toward the adjacent slip at a speed that set alarm bells ringing in Jimmy's head.

Too fast. Way too fast.

The collision wasn't dramatic - just enough contact to snap one of Jimmy's weathered dock lines and shift the *Bering Steel* two feet sideways. Just enough to make a point.

"Sorry 'bout that," Burns called out, his voice carrying across the dock. "Current's tricky today." He killed his engine, the *Nordic Throne* now perfectly positioned in its slip. The kind of parking job that demonstrated decades of experience.

"Current's dead slack," Jimmy said through clenched teeth, already calculating how much a new dock line would cost. Money he didn't have, especially after the repair expenses.

Burns stepped onto the dock with the easy grace of a man who'd done it ten thousand times before. "That right? Guess you've mastered our tides already. What's it been - three weeks?"

Several other captains had stopped their work to watch. Jimmy felt their eyes on him, weighing him, judging his response. He forced his voice to stay level. "Been running boats for eighteen years."

"In Florida," Burns snorted. "Giving sunset tours to tourists. This ain't the Keys, boy. These waters'll kill you if you don't respect them."

"I respect the water fine." Jimmy coiled the broken line with sharp, angry motions. "It's the welcome wagon I'm having trouble with."

A few chuckles from the observers. Not all of them supporting Burns, Jimmy noted. Interesting.

Burns turned to leave, but paused. For a moment, something different flickered across his weathered face - not anger, but something closer to regret.

"Your uncle," he said quietly, "was the best captain I ever knew. First season out, I was green as kelp. Engine seized up fifty miles offshore in January. Every other boat kept moving. Not Rocky. He lost two days of prime fishing to tow me in."

Jimmy blinked, caught off-guard by the sudden shift.

"So why – "

"Because this isn't the Keys, and you're not him." Burns' expression hardened again. "This ocean doesn't forgive mistakes. Rocky earned his place. You've earned nothing."

He walked away, leaving Jimmy staring after him, the broken dock line still coiled in his hands.

One of the watching captains, Ben Greene, a weathered old-timer and captain of the *Merlin* drifted over. "Don't take it too personal. Burns and your uncle had . . . history."

"What kind of history?" Jimmy asked.

The old-timer shrugged. "The complicated kind. Ask me, Burns sees Rocky every time he looks at you. And that scares him more than he'd ever admit."

Jimmy watched Burns' retreating back, suddenly aware that he'd stepped into a story that had started long before he arrived - and that his uncle's shadow might be both his greatest asset and his most dangerous liability.

CHAPTER 12

When he had calmed enough to trust his voice, he called Lily on her cell and spilled his guts, everything - the humiliating welcome at the bar, the decrepit state of the *Bering Steel*, and his near-disaster on the water. He wanted to come home, he admitted, except he no longer had a home to return to.

He half-expected her to invite him to stay in her guest house until he could regroup, but Lily offered little sympathy beyond relief that he and Bella had made it back safely from their "test drive."

"Jimmy, you let those guys get under your skin and made a rash decision," she said, her voice firm but caring. "You know better! This is literally the first day of the journey, and you knew going in it wouldn't be easy. Don't worry about the end result - worry about what you can accomplish today, and only today. Stressing about tomorrow does nothing for your health or your ability to be at your best. This is a journey, not a sprint! Take care of yourself, get the right clothes, get some food in your house, make sure Bella has that healthy weight brand she likes, and take it step by step. You've got this!"

He hung up feeling marginally better. Lily was right, of course. Tomorrow's concerns belonged to tomorrow. What mattered now was getting himself situated and supplied. Everything else could wait.

Jimmy studied his list of immediate needs. The *Bering Steel* required more than just his determination to get her fishing again. He needed parts and supplies - and quickly.

He checked his watch. Still early enough to hit Kodiak Hardware before they closed. The locals might laugh at his boat shoes and Florida layers, but money spent was money welcomed, regardless of the customer's origin.

Jimmy stood in the marine supply aisle of Kodiak Hardware, comparing two different types of deck sealant. His fingers were still numb from the cold despite having been inside for ten minutes. The prices here made his eyes water - everything cost triple what he paid back in the Keys. But when you're the only game in town on an island, you set the prices.

"No, no, no - you don't want that model. Trust me."

The confident voice carried from the next aisle over. Jimmy's ears perked up at the authoritative tone. He edged closer to the shelving divider, telling himself he wasn't eavesdropping, just gathering intelligence about local knowledge.

"But the manufacturer specifically said – " another voice started.

"Manufacturers?" The first voice chuckled warmly. "Half of them have never tested their equipment north of Seattle. Look here . . ."

Jimmy peered through a gap in the shelving. A tall man in his fifties, weathered but well-dressed for Alaska, was holding court with a younger guy - probably early thirties, wearing the standard-issue Grundéns gear of a newcomer to the fleet. The kind of gear Jimmy himself had bought last week.

"See this hydraulic winch system?" The older man pointed to something in the younger man's hands. "They'll tell you it's rated for 2,000 pounds, but I've been repairing boats longer than that salesman's been alive. You put that on your deck, first serious haul you try, you'll be lucky if it just breaks the winch and not your entire deck mounting."

The younger man frowned. "Really? But it's nearly half the price of the Yamaha . . ."

"Exactly." The older man's voice dropped conspiratorially. "They price it low to move product. I've had to repair three deck systems this season alone from captains trying to save a few bucks. Nearly got their crews killed when the pots swung loose."

Jimmy felt a twinge of recognition. He'd used similar lines himself back in the Keys, steering new captains away from cut-rate gear that would fail at the worst possible moment. But something in the older man's smooth delivery set off a quiet alarm in his head.

The younger captain of a research vessel was wavering. "I don't know . . ."

"Tell you what," the older man said, pulling out a business card. "I've got some commercial grade systems back at my shop. Same stuff the big boats use. I could let you have it at my cost, just to keep another captain safe. Jason Carpenter's the name."

Jimmy watched the younger man take the card, nodding eagerly now. He started to make a mental note of the name, but immediately dismissed it. He had bigger problems than overpriced winch systems and overly helpful locals. The *Bering Steel* wasn't going to fix itself.

He grabbed the cheaper sealant off the shelf. Sometimes you had to cut corners to get started. He'd upgrade once the money started flowing in.

Behind him, Jason Carpenter's smooth voice continued dispensing advice, drawing in another shopper who'd wandered too close to his sphere of influence.

Jimmy gathered a few more essentials - marine-grade electrical tape, waterproof caulk, a new multimeter, filters, wrenches, pry bars, and pullers. The weight of the basket grew along with the invisible tally in his head. Ship repair wasn't cheap, even doing it himself.

From somewhere near the back of the store, a voice cut through the aisles - low but carrying the unmistakable gravity of authority.

" - told you twice before. Not welcome in my store, Mitchell."

Another voice responded, too muffled to make out words but with a tone of practiced ease, placating.

"Don't care what you call yourself these days." The first voice again, firmer now. "Or what you're selling. Out."

Jimmy shifted his focus to the shelf of marine fuses before him. Small-town drama wasn't his concern. He had enough problems without getting tangled up in local feuds.

The store's overhead speakers crackled to life with an announcement about a sale in the fishing gear department, drowning out whatever came next in the exchange. By the time the message ended, the conversation had moved outside or dissipated entirely.

Jimmy moved toward checkout, mentally ticking off what these supplies would cover on his endless repair list. He winced at the thought of what a 162-gallon oil change in Kodiak would cost. Probably more than his monthly slip fee back home. But it wasn't like he could take a 110-foot commercial fishing vessel to Jiffy Lube - if such luxuries even existed this far from civilization. Everything here was a punch to the wallet: expensive, inconvenient, slow.

In Florida, time was elastic - stretching lazily through sun-drenched days. Up here, daylight was currency, and he was already burning precious hours.

No time for distractions.

CHAPTER 13

With a trunk full of supplies that cost more than he'd expected and a nagging feeling he'd forgotten something essential, Jimmy returned to the dock. He wasn't sure how to prioritize the mountain of repairs, but at least he could start somewhere.

A few hours into repairs, he noticed a man on the dock studying the *Bering Steel* with what appeared to be professional interest. Something about the stranger's posture triggered a flash of recognition, a strange sense of déjà vu. Had he seen this man before? Around town? At Carl's maybe? The thought slipped away before he could grasp it, lost in the fog of exhaustion and information overload that had defined his first days in Alaska.

Jimmy approached cautiously. Back in Florida, unexpected visitors usually meant tourists hunting for selfies to prove their "best life." But Alaska played by different rules. Maybe this was just a neighbor sizing up the new arrival.

The man turned at Jimmy's footsteps, revealing a weathered face beneath a worn cap pulled low against the wind - different from the clean-cut appearance of the advisor at the hardware store. A toothpick bobbed between his lips, which he nearly inhaled when he noticed Jimmy watching him.

"You must be Rocky Meyer's nephew!" The stranger's voice boomed across the dock. "Gosh, I can't believe the resemblance!"

He extended a gloved hand as Jimmy drew closer. "Name's Jason, Jason Carpenter. Worked with your uncle on and off for fourteen years repairing this big rig you've inherited."

Jimmy shook the offered hand, momentarily distracted by the name. Carpenter. Hadn't he heard that name recently? Between the jet lag, the near-disaster on the water, and the general overwhelm of the past seventy-two hours, his memory felt clouded. The man's face didn't quite connect with anything specific.

"She's a beauty!" Jason continued, gesturing toward the *Bering Steel*. "Oh sure, needs some major overhaul just now, but when you've got her humming, she cuts through the water at a pretty pace! Ol' Rocky always seemed to know how to find the best spots and race ahead of the rest of them."

Jimmy smiled, something warming in his chest despite the cold. "I took her out for a test run earlier and barely made it back in one piece," he admitted.

Jason whistled low in appreciation. "You've got your uncle's balls, that's for sure, kid. You'll do well here with that sort of bravado. Can't be timid out on these seas if you want to find the big crabs first!"

The praise felt good after a day of near-disaster and sisterly lectures. Jason's familiarity with Uncle Rocky seemed genuine, and his enthusiasm was infectious. He spoke of the *Bering Steel* not as the rust bucket she currently was, but as the vessel she could be.

"You mentioned you worked with my uncle on repairs?" Jimmy asked, hope rising cautiously in his chest. "Any chance you could help me fix her up? I can pay, of course."

Jason's face lit up like Christmas morning. "Ya serious? Of course! It's been too long since I've gotten my hands dirty getting this pretty lady up to code." He gestured toward the *Bering Steel*. "Mind if I have a look around now? I've got my clipboard in the truck, can work up an estimate for you."

Twenty minutes later, Jimmy stood at the bow watching Jason emerge from the engine room. The man moved with a knowledge and comfort around the vessel that suggested years of experience. Still, something bothered Jimmy. The inspection had seemed cursory at best - Jason had glanced at components rather than examining them thoroughly, had run his hand over surfaces without testing their integrity.

Too quick, Jimmy thought. Way too quick for a proper inspection. But he pushed the doubt aside. What did he know about Alaskan fishing vessels?

"Well?" Jimmy tried to keep the desperation out of his voice. Every day not fishing was burning through what little capital he had left.

Jason leaned against the gunwale, squinting at the fading afternoon sun. "Well I've got good news and bad news." He paused, studying Jimmy's face. "Bad news is, your timing chain's shot. Probably why you had trouble earlier. Left unfixed . . ." He drew a finger across his throat.

Jimmy's stomach dropped. "And the good news?"

"Let's go inside and I'll show you what else I found."

The two of them were seated in the galley table. Jason had used the calculator on his phone and turned the work order to Jimmy, who inhaled sharply at the long list of items needing work.

"It's not pretty, I grant you, and it's going to take a while," Jason said. "The good news is that with so many ships in these parts, it will be easy to find most of them. Just going to have to put a lot of labor into it."

Jimmy swallowed hard.

Jason continued, "The better news is that I can fix it - and fast. Some things will take until next week but the timing chain I can do and have you running better than new by tomorrow afternoon, or evening at the latest.

"Tomorrow?" Jimmy blinked. Hansen's Marine, which he'd called earlier, had quoted him a week minimum to get parts once they knew what he needed. Pacific Diesel couldn't even spare a mechanic to look at it for ten days. "That fast?"

"I've got most of the parts for that in my shop." Jason shrugged. "And I know these engines. Done so many I could fix them blindfolded."

"You can help if you want, but I'm sure you'll be busy doing captain stuff. Ya know pulling a crew together and getting yourself set up in town, right?"

He pointed to the five-digit sum at the bottom of the page.

"I know it's a big number, but I'm not going to charge you that much. Your uncle was practically a folk hero around these parts, and he never had a bad word for anyone, no matter what he might have actually thought. I'll knock $5,000 off that price for you out of my love for your uncle. But I will need half upfront if that's OK. I've got mouths to feed at home and the old ball and chain hates when I don't collect until the work's done. Cash is preferred to get the best deal on the other parts."

Jimmy chuckled at the face Jason made when referring to his "ball and chain". That was one trap he had avoided falling into so far. But he kind of understood needing some upfront money to source parts.

Through the wheelhouse window, Jimmy could see boats returning to harbor - working vessels with crews unloading the day's catch. Men with purpose, with direction. While he stood here with his inherited junkyard, burning through his dwindling savings.

"Look," Jason said, his voice softening. "I know you're in a bind. New captain, trying to get started . . ." His price that was less than half of Hansen's quote.

Jimmy's instincts flickered. Back in the Keys, if something seemed too good to be true . . .

But this wasn't the Keys. And he wasn't a tourist to be scammed - he was a captain. A real captain, despite what Burns and the others thought.

Jimmy hesitated. "I'm just not confident that . . ."

"Look Captain, I've got other boats lined up next week," Jason added, starting to turn away. "But if you want it done fast, I can squeeze you in. Your call."

Jimmy's eyes drifted to the horizon where the last boats were heading out, probably for night fishing. Another day of sitting here meant another day of falling further behind.

"Do it," Jimmy said.

Jason smiled, pulling out a contract from his jacket pocket. "Smart choice. Just need your signature here . . . and here." He pointed to the bottom line. "And that deposit to cover parts."

Jimmy's pen hesitated for a moment over the paper. Through the corners of his eyes, he saw the harbor master walking past, then stopping, then opening his mouth as if to say something. But the harbor master just shook his head and walked on.

"Something wrong?" Jason asked.

"No," Jimmy signed quickly. "Nothing wrong."

Jason folded the contract into his jacket. "Don't worry, Captain. By this time tomorrow, you'll be heading out with the rest of them."

Jimmy watched Jason walk down the dock, already pulling out his phone to call with the good news about finding an expert to help.

The *Bering Steel* creaked in the falling tide, as if trying to warn him. But Jimmy was too busy calculating how much he could make up for lost time once the engine was fixed to hear it.

CHAPTER 14

Jimmy couldn't believe his luck. After Jason left with a promise to return the next day, Jimmy felt the first glimmer of real hope since arriving in Alaska. A local expert willing to help fix the *Bering Steel* was exactly the kind of support he needed.

The surge of optimism called for celebration. A good meal and maybe a beer to mark this small victory. He headed back to Carl's, hoping for a quieter evening than his first visit. After the day he'd had - nearly crashing into the rocks, getting lectured by his sister, and finally finding someone to help with repairs - he deserved a moment of peace.

The little brown bar was quieter tonight. Jimmy was relieved. Most of the fishing fleet was either at sea or preparing for early departures. Only a handful of regulars occupied the booths along the far wall, their attention fixed on a hockey game playing on the mounted TV. Jimmy claimed the same stool he'd sat on his first night. The familiarity, minor as it was, offered a strange comfort.

Carly appeared before him with a glass and began pulling a beer from the tap.

"Figured you'd be back," she said, placing the glass before him. "You have that look."

"What look?"

"The one that says you either had the best day of your life or the worst." Her green eyes studied him with unsettling precision. "Can't decide which."

Jimmy took a long drink from the glass. "Both, maybe. Nearly crashed the boat this morning."

Her eyebrows rose. "And you're celebrating that?"

"Celebrating that I didn't." He smiled, feeling the day's tension begin to melt. "Hey this is good, what is it?"

"Liquid Sunshine. Local Kodiak brew. If you want to fit in around here you've got to stop drinking that moose drool."

"Yep, I am missing the sunshine. But, in even better news, I found someone to fix up the *Bering Steel*. Nice enough guy. Seems like he worked with my uncle for years."

Something flickered across Carly's face - a subtle tightening around her eyes. She began wiping down the already spotless bar, her movements more deliberate than necessary.

"Oh?" Her voice remained neutral. Too neutral. "Who's that?"

"Guy's name is Jason Carpenter. Says he can have the engine fixed by tomorrow afternoon."

Carly's hand stilled on the rag. The silence stretched a beat too long.

"Tomorrow," she repeated.

"Yeah. Hansen's Marine quoted me a week minimum. This guy says he has the parts ready to go."

She resumed wiping, eyes fixed on some invisible stain. "Hmm."

Jimmy leaned forward. "You know him?"

"I know everyone who comes through that door more than once." She nodded toward the entrance. "Some better than others."

"And?"

Carly sighed, abandoning the pretense of cleaning. She planted both hands on the bar and leaned in, voice lowered. "Look, I'm not in the business of telling people their business, but . . ."

She glanced around, making sure nobody was in earshot.

"This is Kodiak. It's a small place. People here have long memories and even longer winters to nurse grudges." She met his eyes directly. "Not everyone has your best interests at heart. Some people only see what they can take from you."

Jimmy felt a chill that had nothing to do with the Alaska air. "You're saying I shouldn't trust this guy?"

"I'm saying trust yourself first. Your instincts." She tapped her temple. "If something feels wrong, it probably is. Desperate decisions make for expensive lessons."

Jimmy sat back, turning the beer bottle between his palms. "I've already paid him half up front."

Carly's mouth tightened, but she didn't seem surprised. "Cash?"

"A few thousand cash, but mostly card."

"Credit or Debit?"

"Debit"

"Call your bank. Tonight."

The certainty in her voice triggered alarms deep in Jimmy's gut. But he'd seen Jason with his own eyes, talked to him about Uncle Rocky. The man knew details about the *Bering Steel* that an outsider couldn't possibly know.

"He worked with my uncle," Jimmy insisted, hearing the defensiveness creeping into his voice. "They were friends."

Carly shook her head. "Your uncle worked with a lot of people, but Rocky had exactly four close friends on this island. Si Adams, Dr. Jerry Yazzie, Pete Malichek, and Mara Stepanov." She nodded toward an elderly man watching hockey. "Pete's right there. Si's probably home reading tide charts. Dr. J's the Kodiak vet. And Mara died two years ago."

She leaned closer. "Whoever this Jason is, I can promise you one thing - if he was your uncle's friend, he'd have been to his funeral. And he'd have waited at the dock to welcome his nephew, not approached you after you showed up."

Jimmy's appetite vanished. The beer in his hand suddenly tasted bitter.

"You saying he's a con man?"

Carly straightened, her professional demeanor slipping back into place as another customer approached the far end of the bar.

"I'm saying be careful who you trust. And check your card balance." She moved away, leaving Jimmy alone with his thoughts and a beer going warm in his hand.

Through the window, he could see heavy clouds gathering on the horizon. Another storm coming. He wondered if that was some kind of sign.

He'd call the bank in the morning, he decided. Just to be safe. But Jason would be there tomorrow with parts and tools, ready to work. The man had seemed genuinely happy to help. Carly was just being overprotective of the new guy.

Still, as he paid his tab and headed for the door, he couldn't quite shake the shadow that had fallen across his earlier optimism. Something felt off, but he couldn't put his finger on exactly what.

Just paranoia, he told himself as he stepped into the cold night air. This place would make anyone paranoid.

Tomorrow, things would start looking up.

CHAPTER 15

The next morning, confident despite Carly's cryptic warnings, Jimmy was up early. He wanted to be at the dock when Jason arrived to start work. He checked his phone - no messages. The man had said afternoon, but Jimmy couldn't contain his eagerness to begin transforming the rusty hulk into something resembling a working vessel.

He drove down to the harbor, coffee in hand, rehearsing questions about which repairs should take priority. The harbor was grey and still when he arrived, coffee growing cold in his hand.

The *Bering Steel* sat exactly as they'd left it the day before. No tools, no parts, no Jason. A sinking feeling began to form in Jimmy's gut. He pushed it away. It was early yet.

He texted Jason.

9 AM. No response.

10 AM. Again nothing.

11 AM. Silence. None of them showed read yet. Strange.

Noon. The harbor sounds seemed to mock him now - seagulls crying, waves slapping against hulls, other crews calling out as they went about their business.

Frowning, he called the number Jason had provided instead of texting again.

It rang three times before a woman's cheerful voice answered: "Kodiak Daily Mirror, this is Rebecca speaking. How may I help you?"

Jimmy froze, confused. "Uhhhh, can I speak to Jason please?" Did the man moonlight at the local newspaper?

The line clicked, and a deep male voice came on. "This is Jason. What can I do for you?"

"Ummm, hey. Jason? This is Jimmy Meyer. We met on the dock yesterday? I wanted to see if you'd started work on my ship yet."

A long silence followed. Then a hesitant response.

"You said your name is Jimmy? Was the man you spoke to in his mid-fifties with a white beard?"

"Yes! Is that not you?"

"Did he have a toothpick in his mouth?"

"Um, yes . . . this isn't him?"

"Jimmy, you must be new to Kodiak. The man you met is not named Jason. His name is Walter Mitchell. He is a professional con man. He's been using 'Jason' because I've done a series of articles about him over the past few years warning people about his scams. I'm sorry to tell you that it sounds like you're his latest victim. Please tell me you didn't give him any money."

All the positive momentum from the day before drained from Jimmy's body like water from a punctured hull. "I did . . . I gave him half upfront on a bank card and some cash for work on a boat I just inherited."

The real Jason, the reporter Jason, sighed heavily.

"Walter Mitchell is not going to do that work for you, sir. He doesn't know a thing about repair work. And I would check the balance and charges on your card immediately. He has some very impressive skills when it comes to scamming people."

The words hit Jimmy like a falling anchor. He thanked the reporter automatically, his voice sounding distant in his own ears. Ending the call, he stared out at the harbor, at the boats moving with purpose while his sat useless and betrayed.

He thought of his charter business back in the Keys - the life he'd built over eighteen years, knowing every hidden reef, every seasonal current, every charter captain and dock worker by name. A life where he could spot a con artist at fifty yards. A life erased in one violent night.

Now he was the mark. The easy target. The Florida fish out of water.

Jimmy frantically signed into his banking app. There was the original charge for half the work - cleared and gone. Below it, three more charges for similar amounts were pending, each slightly higher than the last.

Rage washed over him in a burning wave. He'd been in Alaska less than 72 hours and had already been taken for thousands. He canceled his card and frantically called the bank's fraud department, hands shaking as he punched in the numbers.

The sea had been his home for eighteen years. He'd weathered storms, sharks, and endless waves of drunk tourists without breaking.

Now he reached for his phone - not to call Lily. He couldn't stomach telling her he'd failed before he'd even started. Instead, he did what he always did when the odds were stacked against him: made a list.

Parts. Costs. Timeline. Step by bloody step.

The ocean hadn't killed him yet. This wouldn't either.

But facing that blank screen, his mind was just as empty. For the first time in his life, there was no clear bearing to follow.

Standing on this alien dock beside a rusted hull that was supposed to be his future, Jimmy Meyer had never felt so adrift on the open ocean.

☸ NAVIGATE

Study the Maps / Full Journey - Continue on to the next page
To Sail the Story - Ride a wave to page 137

STABILITY

THE STABILITY MATRIX™
YOUR FOUR-POINT DEFENSE AGAINST LEADERSHIP ISOLATION

"If you want to go fast, go alone. If you want to go far, go together."
— AFRICAN PROVERB

When was the last time you felt truly alone?

Not physically alone – we're all alone sometimes. I mean that deep, gnawing loneliness that hits you at 3 AM when a major decision is keeping you up. The kind that creeps in during your morning shower when you're rehearsing a difficult conversation. The weight that sits on your chest during that long drive home after a day when everything went wrong. Or a day where something amazing happens and you scroll through all your contacts and connections, but don't really have anyone to share it with.

That feeling? It's universal. And it's killing businesses.

The Power of Strategic Relationships

We love stories of solitary genius - the visionary founder coding alone in their garage, the maverick CEO making bold decisions against all advice, the rugged individualist who needs no one. These narratives feed our ego and fuel our ambitions. They're also incredibly dangerous.

The reality? No one succeeds alone. Not Steve Jobs, not Elon Musk, not Jeff Bezos. Pick your favorite founder hero story or magazine cover. Behind every "solo" success story is an invisible network of relationships that made it possible. The problem isn't that we don't know this intellectually – it's that we don't have a framework for making it actionable.

The data is stark: 72% of entrepreneurs report feeling lonely in their roles. CEO turnover hit record highs in 2024, with isolation cited as a leading cause. Even more telling, a recent Harvard study found that leaders with strong support networks were 40% more likely to succeed through crisis than those who tried to "tough it out" alone.

This isn't just about having people around. Most leaders are surrounded by people - direct reports, board members, investors, and customers. But being surrounded isn't the same as being supported. In fact, *the higher you rise in an organization or profession, the more likely you are to have many contacts but few real connections.*

Traditional networking doesn't solve this problem. You can have thousands of LinkedIn connections and still feel fundamentally alone in your key decisions. You can attend every industry conference and still lack the critical relationships that create stability in turbulent times.

Raw power isn't enough. You can have the strongest team, the best product, the largest funding round - but without stability, that power becomes dangerous. Without the right relationships in the right configuration, all that potential energy is just disaster potential.

For decades, we've been looking at business relationships through the wrong lens. We map them on org charts, sort them into stakeholder matrices, or plot them on influence grids. But these tools miss something fundamental: the human architecture that makes great leaders resilient.

Imagine a map that shows not just who you know, but how they keep you stable. A blueprint that reveals not just your network, but your support structure. A framework that transforms random connections into deliberate strength.

> *The most resilient leaders weren't necessarily the smartest,*
> *the most experienced, or the best funded -*
> *they were the best supported.*

The Stability Matrix

What makes some leaders thrive under pressure while others crumble? After studying and coaching nearly four thousand successful leaders over fifteen years - from startup founders to Fortune 500 executives, from small business owners to nonprofit directors - a clear pattern emerged. The most resilient leaders weren't necessarily the smartest, the most experienced, or the best funded. More striking still, they were often the least stressed, most supportive, and downright joyful in their roles, regardless of their present circumstance.

That is success worth replicating!

At the heart of their resilience was one crucial characteristic: they had built intentional support systems that balanced different types of relationships. The Stability Matrix distills these patterns into a practical framework anyone can use. While created with top-level leaders in mind because they are some of the most isolated and lonely, it isn't just for CEOs or formal leaders - it works for anyone facing challenges that feel too big to handle alone (which is all of us at some point). Whether you're launching a business, leading a team, or navigating a major life transition, the principles remain the same.

At a high level, here is how it looks:

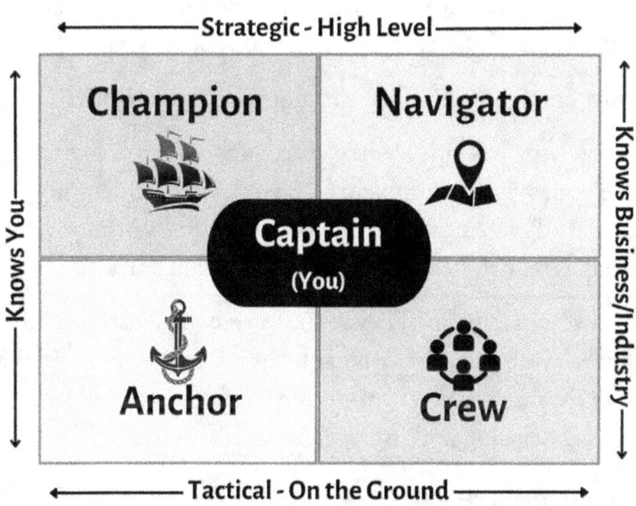

At the center of the Stability Matrix stands the Captain - you. Your role isn't to do everything, but to lead. Just as a ship's captain doesn't personally maintain the engines, plot every course, or handle all the lines, an effective business leader builds and directs a team or support system rather than trying to master every function.

The Stability Matrix identifies four distinct types of relationships, each serving a crucial role where personal and professional worlds intersect with tactical and strategic support:

The Anchor - Your emotional bedrock
The Crew - Your operational backbone

The Navigator - Your strategic compass
The Champion - Your opportunity catalyst

Each relationship type occupies a distinct space in the matrix, defined by two fundamental axes: the personal-to-professional (business) spectrum and the tactical-to-strategic continuum.

When these relationships work in harmony, they create something remarkable - a leader who can weather any storm without losing their course.

The hard truth? Leadership isn't just lonely – it's disorienting. One moment you're making split-second operational decisions, the next you're painting a vision for the next five years. You shift from motivating a struggling team member to negotiating with investors, from solving a customer crisis to reimagining your entire business model.

Each of these moments demands something different from you. Different energy. Different perspectives. Different skills. Try to handle them all the same way, and you'll snap. Try to handle them all alone, and you'll break.

This is why the mix of relationships matters more than any single connection.

Your Anchor keeps you grounded when everything else feels like quicksand. They're not there to solve your business problems – they're there to remind you who you are when those problems threaten to consume your identity. Without an Anchor, success can be as dangerous as failure, because neither defines you correctly.

Your Crew makes things happen. They're in the trenches with you, turning plans into reality, catching what you miss, fixing what breaks. But they're more than just doers – they're your reality check, your practical wisdom, your day-to-day truth-tellers. Without them, vision becomes delusion and strategy becomes fantasy.

Your Navigator sees what you can't. While you're focused on the immediate challenges, they're scanning the horizon, spotting opportunities and threats long before they become obvious. They're not caught up in your daily operations, which lets them ask the questions you're too busy to consider. Without a Navigator, you risk confusing motion with progress.

Your Champion opens doors you didn't even know existed. They believe in your potential more than your current reality, and they put their own credibility on the line to help you achieve it. But they do more than promote you - they challenge you to become the leader they see in you. Without a Champion, you risk settling for good enough.

Matrix Dynamics: More Than the Sum of Their Parts

Each relationship type fills a crucial gap in your leadership capacity. But here's what makes the matrix powerful: these relationships don't just support you - they support each other.

Think of the Stability Matrix not as four separate relationships, but as a dynamic system. Each connection strengthens the others, creating what mathematicians call a "multiplicative effect." When properly aligned, these relationships don't just add value - they multiply it. Often exponentially.

Let me show you what that looks like in action.

When Sophia's manufacturing company faced a critical decision about international expansion, her matrix came alive in ways she hadn't anticipated:

Her Navigator, a veteran executive who'd led global operations, laid out the strategic risks clearly: "The regulatory environment in that region is shifting rapidly. The timing might be wrong."

But her Anchor, her former mentor, reminded her why she started the company: "You built this to bring American craftsmanship to global markets. That hasn't changed."

Meanwhile, her Crew - specifically her logistics director - brought hard data: "We've modeled the supply chain disruptions. They're real, but we've identified three workarounds."

Then something remarkable happened.

Her Champion, an industry connector who knew nothing about logistics or manufacturing, asked the question that changed everything: "What if we partnered with a local firm instead of building our own facility?"

That question - which no one else had considered - led to a hybrid approach that reduced risk by 60% while preserving the expansion timeline.

This is the matrix magic:

Your Navigator and Anchor balance each other - strategic caution meets core purpose.

Your Crew and Champion create a feedback loop - operational reality meets market opportunity.

And diagonally, your Navigator and Crew keep each other honest, while your Champion and Anchor ensure your external success aligns with your internal values.

But here's the critical part: gaps in the matrix don't just weaken one quadrant - they destabilize the entire system.

A leader with a strong Crew but no Navigator ends up executing brilliantly on the wrong things.

A powerful Champion without a solid Crew ready to deliver could potentially push you to heights you're not ready for, setting you up for a dramatic fall.

A Navigator pushing to fulfill your growth mandate may promote a venture that isn't aligned with your core vision when there is no Anchor to prevent mission drift.

The matrix isn't static - it evolves as you and your business grow. Relationships may shift quadrants. People may move in and out of roles. What matters is maintaining the balance, the dynamic tension that keeps you both stable and moving forward.

Your support system isn't accidental – it's architectural.

This is why treating relationships as assets to be collected or networks to be built misses the point entirely.

People aren't objects.
Relationships are not a means to an end.

Quite the opposite.

The Stability Matrix isn't about the quantity of connections or even the quality of individual relationships. It's about the designed architecture of support:

The right relationships, in the right configuration, creating the right dynamics.

In the chapters ahead, we'll dive deep into each quadrant, exploring how to identify, build, and nurture these crucial relationships.

But first, let's talk about how to assess your current matrix . . .

Before you can strengthen your matrix, you need to understand where it stands today. Not just who's in each quadrant, but how these relationships actually function in your life and leadership.

This isn't a comfortable exercise. Many leaders discover they have significant gaps or imbalances they've been compensating for - often in ways that create more problems than they solve. That's normal. What matters is seeing your matrix clearly as it stands currently, without judgment or defensiveness.

Understanding your matrix starts with brutal honesty about who shows up for you in crucial moments. Not who you wish would show up, or who you think should show up - but who actually does. Use these four questions to guide your initial reflection:

1. Anchor - Who do you call first when everything falls apart?
2. Crew - Who makes things happen without you and gives you freedom to focus on things that matter most?
3. Navigator - Who tells you what you need to hear, not what you want to hear?
4. Champion - Who opens doors you couldn't open yourself?

Notice these aren't role-based questions.

I'm not asking about your mentor, your board, your team, or your family. I'm asking about functions - about what these relationships actually do for you. *Someone's title, status, or connection to you matters far less than how they show up in crucial moments.*

Common Leadership Gaps

Simple questions. Difficult answers. As leaders work through these questions (and the deeper assessment available online), four patterns emerge with striking regularity:

1. **The Overloaded Anchor:** Trying to make one strong relationship (often a spouse or best friend) serve all functions. This creates immense pressure on that relationship while leaving critical gaps in professional support.

The danger isn't just organizational – it's deeply personal, as one leader discovered when her perfectly integrated support system began to unravel . . .

Amira built her marketing agency from scratch to a team of thirty in just three years. Her husband David, was her rock - emotional support, strategic sounding board, operational advisor, and networking connection all in one.

When their marriage hit a rough patch, her entire support system crumbled. Not only did she lose her emotional anchor, but she realized she had no independent strategic guidance, no operational mentors, and no professional champions.

She had to piece her life back together and her leadership support system from the ground up, learning the hard way that no single relationship, no matter how strong, can safely carry the weight of all four quadrants.

While an Overloaded Anchor creates vulnerability through over-dependence, the opposite pattern can be equally dangerous. Many leaders surround themselves with tactical support while missing the strategic guidance that prevents costly missteps.

2. **The Missing Navigator:** Plenty of tactical support but no strategic guidance. Leaders often mistake advisors who tell them what they want to hear for true Navigators who challenge their thinking and expand their perspective.

Success can mask this gap until the moment when excellent execution of the wrong strategy leads to spectacular failure . . .

Marcus was crushing it - or so he thought. His tech startup had strong revenue, a solid team, and happy customers. He had plenty of tactical support and operational excellence. What he didn't have was someone to challenge his core assumptions. When the market shifted dramatically, his Crew could execute brilliantly, but no one questioned whether they were executing the right things.

By the time Marcus realized they were optimizing for a market that no longer existed, they had burned through most of their runway. A true Navigator would have helped him spot the shift early enough to adapt.

COMMON LEADERSHIP GAPS

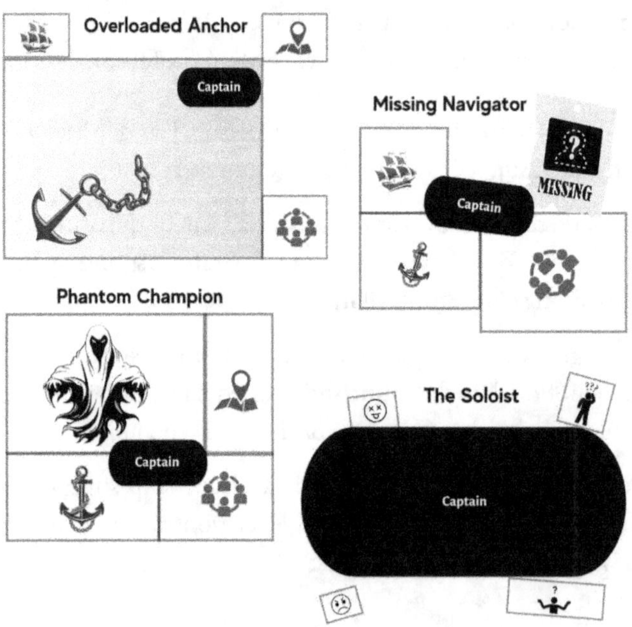

3. **The Phantom Champion:** Assuming someone is in your corner without actively maintaining that relationship. Many leaders discover their presumed Champions aren't actually opening doors or advocating for them in meaningful ways.

The difference between passive approval and an active Champion often becomes clear at the worst possible moment . . .

Natalia assumed her board member Michael, was her Champion. He had opened a few doors early on and made some introductions. But when she really needed high-level advocacy for a crucial partnership, she discovered Michael's support was passive at best. He was happy to endorse her success, but wasn't actively creating opportunities or putting his own reputation on the line to advance her goals. What she had mistaken for championing was merely friendly approval.

The wake-up call came during a make-or-break enterprise deal. Her company needed a strategic partner to scale their healthcare software, and Michael had connections at all the major players. But instead of actively advocating for her, he simply forwarded her pitch deck with a generic "thought you might be interested" note. No context, no personal endorsement, no follow-up. The doors stayed firmly shut.

This forced Natalia to confront an uncomfortable truth: she had no true Champions in her matrix. She had collected impressive names and surface-level connections, but no one was deeply invested in her success. The painful realization pushed her to actively cultivate real Champions - starting with a former client who had witnessed her team's impact firsthand.

This Champion didn't just make introductions; she staked her reputation on Natalia's capabilities, actively sold her vision to key decision-makers, and stayed involved until referral turned into clients. Within eighteen months, Natalia had secured the partnerships she needed, but more importantly, she had learned to distinguish between network connections and true Champions.

4. **The Soloist** - Trying to fill all matrix roles personally while avoiding/delaying/deferring the building of meaningful support relationships. (pick your favorite excuse word)

Leaders become the constraint in their own growth when they insist on wearing every hat rather than building a true support system.

Wait.
I need to pause here.

If you're reading this and feeling personally attacked by that description of The Soloist, good.
That means the message is landing.

I'm not trying to make you comfortable.
I'm trying to make you effective.

And comfort is the enemy of growth.
Always has been.
Always will be.

Being a Soloist makes for a tough life in leadership, not only for you but for your team as well. I've made this mistake more than once. Way more. I had my favorite excuse words for it.

Some of those excuses were even valid.

None of them mattered.

This gap cost me time, killed growth, and great people abandoned ship to move on to places where they felt like their contribution was valued. That what they did mattered.

That actually hurt a little bit to write. But it's true. Of all four leadership gaps, the Soloist is the most common pattern by far.

It's driven by founders who believe in the myth of the solo genius.
Who confuse surrender with failure.
Who mistake control for leadership.

They wear their exhaustion like a badge of honor, their isolation like a sign of commitment, their inability to delegate like proof of their indispensability.

That's not dedication. It's fear dressed as responsibility.

You probably know someone like this.
In fact, you might see that person on a daily basis.

Maybe in the mirror?

I did. For a long time.
I said I didn't, and then acted like I did.
Because I secretly really did!

This one has always been the hardest leadership gap for me. Yeah, I teach this stuff to thousands of leaders, and still struggle with it. Truth.

I joke that I've never let anything go without leaving claw marks all over it. Funny, because there is a grain of truth to it. For me, it's a known issue, and it is something I continue to work on. I probably always will.

It's never easy, but with each successive business and every new stage of growth, it has become better and better. But the tendency to strap on my cape, swoop in, and save the day is always there.

Adam built a genuinely innovative platform with fifteen employees and seven-figure revenue. But every feature, every client communication, every hire required his personal touch. His matrix wasn't just imbalanced - it was nonexistent. He refused to acknowledge he needed one at all.

"Nobody understands the vision like I do," he explained, bags heavy under his eyes.

"Nobody carries the responsibility that I do," he insisted, his phone interrupting dinner for the fifth time.

His words sounded like leadership. They weren't. They were control issues wrapped in vision statements.

The most dangerous part? Soloists often succeed - for a while. Their heroic efforts create remarkable early results. Hustle, grit, and determination work, no doubt about it.

Until they don't.

Founders, entrepreneurs, and executive leaders become the bottleneck in their own business. Until opportunity exceeds bandwidth. Until their body forces the surrender their mind refuses.

Adam's moment of truth arrived via ambulance - a stress-induced collapse that landed him in the hospital for three days.

His company didn't just survive without him. Some things actually improved. Not because his team was smarter. Because they brought perspectives he lacked. Because they finally had space to solve problems their way.

"I realized I wasn't just hurting myself," he told me six months later. "I was hurting the business. My need to control everything was the biggest threat to everything I'd built."

The paradox? Soloists who learn to surrender control don't diminish their impact.

They multiply it.

If you see yourself in any, or all, of these four patterns, take heart. They aren't just common; they're predictable stages in a leader's journey.

I've fallen overboard into all of these gaps. Multiple times.

You too? Congratulations – you're one of us!

We're all leaders in process. If you recognize one or more of these patterns in your own leadership, there is a silver lining.

These patterns represent the natural gaps that form as you outgrow your initial support system but haven't yet built a more robust matrix, or any matrix at all.

More importantly, they present specific opportunities to strengthen your leadership foundation.

Your Support System

Gaps in your support system aren't failures – they're growth signals. They appear precisely because you're evolving as a leader. The relationships, level of thinking, and team that got you here won't automatically take you where you need to go next.

Amira, Marcus, and Natalia's stories illuminate a critical truth: leadership support isn't just about having people around you – it's about having the right people in the right roles. But understanding what's missing is only the first step. The real work lies in building these relationships intentionally, with a clear purpose and mutual value.

In this age of hyper-connectivity, leaders paradoxically face more isolation than ever before. Before examining the key relationships that form a complete support system, we must first understand the central role that makes it all work - the Captain. The myth of the self-sufficient leader has led too many captains to run aground on rocky shorelines.

Here's the thing about transitions:

They reveal whether you're actually going somewhere or just changing scenery.

Most books use chapters like pit stops. Places to pause before continuing the same journey on the same road.

But what if chapters were transformation points?
Not just new information.
But new perspective.

Not just more content.
But deeper understanding.

The Stability Matrix isn't just another framework to memorize.
It's a navigation system for the journey from isolation to integration.

Think about what's actually happening when a leader evolves:
They're not just adding relationships.
They're developing an ecosystem of support that makes their impact possible.

Without this ecosystem, even the most talented founder eventually hits a ceiling.
With it, ordinary leaders accomplish extraordinary things.

Here's the uncomfortable truth:
Your potential isn't limited by your capabilities.
It's limited by your connections.

The isolated genius is a myth.
The supported leader is unstoppable.

Over the next chapters, we'll explore the four relationships that transform founders into leaders:
The Anchor who keeps you grounded when everything else is shifting.
The Crew who amplifies your vision through execution.
The Navigator who expands your horizons beyond your limitations.
The Champion who opens doors you didn't know existed.

Each serves a function.
Together, they create possibility.

Let's begin with the relationship most likely to determine whether you survive the journey:

The Anchor.

REFLECT: Which quadrant of your matrix, if strengthened today, would create the most immediate impact on your leadership effectiveness?
What's the real reason that space remains empty?

ACT: Take one concrete step toward filling your most critical matrix gap this week.

It could be scheduling coffee with a potential Navigator, reconnecting with an Anchor from your past, or delegating a task to your Crew.

One conversation.
One action.
One step forward.

You've got this!

Mapping Your Matrix?

This framework has transformed leadership for thousands who've applied it. Your Reflect/Action work is just the beginning.

I've created deeper assessments, visual mapping tools, and a community of leaders applying these concepts in real time. It's free, my gift to you.

https://TheCaptainsKeys.com/bonus

"I had a few trusted advisors and thought I was good. Seeing it like this rocked my world! I had major gaps, but didn't see them before. Being in community changed my life. I finally found my peeps!"
—ALEX K., CEO

⚓ NAVIGATE

To Sail the Story / Full Journey - Continue on to the next page
Study the Maps - Jump ahead to page 157

CAPTAIN'S LOG

Chart your course forward

Reflections

Action Items

BEYOND THE STORM
Part 4

Every instinct in Jimmy's brain screamed retreat. Go home. Eat something. Sleep. Then methodically plan his next move before this major disaster became a total one.

It was a solid plan.

Which is probably why he did the exact opposite and drove to the restaurant to order a steak and a beer.

Or three.

The familiar weight of failure pressed against his chest as he pushed through the door. The midday crowd was sparse - just a few local captains huddled at a corner table. They glanced up as he entered, and Jimmy caught the flash of a smirk before one muttered something that made the others chuckle.

The sound scraped against his raw nerves like sandpaper.

He steered toward the bar, hoping to find Carly's sharp wit and surprising kindness. But the redhead was nowhere in sight as he approached the polished wood. Then he spotted a hint of copper hair just visible below bar level.

Jimmy perched on a stool and peered down at the top of Carly's head. She was crouched low, focused on something he couldn't see. He opened his mouth to speak when she raised a closed fist without looking up.

"Don't. Make. A. Sound." Her whisper was taut as a mooring line in a storm.

Jimmy froze, suddenly alert to potential danger. His eyes swept the room, searching for threats. Was someone robbing the place? He saw nothing suspicious, just the distant captains nursing their beers.

Carly turned her head just enough to catch his eye, her lips barely moving as she spoke.

"James, I need your help. There is a tundra vole loose in the bar."

The urgency in her voice sent a chill through him despite the room's warmth. *A tundra vole?* He had no idea what that was - beyond bears, crabs, and the occasional wolf pack, Alaskan wildlife remained a mystery to him.

"What do you need me to do?" he whispered back, matching her tone.

"Climb over the bar. Very slowly." The words came through clenched teeth. "You go around right. I'll go left. There's a baseball bat under the bar for anybody who doesn't feel like paying their tab. If you see the vole, go for the head. Hopefully it'll be stunned and we can get it out of here."

"Wait! What does it look like?" Jimmy hadn't signed up for combat with some unknown Alaskan predator. He'd come for steak and beer, not an impromptu gladiatorial match.

Carly's green eyes locked on his. "You'll know it when you see it. Now get your ass over here. If that thing gets by us, it will tear this place apart and cost me money."

Jimmy eased himself over the bar, his layers of clothing rustling too loudly in the sudden quiet. He crouched opposite Carly, who motioned him forward with a silent gesture. The black baseball bat lay against the wall, "Mama Don't Play That" written in silver glitter paint down one side. He gripped it first with one hand, then shifted to two, advancing cautiously.

The bat knocked against the bar twice as he moved, each sound making him wince. His imagination conjured something like a wolverine - fast, vicious, full of teeth. He'd nearly reached the end of the bar when Carly's sharp intake of breath sliced through the silence.

"I see you! I gotcha! I gotcha!" Her triumphant whoop pulled him around the corner.

The beast writhed in her grasp, shrieking in distress. The beast that was . . .

"That's a rat," Jimmy said flatly, adrenaline draining from his body like water from a punctured hull.

"No, James, this is a tundra vole." The first cracks of a smile touched Carly's lips. "They rip into bags of anything they can find down in the cellar, eat what they can, then curl up in a ball and sleep there all winter. You ever reached into a bowl of pretzels and had one of them bite your finger?"

"You acted like it was a monster," he said, his voice climbing to heights that would embarrass a teenage girl. "What exactly was your master plan here? Challenge him to a home run derby for the pretzel stash?"

She smiled sweetly as she carried the creature to the door and shooed it into the snow. When she returned, she calmly took the bat from Jimmy's grip.

"Because when you lose $15,000 to the area con man before you catch your first crab, you need something to take your mind off it, James."

She poured him a beer and handed him the lunch menu. "And I bet it's been a good 7-8 minutes since you thought about that scumsucking lowlife stealing your money and leaving you high and dry, hasn't it?"

Jimmy had to admit she had a point. For those few minutes, he'd forgotten the weight of failure crushing down on him. The brief distraction had reset something in his mind, cleared the fog of despair just enough to think straight again.

"I guess sometimes we all need someone to pull us out of our own head," he admitted, taking a long drink from the cold beer.

Carly nodded. "That's the thing about Kodiak. You can't survive here alone - the cold, the isolation, the sheer danger of it. The ones who try . . ." She glanced toward the harbor where distant masts swayed in the winter wind. "Well, you've seen that wreck out past the breakwater."

He scanned the menu for the largest steak available. "Good news travels fast around here, huh?"

She arched an eyebrow. "You live on an island of 6,000 people, honey. People around here are going to know when you buy a new toothbrush."

CHAPTER 17

As Jimmy waited for his steak, several captains drifted over from their table. Rich Hills led the pack - a man Jimmy vaguely remembered from his first night at Carl's. A tattooed crony with an anchor inked on his neck followed like a shadow, laughing at everything Rich said as if he were witnessing comedy genius.

Jimmy tried to smile and nod along, all while wishing they'd let him eat in peace. He was contemplating asking for a to-go box when Rich decided he wasn't getting the reaction he wanted.

"Now let me ask you a technical question about your boat, Jimmy," Rich said, as Tattoo Neck hovered nearby, giggling in a raspy voice. "Did Walter Mitchell physically bend you over when he took your money, or did you just get down on your knees for him?"

Jimmy felt heat crawl up his neck. From the corner of his eye, he saw Carly moving toward her bat. But before either could respond, a deep tenor voice rang out from across the room.

"HEY HILLS!" The single call silenced the laughing captains. "How's your wife doing these days?"

Jimmy tracked the voice to the far side of the restaurant. Three or four men sat alone at separate tables, nursing beers or eating quietly. He hadn't noticed any of them when he'd entered. The man who had spoken sat solidly built, probably in his sixties, with just a wisp of black hair clinging to his scalp. A well-groomed black mustache and stubbled sideburns framed a weathered face. A shot glass and half-eaten plate of fries sat before him, alongside a neatly folded newspaper.

Rich Hills squinted down the bar. His spine stiffened as he took a half-step away from Jimmy. "Oh, hey Captain Si, didn't see you down there . . . Wait, what did you say?"

Captain Si looked directly at Hills, speaking with deliberate clarity so everyone could hear.

"Your wife, Hills. Remember? You hired Walter Mitchell to teach her yoga back eight, nine years ago, wasn't it? You took your crew out 10 days and left her all alone at home. He must be a great teacher. I heard he had her in a very flexible position when you got home early."

Hills' face flushed purple, like an overripe eggplant. He held Si's gaze for a long moment before breaking the silence. "Ancient history, Captain Si. What of it?"

The older man stood and stretched. "Seems a man who had lost his lady to a con man would be a bit more empathetic to another victim. Why don't you lay off the kid, Hills? Not a one of us save God is perfect down here."

Jimmy wasn't sure he liked being called 'the kid,' but it beat the hell out of the ribbing he'd been taking. Hills glared at Si, then at Jimmy, then at Carly, before whirling toward the door.

"C'mon," he growled to his sidekick. As they left, he called back over his shoulder, "If you're in the market, Meyer, come see me later! I've got some magic beans you might be interested in!"

Jimmy tried to catch Captain Si's eye to nod his thanks, but the older man had returned to his newspaper. Jimmy went back to his steak and his second beer, grateful for the sudden quiet.

He had just finished his meal when Captain Si's voice carried across the room again.

"You're sitting in his seat."

Jimmy blinked, momentarily confused. "Sorry? Does Hills usually sit here? I didn't know guys had assigned seats."

"Not Hills. Your uncle. Rocky used to sit there every time he came in. I used to sit right next to him, and we'd shoot the breeze, tell fish tales. After he passed, I started sitting down here." A shadow passed over Si's face. "Kept turning to tell him something in that old stool and had to remember all over again he was gone."

Jimmy's exhaustion suddenly seemed less important. He gathered his beer and moved down to where Captain Si sat. "You knew my Uncle Rocky?"

The older man folded his paper and tucked it under his arm. "Knew him. Drank with him. Worked with him. Played poker with him. Went fishing with him. Had to haul him back into the boat once when he was convinced he'd hooked the biggest halibut in the history of the world and wouldn't let go of the reel."

A smile softened his features. "Turned out to be an old refrigerator that had fallen off a cargo ship in a storm somehow. He bought me steaks like the one you were chowing down on every Friday night for a month to keep me from telling that story."

Jimmy settled onto the next stool. "Was he as incredible on the ocean as everyone says?"

"No, he was better, truth be told." Si's voice held a quiet reverence. "There's hard work, there's science, there's meteorology, there's biology, and then there's natural instinct. He had them all. But most of all, he had a relationship with the sea that the rest of us could just never understand. It was like he could look out on the water and just know where the biggest load was going to be. Eventually, you just accepted that he had something the rest of us couldn't match. But he was so unbelievably generous, it was tough to resent him."

Jimmy absorbed this honest assessment of his uncle's genius and wished, once again, that he had made an effort to know the man better. "What happened to him?"

Si grimaced. Even months later, Jimmy could see the pain hadn't diminished. "Well, about five years ago, he started getting tired a lot quicker. Started pulling back his hours and relying on guys that were good fishermen but didn't have his instinct. Finally got himself to the doctor, and the cancer was already hard at work. They told him to get off the deck and figure out something to do on land where he could do regular chemo and fight it better. The hours we put in out there are brutal. No place for recovery. It crushed ol' Rocky not to be on the water. He did everything the doc said to fight his way past the disease. His goal was always to get back on the water doing the thing that made him feel most alive."

Si's gaze drifted to the window, where snow was beginning to fall. "We'd still go out on the water now and then, though. You could tell it did him good. Like he was tied to it and always felt better when he was back out on it. We went out salmon fishing up in Kiliuda Bay with a couple of other old codgers. This was about a month before he collapsed. That was our last trip together, and what a trip it was! Rocky caught the biggest King Salmon of the trip. Couldn't stop smiling."

Si smiled like he was reliving the adventure. He paused, and his smile faded.

"I was out with those same guys again, Rocky was tired and skipped it. By the time we got the news and got back home, Rocky had already slipped into a coma. Never saw him conscious again. Two days later he took the final ship."

Silence hung between them, heavy as an anchor chain.

"What about you?" Si finally asked. "Tell me what he was like away from here. Must have been a different guy going home to parties, holidays, summers, eh?"

Jimmy shook his head, sad that he couldn't give Si the answers he wanted. "We met a handful of times when I was a kid. He was larger than life – he'd bring home crazy presents for everyone, handed out money to me and my cousins, would tell stories about some guy getting swept overboard or how they shattered a record for 12 or 24-hour hauls. He never stayed long, though, probably couldn't stand someone else taking all his crabs while he was gone." Jimmy traced the rim of his beer glass with his thumb. "To be honest, I haven't seen him or even heard from him in almost twenty years."

Si shook his head, looking perplexed. "You haven't talked to him in 20 years? And for some reason, he left you everything?"

Jimmy shrugged. He'd been wondering the same thing for more than a month. "Yeah, it doesn't make any sense, does it? The inheritance was a total surprise to me. Although at this point, I'm wondering if it was an inheritance or a curse."

Si raised his eyebrows. "Truck and a home and a business given to you for free doesn't sound like much of a curse to me. You've had a string of setbacks. Lousy luck. No doubts there, but the show is just getting started." His eyes narrowed slightly as he studied Jimmy. "Maybe Rocky saw something in you that you don't yet see? Maybe this is your chance to get out there and silence those jackanapes who keep taking potshots at you. Might just surprise them - maybe even surprise yourself."

"What are you saying?" Jimmy asked, feeling suddenly very tired at the prospect of the unfinished business still waiting at the dock.

"I'm saying it's about time you got some real help, if you're up for it," Si replied. "See if you can give Uncle Rocky something to cheer about when he gets bored playing the harp and flapping with those wings up in Heaven." A grin cracked his weathered face. "Meet at your dock slip tomorrow at 5 a.m. sharp."

CHAPTER 18

Five a.m. in Kodiak, Alaska.

Jimmy Meyer couldn't tell the difference between midnight and morning anymore. The darkness swallowed everything the same.

He'd set two alarms but hadn't needed either. Sleep had come in restless bursts, his mind churning over Captain Si's offer of help. The older man represented something Jimmy hadn't expected to find in Alaska - hope.

The coffee scalded his tongue as he gulped it down. Good. The pain would keep him sharp.

Bella watched him from her crate, golden eyes tracking his movements with calm curiosity. The retriever had adapted to their new life faster than he had. No complaints about the cold. No mourning for the life they'd left behind.

"Just a few hours, girl," he promised, scratching under her chin.

She chuffed when he stopped, retreating deeper into the down comforter he'd bought at the vet's recommendation. A hundred and thirty dollars for a dog blanket. Everything in Alaska carried a premium - especially comfort.

The truck's engine protested as he turned the key, a grinding reminder that even machines struggled against the cold here. Jimmy understood the feeling. Florida had made him soft. Alaska would either harden him or break him.

There would be no middle ground.

The harbor appeared through the rain soaked windshield, a forest of masts swaying against the gray sky. Somewhere among them waited the *Bering Steel* - his inheritance, his burden, his last chance.

And standing on the dock beside it, right where he promised, stood Captain Si.

Waiting.

Jimmy wasn't surprised. Men like Si probably considered 5 a.m. sleeping in. The older captain's breath formed clouds in the frigid air, but his face showed no discomfort - just the calm patience of someone who had long ago made peace with the elements.

"Morning." Si's voice cut through the stillness as Jimmy approached. "Thought you Florida boys needed your beauty sleep."

"Figured I'd better not keep you waiting." Jimmy stamped his feet against the cold that seemed to seep through his boots and into his bones.

Si ran a practiced hand along the hull. "Good to see the old girl again. I own one just like her." He gestured across the harbor to a gleaming vessel that looked like the *Bering Steel* minus twenty years of hard living. "That's mine there - the *Northern Star*."

"Your uncle and I used to joke that we could swap parts in a storm if one of us got in trouble." He smiled at the memory. "Came in handy more than once."

He looked up at the rusted vessel. "She's seen better days, of course, but haven't we all? Let's take a look at that checklist and see what's what - and what isn't."

During their talk at the bar, Jimmy had filled Si in about Walter Mitchell's fraudulent assessment and con job. Now, as they walked the *Bering Steel* together, Si was all business - scratching things off the list, dismissing parts that didn't even exist, adding others he deemed necessary if Jimmy wanted the vessel to last more than a week.

The metal deck beneath their feet rang hollow in spots, solid in others. Si tapped each section with the toe of his boot, listening to the sound with a practiced ear. His weathered fingers trailed over welds and joints, reading the boat's history like braille.

Three hours. That's how long it took Si to complete the inspection - six times as long as Walter had spent on his fake assessment.

Jimmy watched the older man work, noticing things he wouldn't have seen a month ago. The way Si's eyes narrowed when something concerned him. The small nods of approval at signs of sound engineering. The low whistles of surprise when he uncovered unexpected problems.

While Walter had been performing theater, Si was conducting surgery.

"Your con artist had a script," Si explained when Jimmy mentioned the difference. "I'm actually trying to save your life."

The simple truth of that statement settled in Jimmy's gut like an anchor.

Si finally capped his pen and turned the clipboard for Jimmy to review.

"There's good news and bad news"

"That sounds familiar," Jimmy said trying not to dig up the feelings about his recent experience.

"And more bad news and more good news," Si said with a wry smile. "Let's get the bad stuff out of the way. First off, it's going to be a little while before she's seaworthy, which means you're going to be investing more money before you even have one crab to sell.

That means you dip more and more into whatever you brought up here with you. Let's hope it's enough."

A gust of wind cut across the deck, stealing Jimmy's breath. Si didn't seem to notice.

"The other bad news is that your anchor chain is rusted through. We'll get back to that in a minute."

Jimmy's eyes traced the long list of repairs, his savings account mentally draining with each item. The reality of what he'd inherited was finally sinking in. Not just a boat - a responsibility. One that could kill him if he got it wrong.

But Si wasn't finished.

"Now the good stuff. First off, your con man friend doesn't know much about boats, and he put plenty of stuff on here that doesn't need fixing, just a little spit and polish. So it's not going to cost nearly what he said it would."

Relief washed through Jimmy, though it was short-lived.

"Second," Si continued, "I've got a lot of things you need in storage for spare parts for my own vessel. Your uncle and I worked together for a lot of years in the early days, and when we both moved to Captain, we fell in love with the same type of boat. Bought them from the same place at the same time - same model, same manufacturer, hell, the HINs are only three apart!"

The coincidence seemed too perfect. Almost as if Uncle Rocky had planned it this way - setting up connections Jimmy would need decades before he even knew he needed them.

A seagull screamed overhead, its cry cutting through Jimmy's thoughts. He stared in awe at Si's methodical breakdown of the situation, feeling a surge of confidence that had eluded him since his ill-fated meeting with Walter.

"How do you know all this stuff? How do you keep it all in your head?" Jimmy shook his head. "I feel like you're swimming in the Olympic trials, and I'm still putting one foot in the kiddie pool."

Si put a hand on Jimmy's shoulder - the weight of it solid, grounding. Jimmy couldn't remember the last time someone had offered him that kind of reassurance. Maybe never.

"Walter Mitchell knew you had zero experience with these big boats, and he took advantage of it. If I went down to the Florida Keys and tried to get everything I needed for a charter like yours, a greedy vendor could rob me blind just the same."

The harbor sounds faded as Si spoke. The creaking of lines, the lapping of waves, the distant call of a boat's horn, all seemed to dim as the older man's words took center stage.

"Nobody's an expert at everything, Jimmy - not you, certainly not me, not even your uncle. But we're not looking for perfection out here because it does not exist." Si's eyes narrowed, his gaze boring into Jimmy. "What you really need is stability."

Stability. The word echoed in Jimmy's mind like a forgotten song. When had he last felt that? Before Claudette, sure, but maybe years before. Even the fishing charters, predictable as the tides while at sea, were feast or famine on land. One bad storm, an off season, a scary headline about red tide - any hiccup could shut off the money valve.

Si moved to the railing, looking out toward the harbor entrance where waves crashed against the protective breakwater. "It doesn't matter if you're driving the *Bering Steel*, a rowboat in a pond, or an oil tanker in the Suez Canal. If a boat is unstable, it's only good for two things: a warning to others or a house for fish."

He pointed toward the harbor entrance. "That day you took her out when you first got here, you almost ran up on the rocks, right? Saw the old derelict out there, did you?"

Jimmy's stomach clenched at the memory. The looming rocks. The skeletal wreck. The cold certainty that he was about to join it.

"Yeah, Raven's Fortune"

"That's the one. Nobody's bothered to salvage it - makes a better warning system than any buoy. Ocean just keeps taking her piece by piece."

Si continued. "Before you do anything worth doing in business - and especially on the water - you have to make sure all your equipment is functioning. But a boat's got more moving parts than nearly any other machine on the planet. Nobody's brain is big enough to house all that information."

Si tapped the clipboard in Jimmy's hands with a calloused finger. The sound was sharp in the cold air.

"So you need a checklist to inspect it all before you haul anchor. Processes and procedures might seem like the dullest parts of your day when you're going through them, but they are the components that are going to keep you afloat and keep your crew safe when the chips are down."

His voice dropped, each word carrying the weight of hard-earned wisdom.

"If you don't learn that lesson early, you won't learn it until it's far too late."

The wind gusted again, colder this time, cutting through Jimmy's layers like they weren't there. But Si's words had kindled something warm inside him. Purpose. Direction.

For the first time since arriving, he wasn't just reacting to disaster.

He was planning.

Preparing.

Building.

Jimmy felt like he should be recording every word. Si was a fountain of wisdom. He vowed to have checklists, notepads, pens, and markers in his home, his truck, and onboard by this time tomorrow. Getting the boat up to would be an incredible amount of work, but the dread that had been his constant companion since the hurricane was finally being replaced by something else.

Excitement.

Lily was right - he had been living life far too easily.

"You mentioned coming back to the anchor chain earlier," Jimmy said, searching his memory for the thread of conversation.

Si nodded, his expression turning grave. "I don't mean to discount your knowledge of the sea and sailing, James, but things are different up here."

He walked Jimmy to the bow, where the massive anchor chain lay coiled. Rust flaked off at Si's touch, staining his fingers a dull orange.

"In the Keys an anchor holds you in a spot on the reef to let your customers get a good read on a fish and hopefully get you a few more repeat customers. Out here, we use them as an artificial drag mechanism - a sea anchor."

He mimed dropping a parachute behind a moving vessel, his hands telling the story as much as his words.

"Lower it down in your wake, and it will stabilize you against unexpected waves in a storm. Keeps you from taking damage from bow slamming and green water loading. Might make the difference between you coming out of a storm with a full load and them pulling your ship off the bottom."

Si's weathered hands gripped a rusted chain link. "And these anchors - the big brothers to the ones you're used to - they let captains ride out storms in protected harbors. Rest. Sleep. Eat. Safe from dangerous waves, surge, and storms."

"Without one?" His voice hardened. "It's burn fuel and pray."

His fingers traced the metal's corrosion pattern with the unconscious expertise of someone who had handled similar chains thousands of times.

"See this?" He held up the corroded link. "Metal fatigue. Microscopic cracks that grow with every wave until . . ." he snapped his fingers sharply

"Catastrophic failure. Always at the worst possible moment."

Jimmy could almost hear the snap of metal, the shout of panic from a doomed crew, the unforgiving crash of waves against the hull. A chill that had nothing to do with the temperature crawled up his spine.

"You start taking on too much green water, and things get dicey real quick."

Jimmy nodded. He'd seen what happened to boats when they weren't prepared for rough seas. It didn't matter if it was the Haulover Inlet in Florida or an arctic hurricane. Even on reality TV, where events were played up for dramatic effect, there had been times when he was absolutely terrified for the crews.

"Rocky and I got so adept with our positioning and stability we started fishing as a team," Si continued, his eyes far away. "He'd use that natural instinct and pick the best spots, and we'd land on them and use our pots to block the rest of the captains from horning in on the action."

A smile softened his features. "It didn't just happen overnight, though - lots of hard work and dedication got us there over the years."

Si turned to face Jimmy directly, his expression deadly serious. He leaned against the railing, the metal creaking beneath his weight.

"You know why I'm showing you all this, right?"

Jimmy shook his head, rain dripping from his hood.

"Because there's a system to success out here." Si's eyes locked on Jimmy's. "I call it the Stability Matrix. There are four keys that every captain needs, and having a solid anchor is just the first one."

"Four keys?" Jimmy echoed.

Something shifted in Jimmy's chest - a recognition he couldn't name. All those years running his charter alone, handling everything himself, wearing that independence like a badge of honor. What if that hadn't been strength at all? What if it had been his greatest vulnerability?

He thought of his sunken charter boat. The destroyed house. The life erased by a single storm. How quickly everything he'd built alone had washed away.

Si nodded, his face solemn in the gray morning light. "Four relationships that keep you alive and profitable. The difference between the captains who make it and the ones who end up on the rocks."

He held up a weathered finger. "First, the Anchor. Something - or someone - who keeps you grounded, stable. Reminds you who you are when everything else is chaos." Si gestured to the rusted chain. "Out here, it's this. But in life? It might be family. Close friends. Faith. The values you never compromise on."

"That wreck out on the rocks?" Si pointed toward the harbor entrance. Know her story?"

Jimmy shook his head.

"Her captain - guy named Brewer - was known for two things: finding crab and cutting corners. 'Time is money' was his religion." Si's voice hardened. "Three seasons, I watched him ignore maintenance, push his crew past breaking, refuse help from anyone. Pride and profit, that's all he saw."

Si's gaze drifted to the harbor entrance. "Nine years ago, last December, they limped back after an engine failure, just ahead of a major Arctic storm. The harbor was packed full of boats so Brewer anchored up out there."

His fingers tightened around the rusted chain. "That night, their neglected anchor chain snapped clean off. Without it, they were adrift with a crippled engine. Nothing to keep them stable when the waves hit forty feet and more." His voice dropped. "Well, you see the result." He paused, letting the silence speak volumes. "Rolled the Raven over. Three good men. Gone in twenty minutes."

"The warning signs were there," Si continued, "for anyone who cared to look. The NTSB report found three distinct wear patterns in the recovered chain. All of them documented in the maintenance log. All of them marked for replacement."

He turned to Jimmy. "Know what the log entry said?"

"What?"

"'Can probably get one more season out of it.'"

Jimmy turned toward the harbor entrance. Through the morning mist, he could just make out the skeletal silhouette of the Raven's Fortune, still perched on the rocks after all these years. The broken vessel suddenly held new meaning - not just twisted metal, but a monument to failed leadership.

He'd passed that wreck his first day out, seen it as nothing more than bad luck or poor seamanship. Now he understood the deeper warning it represented.

"The most successful captains know they can't do it all themselves. Your uncle understood that better than anyone. Having a good physical anchor will save you, your boat, and your crew in a storm, James. But having these four key relationships? That'll save your business, your dreams, your sanity, and maybe your life."

Si's weathered hand gripped the corroded chain link. "Three good men died because that boat's captain couldn't be bothered to do the right thing. He thought he could handle anything alone. He was wrong."

The parallel wasn't lost on Jimmy. The same could be said about his own life back in the Keys - comfortable, predictable, gradually corroding beneath a sunny exterior. One man handling everything, proud of needing no one.

Jimmy paused, "Si, you said four key relationships. What are the others?"

"We'll get to that Jimmy. The important thing right now is the foundation. All four parts work together in a matrix. I call it the Stability Matrix, and stability starts with the anchor."

Si pulled a grease marker out of his pocket and drew a large plus on the wall mounted whiteboard on deck. Inside the bottom left quadrant he sketched a crude anchor.

"But, Jimmy you need to realize the anchor is more than just a thing; it's a symbol." Si's eyes held a depth of experience that couldn't be faked. "The Stability Matrix isn't some theory I cooked up in a classroom. It's what keeps us alive out here where the ocean doesn't care how strong you think you are."

He paused, his gaze drifting toward the harbor entrance where the wreck lay invisible in the darkness, but always present. Like a ghost. Like a warning.

A cold, rainy gust swept across the deck, but Si was unfazed. "The stories you hear and what you might see on TV is one thing; being out there is entirely different. We aren't out there setting pots and hauling strings for 20 straight hours everyday. We have to have downtime; guys might act tough on shore, but out there, you need space to rest, recharge your personal batteries, and recenter your focus on the task at hand."

Si placed his hand on the rust-flecked chain, his fingers curling around the links as if taking its pulse. "It's not only the boats that need repairing, you understand? The boat keeps us afloat, but the anchor is what really protects us. The weight of command can crush a leader or capsize a ship."

Jimmy turned the words over in his mind. Was he talking to Captain Si from Kodiak Island or Jedi Master Yoda from Dagobah? The man had layers beneath layers.

"Some lessons," Si said softly, "you only need to learn once." He touched the whale pendant at his neck. "But first you have to survive learning them."

"Wow, that's way more than I was expecting. But thank you, seriously, for sharing it. You've given me a lot to think about."

He extended his hand, and Si shook it firmly. The connection felt like more than a simple handshake - a pact, perhaps. A commitment to something neither of them fully understood yet, but both recognized the importance of.

For the first time since arriving in Alaska, Jimmy felt like he might be finding his footing.

CHAPTER 19

That evening, Jimmy spread papers across his kitchen table - parts needed, repair priorities, costs, sources, timelines. His vision blurred. It was 8 p.m., and he'd been at it for 16 hours.

Amazing how an early start changed your perspective.

The room glowed with warmth against the Alaskan night pressing at the windows. Bella snored softly from her bed near the heating vent, her paws twitching as she chased dream rabbits or - more likely now - dream voles.

Jimmy's gaze drifted from the clock to a photo of Lily and her family he'd placed on the windowsill. The only piece of his old life he'd bothered to frame. He did the math in his head and figured it was about 10 or 11 at her home in Miami - worth a call.

She answered on the first ring. "Jimmy? Everything OK? It's midnight."

The concern in her voice made him realize how rare his calls were unless something had gone wrong. That would have to change.

"It's great, Lily. Things are picking up. I met a real old friend of Uncle Rocky who's been helping me see things from a new perspective, and . . . well, I wanted to tell you something I should have said a long time ago."

His sister's breathing was the only sound for a moment. He could picture her settling in for what she probably expected to be a long, dramatic confession.

"What's that, baby brother? That you really were the one who cracked the mirror in the bathroom playing football inside? 'Cause I figured that one out in about two seconds." Her teasing tone wrapped around him like a warm blanket.

"No, this is serious." Jimmy took a deep breath, staring out at the darkness that blanketed Kodiak. "I wanted to thank you for, um, being my anchor all these years. I've been pretty out of sorts for a long time without realizing it, but I've always had you to come to when I needed encouragement or wanted something that made me feel safe. I just wanted you to know that I realized that today, and I wanted to say thanks."

Lily was silent for so long that Jimmy thought the connection had dropped.

"Lil? You there?"

"My goodness, Jimmy." Her voice had softened, all traces of teasing gone. "That Alaskan air must have unclogged your brain. You actually sounded like a grown-up just now." A pause. "And you're welcome. Now let me get my sleep!"

As he set the phone down, Jimmy looked again at the scattered papers before him. Just this morning, they had seemed an insurmountable obstacle. Now they looked like what they actually were: a path forward.

He gathered them into a neat stack, thinking about what Si had said about the anchor being more than just equipment - it was stability in a chaotic sea. Jimmy had always thought independence was strength, that needing no one was the ultimate achievement. But maybe true strength came from something else entirely - from knowing exactly who to rely on, and when.

"Are you seeing this Bella? I think it's a sign. Things are really turning around for us."

Bella walked over and put her head on his lap.

Outside, the northern lights carried out their silent ballet across the Alaskan sky, green tendrils reaching like ghostly fingers toward the stars. Jimmy watched through the window with a sense of awe.

Perhaps he wasn't adrift after all.

He had an anchor. He always had.

And now, maybe, he was finally learning how to use it.

☸ NAVIGATE

Study the Maps / Full Journey - Continue on to the next page
To Sail the Story - Ride a wave to page 179

CAPTAIN'S LOG

Chart your course forward

Reflections

Action Items

THE ANCHOR
SOLID GROUND WHEN THE WORLD IS SHIFTING

*"The most important thing in life will always be family.
The people right here, right now."*
— DOMINIC TORETTO, THE FAST AND THE FURIOUS

Drowning rarely looks like drowning.

The thrashing, the screaming, the dramatic gasps for air? That's Hollywood.

Real drowning is silent. Subtle. Often unnoticed until it's too late.

The call came Saturday evening.

I recognized the tone before I registered the words. The particular quiet that comes when someone's lungs are filling with water while everyone around them sips cocktails.

Not physical drowning. Something worse.

I'd seen it before, but never this complete. A CEO losing everything that mattered in 72 brutal hours.

Not his company. Not his title. Not his market share.
His marriage. His health. His sense of self.

The markets called him "visionary." The business press labeled him "unstoppable." His board considered him "irreplaceable."

None of it mattered now.

He had anchors everywhere - boats in three marinas, a beautiful custom yacht named after his company - but not a single Anchor where it counted. No one who could tell him who he was beyond the metrics. No one who remembered the human beneath the headlines. No one who could speak the truth when everyone else was selling comfort.

By the time he called me, the water had already reached his chin.

He wasn't looking for business advice. He was drowning in plain sight, surrounded by people, even "close friends", and yet completely alone.

This isn't just his story.
It might be yours.
It's definitely a warning.

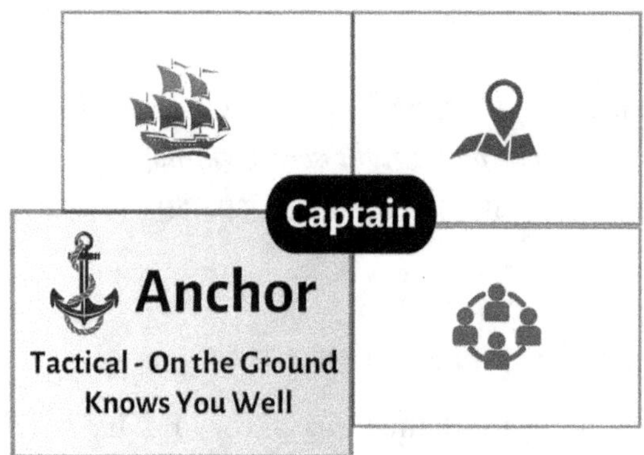

The Silent Crisis

The most dangerous moment in any storm isn't when the waves are highest or the wind is strongest. It's that deceptive pause when you think the worst has passed, when your guard drops just enough to make a fatal mistake.

Leadership today feels a lot like that moment.

We're more connected than ever - smartphones, social media, Slack channels, Teams meetings, virtual happy hours. The average executive receives 156 messages before their morning coffee. Yet among all this noise, something essential has gone missing: true connection.

The statistics are staggering. A 2024 Harvard Business Review study found that 76% of CEOs report feeling "professionally isolated." Another 68% admit to having no one they can talk to honestly about their struggles. Even more telling, 82% say they've made major mistakes they could have avoided if they'd had someone to confide in first.

This isn't just data. It's a crisis.

Every day, capable leaders are drowning in plain sight. They maintain a perfect LinkedIn presence while their marriage crumbles. They post about record quarters while lying awake at 3 a.m., wondering if they're frauds. They inspire their teams with vision talks while secretly planning their escape.

I call this the Tower Principle. Just as a ship becomes more unstable the higher its bridge rises above its hull, a captain elevated above their crew faces unique structural pressures. The taller the command tower stands above the deck, the more it needs the stabilizing support of every level below to remain steady in rough seas.

Think of successful businesses as well-designed vessels. The bridge isn't meant to stand alone – it's integrated into the ship's superstructure, supported by every deck beneath it. But too many leaders try to command from an isolated tower, not realizing that height without foundation is just a capsize waiting to happen.

It's not just the emotional toll we're talking about. Isolation kills businesses. A 2024 study of failed startups found that 67% of founders cited "leadership isolation" as a key factor in their company's demise. Not market conditions. Not competition. Not funding. Isolation.

Here's what makes this crisis particularly insidious: it feels normal. We've romanticized the image of the solitary leader so thoroughly that many mask their isolation as independence.

"It's lonely at the top" isn't just a cliché – it's become a leadership identity.

But here's what they don't teach you in business school: The most successful leaders aren't solo acts. They're deeply, intentionally connected to people who keep them grounded, focused, and aligned with their purpose. They have what we call Anchors.

Not mentors. Not advisors. Not coaches. Anchors.

The difference is crucial. Mentors guide you. Advisors inform you. Coaches push you. But Anchors? They hold you steady when everything else is moving. They remind you who you are when success or failure threatens to redefine you. They provide safe harbor when storms rage, and they keep you from drifting when seas are calm.

Think about actual maritime anchors for a moment. They serve two critical functions: they keep you from drifting in calm waters, and they provide stability in storms. More importantly, they connect you to something solid when everything around you is fluid.

Your leadership Anchor serves the same purpose. They're not there to plot your course or trim your sails. They're there to keep you connected to solid ground - to your values, your purpose, your authentic self - when market forces and leadership pressures threaten to set you adrift.

This isn't just theory. It's survival.

Finding True North: The Anchor Relationship

Every ship's compass points to magnetic north, but every captain knows there's a difference between magnetic north and true north. The same principle applies to leadership support. While many relationships appear to offer guidance, true Anchor relationships point to something deeper.

Let's be clear about what an Anchor isn't:

- It's not your board of directors (though a board member might be your Anchor)
- It's not your executive coach (though they might help you identify your Anchor)
- It's not your mentor (though mentors sometimes evolve into Anchors)
- It's not your therapist (though therapy might help you be ready for an Anchor)

An Anchor is someone who knows both who you are and who you're capable of becoming. They hold space for both your current reality and your future potential. Most importantly, they're connected to you as a person, not just as a leader.

This is why Anchors come first in the Stability Matrix. Without this foundation of authentic connection, other leadership relationships become transactional. Your Crew becomes just employees. Your Navigator becomes just a strategist. Your Champion becomes just a networker. The entire matrix depends on you remaining grounded in who you are and why you lead.

Consider Mikayla, a tech CEO whose company was growing 300% annually. From the outside, everything looked perfect. Revenue soaring. Headcount expanding. Investors happy. But inside, she was losing herself.

"I had advisors telling me to be more aggressive, coaches pushing me to be more visible, mentors suggesting new strategies," she recalls. "What I didn't have was someone who remembered why I started the company in the first place - to make technology more accessible to small businesses. My favorite professor from college became my Anchor. He was the only one who could still see the idealistic student buried deep inside the hard-charging CEO. He helped me reconnect with my purpose when success threatened to pull me away from it."

This highlights the critical difference between advice and anchoring. Advice focuses on what you should do. Anchoring focuses on who you are. Anyone can tell you to cut costs or pivot strategies. Only an Anchor can remind you of your core values when those decisions feel impossible.

This is where positional power actually works against authentic connection. The higher you rise in an organization, the more people want something from you - your time, your influence, your resources. An Anchor wants something for you - your growth, your wellbeing, your authentic success.

The paradox? Just when you need this kind of relationship most - when the stakes are highest and the decisions hardest - it becomes most difficult to find. Power dynamics create artificial barriers. Time pressures make deep connections feel impossible. The very success that makes you "important" makes you increasingly isolated.

This is why intentionally cultivating Anchor relationships early in your leadership journey is crucial. You need these connections established before you need them most. Because when the storm hits, it's too late to start building a harbor.

Anatomy of an Anchor

What makes someone a true Anchor? It's not their title, their experience, or even their wisdom - though these might be present. It's their ability to provide both technical stability and emotional ballast when you need it most.

Think of an actual ship's anchor. Its effectiveness comes from both its design (technical) and its ability to find solid ground (foundational). A leadership Anchor works the same way.

Technical Support:

- Helps you maintain perspective when problems feel overwhelming
- Provides honest feedback without an agenda
- Creates space for reflection and recalibration
- Holds you accountable to your own values and standards

Emotional Ballast:

- Offers unconditional support (not unlimited agreement)
- Creates psychological safety for vulnerability

- Maintains connection regardless of your success or failure
- Remembers who you were before the title

This brings us to what we call the *Stability Paradox: The more successful you become, the more you need grounding in who you really are.* Yet success itself makes authentic connections harder to maintain.

Power dynamics creep in. People treat you differently. You start censoring yourself.

This is precisely why understanding different types of Anchor relationships is crucial.

ANATOMY OF AN ANCHOR

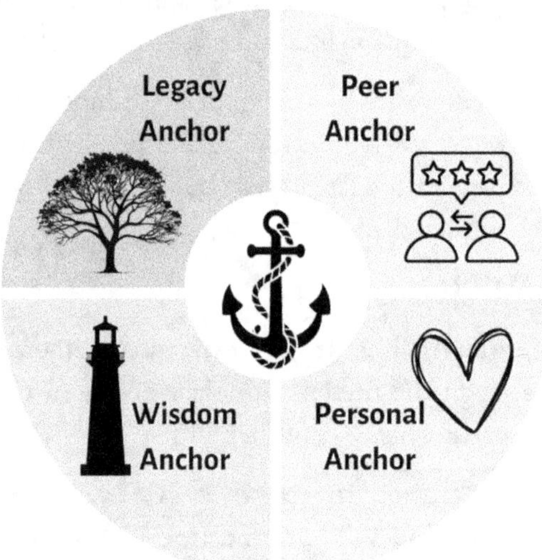

Types of Anchor Relationships:

1. **The Legacy Anchor**
   Often, a family member or lifelong friend who knew you "before." They carry your history and can call you back to your core self. They're immune to your title because they changed your diapers or remember when you worked at the mall.

2. **The Peer Anchor**
   Someone walking a similar path who understands your current challenges from life experience. They provide tactical support because they've faced similar decisions. These relationships often start as networking or peer group connections but deepen through shared experience.

3. **The Wisdom Anchor**

    Usually, someone who's further along their journey and has maintained their authenticity through success. They model life and character you admire, demonstrate what's possible, and provide perspective when you can't see the forest for the trees.

4. **The Personal Anchor**

    Often a spouse, partner, or close friend who holds space for your whole self, not just your professional identity. They keep you connected to your non-work values, hobbies, creative endeavors, and priorities. Sometimes mental health professionals or counselors fill or supplement this role for a season.

Most successful leaders have multiple Anchors, each serving different needs. This prevents overload on any single relationship and provides redundancy when one connection isn't available.

The key is authenticity. You can't manufacture these relationships or force them to develop. What you can do is create conditions where they might flourish:

- Be vulnerable first
- Show up consistently for others
- Maintain boundaries that protect the relationship
- Invest time in non-transactional connection
- Practice reciprocity without keeping score

Remember: An Anchor's power comes not from their ability to solve your problems, but from their ability to help you process and remain steady while you solve them yourself.

The Loudest Storm: Self-Doubt

The fiercest storms don't come from market forces or competitor moves. They rage inside your own mind at 3 AM, when the mask of certainty slips and the questions flood in:

"Am I really qualified for this?"
"What if everyone realizes I'm making it up as I go?"
"Do I deserve this success?"

This is where Anchors prove most vital, not by dismissing these doubts, but by helping you navigate them. They've seen you succeed before. They remember your capabilities when you forget them. Most importantly, they understand that self-doubt isn't weakness – it's often the shadow side of the very qualities that make you effective: self-awareness, humility, and the drive to improve.

Consider Dominique's story: "I was leading a $500 million division, but inside I felt like an impostor. Every success made the feeling worse, not better. My Anchor, my former mentor, helped me see that my self-doubt wasn't about competence - it was about identity. I wasn't struggling with whether I could do the job. I was struggling with whether success had changed who I was. She helped me separate performance from personhood."

Weathering The Storm

Every leader faces storms. Some are sudden squalls that pass quickly - a key employee quitting, a major client leaving, a product launch failing. Others are perfect storms that threaten everything - market crashes, global pandemics, and personal health crises. The difference between those who emerge stronger and those who capsize often comes down to one factor: the strength of their Anchor relationships.

Types of Business Storms

The most dangerous storms are often combinations - like when a personal health crisis hits during a market downturn, or when team conflict erupts during rapid growth. These compound storms test not just your leadership but your very identity.

Consider Mark's story. His software company was growing 200% annually when his marriage began falling apart. "I had advisors for the business challenges," he recalls. "But when personal and professional crises collided, I needed more than advice. I needed someone who could help me stay grounded while everything else was shifting. My Anchor, my former professor turned friend, didn't try to solve either problem. Instead, he helped me remember who I was so I could solve both."

This is how Anchors prevent capsizing:

1. They provide perspective when you're too close to the problem.
    - "Is this really as bad as it feels?"
    - "Have you faced something like this before?"
    - "What's the worst that could actually happen?"

2. They remind you of your capabilities when doubt creeps in.
    - "Remember when you handled that crisis last year?"
    - "You've built something from nothing before."
    - "This isn't beyond your abilities."

3. They hold space for vulnerability without judgment.
    - "It's okay to be scared."
    - "You don't have to have all the answers."
    - "Your worth isn't measured by this quarter's numbers."

4. They keep you connected to your purpose when pressure tempts compromise.
    - "Is this decision aligned with your values?"
    - "What would your best self do?"
    - "Will you be proud of this choice in five years?"

Real-world examples demonstrate this power:

- A CEO whose Anchor helped her maintain integrity during a hostile takeover attempt.
- A founder who relied on his Anchor to navigate ethical decisions during a cash crunch.
- An executive whose Anchor supported her through a layoff and major career pivot.

Here's the thing about storms and anchors:

They reveal what you've built when no one was looking.

The recovery after any storm? It's written in the quiet moments before the clouds gathered. Those anchors you're counting on? They aren't emergency services. They're the relationships you've been cultivating all along.

Why do some weather the same storm differently?

It's simple: They invested during calm seas.

Storm-Ready Relationships aren't built in crisis. They're built in consistency.

The foundation? Regular check-ins. Not when you need something. Not when the waters rise. But Tuesday afternoons and Sunday mornings. The ordinary moments that create extraordinary connections.

Reciprocity matters. Their storms deserve your presence, too. Your strength becomes their shelter. Their vulnerability becomes your trust.

The maintenance isn't glamorous, but it's everything. Small issues addressed quickly. Shifting dynamics acknowledged openly. Relationships renegotiated honestly.

What about boundaries? Honor them religiously. These anchors aren't your on-call therapy. They're people with their own capacity limits.

The professional support? Keep it separate. It serves a different purpose.

Here's the uncomfortable truth most people miss: The time to build your anchors isn't when the storm warnings sound. It's now. Today. In ordinary moments. Every investment in calm seas pays dividends in rough waters.

Are you building anchors now or just hoping they'll appear when you need them?

The Anchor Evolution

Here's the thing about anchors:

They evolve or they become obsolete.
They're well-maintained and cared for, or they get rusty and fatigued.

The captain who refuses to upgrade their equipment eventually finds themselves stranded. The leader who clings to outgrown relationships finds themselves unmoored when they need grounding most.

Your journey has phases. Each demands different support.

Early founders need someone who believes before the evidence exists.
Growth-stage leaders need clarity amid the noise.
Scale-stage executives need truth-tellers when everyone else says yes.
Legacy builders need meaning-makers when the scoreboard no longer satisfies.

What worked yesterday becomes insufficient tomorrow.

Notice the pattern? As your influence expands, your anchors must deepen.

The question isn't whether you need anchors – it's whether you've evolved them intentionally.

Most haven't.

They build relationships for one phase and expect them to serve another. They outgrow their support system but never upgrade it. They wonder why what once steadied them now feels inadequate.

Evolution isn't abandonment. It's acknowledgment.

Sometimes the same people evolve with you. Sometimes new anchors must be found. The constant isn't the relationship – it's your commitment to having the right support at the right time.

Ask yourself:
Have your anchor relationships evolved as you have?
Are you surrounding yourself with what you need now or what you needed then?
Are you drifting because your anchors are outdated?

Your next breakthrough isn't just about what you do.
It's about who's holding you steady while you do it.

LEGACY STAGE

Primary need: Purpose fulfillment and impact
Focus: "Is this what I want my impact to be?"
Anchor role: Supporting transition and succession

SCALE STAGE

Primary need: Identity preservation and values alignment
Focus: "Am I staying true to myself?"
Anchor role: Keeping you connected to your core as your influence grows

GROWTH STAGE

Primary need: Decision support and perspective
Focus: "Am I making the right choices?"
Anchor role: Helping maintain clarity amid complexity

EARLY STAGE

Primary need: Confidence building and basic emotional support
Focus: "Am I cut out for this?"
Anchor role: Believing in you when you don't believe in yourself

WARNING SIGNS AND THE DEPENDENCY TRAP

Watch for the quiet shifts. They start small - a delayed response here, a shortened conversation there. Your once-energetic Anchor seems distant, maybe even frustrated. The warmth that defined your connection feels forced.

These aren't just bad days – they're warning flares of Anchor overload.

It happens gradually, then suddenly. Like a rope fraying under constant tension, the relationship begins to wear. Resentment seeps in where acceptance once lived. Boundaries blur. What was once freely given support starts feeling like an obligation. The depth of your conversations shallow out, becoming more transactional than transformational.

The real danger? Most leaders don't notice until it's too late.

They're too focused on their own challenges to see their Anchor drowning under the weight of their needs. By the time the signs become obvious - when advice turns generic and connection feels forced - significant damage has already occurred.

Then there's the single-point dependency trap.

Relying on one Anchor is like building a house on a single support beam. It might hold for a while, but eventually, the weight becomes too much. When that single Anchor becomes unavailable - through burnout, life changes, or simple capacity limits - the entire structure threatens to collapse.

This dependency creates a paradox:
The more you need support, the more you risk overwhelming your sole source of it. Your Anchor becomes both crucial and crushed, essential and exhausted. It's a pattern that often ends in relationship breakdown just when you need it most.

Smart leaders see these patterns early.
They notice the subtle shifts in energy, the small changes in engagement. They understand that protecting the relationship sometimes means seeking additional support elsewhere. Most importantly, they recognize that preserving the connection might require temporarily stepping back to let it breathe.

Think of it like tending a garden.
Even the hardiest plants need space to grow, time to rest, and multiple sources of support.

Your Anchor relationships are no different. They require attention, care, and most importantly, the wisdom to know when they need room to regenerate.

WARNING SIGNS OF AN OVERLOADED ANCHOR

Healthy Balance	Subtle Shifts	Increasing Strain	Serious Overload	Relationship Breakdown

WARNING SIGNS AT EACH STAGE

Behavioral

			Broken commitments	Complete withdrawal
Clear boundaries	Delayed responses	Avoiding contact		
Reliable responses	Less availability	Making excuses	Unreliable presence	Contact avoidance

Emotional

		Growing animosity or resentment	Hostillity and Burnout	Toxic feelings
Energy after interaction	Occasional fatigue/irritation	Emotional distance		Complete detachment

Communication

			Communication breakdowns and blame	Toxic communication or complete silence
Open and honest dialogue	Less frequent conversations	Surface-level interactions only		

Early intervention prevents relationship collapse and isolation

The solution isn't to need less support – it's to build a broader network of it. Like a well-designed building, your support structure should have multiple points of contact with the ground. Each relationship carries part of the load, preventing any single connection from bearing too much weight.

This is where many leaders face their toughest challenge: admitting they need more than one Anchor. It feels like betrayal, like they're being unfaithful to their original support. But the opposite is true. Building a broader support network doesn't diminish your primary relationships - it preserves them.

Remember: An Anchor relationship's strength isn't measured by how much weight it can bear, but by how long it can remain steady.

Sometimes the best way to honor these connections is to ensure they're not asked to carry more than they can sustain.

The goal isn't to replace existing Anchors but to evolve relationships as needed and add complementary support where appropriate.

Sometimes this means having difficult conversations about changing needs.
Other times, it means expanding your network while maintaining core connections.

BUILDING A NETWORK OF SUPPORT:

1. **Primary Anchors**
   - Deep, long-term relationships
   - Core value alignment
   - Personal history connection

2. **Situational Anchors**
   - Specific expertise or experience
   - Time-bounded support
   - Context-specific guidance

3. **Peer Anchors**
   - Mutual support relationships
   - Shared experience understanding
   - Reciprocal growth focus

4. **Professional Anchors**
   - Structured support roles
   - Clear boundaries and expectations
   - Complementary to personal anchors

Building The Anchor Relationship

Like any critical relationship, finding and developing an Anchor takes intention. But unlike professional relationships that focus on skills or expertise, the Anchor connection develops through something deeper - trust and mutual understanding.

The Stability Matrix shows us why this matters. While your Navigator and Crew operate in the professional sphere, your Anchor relationship must exist in the personal realm, providing tactical, day-to-day emotional stability.

Here's what to look for:

Authenticity

Your Anchor needs to know the person behind the title. Not your LinkedIn profile or company pitch - the real you. The one who sometimes wakes up at 3 AM wondering if you're good enough.

Consistency

While your Champion might appear during big moments, and your Navigator during strategic shifts, your Anchor provides steady, ground-level support. They're there for both the crises and the quiet moments.

Boundaries

The strongest Anchor relationships have clear boundaries. They understand their role isn't to solve your business problems – that's what Navigators and Crew are for. Instead, they help you maintain stability while you solve those problems yourself.

Reciprocity

True Anchor relationships aren't one-way streets. They thrive on mutual trust and vulnerability. While the support may look different at different times, both parties contribute to and benefit from the relationship.

Remember: In the dynamic system of the Stability Matrix, your Anchor doesn't just support you.

They help strengthen your other key relationships by keeping you grounded enough to make the most of them.

Identifying Potential Anchors

The question of who can serve as your Anchor isn't about titles or roles.

It's about trust, stability, and ground-level support. Let's break this down.

Family As Anchors

The short answer? It's complicated.

Family members can make powerful Anchors because they already know your story and have a deep personal connection.

But here's the catch - they need to see you clearly, not just through the lens of family dynamics.

Your spouse may be your biggest fan, and at times your loudest critic. Are they ready to hear the good, bad, and ugly without too much worry, anxiety, or stress? Do they have an anchor themselves, or is that you?

Your mother might be your biggest cheerleader, but can she tell you hard truths when you need to hear them?

Your sister might be your best friend, but does she understand the weight of leadership you carry?

Like I said, it's complicated.

What To Look For

Instead of focusing on categories of people, look for these essential qualities:

1. Someone who knows your core story and values, not just your success metrics
2. A person who shows up consistently - not just for celebrations - but through the storms
3. Someone who can separate you from your business outcomes. Remember, they're anchoring YOU, not your company.
4. A truth-teller who loves you enough to be honest, even when it's difficult

Red Flags To Watch Out For

Avoid potential Anchors who:

- Try to solve your business problems (that's your Navigator's job)

- Only show up for the good times
- Make you question your worth rather than reinforce it
- Blur the lines between personal support and professional advice

The Litmus Test

Ask yourself: "Would I trust this person to remind me who I am when I've completely forgotten?"

If you're struggling to identify potential Anchors, you're not alone. Many leaders dismiss potential connections because of impostor syndrome – "Why would THEY want to help ME?"

The truth is, authentic Anchor relationships often develop naturally over time through shared experiences and mutual trust. The key is being open to these connections when they present themselves.

Getting Out of Your Own Way

That voice in your head? It's the most destructive force keeping you from finding your Anchor. You know the one. That liar has a name. It's called impostor syndrome. It whispers, *"Why would THEY want to help ME?"* or *"If they really knew me, they wouldn't like me."*

It's the same voice that makes you rehearse a casual lunch invitation seventeen times before hitting 'call.' (I may or may not have done this today . . .)

Here's the brutal irony:

When you're starting out, you question whether you deserve support.

You do.

When you finally reach that leadership position? Your impostor syndrome gets promoted right along with you. Doh!

And when big success finally comes? That voice suggests you shouldn't need help anymore.

You do. More than ever! Double Doh!

The real trap? Your self-worth gets tangled up with your net worth.
Your identity becomes wrapped in your title.
Your value becomes measured by your company's success.

You start believing your own press.

And that's exactly when you need an Anchor most.

Let me share Roberto's story. As CEO of a booming fintech, he spent two years admiring his former professor's leadership from afar. "I built this elaborate story about how busy he must be, how many other successful people must want his time." When he finally made the call, his professor's response floored him: "I've been waiting for you to reach out. I've watched your company grow and wanted to connect, but didn't want to overstep."

Sound familiar?

Here are the concrete steps to move past your own resistance:

1. **Start Small**
    Send a simple message: "Your perspective has meant a lot to me. Would you be open to a coffee conversation about leadership challenges?"

2. **Offer Value First**
    Share an article that made you think of them. Comment thoughtfully on their posts. Show you're invested in their thinking.

3. **Be Specific**
    Instead of a vague "we should catch up," try "I'm facing a specific challenge around scaling culture. Could I get your perspective over lunch next week?"

4. **Create Structure**
    Suggest a regular rhythm: "Could we do a quarterly check-in?" This takes the pressure off any single conversation.

5. **Take Imperfect Action**
    Send the message before you can overthink it. Set a timer for 5 minutes. Write. Send. Done.

Remember: You are enough. You are more than enough. When you struggle with that - and we all do – that's precisely when you need to Anchor up and get refueled.

Your worth isn't measured by your business metrics. It's measured by your humanity. And that's exactly what a great Anchor sees in you.

The very self-doubt that makes you hesitate to reach out is exactly why you need to reach out. Your *impostor syndrome isn't a sign you don't deserve support – it's proof you need it.*

Don't let fear keep you from connection and growth. Great relationships are on the other side of fear. Follow the map and cross over.

Fear → Hesitation → Action → Connection → Growth

Being The Harbor

The true measure of leadership isn't just how well you're supported – it's how well you support others. Being an Anchor for others isn't just noble; it's necessary for creating the kind of business ecosystem where authentic leadership can thrive.

Consider the harbor master in any port. Their role isn't just to provide shelter; it's to create conditions where ships can safely weather storms, repair damage, and prepare for their next journey. As a leader, your role in others' lives carries the same responsibility.

A story illustrates this better than any principle: James, a seasoned tech executive, thought he understood leadership until his former employee Darius called him at 2 AM. His startup was imploding, his marriage was strained, and he felt completely lost. "In that moment," James recalls, "I realized being an Anchor isn't about having answers. It's about having the courage to sit in the storm with someone else. It isn't something I was taught growing up. I don't think most guys were."

This is the essence of being worthy of harbor - creating space where others can safely face their storms. *It's not about being perfect. It's about being present.*

But here's the challenge:

As leaders climb higher, people increasingly want something from them rather than for them. Every interaction carries an agenda. Every relationship has subtext. Creating a genuine safe harbor requires intentionally stepping outside these dynamics.

The art lies in setting boundaries that protect both parties while allowing for real connection.

Too rigid, and an authentic connection becomes impossible. Too loose, and the relationship becomes unhealthy for both parties.

Think of it like a real harbor.

It has clear channels for entry, defined areas for anchoring, and established protocols for safety. Yet within these boundaries, ships find the space they need to rest, repair, and prepare for their next journey.

Creating safe spaces in leadership follows similar principles. Establish clear parameters for engagement while maintaining flexibility for individual needs. *Create a structure that supports vulnerability without enabling dependency.*

The enigma? The more successful you become, the more people will seek harbor with you. Yet this same success makes it difficult to provide authentic support. Power dynamics intrude. Time becomes scarce. The temptation to offer quick solutions rather than real presence grows stronger.

This is where many leaders miss the mark. They confuse giving advice with providing harbor. They mistake problem-solving for presence. They rush to fix when what's needed is space to feel.

The truth is simpler and harder: Being worthy of harbor means creating space where others can find their own anchoring. It's about being steady enough in your own foundation that others can safely explore their storms.

To be this kind of leader requires more than skill - it requires continuous inner work. You must tend to your own anchoring so you can offer a stable harbor to others. You must maintain your own boundaries so you can hold space for others' growth.

Most importantly, remember that being an Anchor isn't about having all the answers – it's about being trustworthy enough to hold others' questions.

In the end, this is how leadership ecosystems renew themselves. Today's storm-tossed captain becomes tomorrow's steady harbor.

Today's seeking soul becomes tomorrow's trusted Anchor.

The cycle continues, creating networks of support that make authentic leadership possible at every level.

While your Anchor keeps you grounded in who you are, your Crew determines what you can accomplish. Next, we'll explore how these operational partners transform vision into reality.

REFLECT: Who was your first true Anchor? The person who believed in you before you believed in yourself?

What did they see that you couldn't?
How did they help you see it, too?

ACT: This week, reach out to one person who served as an Anchor in your past.
Not with an agenda. Just with gratitude.
A text, a call, a coffee.
Acknowledge what their stability meant when your world was shaky.

Who's your anchor in the storm?

As you've learned, 76% of CEOs report feeling professionally isolated. I have put together some resources online to help find your emotional ballast. One tool specifically focuses on identifying and strengthening your Anchor relationships. It's free, my gift to you.

Let's end the dangerous isolation of leadership together.

https://TheCaptainsKeys.com/bonus

"I was the 'strong one' who never needed help—until I nearly capsized. It was a dark time, but being in community with like-minded leaders helped me find the Anchor I didn't even know I was missing."

—MORGAN P., CEO

⚓ NAVIGATE

To Sail the Story / Full Journey - Continue on to the next page
Study the Maps - Jump ahead to page 193

BEYOND THE STORM
Part 5

The wrench slipped in Jimmy's half-frozen fingers, the metal so cold it burned against his skin. Another bruised knuckle. Another curse word. Another moment closer to admitting defeat.

The name read Caterpillar, but Jimmy had decided the *Bering Steel*'s diesel engine was actually an "IKEA Prototype" - something deliberately engineered to crush human spirits while appearing deceptively simple. Like those bookshelf instructions that showed three easy steps but somehow left you with sixteen mystery screws and a marriage in crisis.

After two hours of failing to start it with its new components, he was seriously considering printing instruction manuals in Swedish and serving meatballs in the engine room just to make it feel more at home.

He knew the basics of diesel mechanics, but he wasn't actually a mechanic.

Two hours.

Six busted knuckles.

Zero progress.

"You sadistic piece of – "

Jimmy's wrench slipped again, steel kissing steel with a metallic ring that echoed through the engine compartment. Blood welled from a fresh cut across his knuckles. He barely felt it.

"You are officially a thermonuclear grade dumpster fire," he announced to the engine. "With optional cup holders and heated seats."

The words hung in the frigid air of the engine room, crystallizing like his breath. The *Bering Steel*s diesel engine just sat there, radiating the smug satisfaction of a cat that had just knocked your coffee off the counter while maintaining eye contact.

"You can do this," he said out loud, the words hanging in the frigid air. But doubt crept in, cold and insistent as the Alaskan wind.

What if he couldn't? What if Uncle Rocky had made a terrible mistake, believing in a nephew who'd never even sent a Christmas card?

The thought stung far worse than his bleeding hand.

He caressed the gleaming new components he'd installed. Key parts available nowhere else that had cost him a small fortune to overnight from Seattle. Every minute counted.

The engine responded with the sullen indifference of a teenager being asked to clean their room. No matter how much he begged, pleaded, or threatened, it remained stubbornly, deliberately inert.

Back in the Keys, engines spoke to him. A cylinder's misfire had its own language, a signature he could interpret like Morse code. But this massive diesel beast - it spoke a dialect he couldn't decipher, its Arctic accent too thick, too foreign

"It shouldn't be this hard."

Knowing enough to be dangerous and actually rebuilding a massive commercial fishing vessel's power plant were worlds apart, like comparing a paddleboat to an aircraft carrier.

Sweet talk hadn't worked. Neither had cursing, pleading, or the precision torque wrench he'd thrown across the room in frustration a few minutes ago.

Jimmy ran his hand along the cold metal housing. This engine was the heart of everything - his future, livelihoods for his deckhands, and fulfilling the promise he'd made to himself after Hurricane Claudette had wiped out his old life. Without it, the *Bering Steel* was just a floating coffin waiting to be claimed by the sea.

That night, Jimmy sat alone on the edge of his bunk, staring at his raw, oil-stained hands. They trembled slightly - from cold, from exhaustion, from fear. He couldn't tell anymore.

Bella nuzzled his knee, sensing his distress. "What if I can't fix her, girl?" he murmured, scratching behind her ears. "What if all this was for nothing?"

The weight of unrealized expectations pressed down on him like the Arctic night. His livelihood and future hitched to his ability to make this floating rust bucket seaworthy.

He'd never felt so inadequate. So exposed. A memory surfaced - his father teaching him to fix a lawnmower engine when he was ten. "Engines don't respond to panic, Jimmy-boy. They respond to patience."

He took a deep breath. Closed his eyes.

Tomorrow.

He'd try again tomorrow.

CHAPTER 21

Jimmy pulled out his phone, checking the calendar. Three weeks of solo work had produced results measurable only with a magnifying glass. Each day of delay was bleeding him dry - five hundred in docking fees, two thousand in lost potential earnings, not counting the parts he'd ruined trying to install them himself. The math was brutal.

But worse than the financial hemorrhage was the opportunity cost. Other captains were already catching bait, securing their seasonal contracts, locking in the best buyers while he struggled with basic repairs. The invisible clock ticking in his head grew louder by the hour.

He glanced at his hands - blistered, cut, oil-stained. Pride had always been his most expensive possession.

Each failed repair was another whisper in his ear:

You don't belong here. This isn't your world.

Captain Meyer was a title he'd inherited, not earned. Every captain in Kodiak seemed to be watching, waiting for the Florida charter boy to admit defeat and slink back to the sunshine. The thought of proving them right burned worse than the engine room fumes.

Needing a break from engine room frustration, he moved randomly down the list. One minute he was painting name plates - they looked like a child's art project - the next he was trying to reset a massive anchor chain that had nearly crushed his foot.

YouTube tutorials and technical manuals weren't cutting it. At this rate, he'd still be making repairs when hell froze over, which, judging by the temperature in Kodiak, could be any day now.

A hollow knock resonated through the hull, followed by a familiar voice.

"Permission to come aboard, Captain!"

Jimmy climbed out of the engine room, wincing as his stiffened muscles protested. Captain Si stood on the dock, bundled in his trademark layers - same pants, same jacket, same weathered cap pulled low against the wind. The man dressed like he shopped from a single catalog page, year after year.

"Thought I'd come check on how things were going, Jimmy." Si's eyes swept the deck. "Heard you from way down the dock. Having some problems?"

Heat rushed to Jimmy's face. His profanity-laden tirade had apparently carried farther than he'd realized.

"Sure, Si, come aboard, please."

The older man, two thermoses in hand, stepped onto the deck with the easy grace of someone who'd spent more time on boats than land. He handed a thermos to Jimmy who always appreciated coffee.

Si nodded silently, moving around the deck like a building inspector, running his fingers along welds, testing fixtures with gentle pressure. His gaze took in the scattered tools, the half-finished repairs, the general disarray that had become the *Bering Steel's* new normal. His expression gave nothing away, but Jimmy could feel the assessment happening.

Finally, Si turned back to him.

"Looks like the Tasmanian Devil came through here, Jimmy. What's going on?"

Jimmy clenched his jaw, frustration bubbling back to the surface. "I'm in over my head. I keep moving from one problem to the next and nothing's going like it should. I've got my checklists and my schedules but I've fallen way behind and it's getting really frustrating."

"Your uncle had a temper too."

"Yeah, so how long have you been standing there?"

"Long enough to see you're doing it wrong." Si gave Jimmy a knowing smile. "Both the repair and the dealing with it."

Jimmy wiped his bleeding hands on his jeans. "I don't need-"

"A lecture? Help? A friend?" Si set one thermos down near Jimmy. "Pride's a funny thing on the ocean. Won't keep you warm, won't keep you fed, won't keep you alive. But it'll sure as hell kill you if you let it."

The smell of coffee drifted up from the thermos. Real coffee, not the instant stuff Jimmy had been settling for lately. His hands shook as he reached for it.

"I screwed up, Si. I shouldn't be here. I'm letting everyone down. Myself, Lily, Uncle Rocky's legacy . . ."

"Rocky screwed up plenty. Got conned more than once in his early days. Hell, Burns took him for thirty grand his second season with some cockamamie scheme about Russian crab quotas."

Jimmy looked up sharply. "He never bounced back from something like this though."

"No," Si agreed. "He bounced back from way worse. But he didn't do it alone." He gestured at Jimmy's bleeding hands. "This? This is what drowning looks like. And I've watched enough good men drown in their own pride."

"Like that Brewer guy on Raven's Fortune?"

The words were out before Jimmy could stop them.

Si's face tightened for a moment, then softened.

"Yeah, like him. Thought asking for help meant he wasn't good enough. Thought proving himself meant doing it alone." Si's voice caught. "The night we lost him and that crew, he'd refused to radio for help when the storm hit. No one on that boat wanted the other captains to think they were weak."

Si's eyes met Jimmy's. "I think there is some of that in all of us. Ya know?"

Jimmy felt the weight of those words settle on his shoulders. He looked down at his hands, at the blood and grease mixed together.

"I don't know how to fix this, Si."

"No one's asking you to fix it alone." Si picked up a wrench. "Sometimes the strongest thing a captain can do is admit he needs help. A crew. His friends." He paused. "His family."

Jimmy thought of Lily's texts, still unanswered. Of seasoned deckhands applying to other boats, top boats in the fleet, preferring not to wait for leftover jobs. Of Bella, who'd whined at the door to come with him as he'd slipped out before dawn.

"I promised them all I could do this. I promised myself!"

"No," Si corrected gently. "You promised them you'd try. There's no shame in needing help to keep that promise."

Jimmy's vision blurred. The weight of the past few days, the exhaustion, the fear, the anger - it all crashed over him at once. His legs gave out and he sank to the deck, coffee forgotten.

Si's hand found his shoulder, steady and strong. "You're not alone in this, son. But you've got to let other people in."

"I don't even know where to start."

"That's OK, it's not your job to know everything. We'll get you some help. Together we'll figure out how to get the *Bering Steel* back where she belongs - on the water, doing what she was built for."

Jimmy nodded, unable to speak. The first rays of real sunlight broke through the clouds, catching on the scattered tools, the bloodstains, the tears he couldn't hold back anymore.

"Thank you," he managed finally.

Si squeezed his shoulder. "That's what friends and family are for, kid. Now come on - get those hands cleaned up. From all you've told me, she'll have both our hides if she thinks I let you bleed all over your uncle's boat."

For the first time in days, Jimmy felt something close to hope. He wasn't just Captain Meyer anymore, trying to live up to a legend. He was Jimmy - brother, nephew, friend, and captain of a legacy that deserved better than his pride was delivering.

It was time to learn what real strength looked like.

CHAPTER 22

Si's was in the middle of pouring his second cup of coffee when his phone beeped. On checking it, he nearly leaped out of his seat.

"That's enough work for today, Jimmy. Come with me."

Jimmy blinked. "Are you nuts? If I take time off, this is going to take even longer!" The words came out sharper than he'd intended, edged with fatigue and desperation.

Si didn't flinch. Instead, a smile creased his weathered face. "Trust me, Jimmy. It will actually go faster. And this is too good of an opportunity to miss."

Something in the old captain's tone cut through Jimmy's resistance. It wasn't just the confidence in those faded blue eyes - it was the absence of judgment. The calm certainty in those faded blue eyes promised answers to questions Jimmy hadn't even formulated yet.

His father had dispensed advice like medication - precise doses meant to correct deficiencies. His charter boat mentors back in the Keys had taught through ridicule, turning every mistake into a story that haunted the docks for weeks.

But Si offered something different. Not solutions, but perspective. Not criticism, but context. He created space for Jimmy to find his own way through the wilderness rather than handing him a map with only one route marked.

"OK," Jimmy said, surprising himself with how easily he surrendered. "Lead on."

Jimmy locked the door to the bridge, and followed Si down the gangway. The older captain didn't speak as they walked, and Jimmy found himself matching the man's measured pace despite the restless energy still crackling through him.

Si gestured toward Jimmy's truck. "You're driving."

They traveled to another marina, smaller and more sheltered than where the *Bering Steel* was docked. Tied up at the end of the pier was a vessel that sent a pang of nostalgia through Jimmy's chest, a single console fishing boat, not a sport fisher like the one he'd lost, but a very familiar sight. Sleek, efficient, purpose-built for what it did. No identity crisis, no impossible expectations.

"Is this what you and my uncle used to do?" Jimmy eyed Si suspiciously as they approached the boat. "We going fishing in the middle of the day?"

Si tossed him that mysterious smile again, the one that made Jimmy feel like he was missing something obvious.

"Not fishing, Jimmy. Think . . . bigger."

CHAPTER 23

Jimmy's impatience clung to him like a second skin, even as they left the dock. Time wasted. Repairs delayed. But as the first minke whale broke the surface, something inside him stilled. By the time the humpbacks appeared, his watch had stopped mattering entirely.

Jimmy stood transfixed, his body swaying unconsciously with the gentle roll of Si's boat. Less than a hundred feet away, a pod of humpback whales moved through the water with impossible grace, their massive forms synchronized in a ballet no human choreographer could devise.

He'd forgotten everything - the engine problems, the paint job, the crane. All of it faded in the face of these leviathans.

"That is amazing," he whispered.

The words seemed inadequate in the presence of such magnificence.

They weren't the only cetaceans Si had shown him today. Earlier, they'd passed a pair of minke whales - smaller but no less majestic, each at least twenty-five feet long. And just before discovering the humpbacks, Si had pointed silently toward the horizon where a blue whale, the largest creature ever to exist on Earth, had left a wake that could have belonged to a submarine.

But the humpbacks were different. They sang.

Their haunting melodies transported Jimmy back twenty-five years to a forgotten memory: his father kneeling beside him on the bow of a boat off the California coast, arm around his five-year-old shoulders, whispering, "Listen, Jimmy. They're talking to each other." He could still feel his father's presence, the solid warmth of him, the gentle rumble of his voice through his chest.

As Si inched the boat closer, Jimmy realized the whales weren't just singing - they were hunting. Moving in coordination, they arranged themselves in a loose net over a specific area of ocean. At first, he thought they were protecting a calf. Then he saw their massive mouths open in unison, filtering tiny krill too small for the human eye to detect at this distance.

"They're herding," Jimmy murmured, awestruck. "Like cowboys driving cattle to slaughter."

Si nodded, standing beside him at the rail. "What do you think about that?" he asked, reverence evident in his voice.

Each whale had a role - some diving deep to drive krill upward, others boxing the edges to prevent escape, the largest ones sweeping through to claim the harvest. It wasn't just cooperation; it was a living business plan executed with precision refined over millennia.

"By working together, they accomplish far more than any one of them could alone. Sure, they're competing with one another to a degree, but no one humpback could do all of this alone; they'd burn out after a week, maybe make it a month, but eventually they'd fall apart from exhaustion."

Jimmy watched as one massive whale breached slightly, its eye seeming to study the boat before it slipped back beneath the surface.

"Look at them working like that," Si continued. "They've turned a huge problem into a feast. One of the first rules of this ocean is that food is hard to come by; prey is elusive. That's just how it works. Individually, these big boys might burn three times the energy they gain eating krill just looking for krill. But working together, they make it efficient and effective for every member of the pod. They all have a role to play and come together to thrive. You get what I'm saying here, kid?"

Jimmy was mesmerized by the whales. One breached fully now, its massive body defying gravity before crashing back into the sea with a spectacular splash. He had to pull himself back to Si's question.

"I'm sorry, Si, what are you talking about?"

Si's expression tightened, but his voice remained patient. "You're out there chasing bait fish by yourself, kid. Burning out your energy and getting frustrated without any real results. Where's your pod?"

"My pod? Wait, is this about those keys I need?"

Si nodded, his eyes crinkling with approval. "The first key is your Anchor - something that keeps you stable when everything else is chaos." He gestured toward the distant shore. "For these whales, it's their pod structure, their family bonds. But the next one goes far beyond that. It's what we're watching now."

Si looked at Jimmy with a sly smile, "You're missing the next key, one of the biggest components in your operation."

"I need . . . whales? Do they help locate crab or something?" said Jimmy puzzled.

"No, no, no Jimmy," Si laughed, "Think bigger. Where's your crew?"

The question landed like a slap. For a man who had rarely hired a mate in many years on the charter boat, it struck at the heart of his self-image as a captain.

"Uhhhhh . . . does my dog count?" Jimmy attempted humor, but the words rang hollow even to his own ears.

"Well, it does look like a dog could have done that kindergarten fingerpaint job on your hull," Si fired back. "But at the end of the day, we're talking about actual humans. Every captain needs a great crew; it's essential. Otherwise work is hard, lonely, and it takes forever to get done. Does that sound like anyone you know?"

Jimmy grimaced, heat rising to his face. Of course it did. He was trying to do all the work alone because he was stubborn and felt like he had to prove himself. All he was doing was proving that he was a moron.

Si turned back towards the whales, some already darting away from the feeding area in search of the next opportunity. The pod was breaking up, individual members scouting out better prospects elsewhere.

"That's the second key. You need to find a crew to help carry your load. Pick the right people and you'll be able to accomplish amazing things, and do it without burning yourself out over and over."

The words sank deep, finding fertile ground in Jimmy's exhaustion and frustration.

"But the boat has to be ready first, right?" Jimmy heard the uncertainty in his own voice. "At least good enough before I can hire anyone?"

Si studied him for a long moment. "Is this really about the boat being ready? Or about you being ready to commit?"

Jimmy felt exposed under that steady gaze. "How do I get anyone to sign on when I might never make it to the water?"

"How will you ever get to the water if you don't?" Si's logic was simple and brutal. "There's no shame in admitting you're not the best at every job, Jimmy. Not one of us has mastered every skill aboard a ship. Not you, not me, not even your Uncle Rocky."

Si leaned forward. "Play to your strengths. Find your weaknesses. Then surround yourself with people who excel where you don't."

Jimmy thought about the Bulls games he'd watched as a kid with his dad. Michael Jordan, the greatest player ever, but he couldn't win championships alone. Not until he got Scottie Pippen, Horace Grant, and other key players around him. Before that supporting cast arrived, even Jordan's individual brilliance couldn't overcome stronger teams.

Jimmy nodded slowly, understanding blooming. He might not be the Michael Jordan of Alaskan fishing, but he was the one with the boat and the drive to succeed. He just needed the right supporting cast.

"Even Michael Jordan needed help."

Si raised an eyebrow. "Basketball?"

"Yeah. Greatest player ever, but he couldn't win by himself. Needed a team."

"Smart man, that Jordan." Si nodded approvingly. "Before you start advertising for your Dream Team, though, Jimmy, you need to be smart about this. You're going to be hiring from a talent pool that knows all to well you're the new guy in town. You've already been ripped off by one guy and ripped on by all the rest."

Jimmy's face flushed.

"Don't think you can just offer better wages and watch them line up," Si continued. "They need to believe in you and what you're trying to accomplish. Figure out why you're really here, Jimmy. And I don't mean because a hurricane wrecked your old life. That's just desperation."

Si's voice grew quiet. "You're asking them to risk everything on that boat with you. They need a reason they can believe in."

The weight of it settled on Jimmy's shoulders. These weren't just potential employees. They were men who would bet their lives on his judgment.

A distant whale breached, the crash echoing across the water.

Jimmy watched the spray settle, his mind racing. "You said there were four keys every captain needs. What are the other two?"

Si smiled, but didn't answer immediately. He started the engine, letting it idle as he watched the remaining whales continue their coordinated hunt.

"All in good time. But you can put that one in bottom right box next to the anchor."

"Come on, Si. Just tell me what they are."

"Can't build a house from the roof down." The old captain's tone was firm but not unkind. "You master each one in sequence, or you don't master any of them."

Jimmy felt curiosity building, but something deeper stirred beneath it. A need that went beyond intrigue.

"So what's my reason?" he asked. "Why should anyone follow me?"

Si studied him for a long moment, then pushed the throttle forward. "That's something only you can answer, Captain. But I'll tell you this much—when you figure it out, you'll know. And so will they."

The finality in Si's voice told Jimmy the conversation was over. But as they headed back through waters that no longer seemed quite so foreign, Jimmy's mind was already working.

Two more keys. Two more pieces of the puzzle. And somewhere buried in his own motivations, the answer to why any sane person would risk their life following him into the Bering Sea.

The whales were still working behind them, their hunt a living reminder of what was possible when the right people came together for the right reasons.

He just had to figure out what those reasons were.

NAVIGATE

Study the Maps / Full Journey - Continue on to the next page
To Sail the Story - Ride a wave to page 227

CAPTAIN'S LOG

Chart your course forward

Reflections

____

____

____

____

____

____

____

Action Items

____

____

____

____

____

____

____

THE CREW
YOUR UNTAPPED FORCE MULTIPLIER

*"Coming together is a beginning, staying together is progress,
and working together is success."*
— HENRY FORD

My friend Jack runs a successful software company. At least, that's what everyone sees from the outside.

What they don't see is Jack at 1 AM, answering customer emails while his family sleeps.

They don't see him canceling lunch (again) to handle a client crisis.

They don't see the toll of being everything to everyone, all the time.

Jack isn't alone. He's just lonely.

We've all bought into a dangerous myth. The myth of the solo entrepreneur. The visionary who does it all. The captain who needs no crew.

You know the stories – like the one where Mark Zuckerberg single-handedly invented Facebook in his dorm room. Except he didn't.

Elon Musk didn't launch rockets by himself. Sara Blakely didn't create Spanx alone in her apartment. Elon recruited top talent and focused on strategic vision, hiring more top talent. Sara, one of the most savvy founders I know, hired an operator, a CEO, leveraging her genius in product design and driving sales.

But we love these myths. They feed our ego. They tell us we're special. Different. Capable of superhuman feats of entrepreneurial strength. We are the glue that holds the business together. We too want to defy the odds, become legendary. Anyone remember Don Quixote? Funny enough, even Don had Sancho.

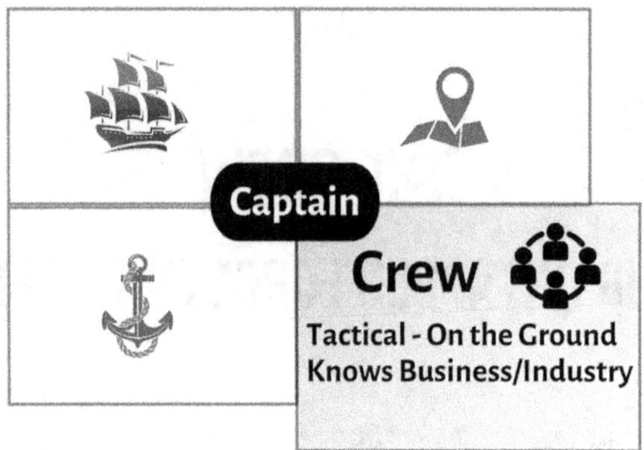

And these myths . . . they're killing us.

Not quickly. Slowly. One missed dinner at a time. One canceled vacation at a time. One "I'll just do it myself" at a time.

Here's what nobody tells you about doing everything yourself:
It's not brave.
It's not admirable.
It's just expensive.

Expensive in time. In energy. In opportunities missed. In relationships strained. In dreams deferred.

I know because I've been there. You probably have too.

The real question isn't "Can you do it all yourself?"

Of course you can.
For a while.

The real question is "What's it costing you?"

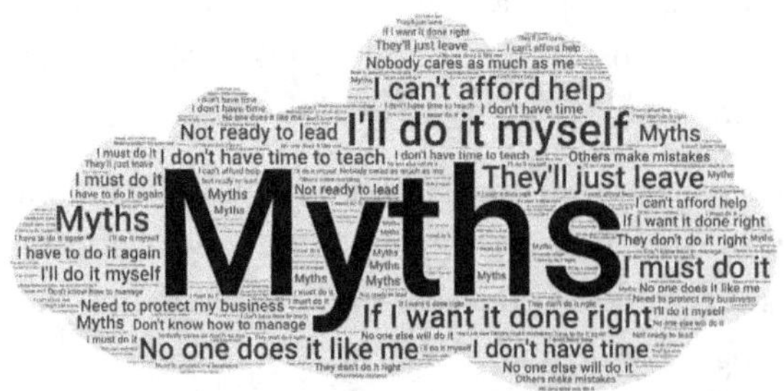

The Captain's Excuses

Every captain has their reasons. Their justifications. Their carefully constructed explanations for why they stand alone at the helm.

Listen closely and you'll hear them:

"I'll just do it myself."

The battle cry of the overwhelmed entrepreneur. The most expensive sentence in business. Not because it's wrong - because it's addictive. Each time you say it, you're buying speed today with tomorrow's growth. Quick fixes that slowly fix you in place.

"Nobody does it quite like I do."

The perfectionist's shield. Of course they don't do it like you. They bring their own magic, their own methods, their own mastery. When you demand carbon copies, you get pale imitations. When you embrace different approaches, you get evolution.

"It takes longer to teach than to do."

The short-term mathematician. Yes, training takes time. Documentation takes effort. Systems require investment. But what costs more - spending a week teaching someone, or spending every week doing it yourself forever?

"I can't afford good people."

The false economy. Translated: I can afford to do everything myself, indefinitely. To cancel every vacation. To miss every dinner. To wake up at 5 AM forever. What's the real cost of "saving money"?

"They'll just leave anyway."

The scarred captain's lament. Yes, some team members will leave just like some customers leave. Some products fail. Markets shift. Roles change. Building no crew because some might leave is like building no business because it might fail.

"I need to protect my business."

The guardian's paradox. You're not protecting it. You're limiting it. Every decision you must make, every problem you must solve, every opportunity you must evaluate - alone - is a ceiling on your growth.

"Nobody cares as much as I do."

The ownership trap. They don't care exactly like you do. They care differently. Sometimes better. Sometimes wider. Sometimes deeper in areas you never considered.

"I don't have time to manage people."

The time traveler's illusion. You don't have time not to. Every hour spent doing what others could do is an hour stolen from what only you can do.

"What if they make mistakes?"

The control conundrum. They will. Just like you did, and probably still do. The question isn't if they'll make mistakes. It's whether those mistakes cost less than the opportunities lost to caution.

"I'm not ready to lead."

The leader's paradox. You become ready by leading. By failing. By learning. By growing. There's no preparation for leadership quite like leadership itself.

Did I miss any? Yes, of course. We all know it, but I'll add it anyway.
"If I want it done right, then I have to do it myself."

Yep. I've used them all. How about you?

These aren't just excuses. They're anchors. (but not the good kind)
Each one reasonable. Each one logical. Each one limiting.

But here's what every successful captain eventually learns:
The cost of doing everything yourself isn't just in time or money.

It's in dreams unrealized.
Impact diminished.
Possibilities unexplored.

Your excuses might be keeping you safe. But they're also keeping you playing small.

The question isn't whether your reasons are valid.

Certainly, some of them are.

The question is whether they're worth it.

The Price of Sailing Solo

Here's the thing about building a Crew: it's always "too early" until suddenly it's "too late."

Every captain has felt it. That moment when you realize the price of waiting. It's steep!

When the opportunity you've been chasing sails past because you were below deck doing tasks someone else should have handled.
When the creative spark dies because you didn't have time to fan it into flame. When you look up and realize another year has passed, and your business is exactly the same size because its growth is capped by your personal capacity. (ouch!)

I watched a brilliant software founder lose his market edge because he insisted on reviewing every line of code. By the time he built his team, three competitors had raced ahead. His perfectionism cost him the market.

I've seen a consultant work herself into the hospital because "clients hired me, not my team." While she recovered, those same clients discovered they actually liked working with her associates. Some never came back.

The math is brutally simple:

Solo operators hit growth ceilings. Micromanagers create bottlenecks. Perfectionists ensure perfect mediocrity.

The cost isn't just in missed opportunities. It's in the slow erosion of what made you start this journey in the first place. Your passion. Your purpose. Your joy in the work.

When you're doing everything, you do nothing well. When you're everywhere, you're nowhere effectively. When you're the answer to every question, you become the biggest question mark in your business.

The irony? The very success you're trying to protect by doing it all yourself is the success you're preventing from happening.

Every day you delay building your Crew is a day your competition is building theirs.

Let me ask you a question:

What's the dream that's dying while you micromanage your team?

What's the opportunity sailing past while you're stuck below deck doing tasks someone else should handle?

What relationship is withering while you "just handle one more thing?"

Write it down.

Seriously.

Stop reading and write it down.

That's the real price you're paying.

Not just time.

Not just money.

But dreams deferred until they die.

Understanding True Crew

Here's where it gets interesting because this isn't just about hiring people.

A few years back, I worked with a startup founder who hired eighteen people in 6 weeks. She was really proud to call me and brag about her fast execution.

"There," she said, "I have a crew now."

Except she didn't.

She had employees. Bodies in chairs. People who showed up for paychecks. But she didn't have a Crew.

The difference? It's not in the hiring. It's not in the org chart. It's not even in the skills.

It's in the mission.

A true Crew isn't just interested in your mission – they're committed to it. They don't just know where the ship is going - they help plot the course. They don't just show up - they show up ready to make history.

Think about the best team you've ever been part of. Maybe it was in business. Maybe sports. Maybe a volunteer project. What made it special wasn't just what you did - it was how it felt. The shared purpose. The collective energy. The sense that you were part of something bigger than yourself.

That's what a true Crew feels like.

You can hire differently. You can recruit complementary talents. You can assemble the perfect blend of skills and experiences.

And still watch it all fall apart.

Because *diversity without direction is just chaos in slow motion.*

The Crew Test

Want to know if you have a crew or just employees? Watch what happens when you're not there.

Employees follow instructions. A Crew follows the mission.

Employees need supervision. A Crew needs clarity.

Employees ask, "What should I do?" A Crew asks, "What needs to happen?"

Employees wait for permission. A Crew creates possibilities.

The Invisible Contract

Every Crew operates on an unwritten agreement that goes beyond employment contracts and job descriptions.

It sounds like this:

"I'm not just here for a paycheck. I'm here for a purpose."

"I don't just work with these people. I succeed and fail with them."

"This isn't just what I do. It's part of who I am."

When these words remain unsaid, you have staff.
When they're spoken, you're on your way. You may have a team.
When they become the hardcore truth, then you have a Crew.

Note: As part of the bonus items with this chapter, I have specific ways to make this invisible contract visible and out loud. Details are at the end of the chapter.

The Commitment Spectrum

Not everyone on your team will show the same level of commitment. That's not a problem, that's normal. Reality.

The problem? Most captains don't recognize where their people stand. They treat the All-In like the Transactional. They expect the Contractual to act Invested. Then they wonder why their ship keeps drifting off course.

The crew member's commitment level isn't just about them. It's about you. It's about your leadership. It's about what you're willing to see.

Five levels. Five different relationships. Five different approaches.

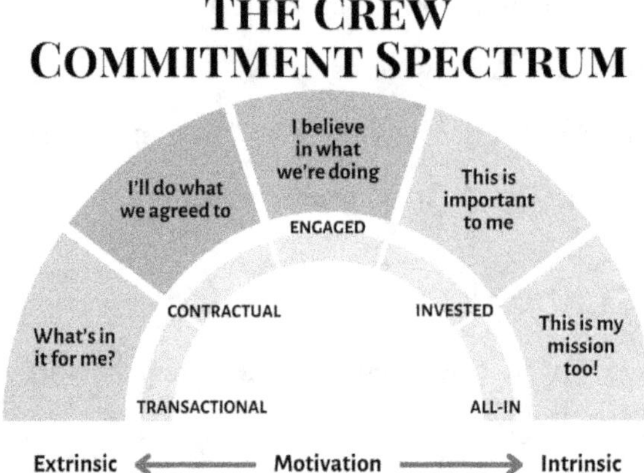

Transactional: "I work, you pay me."

The simplest exchange. The lowest commitment. They give to get. Nothing more.

These mercenaries operate on pure extrinsic motivation. Minimum effort for maximum compensation. No immediate benefit? No reason to act.

This isn't leadership territory. It's management purgatory. High monitoring. Low return. Endless frustration.

Captain's Question:

Is this a values mismatch or a connection failure?

Action Plan:

- Move Quickly: Values mismatches don't improve with time. Navigate them out today.

- Set Boundaries: If removal isn't possible or there is a values match, create crystal-clear expectations.
- Check Yourself: Sometimes transactional behavior reflects transactional leadership.
- Critical Timeline: Three months to show movement. My two cents: replace them now.

Contractual: "I do my job and meet expectations."

One small step from transaction to obligation. Still miles from commitment.

These staff members fulfill their duties as written. They meet expectations as long as those expectations don't grow. Ask for extras, and watch satisfaction plummet.

The telltale sign? Clock-watching. They arrive at X. They leave at Y. End of story.

Captain's Question:

Have I connected tasks to meaning and shown why the work matters?

Action Plan:

- Connect to Purpose: Share the "why" behind tasks, not just the what.
- Expand Perspective: Show them the impact beyond their station.
- Look for Sparks: Do their eyes light up when seeing the bigger picture?
- Set a Timeline: Give them 6 months to move toward Engaged.
- Be Realistic: Some solid performers remain Contractual by choice.

Engaged: "I believe in what we're doing and want to excel."

This is where leadership begins. Where management ends and inspiration starts.

These budding crew members catch the vision. They align with the mission. They're willing to go beyond the contract.

The difference? They take pride in outcomes, not just duties. They spot problems before you do. They bring solutions, not just questions.

Captain's Question:

Where can I give them room to shine and recognize their contribution?

Action Plan:

- Increase Ownership: Delegate decisions that actually matter.
- Build Community: Connect them with your Invested and All-In crew.
- Show Impact: Provide direct feedback about how their work moves the ship forward.
- Provide Growth: Assign projects that test their limits and increase their visibility.

Invested: "This is important to me."

These aren't employees. They're partners.

They don't just show up for the mission. They take personal ownership of it. They don't just identify problems. They hunt for solutions.

The difference between Engaged and Invested?
Initiative. Anticipation. Ownership.
They're emotionally connected to results.

Captain's Question:

How can I remove every barrier between them and their maximum impact?

Action Plan:

- Develop Leadership: Move them from doer to developer of others.
- Eliminate Bureaucracy: Cut every rule that frustrates their initiative.
- Create Challenges: Offer opportunities that stretch their abilities.
- Tailor Recognition: Generic praise insults specific excellence.

All-In: "This is my mission, too!"

The rarest crew members. And the most valuable.

They don't see your organization's success as separate from their own. They tackle problems without being asked. They anticipate needs before they arise. They recruit others to the mission. They embody your values even when no one's watching.

They're not working for you. They're working for the same purpose you are. They are owners, whether they have equity or not.

Captain's Question:

Am I worthy of their commitment level?

Action Plan:

- Prevent Burnout: Their greatest risk is their greatest strength - their commitment.
- Create Legacy: Ensure they're developing the next generation.
- Strategic Input: Bring them into the captain's quarters for the big decisions.
- Personal Growth: Find challenges worthy of their capabilities.

The question isn't whether you have people at each level. You do.

The question is whether you know who they are. And whether you're leading each one accordingly.

A true Crew lives in the last three zones - Engaged to All-in. Not because you demanded it. But because you created conditions where it could grow.

Jim Collins talks about getting the right people on the bus and in the right seats. Good start. Wrong focus.

When I speak on building a committed crew, I'm always asked:
"How do I find people who are already committed?"
"How do I get the right committed people in the right seats on the bus?"

Makes complete sense. And misses the entire point.

The better question:
"How do I build something worth committing to?"
"How do I build a bus people are fighting to get on?"
"How do I create a ship people align with so deeply they recruit others to join?"

It starts with you. With your clarity. With your consistency. With your commitment to something bigger than yourself. With your vision that creates purpose beyond a paycheck.

Because here's what every successful Captain knows: You can't have a committed Crew without being a committed Captain first.

The level of commitment you receive will never exceed the level of commitment you demonstrate.

Your Crew isn't failing you. Your leadership might be failing them.

Where are you on the commitment scale?

For a while, mine fluctuated, as other parts of my Stability Matrix faltered. I blamed it on all sorts of things. The bottom line was that I had to raise my own standard. I had to raise my commitment and be consistent.

Amazingly, when I did, my Crew revealed itself in a new way. Everyone moved up a level, and the bottom tier fell out. It didn't require hiring new talent. Just leading the team I had with clarity of vision, irresistible mission, and a higher level of trust.

Raise the standard. Accelerate outcomes more easily than ever.

The Binding Force

Here's the thing about commitment: it's impossible to commit to something you don't understand.

Have you ever wondered why some teams move mountains while others barely shift pebbles? The difference isn't talent. It isn't resources. It isn't even leadership, at least not directly.

It's clarity of mission.

A mission isn't just words framed on a wall. It's the invisible thread that pulls your entire operation forward. It's what transforms a bunch of people collecting paychecks into a Crew willing to brave storms together.

But here's the uncomfortable truth: most businesses don't have missions. They have wall decorations.

The Wall Art Trap

I walked into a coffee shop last month with a beautifully framed mission statement: "To provide exceptional beverages and superior customer service in a welcoming environment."

I asked the barista what it meant.

He stared at me like I'd asked him to explain quantum physics in Mandarin.

"We make good coffee and are nice to people," he finally mumbled.

Two blocks away, another coffee shop has no mission statement on display. But when I asked the barista why she loves working there, she lit up: "We're building community here. One cup, one conversation at a time."

Which shop has a mission?

Which shop has a Crew?

The Invisible Thread

A real mission isn't a marketing slogan. It's a magnetic field that aligns every action, every decision, every innovation toward a shared purpose.

But here's where captains get it wrong: They create the mission, frame it beautifully, hang it prominently, and then . . . assume it's done.

Done? You've barely started.

Advertisers have a rule called the "Rule of 7" – a person needs to hear a message seven times before they truly hear it once. For missions, multiply that by ten.

Want to know why your team isn't committed to your mission? Because they don't actually know what it is.

Not really. Not deeply. Not in their bones.

The Mission Manifested

Great missions have three qualities:

They're understandable. A child should grasp them.

They're memorable. They stick without effort.

They're repeatable. They spread through conversation.

But the fourth quality? That's the game-changer:

They're constant.

Not mentioned once a quarter in all-hands meetings. Not reserved for onboarding and exit interviews. Not saved for crises and celebrations.

Every. Single. Day.

When Mission Takes Hold

Here's what happens when a true Crew catches fire with a real mission:

The accountant doesn't just track numbers - she finds ways to fund the dream.

The customer service rep doesn't just handle complaints - he builds relationships that last decades.

The delivery driver doesn't just drop off packages - she becomes the face of your promise to the community.

This is when business math gets weird. Really weird.

I watched a small marketing agency triple their impact (and revenue) in eight months. Not by working harder. Not by hiring more people. But by aligning their existing team around a mission that mattered.

They stopped trying to serve everyone and started serving schools exclusively. Their mission? Help educators tell their stories better. Suddenly, every team member became an education advocate. They read education journals. Attended school board meetings. Volunteered at local schools.

Their work got better because their mission got clearer.

The strongest missions become the default language of your organization. They shape decisions without being referenced. They answer questions before they're asked. They resolve conflicts without mediation.

But only if the mission is alive, not framed or a drawer liner.

The Echo Effect

Want to know if your mission is alive? Listen to how your team talks when you're not in the room.

Do they reference the mission naturally? Do they defend decisions based on it? Do they challenge actions that contradict it?

If not, your mission isn't failing. It's already dead.

Resurrection requires repetition. Not just from you – from everyone. The mission must echo from every corner of your organization until it becomes the natural language of your business.

This isn't about posters. This is about practice.

The Captain's Choice

Here's what every successful captain eventually learns: Your Crew doesn't commit to words on a wall. They commit to the world those words create when lived daily.

They're watching what you do, not what you say. They're measuring consistency, not creativity. They're seeking proof, not promises.

The question isn't whether you have a mission. The question is whether your mission has you.

Does it guide your smallest decisions? Does it determine your toughest tradeoffs? Does it define your development plans? Does it shape your hiring choices?

If not, you don't have a commitment problem. You have a clarity problem.

The Commitment Catalyst

A great Crew isn't just excited about the mission. They're invested in it. It's an obsession. They own it. They defend it. They advance it. They bet their livelihood on it, and in some cases, they even put their lives on the line for it: Firefighters, law enforcement, military, lifeguards, missionaries, and teachers immediately come to mind.

All-in investment like that requires understanding.
Understanding requires clarity.
Clarity requires repetition.
Repetition requires intention.

The simplest path to a committed Crew?

1. Make your mission simple enough for everyone to understand
2. Repeat it until you're sick of hearing yourself say it
3. Then repeat it ten more times (twenty is better)
4. Connect every victory, every challenge, and every decision to it
5. Live it so visibly that hypocrisy becomes impossible

Because here's what separates legendary Captains from the rest: They don't command commitment. They inspire it through relentless clarity.

They know the strongest crew isn't bound by ropes, but by purpose. Not by obligation, but by shared direction. Not by authority, but by alignment.

Your mission isn't words on a wall. It's the reason your Crew shows up when storms hit. It's why they stay when competitors call. It's how they know which way to row when you're not there to point.

The question isn't whether your Crew will commit to your mission. The question is whether your mission is worth committing to.

And whether you've made it impossible to miss.

> If you would like to uplevel your mission, vision, purpose, and core values, check out this resource from my first book, *Small Fish Big Pond: Building a World-Class Business That Swims Circles Around Competitors.* The tool is called "The Business Identity Blueprint." It's free.
>
> Download it at https://smallfishbigpond.com/resources
> Grab a copy of that book here. All profits go to charity.
>
> 

The Power of Different

Every captain faces the same temptation. It whispers in the back of their mind during every interview, every hire, team-building moment: "Find someone like you. Someone who thinks like you. Someone who works like you."

It's a siren song of sameness, and it's killed more businesses than any market crash.

You see it in startups that scale into stagnation. Their leadership team is a mirror image of the founders. You see it in corporate boardrooms where innovation goes to die, surrounded by nodding heads and echoing perspectives. You see it in the quiet death of companies that mistake harmony for strength.

The myth of the perfect crew runs deep. We imagine a seamless machine, parts moving in perfect synchronization, everyone anticipating everyone else's thoughts. No friction. No conflict. No mess.

But watch any truly great company in action. Listen closely. You'll hear the productive clash of different minds approaching the same problem. You'll see the creative tension of diverse perspectives pulling solutions into new shapes. You'll feel the energy that comes not from agreement but from intelligent disagreement.

Consider what happens when you build a crew of sameness:

"I need someone who thinks exactly like me," says the visionary founder, not realizing she's hiring someone who'll share her blind spots.

"We want people who'll fit our culture," says the hiring manager, unconsciously translating culture fit into comfort fit.

"This candidate really gets how we do things," says the team leader, missing the opportunity to discover better ways of doing things.

The true power of a crew lies not in how well they blend but in how effectively they complement. Like a master chef building flavors, it's the contrasts that create the magic:

The visionary needs the pragmatist - not to clip their wings, but to build runways for their ideas to take flight.

The risk-taker needs the analyst - not to say no, but to illuminate the path to yes.

The accelerator needs the brake - not to stop growth, but to make it sustainable.

These aren't compromises. They're amplifications. Each strength is made stronger by its counterpart. Each perspective is made clearer by its contrast.

Look at the great partnerships that built lasting empires:

Walt Disney's boundless imagination needed Roy Disney's financial acumen. Together, they didn't just create stories - they built a legacy that outlived them both.

Steve Jobs' revolutionary vision required Steve Wozniak's engineering brilliance. Their differences didn't divide them - they multiplied their impact.

This isn't about arbitrary diversity. It's about intentional composition. About understanding that your crew's strength comes not from their similarity to you, but from their difference from you. Not from their ability to echo your thoughts, but from their power to expand them.

The most dangerous moment for any captain isn't when they face external storms. It's when they look around their crew and see only themselves reflected back. When every voice speaks in the same tone, every mind moves in the same groove, and every solution comes from the same playbook.

DANGER WILL ROBINSON!

Because here's what every successful captain learns: If everyone in your crew thinks like you, someone isn't thinking. If everyone approaches problems your way, most problems aren't getting solved. If everyone shares your strengths, you're all sharing the same weaknesses.

Build a crew of different. Not because it's fashionable. Not because it's right. Do it because it is precisely how you build something bigger than yourself. Something that lasts longer than your own vision. Something that grows beyond your own limitations.

The power isn't in the harmony.
It's in the symphony.
Each instrument is distinct. Each voice is clear.
Creating something together that none could create alone.

That's not just crew composition.

That's Crew magic.

The Control Evolution

I'm currently writing this while sitting in Martha's frozen yogurt shop.

Martha made the best frozen yogurt in three counties. The lines were out the door every weekend. She worked sixteen-hour days, perfected every flavor, and handled every customer complaint. Her yogurt was amazing. Her life? Not so much.

"No one can make it quite like I do," she'd say. And she was right. The product was exceptional! She was also stuck.

Here's the thing about control: It's like holding onto a handful of sand. The tighter you squeeze, the more slips through your fingers.

This isn't just about yogurt. I see this pattern everywhere.

The graphic designer who can't delegate because "clients expect my work."
The consultant who won't build a team because "my reputation is on the line."
The restaurant owner who hasn't taken a vacation in five years because "nobody does it right."

They're all telling themselves the same story:
If I want it done right, I have to do it myself.

It's the most expensive story in business.

The Evolution Nobody Talks About

Here's what really happens when you start letting go:

First, someone does it differently from you. This feels wrong.
Then, they make a mistake you wouldn't have made. This feels terrible.

Then, they find a better way to do it. This feels . . . interesting.
Finally, they transform it into something you never could have created alone. This feels amazing.

But getting there? That's the hard part.

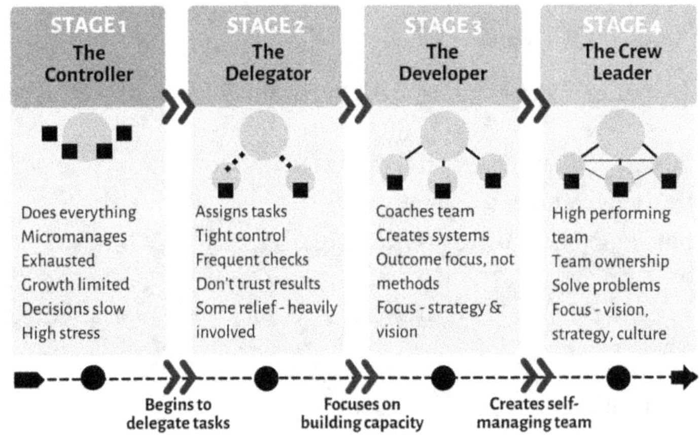

American Idol Syndrome

Remember William Hung from American Idol? It has been a while. Think all the way back to the early days when it was so bad that it was actually good. Contestants were delusional. Hung became famous for singing with amazing enthusiasm, unwavering confidence, and zero ability. The judges could not convince him he wasn't a great singer. He was completely convinced he was amazing - and viewers across America voted for him repeatedly. Many found it hilarious to vote for someone so horrifically bad, and at the same time, he was incredibly entertaining and charismatic. Most of all because he had zero self-awareness! (and/or just didn't care)

Here's the thing: we're all William Hung in some area of our business.
Yep, just like some of those singers, we are delusional.

Maybe you think you're great at sales when you're just okay. Or you believe you're an excellent project manager when you're actually creating bottlenecks. Or you insist on doing the books because "it's easier than explaining it to someone else."

This is American Idol Syndrome: The inability to see our own limitations.

The cure isn't pretty, but it's necessary:

1. Ask for honest feedback (and try not to cry when you get it)
2. Track your time ruthlessly (where are you really spending your hours?)
3. Calculate the real cost of doing it all (hint: it's more than money)
4. Find people who are actually great at what you're just okay at
5. Let them teach you a better way

Finding Your Genius Zone

Here's a simple exercise: For one week, track every task you do. Mark each one as:

- Energizing (you feel better after doing it)
- Neutral (you could take it or leave it)
- Draining (you need coffee just thinking about it)

Your Genius Zone lives in the Energizing category. That's where you should spend most of your time.

Everything else? That's what your Crew is for.

The question isn't whether you can do it all. Of course you can, for a while.

The real question is what's it costing you? In dreams deferred. In opportunities missed. In relationships strained.

Your job as Captain isn't to row every oar. It's to set the course and build a Crew that can navigate any waters.

Even the ones you've never sailed before.

The Daily Dance of Trust

Let me tell you about Alex. She runs a $25M software company that's growing 80% year over year. Last month, her team deployed 47 product updates.

She learned about 43 of them after they happened.

"Isn't that terrifying?" I asked her, smiling.

"Maybe a little scary some days," she joked back, then completely serious, "What's truly terrifying is being the constraint in your own company's growth."

The Permission Paradox

Here's what happens in most companies: A junior developer has an idea. She asks her team lead. The team lead consults the director. The director puts it on the agenda for the next leadership meeting. The leadership team decides to "think about it."

Six weeks later, their competitor launches the exact same feature.

Sound familiar?

Now, look at what happens in companies built on trust: A junior developer has an idea. She tests it. It works. She deploys it. The team learns from the results.

Six hours later, customers are already using it.

The difference isn't process. It's permission.

The Morning Question

Every day starts with team leads asking their people one question: "What do you need to remove to move faster?"

Not "what do you need to add?" Not "what do you need to do?" What needs to go away?

Sometimes it's a redundant meeting. Sometimes it's a clunky approval process. Sometimes it's fear of making the wrong call.

Remove the barriers. Speed follows.

Scaling up is rarely about doing more. It's usually about killing off the time-sucking projects that inevitably creep in. As businesses grow, they naturally become more complex. They have more moving parts, more approvals, more redundancy, and far more steps.

Left unchecked, these little complexity monsters multiply. Simplicity scales. Kill the complexity monsters. The sooner the better. If not, those little monsters grow up.

The Trust Accelerator

Here's what happened when one of Alex's junior developers pushed a bug to production:

Nothing.

No emergency meeting. No blame game. No new approval process.

Instead, she asked three questions:

1. What did we learn?
2. How do we share that learning?
3. What will you do differently next time?

The bug got fixed in 20 minutes. The lesson got shared in their weekly tech talk. The team got stronger.

That's how trust compounds.

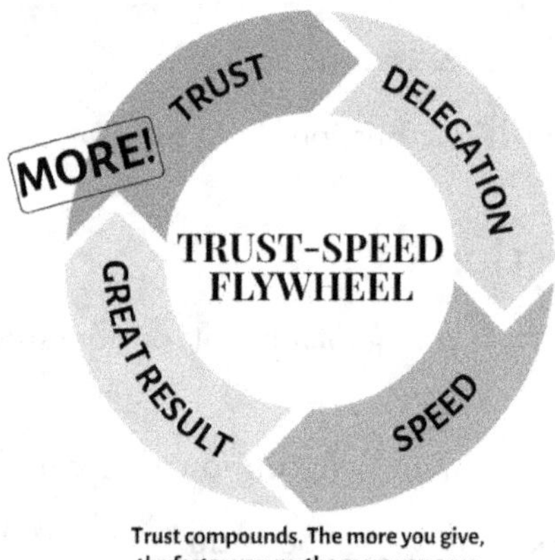

Trust compounds. The more you give,
the faster you go, the more you earn.

The Decision Protocol

They have a simple framework for decisions:

Reversible decisions: Make them fast. Make them now.
Irreversible decisions: Make them together. Make them well.
But here's the key: Most decisions we think are irreversible actually aren't.

That new feature you're worried about launching? Reversible.

That hire you're thinking about making? Reversible.

That process you want to change? Reversible.

Speed comes from knowing the difference.

DECISION VELOCITY MATRIX

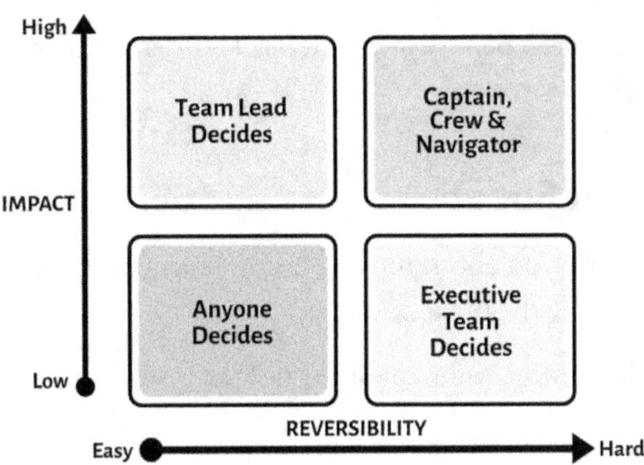

The Reality Check

Now, you might be thinking: "This sounds great, but it would never work here."

That's what Tom thought too. He runs a $40M cybersecurity firm. High stakes. Serious consequences for mistakes. The kind of place where "move fast and break things" sounds like a recipe for disaster.

But even there, he found places to trust. Decisions to delegate. Speed to enable.

He started small:

- One team
- One project
- One month

The result? That team delivered 3x more than others. With fewer bugs. Higher client satisfaction. Better security metrics.

Because trust isn't just about feeling good. It's about moving fast.

The Daily Choice

Every day, you make hundreds of micro-decisions about trust:

- Do you ask to see that email before it goes out?
- Do you need to be in that meeting?

- Does that decision really need your approval?

Each one is a choice between being a multiplier or a bottleneck. Between building a team that runs with you or waits for you.

The Truth About Speed

Here's what nobody tells you about moving fast in business: Speed isn't about running faster. It's about removing the brakes.

And the biggest brake in most companies? It's not the systems. It's not the processes. It's not even the people.

It's the leaders who can't let go.

Navigation Hazards

Even with the best charts, every journey has its hazards. Exposed rocks and reefs hidden just below the surface. Here are the warning signs your crew-building efforts are drifting off course:

The Dependency Trap: You're in meetings all day. Your inbox is overflowing. People are standing in line outside your office. Everyone needs "just a quick decision" from you.

Sound familiar? That's not leadership. That's dependency.

And you likely created it. With every "let me see that before it goes out" and "check with me first," you've trained your team to need you. Now they're just following those instructions.

The Information Desert: You're in a meeting when someone mentions a major client issue. "When did this happen?" you ask. The uncomfortable response: "Two weeks ago."

Or perhaps you discover a new initiative already underway, a hire already made, or a decision already implemented - all without your knowledge.

This isn't a lack of transparency. It's a lack of clarity. Your team either doesn't know what information you need, or they're afraid to bring you certain types of information. Both are dangerous.

The Decision Delay: "We're waiting for your approval." "It's been in your inbox since Tuesday." "We can't move forward until you weigh in."

These aren't scheduling issues. They're symptoms of a decision culture that's built around permission rather than purpose.

The Echo Chamber: Everyone agrees with your ideas. Meetings feel harmonious. There's never any pushback.

This isn't alignment. It's avoidance. When teams fear offering different perspectives, you get artificial agreement and real disengagement.

The Rescue Routine: You find yourself repeatedly saving projects at the last minute. Jumping in to handle client escalations. Fixing problems that should have been caught earlier.

This isn't heroic leadership. It's enabling. And it teaches your team that they don't need to develop these skills because you'll always be there to save the day.

The good news? Each of these hazards has a simple course correction:

For dependency: Ask "Who else could decide this?" before answering. For information deserts: Clarify what information needs to flow where. For decision delays: Create default decision rights that don't include you. For echo chambers: Reward constructive disagreement publicly. For rescue routines: Let small fires burn occasionally so others learn to prevent them.

These course corrections aren't complex. But they require something many captains find challenging:

The courage to be temporarily unnecessary.

That can be scary!

Hang on.

Let's be brutally honest for a moment.

You don't actually want a Crew.

You want employees who do exactly what you tell them to do.
You want people who execute your vision without questioning it.
You want the comfort of control without the pain of genuine collaboration.

How do I know?
Because that's what I wanted too.

Until I realized that kind of control is just another word for limitation.

My limitation.
My ceiling.
My constraint on what's possible.
That was scarier to me than being temporarily unnecessary!

Real Crews aren't extensions of the Captain.

They're multipliers of the Captain.

Let that sink in for a minute.

Creating a Cohesive Crew

Let's talk about Tamara's first week at her dream job.

In a team meeting, she spotted a flaw in the new product launch plan. She had an idea that could save weeks of work. But she stayed quiet. Why? Because in her last job, pointing out problems got you labeled as "not a team player."

This is what happens without psychological safety.
Good ideas die in silent throats.

Problems grow in dark corners. Innovation suffocates under the weight of "that's how we've always done it."

Building safety isn't about being nice. It's about being real.

It looks like:

- The CEO admitting, "I was wrong about that approach."
- The team lead saying, "I don't know, what do you think?"
- The new hire feeling safe to ask "dumb" questions.
- Everyone knowing that failed experiments are celebrated as learning opportunities.

The Real Work Begins

Building a true Crew isn't like hiring employees.
It's more like growing a garden.

You can't force it to happen faster, but you can create the conditions for growth.

Start here:

1. Clear the Weeds
   - Stop doing everything yourself
   - Identify what actually needs you
   - Let go of tasks that drain your energy
   - Make space for others to step up

2. Plant the Seeds
   - Share your vision. Then share it again
   - Tell stories that bring the mission to life
   - Look for light in people's eyes when they hear about the work
   - Hire for resonance, not just resumes

3. Nurture Growth
   - Give trust before it's "earned"
   - Celebrate small wins loudly
   - Make it safe to fail forward
   - Let people surprise you with their capabilities

The Permission Paradox

Here's something fascinating: The more permission you give others to lead, the more leadership you actually have.

I watched a tech company founder struggle with this. He was holding weekly "alignment meetings" that were really just him telling everyone what to do. His team was capable, but careful. Cautious. They waited for permission for everything.

Then he got sick.
Really sick.
Had to step away for two months.

Something remarkable happened: His team didn't just maintain - they thrived.
They made decisions.
Solved problems.
Innovated.

When he returned, the business was stronger than when he left.

Not because they finally had permission to lead, but because they finally had to.

The Three Questions

Want to know if you're building a true Crew? Ask these three questions:

1. If you disappeared for a month, would your mission continue without you?
2. Do people bring you solutions, or just problems?
3. When someone says "we should try _______" Do others lean in or look down?

The answers tell you everything about where you are on the journey.

The Horizontal Power

There's a secret about great crews that mediocre ones miss entirely: The strongest bonds aren't between captain and crew. They're between crew members themselves.

Think about the last time you saw a remarkable team in action. The restaurant staff who flow around each other without colliding. The surgical team that communicates with glances and nods. The product team that finishes each other's sentences and builds on each other's ideas.

That magic doesn't come from vertical leadership. It comes from horizontal connection.

I watched a tech startup triple their output after implementing one simple change: They stopped routing all communications through the founder and started talking directly to each other.

Teams that need the captain as a constant intermediary aren't teams at all. They're just collections of individual relationships with the leader.

Real Crew power happens when:

- Team members solve problems together without escalation
- Skills and knowledge flow freely between departments
- People cover for each other without being asked
- Feedback moves in all directions, not just top-down
- Celebration comes from peers, not just from leadership

In the strongest crews, the captain becomes less central over time, not more. The team's reliance on any single person - even the leader - decreases as their interconnection increases.

This isn't abdicating leadership. It's evolving it.

From controller to connector. From bottleneck to bridge-builder. From answer-provider to question-asker.

Want to test if you're building peer strength? Ask this: If you removed yourself from your team for a month, would communication improve or collapse?

If it would collapse, you're not building a Crew. You're building dependencies.

The most powerful question you can ask isn't "How can I lead better?"
It's "How can I connect my crew more effectively to each other?"

Because here's the truth about leadership: Your ultimate success isn't measured by how well your team follows you.

It's measured by how well they lead without you.

When Storms Hit

Remember March 2020? When the world turned upside down?

Some businesses fragmented under pressure. Others got stronger. The difference wasn't their business model or their cash reserves. It was their Crew.

I watched a local restaurant transform overnight from dine-in to community kitchen. Not because the owner ordered it. Because the Crew saw a need and said, "We can help."

The servers became delivery drivers. The chef created family-style meals. The dishwasher organized a phone bank to check on elderly customers.

That's what a mission-driven Crew does in crisis. They innovate. They adapt. They find ways through, over, or around obstacles.

They don't just survive - they serve.

Your Next Move

Building a Crew isn't a destination – it's a practice. It's something you choose every day, in small moments and big decisions.

It's choosing to:

- Listen more than you speak
- Ask instead of tell
- Trust before you have "proof"
- Let go before you're completely comfortable
- Serve the mission more than your ego

Because here's what I know for sure: The size of your impact will always be limited by your ability to build and nurture a true Crew.

Your mission matters too much to do it alone.
Your dreams are too big for solo sailing.
Your impact is too important to keep it small.

It's time to build your Crew.

Not just to help you carry the load.
Not just to multiply your impact.
But to create something none of you could create alone.

Because that's how great things are built.
That's how missions come alive.
That's how dreams become reality.

One person at a time.
One connection at a time.
One shared purpose at a time.

Your Crew is waiting.
What's your next move?

REFLECT: Are you operating as a True Captain, Team Builder, Working Manager, or Solo Sailor?

Where are you still rowing alone when you should have a Crew?
What's the real reason you haven't let go?

ACT: Tomorrow morning, identify one task, outcome, or decision you've been holding onto that someone else could handle. Hand it over completely. No hovering, no checking in. Just transfer it and trust.

From Employees to Crew

You now understand the difference between employees and true Crew members. I put together some tools and resources to help you build the operational backbone that turns your vision into reality.

One of them is the "Invisible Contract" that transforms transactional relationships into committed Crew connections - without doing everything yourself. It's free, my gift to you.

Join leaders who have escaped the "I'll just do it myself" trap.

https://TheCaptainsKeys.com/bonus

"Thank you! This helped me build a Crew that's not just interested in our mission—they're committed to it. The process worked like magic."

—JAMIE T., FOUNDER

⚙ NAVIGATE

To Sail the Story / Full Journey - Continue on to the next page
Study the Maps - Jump ahead to page 245

CAPTAIN TO CAPTAIN:

You are X here

Here's the thing about journeys - you can't plot a course if you don't know your starting position.

Every captain falls somewhere on this map. Be honest about where you are, not where you wish you were. The shortest path to your destination starts with the truth about your current location.

Solo Sailor

- You make nearly all meaningful decisions
- Your days are spent firefighting
- Vacations mean answering emails remotely
- Growth is directly limited by your hours
- The business struggles when you're absent

Working Manager

- You delegate tasks, but keep decisions
- You review most work before it goes out
- You're the bottleneck for most innovations
- Team members check with you before acting
- You know you need to let go, but struggle to do it

Team Builder

- You've let go of how, but still control what
- You have pockets of real delegation
- Some team members own entire functions
- You're building systems, but they're incomplete
- You still feel responsible for everything

True Captain

- You focus on strategic direction, not operations
- Your team brings you solutions, not problems
- The business grows when you're not there
- Mission drives decisions at all levels
- Your job is setting conditions, not controlling outcomes

Most leaders overestimate where they are on this journey. The true test isn't what you think – it's what happens when you're not in the room.

Where are you today? More importantly, where will you be in 90 days?

"NAVIGATING
UNKNOWN WATERS"

BEYOND THE STORM
Part 6

Jimmy didn't leave the house for the next two days except to grocery shop and walk Bella. The isolation wasn't about avoidance this time - it was about clarity.

He spent hours on the second-floor deck, bundled against the cold, watching waves crash against the Alaskan shore. Bella would curl at his feet, her golden coat collecting snowflakes that melted into tiny dark spots. Sometimes he'd reach down and brush the dampness away, and she'd look up at him with those soulful eyes that asked nothing and accepted everything.

"What do you think, girl?" he asked her as the sun dipped toward the horizon, painting the water in copper and gold. "Who would be crazy enough to follow a Florida transplant into the deadliest waters on Earth?"

She thumped her tail twice against the deck boards, then laid her head on his boot.

The truth was, he loved the water more than he dared admit. Not being able to see it, to spend his days on or near it - that was unthinkable. He needed crewmembers who felt the same way, men who weren't just chasing a paycheck but something deeper.

The money could be insane if everything went right - $80,000 per man for a successful 3-4 month season wasn't unusual. But money alone couldn't sustain you through sixteen-hour shifts in freezing spray, bone-deep exhaustion, and constant danger. When waves crashed over the bow at 2 a.m. and hypothermia was just one mistake away, a man needed more than dollar signs to keep him going.

In a moment of real clarity Jimmy realized that he wasn't particularly motivated by money himself right now. The final insurance settlement, the house, the boat, the truck - he had more assets now than in the rest of his life combined. It was far more than money. He needed the challenge, the purpose. Everything else was secondary.

He finally came to the conclusion that he had to appeal for crewmembers based on the one commodity he did have: the family name. He was every bit as much a Meyer as Uncle

Rocky, and while he had chased marlin and swordfish instead of crab, his essential business had been the same.

Pride would be a factor for the men he hired; either they had lost it or they were still in search of it. He felt the same way after his constant ribbing by the other captains. Pride could be a bad thing if you had too much, but a man needed something to hang his hat on. He hoped to find a crew with that same ambition he was feeling, inspire them with his uncle's story, and get out into those treacherous waters and start feeling alive again.

On the third day, he drove to the local copy shop and designed his hiring advertisements. No fancy language, no corporate BS. Just bold colors and clear purpose:

It might chafe a few of the other captains, but Jimmy no longer cared. This was about him and his crew, not the guys who were worried about a newcomer and sought to bully him out of town before he got his feet wet.

Back at home, Jimmy sketched out a simple grid on the back of an old envelope. From his many years as a charter captain he learned you could tell everything about a person by three things: how they handled sleep deprivation, how they reacted to disappointment of being skunked at a particular fishing spot, and how they treated people who could do nothing for them.

Jimmy added a fourth criterion: adaptability. The Bering Sea would throw curveballs no one could anticipate. He needed men who bent without breaking.

He studied his impromptu rating chart. Not just skills, but character. Not just experience, but temperament. He'd hire for the qualities no training manual could teach, then build around them.

CHAPTER 25

Purpose had more power than Jimmy imagined. His phone lit up with calls and text messages from potential crew members. With each candidate, Jimmy asked the same question last: 'Tell me about your worst day at sea.' The lies stood out immediately - too polished, too heroic. The truth came ragged, raw, and real, revealing how a man handled not just danger, but failure.

Tom Lance had been his first hire. At thirty-nine, the Sun'aq tribe member carried generations of Kodiak history in his blood. His people had settled where the city of Kodiak now stood more than 2,500 years ago, and had first come to Alaska more than 8,000 years ago. Tom had been hunting and fishing since he could walk, an intimacy with the island and its waters that no amount of book learning could provide.

He'd shown up to the interview wearing a short-sleeved shirt when it was 27 degrees outside. Jimmy had taken this as either madness or a power move, but the truth was simpler: the cold simply didn't register for Tom the way it did for others.

"Why aren't you on another boat?" Jimmy had asked him directly.

Tom's eyes had shifted away, the first sign of discomfort he'd shown. "Got in a fight with another crewmate. Got branded a hothead."

It had taken more questioning to get the full story: how an overwhelming number of the fishermen were white, how different standards were applied to native crew members, how one heated exchange had followed him from boat to boat like a shadow.

"I worked for your uncle a few times," Tom said, his expression warming at the memory. "Rocky Meyer was fair. Demanding, but fair. Didn't matter where you came from, only what you put in."

Tom's references spoke of grace under fire, a sure hand in a crisis, and, despite his reputation, someone who could negotiate arguments effectively. The bias some captains held against him resonated deep inside Jimmy, who had felt a similar dismissive judgment since arriving in Alaska.

Jimmy's second hire was another Kodiak native, but Richie Knapp was neither Sun'aq nor experienced. At twenty, he was already married with a baby on the way. His wife, Lori, worked at their old high school as a coach and teacher.

"Construction work is feast or famine around here," Richie had explained, fidgeting with his wedding band. "It pays well when jobs are hot. It was fine when it was just me, but tougher with a wife and a little one on the way. I've got to step up my game."

His family had been crabbing for generations, but his two relatives in the trade were already at sea when he'd learned he was going to be a father. The kid was desperate to provide and to honor his family legacy.

Jimmy had taken him aboard the *Bering Steel* to see how he'd react. Without prompting, Richie had started fixing things - repairing splits in pot mesh, replacing ropes, asking if he could repaint sections of the hull where Jimmy had botched the job.

"Whoa, hold on," Jimmy had interrupted. "We haven't talked about salary or hours yet."

Richie had just shrugged. "As long as I can take care of my family, I don't care what it is."

The kid was a natural with uncanny mechanical aptitude, hungry for knowledge and willing to learn. Jimmy recognized the look in his eyes - it was the same one he'd seen in his own reflection when he'd first started captaining in the Keys.

Jimmy had almost rejected Aidan Beagle on first impression alone. The twenty-five-year-old's dazzling shock of blonde hair stood almost straight up from his massive six-foot-six frame. At 250 pounds of pure muscle, he looked like he belonged in a skate park or on a surfboard, not on a commercial fishing vessel.

But Jimmy had promised himself to hear everyone out. Turned out Aidan was a Colorado Springs transplant and a certified adrenaline junkie who had already mastered mountain climbing, base jumping, cliff diving, and cave diving - activities that sounded to Jimmy about as appealing as being eaten alive by scorpions.

"I watched every season of 'Deadliest Catch' three times," Aidan had said, leaning forward with intense focus. "I know it's TV, but man, that rush when they're pulling pots in a storm? That's real. That's what I'm after."

Despite his extreme sports persona, Aidan had methodically prepared for this career pivot. He had his state license and all required certifications. He'd studied vessel operations and weather patterns. Jimmy was impressed - looks were definitely deceiving with this one.

The last hire was Bob Sanders, whom everyone called "Old Bob" despite the fact that he was just fifty-one. The lines etched into his face suggested a man pushing seventy who had done some profoundly hard living.

He'd surprised Jimmy by bringing another man to the interview - his Alcoholics Anonymous sponsor. Bob had wordlessly laid six sobriety chips on the table, arranged in chronological order. Six years clean and sober.

"I need you to know who I am before anything else," he'd said, his voice steady despite the vulnerability of the gesture.

Bob had been a mechanic once, a talented one, before alcohol had consumed him. It had cost him his license, his career, and ultimately his wife. Rock bottom had come when his thirteen-year-old daughter found him blacked out in their front yard, suffering from hypothermia. The hospital had nearly pronounced him dead, but she'd stayed by his side and talked him back to the land of the living.

Now she was nineteen and lived with him while working as an artist. Jimmy had looked up her work online - paintings and sculptures of local wildlife, landscapes, and portraits. She was incredibly talented and was paying most of their bills with sales to locals and tourists.

"She's been accepted to a program in Seattle," Bob had explained. "Partial scholarship, but her loan application was denied. I need to do right by her."

He'd pointed to Jimmy's advertisement, still visible where it lay on the desk between them. "That word 'pride' there? That's what I need. Not just the money. A chance to be the man my daughter deserves."

Jimmy knew alcoholics were never "cured," only in recovery. He understood the inherent risk of taking a recovering alcoholic to sea, where long hours, stress, and isolation could trigger relapse. He'd need to keep an eye on Bob until trust was established, but the man's drive to redeem himself was palpable.

He had four men ready to sail into hell with him - at least in words. Action would prove whether he had a crew or just employees. Jimmy was the captain bridging two greenhorns and two seasoned hands, all five carrying chips on their shoulders and purpose beyond a paycheck.

The night before they all reported for work, Jimmy stood at his window staring at the distant outline of the *Bering Steel*.

What if he'd chosen wrong?

What if his judgment was as faulty as that engine?

What if they never made it out to sea?

Four men's livelihoods, possibly their lives, now rested on his decisions.

CHAPTER 26

Within days, the metamorphosis of the *Bering Steel* was remarkable. The rusty, temperamental Caterpillar (engine) was turning into a butterfly - or at least a dusty moth. Where Jimmy had struggled alone for weeks, his crew attacked problems with coordinated efficiency. Between the four of them, they had connections for parts and equipment that saved thousands compared to what Jimmy would have paid on his own.

He deliberately paired Old Bob with Richie, and Tom with Aidan. He didn't want the crew splitting into young guys versus old guys, dividing morale along generational lines. More importantly, he knew Richie was the cleanest living of the four - a straight arrow right out of high school with a pregnant wife wasn't hitting the bars every night. Bob seemed to see something of his own daughter in Richie's work ethic and sincerity. They were working in tandem within hours.

It took Aidan and Tom longer to find common ground, but when they did, they became nearly inseparable. Aidan learned that the experiences he was traveling the world seeking - swimming in frigid waters, wilderness survival, hunting with primitive weapons - Tom had mastered as a child. He was fascinated by how the native man had accomplished naturally what Aidan had spent fortunes chasing. The blonde giant might have looked out of place in Tom's village, but there was no question both men shared a deep respect for the untamed world and the discipline required to survive in it.

Jimmy watched in disbelief as Tom and Aidan tackled the hydraulic system he'd fought with for three days. Tom's hands moved with intuitive precision while Aidan provided the raw strength to hold components in place. They barely spoke – didn't need to. Within two hours, the system hummed to life as if it had never been broken at all. What had defeated him alone was easily conquered by them together.

What had once been a months-long repair schedule now appeared achievable in weeks. The *Bering Steel* was coming back to life, shaking off rust and neglect with each passing day.

Jimmy caught himself watching his crew with a mixture of pride and unease. They worked with an easy competence he hadn't yet mastered on his own vessel. Even the greenhorns we're settling in quickly. What if they realized how much more he needed them than they needed him? The balance of power on any ship was delicate - respect had to be earned, not assigned with a title. He pushed the thought away and focused on long list of jobs to be done.

Still, Jimmy noticed the small things - how Tom's jaw tightened when Bob gave unnecessary instructions, how Aidan's impatience flickered when Richie needed explanations repeated, how conversations chilled when talk turned to money or risk. Tiny fault lines beneath the surface solidarity.

Jimmy found himself missing the simplicity of his single furry crew member. Yet despite the friction, every project moved significantly faster with human help. His biggest challenge now was learning to lead through conflict rather than firing everyone and retreating to the old way.

Si coached him that every crew faced its breaking point. Not from the sea or the work, but from the pressure-cooker of proximity - men with different histories and habits confined in a floating metal box for weeks on end. The question wasn't if cracks would appear, but whether the foundation was strong enough to hold despite them.

Jimmy filed these observations away and resolved to focus on today's victories. Tomorrow's challenges could wait. For now, the gains far outweighed the squabbles. The *Bering Steel* was coming back to life, and so was the pride of Kodiak Island - one day at a time.

Ten days into the transformation, Captain Si appeared on the dock with lunch for all five men - and a massive beef shoulder bone for Bella. The crew greeted him with warm familiarity. Bella found a new best friend, at least temporarily. The entire crew seemed to know Si in some capacity either through interaction or reputation. Si exchanged quick words with each man before joining Jimmy in the wheelhouse.

For once, Jimmy did all the talking - gushing about the progress, the innovative solutions his crew had developed, and their upcoming three-day cod fishing "test run" once final repairs were complete. Si nodded, offered occasional compliments, and smiled to himself with quiet satisfaction.

As they watched the crew work through the wheelhouse window, the older captain placed a weathered hand on Jimmy's shoulder.

"He saw greatness in you," Si said softly, almost to himself. "Rocky would be proud of the man you've become - and the Captain you're turning into."

CHAPTER 27

Bering Steel

Gulf of Alaska, Cod fishing grounds

53 miles east of Kodiak

Icy spray cut across Jimmy's face as he stepped onto deck. His eyes burned from sixteen hours of vigilance, but pride held him upright. The engines had passed their test. Now it was the crew's turn.

The crew gathered in the galley in exhausted silence. Their first day of backbreaking work leaving them hollow-eyed and snappish. The tension in the galley was thick enough to cut.

Tom studied them for a moment, then silently rose and went to his bunk. He returned with a small wooden box, intricately carved with symbols Jimmy didn't recognize.

"My grandfather made this," Tom said, his voice cutting through the heavy silence. "Inside is red ochre from our sacred caves. Before each fishing season, our tribe would mark their faces with it. Not for luck." His dark eyes swept the room. "For connection."

He opened the box and dipped his finger in the rust-colored powder, then drew a simple line across his forehead.

"This reminds us that no fisherman faces the sea alone. The tribe's strength flows through each person." He offered the box to Aidan. "In my people's way, we are already a tribe. Now we make it visible."

One by one, each man marked himself with the ochre. When Tom reached Jimmy, he paused.

"For captains, the mark is different." He drew a circular pattern on Jimmy's forehead. "This symbol means 'one who listens to both the sea and his people.'"

The tension in the room had evaporated, replaced by something Jimmy couldn't name but instantly recognized. The same feeling he'd had as a boy when his father gathered the family before a storm - safety within chaos.

"In my culture, we say a warrior alone is food for wolves," Tom said quietly.

"Si calls it the Stability Matrix," Jimmy replied.

"Different words, same truth." Bob nodded. "Recovery taught me that. You're only as strong as your support system."

"Tomorrow," Tom said, "we will be stronger than today. Not because the work will be easier, but because we face it together."

The following day, things were . . . different. Shifted. The crew operated as a unit. It was hard to explain. The work was still grueling. The roles and responsibilities were the same. This day, the execution was smooth. Attitudes, relaxed.

As the last cod pot of the string came over the side, a collective cheer came from the crew. They'd done it.

The hold beneath his feet vibrated with the weight of their catch - tanks stuffed with thousands of pounds gleaming cod, the first real test of his inherited vessel. Not crabs yet, but proof the old girl could take whatever the Gulf and Bering Sea threw at her.

And God knew it had thrown plenty on this first brief run.

"Captain." Richie appeared at his shoulder, the youngest crew member's face etched with exhaustion but beaming with the particular satisfaction that comes only from honest labor. "Tom says we're about forty miles out from St. Herman harbor."

Jimmy nodded, the simple motion sending pain through his stiff neck. "Tell the boys well done. First round's on me tonight."

As Richie disappeared below, Jimmy's thoughts drifted to the past twenty-four hours. He'd never admit it aloud, but they'd come closer to disaster than anyone but Tom and perhaps Old Bob realized.

A storm had blindsided them - not unusual in these waters, where weather forecasts were educated guesses at best. High seas had driven them further off course than planned, burning precious fuel as they fought the current. What should have been a simple day's sail had stretched into an endurance trial.

Jimmy made a rookie mistake. To save money he had only added enough diesel to run the boat a few days. At forty-two gallons an hour, they would be cutting it close.

Standing alone in his quarters, Jimmy spread the charts across his small desk, the worn paper crinkling beneath his calloused fingers. Lamplight cast deep shadows across the topographical lines as he traced potential routes with his thumbnail. No one to consult. No experienced voice to weigh in. Just him, the charts, and a decision that could kill them all on their first trip.

Risk overstressing the transmission fighting the currents and potentially running out of fuel, or attempt the narrow Chenega Bay pass that local charts marked with warnings that made insurance adjusters wake up sweating. Rocky's chart noted it was usually passable at high tide, as long as there was no weather. High tide was an hour ago.

Two bad options. One key choice.

This isn't the Keys, the voice of reason had whispered.

But another voice - one that sounded suspiciously like his late uncle - had countered: *Water is water, and a captain is a captain.*

When he'd emerged from his quarters to announce his decision, he'd looked each crew member in the eye.

He chose the pass.

Tom and Bob had exchanged glances, their weather-beaten faces betraying concern they wouldn't voice in front of the younger men.

That was the code. Dissent in private. Unity on deck.

The pass was even narrower than the charts suggested - a throat of water barely wider than the *Bering Steel* herself, with razor-sharp volcanic rock lurking just beneath the surface. Three times, the keel had scraped something solid, the sound echoing through the hull like the cry of a wounded animal.

Each time, Jimmy had felt the vibration through the soles of his boots, a silent prayer rising in his throat.

But they'd made it through.

The *Bering Steel* dropped anchor in St. Herman harbor at dusk, the sky bleeding crimson across the western horizon. They were safe and secure, a stones throw away from the cod processor on Near Island. While the rest of the crew straightened up the boat Bob disappeared below into the galley.

An hour later, aromas of red beans, rice, and spicy sausage filled the mess as Jimmy called the crew down to a feast fit for a celebration - not just their successful first haul, but turning near-disaster into safe passage. The simple meal had the whole crew groaning with pleasure as they stuffed themselves.

Bob demonstrated exceptional talents in the kitchen so the crew made him the honorary *Bering Steel* chef. Then the real surprise: Slipping down to his cabin Bob returned with a battered old ukelele like a treasured relic. His gnarled fingers had coaxed melodies that transformed the cramped quarters into something different - something like home.

One by one, the crew had joined in, voices rough but earnest. Even Tom, the Sun'aq tribesman who rarely spoke more than necessary, had contributed a traditional song, its haunting melody silencing the others with its raw beauty.

Jimmy hadn't realized until that moment what he'd assembled. Yes, way more than employees, this bunch had become a Crew. However, there was something more here.

The beginnings of a bond that had been missing from his life for longer than he cared to admit.

Family.

The next morning Jimmy woke to the sounds of processing plants emerging through the mist outside his cabin window. The weight of responsibility settled deeper into his bones.

These men had trusted him with their livelihoods - and if yesterday was any indication, their lives. They'd believed in him with nothing but his word and a dead uncle's legacy to go on.

He wouldn't let them down.

CHAPTER 28

Jimmy's key scraped in the lock of his inherited house, the sound triggering a storm of joyful barking from the other side. The moment the door swung open, ninety pounds of golden fur launched toward him.

"Hey, girl." His voice broke with unexpected emotion as Bella's warm body collided with his. "Missed me, huh?"

Her answer was a frantic dance, circling and sniffing and pressing against his legs as if making sure every part of him had returned intact.

For the last ten years in the Keys, Bella had been his constant companion on the water. His charter guests had loved her - the friendly retriever who would solemnly accept the role of first mate, sitting at attention beside Jimmy as they motored out to the fishing grounds.

But that was the Keys, with its bath-warm waters and gentle swells. This was the Bering Sea, where water killed in minutes and waves could sweep a grown man overboard without warning.

"I know, girl." He scratched behind her ears, her favorite spot. "Wish you could've come this time. Maybe someday."

But even as he said it, he knew the day might never come. The image of her paddling in that killing cold, confusion in her loyal eyes as hypothermia took hold - he couldn't bear it.

Better she hate him for leaving her behind than risk losing her to the sea's indifference. Thankfully his next-door neighbor, Jerry aka "Dr. J", ran the friendliest vet clinic in Kodiak. A long time friend of Uncle Rocky, "Dr. J" volunteered to care for Bella while Jimmy was out fishing. He took her along on the occasional field trip so she wasn't stuck at home which Jimmy appreciated, and Bella even more so.

An hour later, freshly showered and with Bella curled at his feet, Jimmy scrolled through his messages. Three missed calls from Si. Two from Bob. None from his last conversation with Lily, weeks ago.

Guilt pressed against his ribs. He'd promised to call more often.

The number rang four times before his sister's familiar voice answered, slightly breathless.

"Jimmy? Is everything okay?"

"Everything's great, Lil. Just got back from a successful fishing run. Thought I'd check in, see how you and the kids are doing."

The relief in her laugh warmed him. "Well, that's a nice change. Usually, you only call when you're sinking or broke or both."

They fell into easy conversation, the miles between Florida and Alaska seeming to shrink with each shared story. She told him about her youngest's science fair project and her husband's promotion. He described the aurora borealis he'd seen two nights ago, how the sky had danced with colors no painter could capture.

"You sound different," she said abruptly, interrupting his description of Bob's harmonica playing. "Happier."

Jimmy paused, surprised by the observation. "Do I?"

"Mmm-hmm. Like you've found something you didn't know you were looking for."

The insight struck deeper than she could know. All those years running charters, he'd told himself he was free. No boss, no schedule but nature's, no responsibilities beyond the daily catch. But now he recognized it for what it really was.

Not freedom.

Drift.

"Maybe I have," he admitted. "These guys, Lil - my crew – they're something special. It's like they each bring something I didn't even know I was missing."

"That's called a team, little brother. Most people discover them before forty."

He laughed, accepting the jab. "Better late than never, right? And hey, I'm not forty yet sis!"

Their conversation wound down, promises to call more often exchanged. As he hung up, Jimmy felt the familiar steadiness she always brought him. He'd spent years taking that gift for granted. Not anymore.

He made a silent vow to honor that gift - and return it.

CHAPTER 29

The town bar pulsed with the particular energy of working men unwinding. The air hung thick with wood smoke and the salt-sweat scent that clung to fishermen no matter how they scrubbed. Laughter erupted from a back table where a story was reaching its punchline, the kind of tale that grew more outrageous with each telling.

Jimmy pushed through the door, cold air following him inside like a stalking predator before the heavy wood swung shut. His gaze swept the room, landing on Captain Si seated at the bar, a gift box at his elbow.

Si's weathered face cracked into a smile that deepened the crow's feet around his eyes. Beside him, Carly mirrored the expression, her copper hair catching the amber light from the overhead fixtures.

Something in Jimmy's chest loosened at the sight of them waiting for him. It was a small thing - a welcome, a celebration - but it struck him with unexpected force.

They missed me.

In Florida, he'd come and gone as he pleased, his absence barely noted except by Bella. Here, people tracked his movements, remembered his preferences, anticipated his return. The theme song from Cheers began playing in his head as he sauntered toward the "Meyer seat" at the bar.

"Welcome back, Captain!" Si clinked his beer against the one Carly smoothly placed in Jimmy's hand. "Heard you got a nice big haul of bait cod out there. Any troubles?"

For a heartbeat, Jimmy considered the easy lie. *Smooth sailing. No problems.* The kind of answer that maintained the illusion of effortless competence.

But Si had earned more than that.

"Actually, we hit some rough patches." Jimmy settled onto a barstool, the wood worn smooth by generations of sea-toughened bodies. "Had to thread the needle through Chenega Bay Pass when the current turned against us."

Si's eyebrows shot up, but he said nothing as Jimmy recounted the trip, detail by careful detail. The older captain winced visibly at the mention of the pass, his fingers tightening around his glass.

When Jimmy finished, Si patted his arm. "We're proud of you, kid. Taking risks is one thing. Calculating them is another."

Carly set another beer in front of them. "Speaking of calculations, how would you rate your chances of surviving our little gift without squealing like a six-year-old girl?"

Jimmy eyed the box suspiciously. "What is this, initiation?"

"Something like that." Si's eyes twinkled with mischief that shaved decades off his face. "Go on, open it. Carly's recording this for posterity."

Sure enough, she had her phone out, a smile playing at the corners of her mouth as Jimmy untied the ribbon and lifted the lid.

The box was filled with decorative paper. Jimmy played along, making a show of digging through it. "I can't wait to see what it is, guys. It's so kind of you to - SWEET MOTHER OF - "

The box rocked violently beneath his hands. Something inside was alive and moving.

Jimmy jerked back so quickly he nearly toppled his barstool, heart thundering against his ribs.

Carly doubled over, tears streaming down her face as silent laughter shook her shoulders. Si wasn't much better, his weathered face creased with delight at Jimmy's reaction.

Recovering his composure, Jimmy cautiously peered into the box. Two pairs of beady eyes stared back at him from furry faces.

"Tundra voles?" His voice emerged higher than he intended. "You put rodents in a gift box?!"

The other captains in the bar were openly laughing now, several raising bottles in a mock toast to Jimmy's discomfort. Heat climbed his neck, but it was good-natured ribbing, not the cutting mockery he'd faced when he first arrived.

"Thought Bella could use some company." Carly suggested innocently. "How about naming them Port and Starboard? Or maybe King and Blue?"

Jimmy flicked a French fry at her, which she caught deftly in her mouth, eyes dancing.

"Dunge and Ness?" she continued, undeterred. "Florie and Keys? Marlin and Nemo?"

As their laughter subsided, Si leaned in, his expression shifting to something more serious. "Speaking of names, I've got one you should know."

The change in tone caught Jimmy's attention. "What's that?"

"Scott Kaiser." Si swirled the amber liquid in his glass. "One of the best navigators to ever sail these waters."

"Navigator?" Jimmy repeated, the unfamiliar term catching in his mind.

Si nodded, his eyes taking on that distant look they got when he was pulling knowledge from decades of experience. "That's the third key, Jimmy. You've got your Anchor keeping you stable. You've assembled a whale of a Crew to execute the mission. But you're still missing someone who knows the terrain better than you ever could. That's a navigator."

Jimmy quickly grabbed a cocktail napkin and drew a plus like before. Si said, "That one goes in the top right." Jimmy added in all three parts in their quadrants and asked, "Why do I need a navigator? The boat has decent electronics."

Si gestured toward the harbor through the frost-edged windows. "I've seen how you handle that boat every time you're out. You've got instincts. Gifted. Making that pass takes guts, and skill. No doubt about that. But those will only take you so far in waters that have been killing experienced sailors for centuries."

Jimmy considered this, remembering how close they'd come to disaster. If that hidden shelf of rocks had been a few feet to the west . . .

"The fleet here saw three shipwrecks during the season last year," Si continued. "Good captains with years of experience. The sea doesn't care about your resume or your electronics. It'll kill you just the same."

"So this Scott Kaiser – he's available?" Jimmy asked, mind already calculating the additional salary against projected earnings.

A shadow crossed Si's face. "He's available. Whether he's willing is another matter."

"What do you mean?"

Si took a long pull from his beer. "Scott's been on dry land for two years now. Won't go near the water."

"Why not?" Jimmy leaned forward, intrigued.

"He let some friends take his boat out. Deep-sea charter, south of here." Si's voice lowered. "There was a hurricane brewing, but they were keeping an eye on it. You know how these things are - track projections, probability cones."

Jimmy nodded, phantom rain stinging his face as memories of Claudette surged unbidden.

"The storm accelerated. Caught them at night. Hundred and forty mile-per-hour winds." Si's eyes had gone flat, seeing something far beyond the bar's walls. "Ship went down with all hands."

Jimmy exhaled slowly, understanding dawning. "And he blames himself."

"Wouldn't you?" Si asked, but it wasn't really a question.

The silence stretched between them, filled with the phantom voices of all those the sea had claimed.

"Scott was like you once," Si finally continued. "Natural talent, instinctive understanding of the water. Could read currents like you and I read street signs. Plus, he had something most never develop - a sixth sense for weather. Could feel a storm coming before the barometer dropped."

"And now?"

"Now he sits in his cabin and stares at charts of waters he'll never sail again." Si's weathered hand closed around Jimmy's forearm. "Or so he believes."

The implication was clear. "You want me to change his mind."

Si's eyes, pale blue as a winter sky, fixed on Jimmy's. "I want you to offer him redemption."

The word hung in the air between them, heavy with meaning. Not just a job. Not just a paycheck.

A second chance.

Jimmy swallowed, the weight of what Si was asking settling across his shoulders. "What makes you think he'd listen to me?"

"Because," Si said softly, "you're Rocky Meyer's nephew. Scott and your uncle go back a long way."

In the harbor beyond the frosted glass, boats rocked gently at their moorings, waiting for the dawn that would send them hunting again. Among them, the *Bering Steel* sat dark and patient, already becoming more than just a vessel to Jimmy.

She was becoming a promise.

Jimmy's jaw tightened. "Where do I find him?"

> ## ⚓ NAVIGATE
>
> Study the Maps / Full Journey - Continue on to the next page
> To Sail the Story - Ride a wave to page 273

THE NAVIGATOR
SEEING BEYOND THE HORIZON

"We navigate by the stars, not by the lights of every passing ship."
— GENERAL OMAR N. BRADLEY

February 2019.
Atlantic Ocean. 50 miles East of Grand Bahama Island.

They found the yacht drifting.
Pristine and empty.
Engines perfect. Hull intact.
Weather had been clear for days.
Navigation system state-of-the-art.

The owner was a brilliant entrepreneur worth nine figures.

He was gone - along with three passengers aboard.

What happened?

The Coast Guard investigation revealed a simple, devastating truth:

The CEO had been warned repeatedly about rough seas and crossing the Gulf Stream.
At night.
Solo.

Several experienced captains had offered to accompany him.

"I've read three books on navigation," he'd told a harbor master the day before. "And I've got the best equipment money can buy. I'll be fine."

He had every instrument needed to navigate safely, but he trusted his novice instincts instead.

He rejected the voices of experience because they contradicted his confidence. Made him look "weak" in front of his friends.

Confidence without competence can be deadly when traveling in unknown waters.

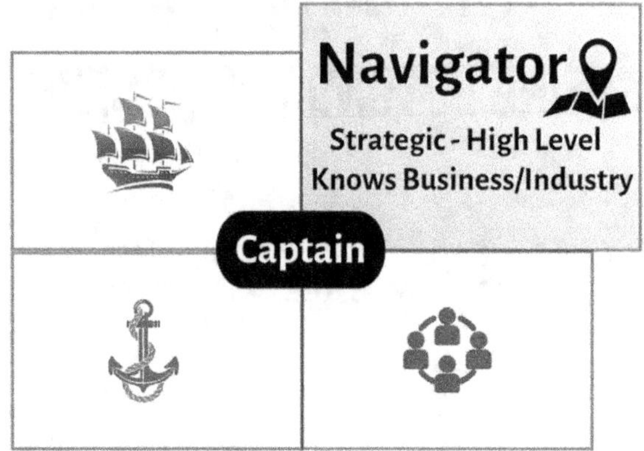

The Courage to Be Guided

Here's the thing about Navigators: Everyone thinks they want one until they get one.

They say they want guidance. What they actually want is validation.
They ask for direction but bristle at being directed.
They seek wisdom but reject the parts that don't confirm what they already believe.

Sound familiar?

The most dangerous words in business aren't "we're going bankrupt" or "our competitors are beating us." The most dangerous words are far simpler:

"I already know that."

Those four words have sunk more businesses than recessions, competitors, and market shifts combined. They're the verbal equivalent of locking your ship's wheel in place and throwing away the key.

Is that what you're doing?

The Navigator's Challenge

Here's the brutal truth about navigation: The most successful entrepreneurs aren't the ones with the best ideas.

Or the most charisma

Or the biggest risk appetite.

They're the ones who know what they don't know.

And the courage to act accordingly.

Everyone else? They're just confidently sailing toward disaster.

What you don't know will sink you faster than what you do know will save you. This isn't pessimism; it's mathematical certainty. The universe of what any of us doesn't know will always vastly exceed what we do know.

Yet most business leaders operate as if the opposite were true.

Why?

Because admitting we don't know feels like weakness. It feels like vulnerability. It feels like we're undermining our authority.

But here's the paradox:

The most powerful phrase in leadership isn't "I know." It's "I don't know, but I'll find out."

This is where your Navigator becomes essential.

Not optional. Not a nice-to-have. Essential.

Your Navigator isn't there to make you feel good about your decisions. They're there to make your decisions good. Sometimes that means challenging beliefs you hold dear. Sometimes that means questioning strategies you've bet your company on.

And yes, sometimes that means telling you you're wrong.

The Navigator brings something irreplaceable: experience you haven't had to pay for yet.

They've seen the patterns. They've witnessed the failures. They've observed the recoveries.

Their wisdom isn't theoretical. It's scarred, battle-tested, and proven.

Industry expertise matters more than general business knowledge because context is everything. A Navigator who knows your specific terrain - its hidden currents, its seasonal patterns, its unique dangers - brings value that no general business advisor can match.

Has your ego been getting in the way of your success?

Are you confusing motion with progress?

Could you be confidently sailing in the wrong direction?

These are questions only a Navigator can help you answer honestly.

The Navigator is the voice you need, not just the one you want.

Here's the thing: Truth-tellers are rare.

Most people in your life have incentives to tell you what you want to hear:

Employees fear for their jobs.
Friends fear for your feelings.
Family fears for your stress levels.
Vendors fear for your business.

Your Navigator fears only one thing: that you'll fail because they didn't speak up.

This creates a relationship fundamentally different from mentorship. Mentors nurture. Navigators challenge. Mentors comfort. Navigators confront.

Both have their place, but don't confuse them.

The best time to seek guidance isn't when you're already in trouble. It's when things seem to be going well. When you're confident. When you're comfortable.

That's precisely when you're most vulnerable.

Success creates a dangerous illusion of invulnerability. It tricks you into believing that what worked yesterday will work tomorrow. It convinces you that good outcomes mean good decisions, when often they simply mean good luck.

Your Navigator cuts through this illusion.

They ask the questions you're not asking yourself:

What could go wrong?
What are you missing?
What assumptions are you making?
What would happen if . . .?

The professional relationship with your Navigator transcends personal results because it's not about friendship – it's about improvement. It creates a space where truth isn't personal. Where feedback isn't an attack but a gift.

When was the last time someone told you something about your business you didn't want to hear but needed to?

If you can't remember, you don't have a Navigator.

Navigation as Discipline

Business leaders make dozens of significant decisions daily in conditions of incomplete information.

It's like setting a course in fog.

You never have perfect clarity. You never see the entire picture. You never have all the data you want.

But you must decide anyway.

This is where navigation becomes discipline - a systematic approach to uncertainty.

Strategic frameworks aren't constraints on creativity; they're enablers of it. They create boundaries within which innovation can thrive. They establish decision-making protocols that prevent tactical chaos.

The most successful entrepreneurs don't make better individual decisions. They establish better decision-making systems.

Your Navigator helps you build these systems.

They teach you which instruments to trust when visibility is low. They show you how to establish reliable reference points. They train you to distinguish between signal and noise in your industry.

Most importantly, they help you develop the discipline to trust these systems even when your instincts scream otherwise.

Because here's the uncomfortable truth:

Your instincts were formed in past conditions.
They were shaped by previous experiences.
They were calibrated for yesterday's challenges.

But you're navigating today's waters toward tomorrow's opportunities.

Do you have the discipline to trust your instruments when they contradict your gut?

That's the test of true leadership.

> ## CAPTAIN TO CAPTAIN:
>
> There will be a moment when your Navigator's guidance contradicts your deepest instincts. That moment will define your leadership more than any other decision you make.

Borrowed Wisdom

US President Woodrow Wilson said something that changed everything for me: *"I use all the brains I have, and all the brains I can borrow."*

Here's the thing about wisdom:
You can get it two ways.
Experience everything yourself.
Learn from others' experiences.

The first approach is heroic, admirable, and profoundly stupid.
It's also how many leaders operate.
They confuse scars with trophies.
They mistake struggle with accomplishment.
They wear their exhaustion like proof of commitment.

And then they wonder why they keep running into the same freakin' rocks.

My early leadership experiences were "rocky" to say the least. I thought I was pretty smart. Turns out I was just stubborn. I ignored advice and counsel. I thought I knew better and made a bunch of mistakes myself.
That's the way kids learn, not Captains.

You don't have enough time for that nonsense.
You don't have enough resources.
You don't have enough lives to make all the mistakes yourself.
I didn't either.

Your Navigator brings borrowed wisdom - lessons extracted from experiences you haven't had to suffer through.

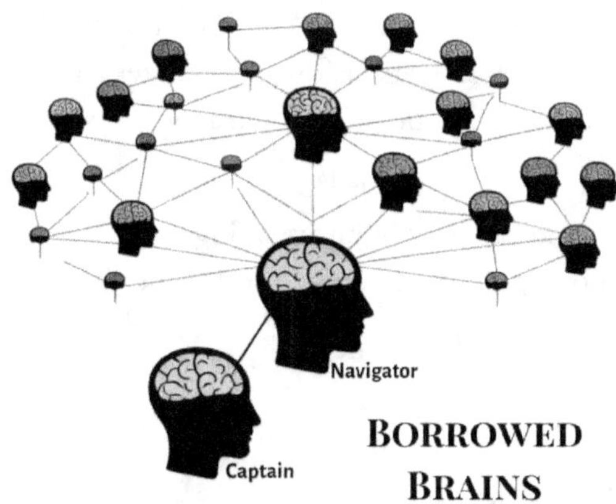

This isn't about avoiding all mistakes. Mistakes are inevitable, and the right mistakes can often be valuable. It's about avoiding the preventable ones. The dumb ones. The mistakes that cause major damage and trauma.

Most entrepreneurs don't lack goals.
They lack milestones that drive behavior.
There's a difference.

Goals tell you where you want to go. Milestones tell you whether you're actually going there. They're not just markers of progress; they're creators of progress.

The right milestones don't just measure activity; they generate it.

Your Navigator helps you create milestones that matter - ones that drive daily decisions rather than just quarterly reviews.

Most entrepreneurs also misunderstand accountability.
They see it as a constraint when it's actually freedom.

Proper accountability systems don't restrict; they liberate. They take the pressure of remembering, tracking, and checking off your shoulders so you can focus on moving forward.

And your Navigator helps you get the opportunity/risk equation right.

Most leaders evaluate opportunities based on potential gain and risks based on potential loss. The correct approach? Evaluate both based on their impact on your strategic direction.

It's not about the size of the gain or loss. It's about the direction.

Your Navigator recognizes patterns you can't see because they've seen them before in different contexts. They sense threats before they materialize - particularly valuable because most dangers appear as opportunities, as innovations, as can't-miss chances.

Is your wisdom self-generated or borrowed?
Are your milestones driving behavior or just marking time?
Are you evaluating opportunities based on size or direction?

Your Navigator helps you see the difference.
Then act on it.

The Captain's Blindspot

I've guided countless entrepreneurs through treacherous waters over the years.

The ones who thrive? They share one trait.

They understand a profound truth: being the Captain doesn't mean you see everything.

The best Captains know they have blind spots. The worst pretend they don't.

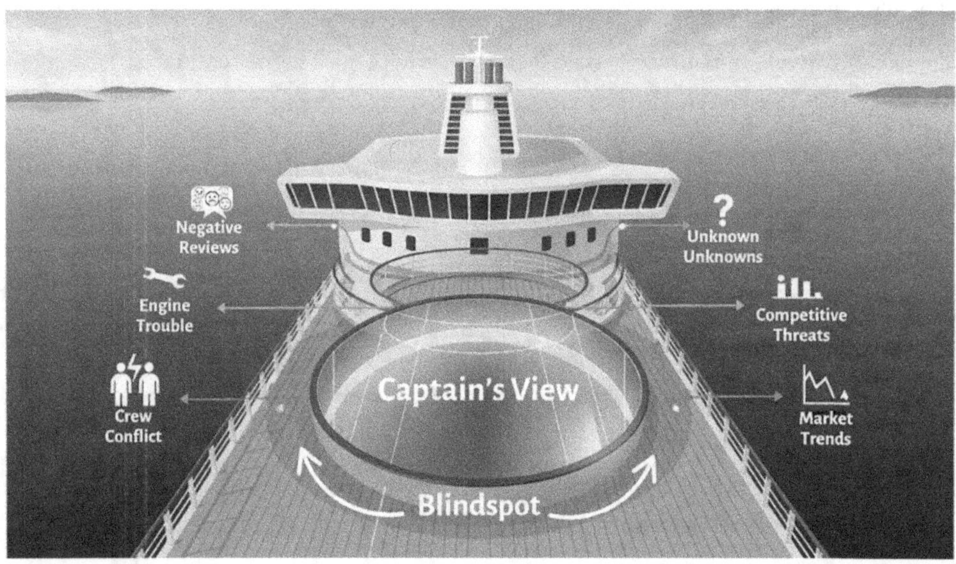

Here's what I've learned from decades of navigating businesses through storms and calm seas alike:

The most dangerous decisions aren't the ones you know are risky.

They're the ones you don't know are risky.

The hidden reefs.
The underwater currents.
The storms that are building, just over the horizon, that your instruments haven't picked up yet.

I remember working with a manufacturing CEO who was absolutely certain his team was aligned on their growth strategy. "Everyone's on board," he assured me. "We've discussed it to death."

During my first week as his Navigator, I interviewed his leadership team one by one.

Seven people.
Seven different directions.
Zero alignment.

The CEO was stunned. "But we all agreed in our meetings!"

They'd agreed to words, not meaning.
They'd nodded at concepts, not commitments.

His blind spot wasn't that he had disagreement in his ranks. It was that he couldn't see the disagreement that was already there.

As a Navigator, I don't bring magic answers. I bring perspective you can't have from where you stand.

I see the business map from a different angle.
I notice the reefs that don't appear on your charts.
I've watched other ships run aground where you're headed.

You're the Captain. The decisions are yours. The ship is yours. The glory of success is yours.

But no Captain navigates alone. Not if they want to reach their destination.

I'm no different. I have several Navigators because I can't see my business from where I stand either. I need their perspective. So do you.

Storm Navigation

Every business faces storms.
Not every business survives them.

The difference often isn't resources or luck.
It's navigation.

When everything is going wrong, most leaders make the same mistake: they speed up. They make more decisions faster. They react to symptoms rather than causes. They confuse activity with progress.

Your Navigator teaches you the counterintuitive power of slowing down during a crisis.

Not paralysis. Not indecision. But deliberate, focused action based on clear priorities rather than a frantic response based on immediate pressures.

They help you implement rapid course correction without losing direction. Because there's a difference between adjusting to conditions and abandoning your destination.

And they ensure you don't skip the step most leaders miss: recovery planning.

Recovery isn't just getting back to where you were. It's integrating what you've learned. It's strengthening what was exposed as weak. It's preparing for the next storm while the memory of this one is still fresh.

Your Navigator has weathered storms you haven't seen yet. They've witnessed the difference between businesses that merely survive crises and those that emerge stronger from them.

The key difference?
Survivors react.
Overcomers respond.
Captains, own their response.

Reaction is emotional. Response is strategic.
Reaction focuses on symptoms. Response addresses causes.
Reaction aims at relief. Response targets resilience.

Does a crisis make you speed up or slow down?

Do you correct course based on actual conditions or change the destination based on fear?

Do you have a recovery plan or just a survival instinct?

Your Navigator helps you navigate storms by keeping your eye on what matters when everything is screaming for attention.

STORM NAVIGATION
Instruments vs Instincts
Navigating business decisions with data and intuition

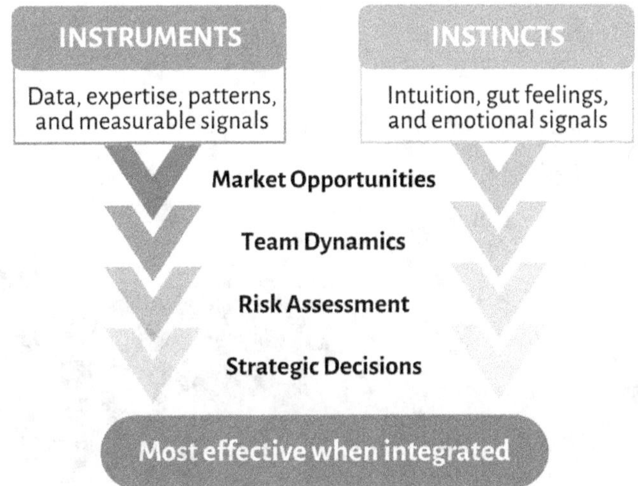

The Uncomfortable Truth: Feelings vs. Instruments

The most dangerous phrase in aviation isn't "I don't know how to fly this thing."

It's "That doesn't feel right."

When pilots fly into clouds or darkness, their sense of direction becomes instantly unreliable. Up feels like down. Turning feels like going straight. Straight feels like turning left. It's incredibly bizarre. The brain, missing visual references, creates phantom sensations that feel absolutely real - and are absolutely wrong.

This phenomenon kills experienced pilots every year.

The cure? Learning to trust instruments over instincts.

This was one of the hardest things for me to adjust to when I was learning to fly. My senses were telling me *"We're descending and turning left,"* overloading my brain, screaming, *"If you don't ascend and turn right, you're going to die".*

True? Nope.

The instruments said we were straight and level.

In the air, feelings can be deadly.

The parallel to business is perfect.

How often have you said:
"I have a gut feeling about this candidate."
"This deal doesn't feel right."
"I sense an opportunity here."

Feelings have their place. But when the stakes are high and visibility is low, instruments trump instincts every time.

Your Navigator is your instrument panel.

I've seen founders make million-dollar decisions based on how they felt in a meeting. I've watched CEOs ignore market data because it didn't match their instincts. I've observed owners reject profitable strategies because they didn't "feel right."

I've also seen what happens next.

The right Navigator doesn't dismiss your feelings. Like my awesome flight instructor Frank, they help you calibrate those feelings against objective reality. With the right guidance, you learn what's real. *They teach you when to trust your gut and when to override it.*

Because sometimes your instincts are right.

And sometimes, they're just phantom sensations in the dark.

The difference between success and failure often comes down to knowing which is which.

CAPTAIN TO CAPTAIN:

The test of a Navigator relationship isn't when they confirm what you already believe - it's when their hard-won widsom clashes with your gut feelings. How you respond in that collision will shape every decision that follows.

The Navigator Relationship

The hardest thing about working with a Navigator? Learning to receive feedback without defensiveness.

It's nearly impossible because our brains are wired to protect our self-image. To justify our decisions. To defend our actions.

But defensive listening is the enemy of growth.

When you're defending, you're not learning.
When you're justifying, you're not changing.
When you're explaining, you're not improving.

Your Navigator relationship works when you master the art of open listening - hearing feedback not as judgment of past actions but as guidance for future ones.

This doesn't mean blind acceptance. It means thoughtful consideration.

The goal isn't Navigator dependency. It's Navigator-enabled independence. This happens when you don't just follow advice but understand the thinking behind it. When you don't just implement suggestions, but internalize principles.

Your Navigator succeeds when you need them less, not more.

This requires a delicate balance between confidence and humility. Confidence in your ability to lead. Humility about your limitations. Confidence to make decisions. Humility to reconsider them.

And it requires embracing deliberate discomfort.

Truth: When your Navigator first challenges you, you'll hate it.
Your body will tense.
Your mind will race to defend.

Your ego will scream for justification.

This is normal.
This is human.
This is also the moment where growth happens.
Or doesn't.

Growth happens at the edge of your comfort zone. Not in the center, where everything feels familiar and safe. Your Navigator pushes you to that edge - not to stress you, but to stretch you.

Are you listening to defend or to learn?

Are you becoming more dependent on guidance or more equipped by it?

Are you seeking comfort or growth?

These questions define whether your Navigator relationship is transformational or just transactional.

What I've Learned From The Captain's Chair

Let me tell you something most business advisors won't admit:

I've made every mistake I warn my clients about.

Every single one.

I've ignored instruments when my gut felt otherwise. I've mistaken motion for progress. Pretended activity equaled outcomes.

When the data said the business model wouldn't work, I changed the assumptions or the data until it did. Guess what? That playbook bombed.

I've confused good luck with good strategy. I've been blindsided. I've sailed straight into storms I saw clearly and knew I should have avoided.

The difference? I've made them all before. You don't have to.

That's why I don't teach theory. I teach experience.

I don't offer perfect answers. I share battle-tested wisdom.

When you work with me as your Navigator, you're not getting abstract principles. You're getting scars translated into strategies. You're getting failures transformed into frameworks.

The $15 Million Lesson

Here's a key truth I paid dearly to learn:

The most expensive decisions are the ones that seem obvious.

A few years back, one of my companies had the opportunity to expand internationally. The market was ripe. The demand was clear. The numbers looked incredible. The decision seemed like common sense. I checked with a couple of advisors who agreed.

So I did it.

I poured $15 million into that expansion. That's not a typo.

Fifteen million dollars down a beautiful, well-designed gold-plated drain.
And smiled confidently while I did it.

Why? Because while I understood the mechanics of international expansion, I completely missed the regulatory landmines specific to our industry. I underestimated the need for local market knowledge. Landmines that were well-known to anyone who'd navigated those waters before.

I had "experts" who were familiar with international business. In reality, I needed a Navigator who deeply understood the nuances of international business in MY industry. Sometimes the clearest waters hide the deadliest reefs.

That $15 million blunder taught me three things:

1. Context-specific experience is worth more than general expertise
2. The most dangerous risks aren't the ones you're evaluating – they're the ones you don't know exist
3. Industry pattern recognition isn't a luxury – it's survival

I don't share this to impress you with the size of my blunder. I share it because it fundamentally changed how I approach business navigation. *What's obvious in hindsight is often invisible in the moment.*

And it's why my clients don't make the same mistake.

The Voice That Changed Everything

When my business hit $20 million in revenue, we were growing 40% year over year. Everyone thought we were crushing it. I was featured in magazines. Speaking at conferences. Living the entrepreneurial dream.

Except for one thing:

We were 90 days from sinking.

Growth was destroying our cash flow, but nobody saw it. Nobody except my Navigator, Ben. The dude has night vision built into one eye and a thermal scope for the other. I swear he can see around corners. Bonafide freakin' genius.

During our monthly review, while everyone else was celebrating our growth metrics, Ben asked one question:

"What's your cash conversion cycle?"

"My what?" I didn't have a good answer. It's kinda embarrassing, but I had to Google the term.

That night, he sent me a simple spreadsheet model. It showed that our current growth trajectory - the one everyone was celebrating - would send the company off a cash flow cliff in about 90 days.

That ain't good.

We made four small, but very specific, changes to our operations based on his model.

Three months later, we weren't doing the 'Thelma & Louise'. We were more profitable, and our cash flow position was solid. We weren't going to grow ourselves to death.

No bank would have caught this. No general advisor would have seen it. No growth consultant would have even looked for it.

It took someone who had navigated that exact challenge in our specific industry to spot the pattern before it became a catastrophe.

That's the difference between advice and navigation.

The Counterintuitive Move

One of my high-tech manufacturing clients was struggling with fierce competition and eroding margins. Every consultant told him the same thing:

Cut costs. Automate more. Reduce headcount. You know, the obvious stuff.

Standard playbook. Logical advice. I told him to raise prices by 30%.

He thought I was insane.

But I'd seen this exact pattern play out in three similar businesses. I knew something the consultants didn't:

In his specific market segment, price was being used as a proxy for quality. His low prices were actually scaring away his ideal customers.

He reluctantly tested my approach with one product line. Sales increased 40%. Margins doubled. Within six months, he'd implemented the strategy across his entire catalog.

That's not general business wisdom. That's not something you learn in business school.

That's pattern recognition from having seen the same specific challenge in the same specific context multiple times before. It was understanding buyer psychology in that particular market.

Could another Navigator have given that advice? Maybe. But not one who hadn't navigated that exact terrain before.

The Best Navigators Have Been Captains

Every great Captain needs a Navigator. But the best Navigators have been Captains themselves.

They know what you're feeling because they've felt it. They understand your challenges because they've faced them. They respect your decisions because they've made them.

This is the difference between advice and wisdom.

Between theory and truth.

Between what works in books and what works in the storm.

I've built and sold multiple 8-figure businesses. I've raised venture capital and bootstrapped. I've hired hundreds and fired dozens. I've expanded internationally and contracted strategically.

Not because I'm special. Because I've been at this a long time.

And every scar, every victory, every lesson becomes part of what I bring to your bridge.

Not to take the wheel from you. But to help you see what's beyond the horizon.

The Acceleration Effect

Here's the thing about entrepreneurial progress:

It's not linear. It's not even exponential. It's compounded by relationships.

I don't just believe in having a Navigator. I've lived the difference.

My business quadrupled with the right experts in my corner. Not doubled. Quadrupled. When I could learn from their mistakes instead of making them myself, my progress accelerated 20x with far less stress.

Do you understand what that means?

Twenty times faster progress. Twenty times fewer costly detours. Twenty times the clarity.

That's not incremental improvement. That's a different game entirely.

The math of Navigator relationships is ruthlessly simple:

Every significant mistake costs you three things: time, money, and momentum. The average entrepreneur pays this tax over and over, thinking it's just the price of doing business.

It's not. It's the price of navigating alone.

When I finally got serious about surrounding myself with the right Navigators, I stopped paying the "Dumb Tax," as my friend Keith calls it.

OK, not completely - I still made mistakes (and I still do) - but I made different mistakes. New mistakes. Smarter mistakes. Higher-quality mistakes that actually moved me forward.

My Navigators' experience became my experience. Their wisdom became my wisdom. Their pattern recognition became my shortcut.

And here's what I've learned: The true value of a Navigator isn't just their personal experience – it's their network of experiences. We all stand on the shoulders of giants.

Over the years, I've had the privilege to work with some world-class Navigators! I've spent a few million dollars on them, and in turn made tens of millions, and saved tens of millions more, avoiding the "Dumb Tax."

For the founders I work with, they aren't just getting my mistakes and victories. They're getting the distilled wisdom of every Navigator, mentor, and influence I've ever had. They're getting the collective intelligence of hundreds of business journeys, refined and translated into frameworks that actually work.

It's borrowed brains at scale.

It's decades of trial and error compressed into actionable strategies.

It's the difference between reading about storms and having someone who's survived them sitting next to you when yours hits.

That's why I'm not just suggesting you find a Navigator.

I'm telling you *it's the single most valuable relationship decision you'll make as an entrepreneur or leader.*

Because the alternative isn't just slower growth.
It's unnecessary pain.
Avoidable setbacks.
Preventable failures.

And life's too short for that.
Your business is too important for those.
Your impact is too valuable for those.

The Navigator's ROI: Measurable Value on Borrowed Wisdom

Here's the thing about expensive lessons:

You only have to pay for them once.

Unless you insist on paying for them yourself.

It's weird, but most entrepreneurs do.

They pay the full retail price for every mistake, every setback, every missed opportunity - in cash, time, momentum, and emotional capital.

Then they wear these payments like Olympic medals.

"I learned the hard way."
"I had to figure it out myself."

"School of hard knocks."

Congratulations. You've just paid the highest tuition in the school of business.

And for what?

The privilege of making the same mistakes that thousands of entrepreneurs before you have already made?

The right to rediscover fire?

The Navigation Premium

When I ask business owners about their biggest mistakes, they don't struggle to answer.

"Hired the wrong people."
"Scaled too quickly."
"Trusted the wrong partner."
"Ignored the market signals."

Then I ask a follow-up question: "How much did that mistake cost you?"

The numbers are staggering.

$400,000 on a failed product launch.
18 months of stalled growth.
$1.2 million on the wrong technology platform.
Three years rebuilding a damaged culture.

Those were just a few stories from new clients onboarded last year and the pain that prompted a conversation.

Now for the question that matters: "Would you have paid 5% of that cost to avoid it entirely?"

Of course they would. Anyone would.

That's the Navigator Premium. The price you pay for borrowed wisdom. The investment that delivers returns measured in:

- Mistakes avoided
- Years saved
- Growth accelerated
- Pain prevented

The ROI isn't theoretical. It's mathematical.

One manufacturing client saved $1.4 million in the first six months with a simple inventory layout change that their Navigator suggested.

A tech founder avoided a disastrous acquisition that would have saddled him with $3 million in hidden technical debt.

A service business owner restructured her offering based on her Navigator's advice, doubling her margins without losing a single client.

Over the years, my Navigators have delivered massive returns from avoiding bad acquisition deals, skillfully navigating international expansion, passing on disastrous hires, and adding some of the best team members (true Crew) that I have ever worked with.

These weren't magic insights. They were pattern recognition - the kind that only comes from having seen the same movie play out dozens of times before.

The Captain's Compass: Four Questions That Cut Through The Fog

Here's the thing about navigation:

The quality of your decisions depends entirely on the quality of your questions.

Most business leaders ask themselves the wrong questions: "Can we afford this?" "Will this increase revenue?" "Is this what our competitors are doing?"

Surface questions get surface answers.

Your Navigator brings deeper questions - the kind that reveal what's beneath the waterline.

I've distilled decades of navigation experience into four questions that will improve any major business decision. I call it the Captain's Compass:

1. **The Direction Question**: "Does this move us toward our true north, or just toward a shiny object on the horizon?"
2. **The Pattern Question**: "Have I seen this situation before, and if so, what pattern am I missing?"
3. **The Risk/Reward Calculation**: "If this fails completely, can we survive? If this succeeds completely, will it matter?"
4. **The Honest Assessment**: "Am I making this decision based on data, or based on what I hope the data says?"

THE CAPTAIN'S COMPASS
Four Questions That Cut Through The Fog

Direction Question
Does this move us toward our true north, or
just toward a shiny object on the horizon?

Honest Assessment
Am I basing this decision
on data, or on what I
hope the data says?

Pattern Question
Have I seen this situation
before, and if so, what
pattern am I missing?

Risk/Reward Calculation
If this goes south, can we survive?
If this succeeds completely, will it matter?

These aren't just questions. They're navigation instruments. They're course correctors. They're truth detectors.

Most importantly, they're decisions in disguise.

Because *the right question doesn't just lead to the right answer, it makes the answer obvious.*

Try this: Before your next major decision, write these four questions at the top of a blank page. Answer them honestly. Then see if your decision has already made itself.

That's navigation at work.

The Cost of Navigation Avoidance

The opposite of the Navigator Premium is the Solo Tax. I like to think of it as a subcategory of "The Dumb Tax" I mentioned earlier.

It's what you pay when you navigate alone.

And unlike most taxes, this one is entirely optional.

The Solo Tax manifests in three specific ways:

1. **The Opportunity Cost**
   When you're solving problems others have already solved, you're not creating new value. You're stuck in remedial business class while your competitors are inventing the future.

2. **The Time Delay**

   Business growth isn't linear. It compounds. A six-month delay doesn't cost you six months - it costs you everything that would have been built during those six months. A mistake at $5 million in revenue costs exponentially more than the same mistake at $500,000. In an AI-accelerated world, six months is like a decade.

3. **The Energy Drain**

   Every unnecessary setback takes an emotional toll. It doesn't just cost money and time. It costs confidence, momentum, and creative energy. These are your most precious and finite resources.

I worked with a CEO who was considering a Navigator relationship for two years before pulling the trigger. When I asked why she finally decided to move forward, her answer was simple:

"I calculated what the last two years of mistakes had cost me. It was over four million dollars and countless sleepless nights. Your Navigator fee was less than 3% of that. The math became obvious."

The Third-Party Effect

There's another Navigator advantage that's harder to quantify but just as valuable:

Authority leverage.

Here's how it works:

You know exactly what your business needs to do. You've been saying it for months. Maybe years. But your team isn't moving with the urgency you need.

Then your Navigator says essentially the same thing.

Suddenly, everyone's on board.

It's not fair. It's not logical. But it's real.

One CFO told me, "We paid you to tell us what we already knew, but in a way that made us actually do it."

That's not actually what happened. What I did was validate the direction, remove doubt, and create the psychological safety for action through external expertise.

But the result was the same: momentum where there had been stagnation.

The Compounding Advantage

The financial ROI of a Navigator relationship happens instantly - the moment they help you avoid one significant mistake or seize one hidden opportunity.

But the true value compounds over time in ways that don't show up on a balance sheet:

- Decision confidence increases
- Strategic clarity improves
- Execution speed accelerates
- Team alignment strengthens
- Leadership capacity expands

These aren't soft benefits. They're fundamental business advantages that create tangible results.

I've watched founders transform from reactive to proactive, from tactical to strategic, from working in their business to working on it.

The catalyst wasn't just information. It was the Navigator relationship itself - the regular cadence of accountability, the trusted space for vulnerability, the consistent exposure to higher-level thinking.

The Simple Math

Still wondering about the Navigator ROI?

Try this exercise:

1. Write down your three biggest business mistakes from the past two years
2. Calculate their total cost in dollars, time, and opportunity
3. Estimate how many of them could have been prevented with the right guidance
4. Multiply that by your growth ambitions for the next two years

That's your potential Navigator ROI.

Now ask yourself a simple question:

Can you afford to keep paying the Solo Tax? Or as I call my mistakes, "The Dumb Tax."

Or is it time to invest in the Navigator Premium?

Your ship. Your call, Captain.

But the waters ahead aren't getting any calmer.

Remember that empty yacht? That could be your business.

Perfect systems.
Pristine operations.
No Captain in sight.

Or it could be something else entirely.

A vessel with purpose.
A journey with direction.
A Captain with vision.
And a Navigator who sees what you can't.

The water doesn't care which you choose. But you should.

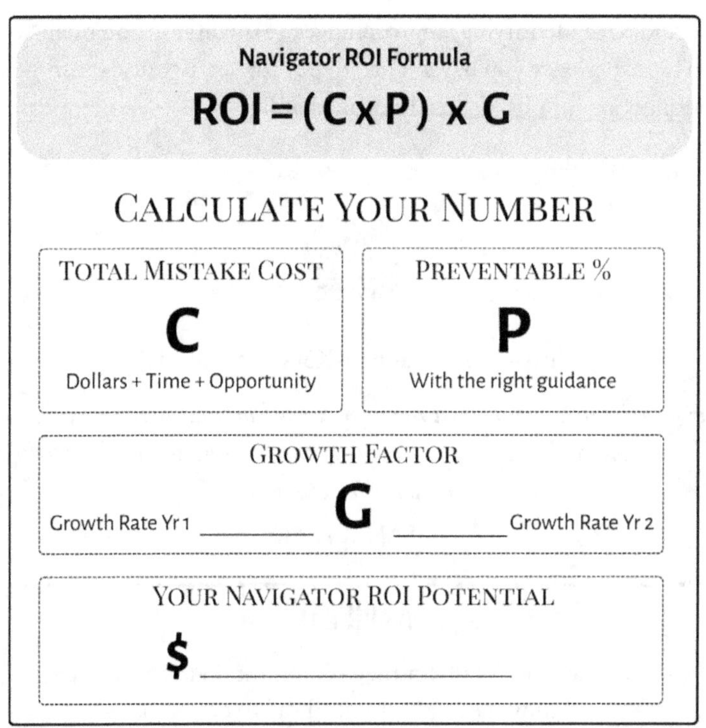

CAPTAIN'S COMPASS

REFLECT: When was the last time someone told you something about your business you didn't want to hear but needed to?
If you can't remember, your ship might be off course.

ACT: This week, find one person with deep expertise who will tell you what you don't want to hear.
Then listen. Just listen.
Don't defend.
Don't explain.
Just listen.

Whose scars are saving you from your own?

Finding someone who has already sailed your waters can help you avoid the rocks that have sunk others. Borrowed wisdom is the cheapest education you'll ever get.

I've created guides for identifying, approaching, and qualifying potential Navigators—people with the experience you haven't had to pay for yet. Because the most dangerous words in business are simply: "I already know that."

It's free, my gift to you.

https://TheCaptainsKeys.com/bonus

"My Navigator relationship saved me from a million-dollar mistake I was about to make. These resources helped me find exactly the right person with exactly the right experience. Thank you!"
—SAM R., CEO

⚓ NAVIGATE

To Sail the Story / Full Journey - Continue on to the next page
Study the Maps - Jump ahead to page 291

CAPTAIN'S LOG

Chart your course forward

| Reflections

| Action Items

NORTHERN STAR

BEYOND THE STORM
Part 7

Dawn hadn't yet broken when Jimmy pulled up to the address Si had scrawled on a bar napkin. The cabin sat isolated at the edge of a small clearing, half-hidden by wind-stunted pines that leaned away from the prevailing gales.

No smoke rose from the chimney. No path had been cleared through the fresh snow that had fallen overnight. The place had the abandoned look of a site long forsaken - except for a single set of boot prints leading from the covered porch to a weathered shed and back.

Someone was home. Someone who wanted to be left alone.

Jimmy's knuckles rapped against the door, the sound sharp in the brittle morning air. When no response came, he knocked again, harder.

The door eased open just enough to reveal a single blue eye, startling in its intensity, set in a face mostly hidden by shadow.

"Whatever you're selling, not interested." The voice was gravel wrapped in velvet - educated but hard-edged, with vowels that still carried the faintest hint of Wisconsin flatlands.

"Not selling anything." Jimmy pulled his collar higher against the biting wind. "Captain Si Adams sent me. I'm looking for Scott Kaiser."

The eye narrowed, something flashing behind it. "Si needs to mind his own business."

"He said you're the best navigator in Kodiak."

"Was." The door began to close.

Jimmy's boot shot out, wedging into the narrowing gap. It was a risk - both to his foot and to whatever fragile opportunity existed here.

"My uncle was Rocky Meyer."

The pressure against his boot eased. The door stilled, then reluctantly widened.

Scott Kaiser emerged from shadow into the gray morning light - a tall man with the rangy build of someone who'd once been powerful before life had hollowed him out. Hair once dark had silvered at the temples and swept back from a broad forehead. Eyes the color of deep water regarded Jimmy with calculation that bordered on suspicion.

"Rocky Meyer's nephew?" He studied Jimmy's face, looking for traces of resemblance. "You don't look much like him."

"So I've been told."

"What's your angle?" Direct, no preamble. "Rocky's been gone seven months. If you're here about money, he and I were square."

"No angle. No money." Jimmy forced himself to meet that penetrating gaze without flinching. "I inherited his boat. The *Bering Steel*. I'm hoping to inherit his navigator too."

Something shifted in Scott's expression - not softening, exactly, but a fractional change in the tectonic plates of his reserve.

"Come in," he said finally. "Before you freeze your key limes off."

The cabin's interior was a study in austere functionality. A single room with a curtained-off sleeping area. A woodstove radiated welcome heat. Every surface gleamed with military precision, nothing out of place.

One wall stood apart - covered in navigational charts, their edges curling with age and use. Faded pencil notations crowded the margins, a cryptic language understood only by their author. A half-assembled sextant lay on a coffee table beside a mug of coffee gone cold.

Scott didn't offer a fresh cup.

"Sit," he indicated a worn armchair. He remained standing, arms crossed, a man accustomed to interrogation rather than conversation.

"Why are you here?"

Jimmy considered the canned pitch he'd mentally rehearsed on the drive over. Something about opportunity and fresh starts. One look at Scott's face told him it would be received about as well as a marketing call during dinner.

"I nearly sank that boat my first time out," he said instead. "Almost became part of the scenery on that breakwater reef beyond the harbor."

Scott said nothing, but his stance shifted imperceptibly.

"I've been on the water my entire adult life," Jimmy continued. "Eighteen years running charters in the Florida Keys. Thought that meant I knew what I was doing."

A ghost of a smile touched Scott's mouth. "The Bering Sea has a way of correcting that assumption."

"I assembled a crew. Good men. They're counting on me." Jimmy leaned forward, elbows on knees. "But I'm still missing someone who really knows these waters."

"There are plenty of experienced hands in Kodiak."

"Not according to Si."

"Si exaggerates."

"Si told me what happened to your boat." Jimmy watched the words land like body blows. "To your crew."

Scott's jaw tightened, a muscle flickering beneath the skin. "Then you know why I don't go out anymore."

"I know why you think you shouldn't," Jimmy countered. "But running from the sea won't bring them back. Neither will letting their deaths be the end of your story."

"You don't know what you're talking about."

"Don't I?" Jimmy's voice hardened. "I lost everything in a hurricane. My charter business. My home. Nearly lost my dog. Had to decide if I was going to let that be my ending too."

He gestured around at the isolated cabin. "This? What you're doing? It's a slow death. Trust me, I tried it back in Florida. All it brings is more regret."

Scott turned away, moving to the window where dawn was beginning to lighten the eastern sky. His fingers traced unconscious patterns on the glass - plotting invisible courses only he could see.

"Rocky used to say the sea gives us second chances," he said finally, his voice distant. "But only if we're brave enough to take them."

Jimmy waited, sensing the conflict raging behind Scott's calm exterior.

"You said Si recommended me?" Scott asked, still facing the window.

"Said you're the best."

"Was the best." The navigator's calloused fingers drifted to a photograph on the mantel - a younger version of himself with his arm around a teenage boy whose smile mirrored his own. "But maybe . . . maybe it's time to find out if that's still true."

He crossed to a bookshelf, pulling down a thick leather-bound volume. The weight of it in his hands seemed to center him, like a man reconnecting with a part of himself long abandoned.

"Before we discuss terms, you need to understand how I work." He placed the book on the coffee table between them. "This isn't about just pointing the boat in the right direction."

The book fell open to reveal pages filled with meticulously documented data - ocean patterns, current flows, weather systems. A lifetime of knowledge preserved in precise handwriting.

"The Bering Sea isn't just water," Scott continued, his voice taking on a teacher's cadence. "It's a living thing. Most captains treat it like an enemy to be conquered. That's how people die."

His eyes, sharp with intelligence that couldn't be learned from books, found Jimmy's. "Your uncle understood that. Question is - do you?"

Jimmy thought about the rocks he'd nearly hit his first time out. About the wreck that still sat on them as a warning to the unwary.

"I'm ready to learn."

Scott nodded slowly, something resolving in his expression. "One condition. A special request."

"Name it."

"When the season's over . . . " Scott paused, choosing his words carefully. "I want you to take me deep-sea fishing in the Keys. You know tarpon, marlin, sailfish, and big 'uns like that. Never been. Always wanted to go with . . . " His eyes flickered to the photo on the mantel. "Well, I just always wanted to try it."

Understanding clicked into place. Like the last tumbler in a lock falling.

"I love that. Deal." Jimmy extended his hand.

Scott took it, his grip firm and certain.

"And if it isn't too much trouble, one of those tropical drinks with an umbrella in it."

"Well, now it's a party. You got it."

CHAPTER 31

Bering Steel

Bering Sea, Cod fishing grounds

110 miles northwest of Kodiak

Scott hunched over the chart table, the amber glow of the navigation lamp casting deep shadows across his weathered face. His fingers traced invisible patterns across the paper - routes only he could see, currents only he could feel. Less than two weeks until crab season opened, and everything depended on this.

Jimmy watched, mesmerized by the navigator's confidence. Around them, the crew worked the final cod run with machine-like precision, but Jimmy's focus was entirely on the man who held their future in his calloused hands. Outside, the Bering Sea stretched black and endless, stars reflecting off its surface like scattered diamonds.

"There." Scott tapped a seemingly empty spot on the chart. "That's where we'll find them."

"There's nothing there," Jimmy said.

Scott smiled - the small, patient smile of a man used to knowing things others didn't. "Exactly why it's perfect."

He pulled it up the map on the boat's GPS chartplotter. The screen showed the same map digitally overlaid with the contour lines of the seabed.

"Look here. Two underwater canyons intersect at this point. The deep currents collide, forcing nutrients from the bottom up toward the surface."

Jimmy leaned closer. "Creating a feeding zone."

"Creating an opportunity." Scott's voice softened. "Navigation isn't just about avoiding the dangers, Jimmy. It's about seeing patterns others miss. The currents beneath the currents. The weather behind the weather."

Outside, the engine's rhythm changed slightly as they altered course. The Bering Steel responded instantly to the new heading, as if she too trusted Scott's judgment without question.

"How did you learn to read water like this?" Jimmy asked.

Scott was quiet for a moment, his eyes distant.

"My father was colorblind. Couldn't see red at all. But he could smell a storm coming before anyone else. Said his other senses compensated."

He tapped the chart again. "I learned to look deeper. Past what's obvious. Past what everyone else is chasing."

"While all those other captain's out there fight over the known grounds . . ."

"We'll be harvesting what they can't see."

Scott nodded. "You're getting' it, Cap. In business, in fishing - my gosh, in life – everyone's fighting over the same visible resources. The real advantage comes from discovering what's hidden."

The radio crackled with chatter from other boats. Captains sharing locations, competing or collaborating depending on past favors and alliances. A complex dance Jimmy was still learning. Scott muted it.

"Too much noise. Follow the wrong voices, you end up where everyone else is going. Follow your instruments, you end up where you need to be."

Jimmy thought about the weeks since his arrival. How many times had he nearly failed by following conventional wisdom? How often had his instincts been wrong about these unfamiliar waters?

"Back in the Keys, I knew every sandbar, every reef." Jimmy's voice had an edge of frustration. "Here, I'm flying blind."

"No." Scott straightened, fixing Jimmy with a piercing look. "You're just trusting the wrong instruments."

He gestured toward the radio. "That's what most captains use to navigate. Rumors. Gossip. Following the crowd."

He pointed to the radar, the sonar, the charts spread before them. "These tell you what's actually happening. But they're only useful if you know how to interpret them."

Scott crossed to the window, staring out at the moonlit water. "A good Navigator doesn't just tell you where to go. He helps you understand why that's the right direction."

The ship's bell chimed softly with the hour. Two a.m. The rest of the crew was asleep below, trusting the course these two men charted.

"The sea doesn't reward the captain who chases every opportunity," Scott said after a long silence. "She rewards the one who knows which opportunities to chase - and which to let sail by."

Jimmy moved to stand beside him at the window. Beyond the glass, the endless ocean stretched toward tomorrow's fishing grounds. Toward uncertainty. Toward possibility.

"Like a strategic advisor," Jimmy said quietly, understanding dawning.

"Exactly." Scott's reflection nodded in the glass. "Some captains think navigation is just about avoiding rocks and catching red gold. But it's really about seeing the whole board when others only see what's directly in front of them."

He turned back to the charts. "Look here. Weather system moving in from the northwest. Will hit these grounds" - his finger traced a circle – "in about ten hours. Most boats will run for shelter."

"But not us?"

"No. We'll be here." He pointed to another intersection of the underwater canyons. "Protected by this underwater ridge. We'll have the cod fishing grounds all to ourselves for another ten or twelve hours because everyone else will only see the danger, not the opportunity behind it. Set one more string and then find cover."

Trust. That's what this was about. Trust not just in Scott's technical expertise, but in his decades of borrowed brains - the accumulated wisdom of every captain, every navigator, every fisherman who'd shared their knowledge with him. A golden opportunity to transform uncertainty into advantage.

"In the Keys," Jimmy said, "I never needed anyone to help me find my way."

"And now?"

Jimmy thought about the vastness of the Bering Sea. The complexity of these waters. The cost of wrong decisions.

"Now I'm starting to understand why every great captain needs someone who sees what they can't."

Scott smiled - a real one this time, crinkling the corners of his eyes. "There's hope for you yet, Captain Meyer."

Outside, the first hint of dawn touched the eastern horizon. Another day of decisions. Another day of risks and rewards.

But now, Jimmy realized, he wouldn't be navigating alone.

CHAPTER 32

True to his reputation, Scott nailed the forecast perfectly. While other captains abandoned their fishing early to seek shelter, the *Bering Steel* remained well-positioned to complete one final haul and reset their pots before the weather turned nasty.

"Storm's building faster than predicted," Scott announced, studying the radar's green glow. "But we've got a three-hour window. Maybe four if we're smart about it."

Jimmy made the call. "Finish the set, then we run for cover."

The crew worked with practiced efficiency, harvesting the cod from their pots, adding fresh bait and setting them back again before sprinting to safety. By the time they finished, the first whitecaps were already forming.

Scott had plotted their course to Humboldt Harbor near Sand Point—a natural refuge that could shelter them while the storm passed. As they raced toward the harbor entrance, the wind began to howl and the seas built behind them like pursuing wolves.

The *Bering Steel* groaned as waves struck her stern, pushing them toward safety with increasing urgency. What had started as moderate chop was evolving into a full-blown tempest, the storm intensifying exactly as Scott had predicted—but now they were prepared for it.

They slipped into Humboldt Harbor just as the weather reached its full fury. Outside the protected waters, waves crashed against the breakwater with thunderous force. Inside, the *Bering Steel* rode gently at anchor, safe from the storm's rage.

The crew gathered in the warm, dry galley, the contrast between their snug shelter and the chaos outside making their refuge feel doubly secure.

"Seven, maybe eight hours until it passes," Scott said, checking the radar. "Right on schedule."

A particularly violent gust of wind howled across the harbor, but the protective breakwater kept the worst of it at bay. Jimmy felt the tension in his shoulders finally release.

"Might as well get comfortable," Bob said, settling onto the cramped bench. "Not going anywhere for a while."

Aidan had stopped his restless pacing now that they were safe. "Hate waiting, but I'll take this over being out in that mess."

"Smart mariners live to fish another day," Richie said, still warming his hands around a mug of coffee.

The cabin fell into comfortable silence except for the distant sound of wind and waves beyond their protective harbor. Each man lost in his own thoughts, grateful for Scott's accurate forecast and Jimmy's decisive leadership.

"My dad died in a storm like this," Tom said suddenly. His voice was quiet but carried clearly in the small space. "Not here—back home near the village. His boat was smaller, but the storm wasn't much different. I was twelve. They never found him."

The others turned to look at him. Tom rarely spoke of his past.

"That why you became a fisherman?" Bob asked. "To face it down?"

Tom shook his head. "To understand it. To learn its ways. My people believe the sea is a living thing. She takes, yes, but she also gives. The trick is learning her moods, earning her respect."

"Respect," Aidan said thoughtfully. "Hard to respect something that can kill you."

"That's exactly when you need to respect it most," Scott said, turning from the radar. "Lost my whole crew once thinking I was stronger than the sea. Thought I knew better than the weather reports, the signs, everything. Pride makes you stupid out here."

The cabin grew quiet again as Scott's words sank in. Everyone knew his story now, but he never spoke of it directly.

"You know what scares me most?" Richie said, breaking the silence. "Not making it home to Lori and the baby. Having them wait and wait and never know what happened to me. Like your dad, Tom."

Bob nodded. "When I was drinking, I never worried about dying. Now . . ." He pulled out his six-year chip, turning it over in his hands. "Now I've got reasons to live. My daughter, this crew, this chance to make things right. Funny how that makes everything scarier."

"What about you, big man?" Jimmy asked Aidan. "What keeps the adrenaline junkie up at night?"

Aidan considered the question. "Failing. Not the kind where you try something crazy and it doesn't work out. The kind where people are counting on you and you let them down. Like my sister." He swallowed hard. "That's why I always worked alone before. Can't fail anyone if no one's depending on you."

The words hit Jimmy like a punch to the gut. Lightning flashed outside the harbor, illuminating their faces in stark relief, and for a moment he was sure everyone could see right through him. The thunder that followed seemed distant now, muffled by their protective anchorage.

"Captain?" Scott's voice was gentle. "What about you?"

Jimmy looked around at his crew—his family now, really. Men who had trusted him with their lives, their futures. Men who had just laid bare their deepest fears.

"I'm afraid I'm not the captain you all deserve," he said finally. "That I'm just playing at being Uncle Rocky's successor. That one of these days I'm going to make a call that gets someone hurt. Or worse." He ran a hand through his hair. "Back in the Keys, it was simple. Just me and the tourists and Bella. Out here . . . every decision affects all of you. Your families. Your futures. Sometimes I wake up wondering if I'm really cut out for this."

"That's exactly why you are," Tom said firmly. "A foolish captain never questions himself. A wise one always does."

"You think your uncle never had doubts?" Scott added. "He told me once that the day you stop being scared is the day you should quit. Fear keeps you sharp. Keeps you honest."

"Besides," Bob said with a slight smile, "you think any of us aren't scared? That's why we work so well together. We each carry part of the load. No one has to bear it alone."

Richie nodded. "Like getting the boat ready before the storm hit. Any one of us might have hesitated, but together? We just did what needed doing."

"Synergistically stable," Aidan said thoughtfully.

The others stared at him blankly.

"Uh, can you explain that one to us, professor?" Scott said with a grin.

"That's what we are, right? Each of us supporting the others. You know, synergy. Making the whole stronger than its parts."

Another gust of wind howled across the harbor, but the *Bering Steel* barely shifted in the protected waters. Jimmy felt something settle in his chest—not just relief, but a new understanding.

"Alright then," he said, straightening up. "Scott, keep monitoring that system. Bob, once this passes, give the engine room a quick check. Tom, Richie, Aidan—get some rest. We'll need everyone fresh when we head back out."

As his crew moved to their tasks, Jimmy felt a new certainty settle over him. They were right—no captain could carry the weight alone. But together? Together they could weather any storm.

The *Bering Steel* rode out the night in perfect safety, her crew stronger for having shared their burdens, their trust in each other deeper than ever.

When dawn finally broke, the storm had passed completely. They emerged from Humboldt Harbor into seas so calm they looked like green glass. The crew made quick work of hauling in their final cod bounty, stacked their pots on board, and headed for home.

Another successful trip, with a crew now truly ready to face whatever challenges lay ahead.

CHAPTER 33

The call came as Jimmy sprawled on his couch, one hand absently scratching Bella's golden head as she snored gently against his thigh. Afternoon light slanted through the blinds, painting stripes across the worn hardwood floor of his inherited home.

He'd meant to make a proper lunch, but had settled for a sandwich eaten standing over the sink, his mind filled with preparations for their first real crabbing run. The manifest. The supplies. The crew assignments.

Details that never would have mattered when he ran a thirty-foot charter boat now kept him awake at night.

His phone vibrated against the cushion, an unfamiliar number with a Kodiak area code. Jimmy considered letting it go to voicemail. Telemarketers had found him even here, at the edge of the world.

Something made him answer anyway.

"James Meyer?"

The voice was male, precise, with the particular cadence of government bureaucracy.

"Speaking."

"This is Linda Holloway, North Pacific Fishery Management Council."

Jimmy sat up straighter, dislodging Bella. She grumbled and repositioned herself against his leg.

"There's an issue with your vessel's crab fishing permit and quota allocation."

Words that turned his stomach to ice.

"What kind of issue?" His own voice sounded distant to his ears.

"The application submitted under your name has been flagged for review." Paper rustled in the background. "Our records show the *Bering Steel* hasn't actively fished in two seasons. Under current regulations, this makes the vessel ineligible for automatic quota renewal."

Jimmy closed his eyes. Of course. Nothing could be simple. Not here. Not now.

"But my uncle had a quota. He was still receiving one every year."

"Your uncle had grandfather status last year based on his historical contributions to the industry. There were . . . irregularities in his final filings. Questions the council is still investigating."

Holloway's voice softened fractionally, human empathy breaking through the bureaucratic shell.

"Unfortunately, that status doesn't automatically transfer with vessel ownership. You'll need to submit an appeal before the council, which meets next quarter."

Next quarter.

Three months from now.

After the season ended.

The implications crashed through his mind like a rogue wave hitting a vulnerable stern.

Jimmy's mouth went dry. No permit meant no legal right to fish.

No permit meant no quota.

No quota meant no crabs.

No crabs meant no income for the season..

No income meant he couldn't pay his crew, couldn't maintain the boat, couldn't recover the small fortune he'd sunk into this new life.

His entire future - evaporating in a single phone call.

"Let me get this straight," he said, fighting to keep his voice level. "Without this permit, we can't drop a single pot in the water? Even though I own the boat?"

"Commercial crab fishing in the Bering Sea is strictly regulated. The permit system controls who can harvest how much and where. It prevents overfishing and protects the resource."

She lowered her voice. "These permits are more valuable than gold up here. Some captains pay millions for them. They're limited by design - no new ones being issued. You either inherit an active one or lease quota from another boat."

"There has to be another way," Jimmy said, fighting to keep his voice level.

"We're ready to go out. The boat's repaired, crew assembled . . . "

"I understand your position, Mr. Meyer." A pause, then: "But regulations are clear."

Regulations. The word burned like acid.

"I suggest you contact legal counsel familiar with fishery management appeals," Holloway continued. "The process can be expedited in some cases."

Jimmy wrote down the official's contact information, his hand moving mechanically while his mind calculated survival scenarios. How long could he keep the crew together with no income? How much of his savings could he burn through before financial reality forced him back to Florida?

When the call ended, Jimmy stared at the wall, seeing not the faded paint but the disappointed faces of his men when he told them.

Men who had trusted him.

Followed him.

Men who would now pay for his ignorance.

The reality crashed over Jimmy like a rogue wave. He wasn't just fighting for his place in the fleet. He was fighting for his legal right to even compete.

Something cold and slick settled in the pit of his stomach, an old familiar companion from childhood. Failure dressed in his father's clothes. The ghost that whispered in his darkest moments.

You don't belong here. You never did.

Jimmy shook his head hard, banishing the voice. He grabbed his phone and called the only person who might understand the full scope of the disaster.

Si answered on the second ring.

"Hey Jimmy, what's wrong?"

Of course Si would know something was wrong. The man possessed an intuition that bordered on the supernatural.

Jimmy unloaded, trying to explain the situation in clipped sentences, tension building with each word.

Si's line went quiet - not the silence of surprise, but the calculating quiet of a mind assembling options.

"I've got to run some errands for my own vessel," he said finally. "Meet me at your boat in two hours. We'll sort this out."

The confidence in his voice was a life raft in a stormy sea.

Jimmy showered and changed, needing to feel the illusion of control. When he arrived at the marina, the late afternoon sun hung low over the mountains, casting the harbor in copper light.

The *Bering Steel* creaked gently at her moorings, massive and patient. Richie, Aidan, and Old Bob were already aboard, fine-tuning systems and preparing for what they still believed would be an imminent departure.

Jimmy watched them from the dock, guilt burning a hole in his chest. These men had families, expenses, lives that depended on the promises he'd made.

When Si arrived, he brought lunch for the crew - he somehow always knew when people would be hungry.

"Thought you boys might need fuel," he called, handing out wrapped sandwiches with the same care a priest might distribute communion wafers.

While the men ate in the galley, Si drew Jimmy into the wheelhouse, closing the door behind them. The small space smelled of polish and steel, the scent of a vessel prepared for battle with the sea.

"Remember when I told you there were four keys a captain needs?" Si asked, lowering himself into the navigator's chair, his movements betraying the arthritis he never complained about.

Jimmy had been so preoccupied with the quota issue that the question momentarily threw him.

"Um, yes." Jimmy pulled out a folded up piece of paper with a cross on it like Si had drawn each time he revealed a part.

"Look it's right here, the Anchor, the Crew, and the Navigator just like you showed me."

Si watched him expectantly.

"Well, that's only three," Jimmy realized. "I'm guessing number four is about to be revealed?"

Si nodded, pulling out his phone. "Indeed. The fourth is what you need right now." he said with a wink.

"A crab quota?" Jimmy's words had the sharp edge of a man running out of patience. "Is that the fourth one? Because if you're going to pull that out of your keester, you might want to stand up first."

Si didn't rise to the bait. With the same unhurried precision he used to tie his knots, he pulled out his phone and made two calls. Each conversation was a masterclass in efficiency - explaining the situation in measured tones, offering thanks, then ending the call with the crisp finality of someone who'd never learned the art of goodbye.

"What's going on?" Jimmy asked, impatience fraying his tone.

Captain Si's weathered face creased in a smile that had weathered a thousand storms.

"That was number four, Jimmy. You need a Champion."

The word hung in the air between them, simultaneously ancient and immediate.

"A Champion? Sounds like something out of '*Game of Thrones*' - definitely not a nautical term I've ever heard."

"That's because you spent your life in tourist waters where the biggest threat was a sunburned lawyer threatening to sue you over a seasick wife." There was no malice in Si's voice, just matter-of-fact observation.

He leaned back in the chair, settling into storytelling mode, his voice dropping to the particular cadence that made men lean forward to listen.

"It's more nautical than you might think. Go back to the age of exploration. Ponce de León, Columbus, Magellan, all those guys who crossed the Atlantic and carved out new settlements."

Si's eyes took on a faraway look, seeing across centuries with the particular vision of a man who read history not as academic exercise but as practical manual.

"Once they established those colonies and trade routes, they faced constant threats - pirates, privateers, rival nations, raiders looking for easy targets. Kings and monarchs funded those voyages, expecting profits beyond imagination in return."

His gnarled fingers traced an invisible map on the arm of the chair.

"So they equipped their captains with letters of credit, letters of authority, and most importantly, their flags and coats of arms to display on the ship."

Jimmy could almost see it - battered wooden vessels on wine-dark seas, sails billowing with promise and fear.

"Imagine you're a pirate in the 1650s off the coast of Cuba," Si continued. "You spot a fat merchant vessel loaded with goods, ripe for the taking. You turn to pursue - but as you draw closer, you see a golden anchor emblazoned on the hull and a red flag with a gold crown flying above the sails."

The old captain's voice dropped, compelling Jimmy to lean in.

"Suddenly, you're not just looking at a merchant ship. You're looking at a vessel under the personal protection of King Philip V of Spain - a man currently waging war against Austria, France, and England simultaneously." Si's index finger jabbed the air for emphasis. "Attack that ship, and you're not just committing piracy. You're declaring war on Spain itself."

The implication crystallized in Jimmy's mind.

"So my Champion . . . "

"Is already fighting for you." Si glanced at his watch. "Sometimes Champions become the door between you and failure. Other times, they save you from enemies you didn't even know you had. Keep your chin up, we should hear something within the next few hours."

"The people you called - who were they?"

"First was an old sea dog who knew your uncle but doesn't know you from Adam. Wasn't much help." Si's smile widened, creasing the weathered terrain of his face. "Second was a senior member of the North Pacific Fishery Management Council."

Jimmy's brow furrowed.

"And . . . they know me?"

Si nodded.

"Is that a good thing? Is that a . . . how do they know me?"

"In this case, it's a very good thing." Si's eyes gleamed with something like mischief. "You see this person at least weekly, as a matter of fact."

Jimmy mentally scrolled through the regulars at Carl's. None seemed to fit the profile of a fishery management official.

"Another captain?" He shook his head. "Those guys barely tolerate me. Can't be one of the dock workers? The processing plant?"

"Jimmy," Si interrupted, amusement crinkling the corners of his eyes. "You've got to think bigger."

Study the Maps / Full Journey - Continue on to the next page
To Sail the Story - Ride a wave to page 319

BERING STEEL

THE CHAMPION
THE INVISIBLE WIND IN YOUR SAILS

"Help me help you. Help me, help you!"
— JERRY MAGUIRE

I learned what it really means to have a Champion the day someone else told my story.

Not just any someone.
Not just any story.

My biggest competitor told my story to my dream client.
And he told it better than I ever could.

I was sitting in the back row at the biggest tech conference in our industry, exhausted.

The venture capital round I'd been chasing for months had collapsed that morning. My biggest enterprise client had just cut their budget in half. My lead developer was entertaining offers from a FAANG company. Back-to-back SHTF moments were the order of the day. It really sucked.

The numbers weren't adding up. The runway was getting shorter. The weight of it all kept my eyes fixed on my laptop screen rather than the keynote stage.

Then I heard it.

My company name. From the main stage. " . . . architected a security implementation that transformed this entire infrastructure."

Who is this panelist?

As the fog in my brain lifted and my eyes adjusted for distance, I saw it was Martin Chen, CTO of an enterprise whale I'd been pursuing unsuccessfully for over a year.

He was telling three thousand people about our methodology. Our approach. Our results.

But we'd never worked directly with them.

I cornered Martin afterward, confusion and hope wrestling for control of my voice.

"That was . . . unexpected," I managed. "We've never actually worked together."

Martin's smile was knowing. "Not directly. But Alex Coleman showed me everything your team did. Walked me through the entire implementation. Said you solved in three weeks what his previous vendor couldn't crack in six months. It was the perfect case study for today's presentation."

Alex Coleman.

The company that tried to poach my security lead last year.
The same guy whose business I'd helped rescue after a devastating data breach.

I hadn't asked him to speak on my behalf. I hadn't mentioned Martin or his company. I hadn't even talked to Alex in months.

He just did it.

That's what Champions do.

They raise your flag when you're not even in the room.
They stake their reputation on yours when you're not there to defend it.

They tell your story when you've run out of energy to tell it yourself.

Here's the thing about flags.

They don't do much when nobody sees them.

A flag hidden in your pocket might as well not exist. A flag flying in an empty forest signals nothing to no one. A flag at half-mast tells a story of loss, but a flag at full height declares confidence, presence, and pride.

Most entrepreneurs are flying with their flag at half-mast - or worse, they haven't raised it at all.

But Champions - they don't do half-mast. They raise your colors to the top where everyone can see them. They make sure your signal can be spotted from miles away.

And they do it because of who they are, not what they want.

The Courage Factor

Here's the thing about Champions: They require you to be brave first.

What I didn't tell you was that six months earlier, I'd championed Alex to a strategic partner when his company was struggling to break into the healthcare vertical.

Not because I expected anything in return. Simply because his solution was genuinely excellent for that market.

Champions don't calculate ROI on their advocacy.

They just give first.
And somehow, it always comes back multiplied.

Most entrepreneurs claim they want Champions. But they're lying.

Not to you. To themselves.

Because Champions don't just bring opportunity - they bring exposure. They put you on stages you haven't earned yet. They create chances you might not be ready for. They raise your flag so high that everyone can see the rips and tears in the fabric.

And that terrifies the mediocre.

What if I can't deliver? What if I'm found out? What if my flag flies so high that everyone can see my flaws?

These aren't spoken fears. They're lurking fears. The kind that hide behind reasonable excuses.

"I just need to perfect our platform first." "We need more case studies before approaching enterprise clients." "Our API documentation isn't quite ready for that level of scrutiny."

Sound familiar?

These aren't planning statements. They're hiding statements. The battle cry of the almost-great. The comfort blanket of the could-have-been.

Champions don't champion hesitation. Champions don't advocate for "good enough." Champions don't raise half-flags.

They champion courage. They advocate for excellence that refuses to hide. They raise banners that can be seen for miles.

Which is exactly why we resist them.

It's safer to network than to be championed. Networking keeps you in control. Having Champions puts your reputation in someone else's hands.

It's safer to self-promote than to be championed. Self-promotion lets you manage the message. Having Champions means someone else tells your story.

It's safer to grow slowly than to be championed. Slow growth means predictable challenges. Champions create opportunities that might stretch you beyond your comfort zone. Sometimes way beyond.

Safety or Champions. You can't have both.

The choice is yours.

So the real question isn't whether you want Champions.

It's whether you're brave enough to deserve them.

Are you?

Champions vs. Networking: The Fundamental Difference

Most people think they understand networking.

They don't.

They understand collecting business cards.
They understand awkward small talk over warm chardonnay.
They understand the transactional exchange of "you scratch my back, I'll scratch yours."

But that's not a Champion.
That's sophisticated begging.

Networkers are go-getters. They want something from you.
Champions are go-givers. They want something for you.

The difference?
Everything.

The networker asks, "What can I get?" before extending a hand.
The Champion asks, "What can I give?" without looking for returns.
This isn't idealism. It's strategy.
The Champion role always begins with giving, not taking.
Always pushing others forward, not pulling yourself up.

A networker will connect you if there's something in it for them.
A Champion will connect you because there's something in it for you.

A networker's Rolodex is a commodity to be leveraged.
A Champion's network is a community to be served.

A networker asks, "What can you do for me?"
A Champion asks, "Who do you need to meet?"

When Alex championed my company, he gained nothing. He risked his reputation by recommending a former competitor. He did it anyway.

Why? Because Champions operate from abundance, not scarcity. Because Champions understand that the ecosystem thrives when good businesses succeed. Because Champions know that today's beneficiary becomes tomorrow's benefactor.

But here's the warning:

The business world is full of Phantom Champions - people who promise advocacy but deliver nothing. They're easy to spot. They say things like:

"I know everybody in this industry."
"I'll definitely connect you with some people."
"Let me see what I can do."

And then . . . silence.
Ghosted . . . again

A real Champion makes specific introductions to specific people for specific reasons. A real Champion follows through. A real Champion puts skin in the game.

The most powerful Champions often emerge from unexpected relationships. Like Tony, a casual acquaintance who became a critical ally. Like clients who become advocates. Like employees who move to new companies and bring you with them.

Champions cannot be scheduled, bought, or manufactured. They emerge organically from authentic relationships and consistent positive interactions.

They can be cultivated.

There will always be takers, networkers, snakes, and phantoms.

Who cares? Give anyway.

THE CHAMPION CYCLE

Being a Champion begins with giving, not receiving

The most championed people didn't start by attracting Champions. They started by being Champions when they had nothing to gain

Phantom Champions: Beware the Ghost Flag

Here's why the Champion role is difficult to find: The promise is often more common than the practice.

The business world is full of Phantom Champions - people who signal advocacy but deliver abandonment.

They're the ones who talk big but act small. They're the ones who promise connection but create disappointment. They're the ones who leverage hope but never deliver help.

You've met them. You've believed them. You've been disappointed by them. Sometimes they are well-meaning and lack follow-through. Sometimes you're just a means to an end. Ugh.

But have you learned to spot them before they waste your time?

Warning Signs of Phantom Champions

They talk more about who they know than how they can help. Real Champions focus on your needs and how their network might serve you. Phantoms focus on their impressive connections and how you should be grateful for their attention.

They make vague offers rather than specific introductions. Real Champions say: "I'm having lunch with Mike next Tuesday. He needs exactly what you provide. Can I make that introduction today?" Phantoms say, "We should definitely connect you with some people. Let me think about who would be good."

They name-drop but never name-connect. Real Champions create actual meetings, calls, and relationships. Phantoms mention impressive names to enhance their own status, but never create the bridge.

They promise future value but deliver none present. Real Champions start small: a useful article, a relevant connection, a piece of valuable feedback. Phantoms always position value just beyond the horizon: "Once you do X, then I can really help you."

They take credit for success they didn't create. Real Champions celebrate your wins without inserting themselves into the narrative. Phantoms retroactively claim they were the catalyst for opportunities they had nothing to do with.

They're enthusiastic in person but disappear afterward. Real Champions follow through regardless of the environment. Phantoms are champions only in the room, never once you've left it.

The most dangerous Phantom Champions believe their own mythology. They aren't consciously deceiving you. They've deceived themselves first.

They genuinely believe they're more connected, more influential, and more helpful than they are. They confuse intention with action. They mistake goodwill for good works.

WARNING SIGNS

The promises sound real.
The results never materialize.

Talk more about who they know than how they can help

Real Champions focus on your needs
Phantoms focus on their connections

Make vague offers rather than specific introductions

Real Champions name names and dates
Phantoms "will connect you sometime"

Name drop but never name connect

Real Champions create meetings
Phantoms mention impressive names

Promise future value but deliver none present

Real Champions start small today
Phantoms will start "tomorrow"

Take credit for success they didn't create

Real Champions celebrate your wins
Phantoms insert themselves in your story

How do you handle Phantom Champions?

Don't confront. Don't accuse. Don't burn bridges.

Simply categorize accurately and invest accordingly.

Give them opportunities to prove themselves with small requests. Watch what they do, not what they say. Allow them to earn trust incrementally rather than assuming it completely.

Remember this: A known Phantom is less dangerous than a misidentified Champion. Accurate categorization prevents disappointment. Realistic expectations prevent wasted opportunity.

The business world doesn't lack potential Champions. It lacks the discernment to distinguish real from phantom.

Develop that discernment. Protect your time. Invest in proven advocacy.

Your flag is too important to be carried by ghosts.

The Multiplication Effect

Here's the math of a Champion:

One strong Champion equals dozens of cold calls. One respected voice carries more weight than a thousand marketing dollars. One strategic introduction opens doors that might have remained forever closed.

When Champions speak on your behalf, they transfer their trust to you. They loan you their credibility. They extend their reputation to cover yours.

This creates what I call the Multiplication Effect.

When Tony vouched for me at an executive summit, he wasn't just saving one day or one reputation. He was creating ripples that extended far beyond that moment. The executives there that day didn't just become clients - they became references who brought in other clients. The methodology we discussed there became a case study that attracted industry attention.

This isn't a coincidence.

This is the ripple effect of true championship.

Champions don't just open one door - they create a pattern of doors opening. They don't just make one introduction - they trigger cascades of opportunity. They don't just speak well of you once - they create ongoing conversations about your value.

The traditional sales funnel is linear. The championship effect is exponential.

And the most powerful part? You can't buy it. You can only earn it.

When Alex spoke up for me at that conference, he wasn't following a script. He wasn't fulfilling an obligation. He was responding naturally to the value he'd experienced.

That's the difference between marketing and championship.

Marketing says, "Here's why we're great." Champions say, "Let me tell you how they changed everything for me."

Which would you believe?

The math is clear. Champions create exponential results.

So why aren't you surrounded by them already?

Finding Your Champions (When You're Not Looking)

The uncomfortable truth about Champions?

You can't find them. They find you.

More specifically, they find you when you're being championship-worthy.

I spent years attending networking events looking for Champions - powerful people who could advance my business. I collected business cards. I followed up diligently. I tried to impress.

It never worked.

My most powerful Champions emerged when I stopped looking for them and started deserving them.

When I focused on creating exceptional value. When I helped others without expectation of return. When I became reliable, consistent, and worthy of recommendation.

Champions are attracted to excellence. They align themselves with integrity. They advocate for people who deliver.

They also emerge from unexpected places.

Like Tony, a casual industry acquaintance. Like Elaine, the client who fired me then championed me to a bigger client three years later. Like Jorge, the banker who denied my loan but connected me with an investor.

The path to Champions is rarely direct. It's circuitous, surprising, and often invisible until the moment of revelation.

So, how do you find Champions when you can't actually look for them?

The first way is becoming the kind of person Champions want to advocate for. Do it by solving real problems instead of chasing recognition.

The second way is by helping others. Be a Champion first. It is by building relationships first and leveraging them never.

Developing Champions is a byproduct of excellence and service, not a target to be acquired.

It's what happens when you focus on being remarkable instead of being promoted.

Champion Archetypes: Know Your Flag Bearers

Here's the thing about Champions: They come in different flavors.

Each raises your flag in a different way. Each amplifies your signal through a different channel. Each supports your success through a different strength.

Most entrepreneurs make the mistake of looking for generic Champions. They miss the specific types that would transform their business.

Know these four archetypes. Find them in your network. Cultivate them intentionally.

The Industry Authority

They don't just have a reputation. They are the reputation standard.

The Industry Authority doesn't just endorse you. They validate you.

Their word carries weight because they've earned it. Their approval transfers credibility because they rarely give it. Their advocacy opens doors because people trust their judgment.

When an Industry Authority champions you, they're saying: "I've seen everything in this space, and this is worth your attention."

They're not impressed by hype. They're immune to trends. They're allergic to mediocrity.

Which means their championship must be earned through undeniable excellence.

You recognize them by:

- Their name precedes them
- Their opinion changes markets
- Their recommendation eliminates hesitation
- Their validation supersedes due diligence

The Connected Catalyst

They don't just know people. They know exactly who needs to know you.

The Connected Catalyst lives at the intersection of networks. They're not just well-connected – they're strategically connected. They're not just introducers – they're connection architects.

When the Connected Catalyst champions you, they're saying: "I know exactly where this solution belongs in the ecosystem."

They see patterns invisible to others. They spot complementary needs across industries. They identify connection points that create exponential value.

The Connected Catalyst doesn't introduce you to everyone. They introduce you to the right someone.

You'll recognize them instantly because:

- Their introductions feel precisely targeted
- Their network spans multiple industries
- Their connections become lasting relationships
- Their championship creates chain reactions of opportunity

The Success Story

They don't just like your solution. They've been transformed by it.

The Success Story champions you through their results, not just their words. They're the living proof that your promise is real. They're the case study that breathes, speaks, and advocates.

When a Success Story champions you, they're saying: "This changed everything for me - it can do the same for you."

They speak with a conviction no marketing can match. They share details no case study could capture. They answer objections before they're raised.

The Success Story doesn't just describe outcomes. They embody them.

You recognize them by:

- Their enthusiasm is infectious
- Their results are measurable
- Their story contains specifics that resonate
- Their championship creates emotional investment

The Crisis Companion

They don't just show up when it's convenient. They show up when it matters.

The Crisis Companion proves their championship when everything falls apart. When reputations are at stake. When solutions are scarce. When others are running away.

When the Crisis Companion promotes you, they're saying: "I believe in who you are, not just what you've achieved." They offer resources without being asked. They provide support without tracking the debt. They champion you precisely when you feel least championable.

And in doing so, they create a bond that transcends transaction.

You recognize them by:

- Their support arrives without prompting
- Their help comes with no strings attached
- Their faith in you exceeds your own
- Their championship creates profound loyalty

Most businesses have one or two of these champions. The exceptional have all four.

Which ones are missing from your arsenal? Which ones have you failed to recognize? Which ones are you failing to cultivate?

Your future growth depends on your answers.

The Anti-Champion Environment

Most business cultures actively prevent Champions.

This isn't an accident. It's by design.

They reward internal competition over communal success. They celebrate individual achievement over collective advancement. They measure personal metrics over ecosystem health.

And then they wonder why Champions are rare.

Look at your own organization:

- Do you celebrate the salesperson who closes the deal or the support person who makes them look good and retains business for years?
- Do you reward the executive who claims credit or the team that created the result?
- Do you promote the visible or the valuable?

The answers reveal whether you're building a Champion culture or crushing it before it can emerge.

Champions thrive in environments of abundance, not scarcity. They flourish in cultures that value connection over transaction. They multiply in systems that celebrate others' success as vital to the whole.

The math is simple:

Scarcity thinking + Individual metrics = Champion prevention

Abundance thinking + Collective success = Champion creation

Here's the inconvenient question: Is your organization structured to create Champions or to prevent them? Is your leadership style designed to foster advocacy or to stifle it? Is your success metric based on what you achieve or what you enable?

These aren't theoretical questions. They're the difference between businesses that scale through Champions and those that stall through isolation.

The irony? The more desperately you need Champions, the more likely your environment is preventing them. The more you focus on self-reliance, the less championable you become. The more you emphasize personal achievement, the less champion potential you create.

Changing this isn't about better networking. It's about better environment-building.

Champions emerge from cultures of mutual success. They arise from systems that reward the elevation of others. They appear when leadership models the championship behavior it seeks.

Build that environment first. Then watch as Champions emerge naturally from the fertile ground you've created.

Cultivating Your Champion Network

Here's the paradox of Champion relationships:

The moment you try to formalize them, you break them.

Champions aren't part of your sales team. They're not your unpaid marketers. They're not extensions of your business development department.

They're independent advocates who choose to speak on your behalf.

You can't control them. But you can cultivate them.

First, be specific about who you serve. When Tony recommended me to those executives, he knew exactly what problem I could solve for them. Champions need clarity to champion effectively.

The worst thing you can say to a potential Champion is, "I can help anyone with anything." Or one of the most common "My ideal customer profile is entrepreneurs . . . and enterprises . . . and small businesses . . . and sometimes medium-sized companies too.

The best thing is "I transform logistics operations for shipping companies with 50+ vessels that are struggling with regulatory compliance."

Specificity breeds results.

Second, maintain engagement without exploitation. Champions need to stay connected to your story, your growth, and your impact. But they shouldn't feel used.

Share victories. Ask for advice. Provide updates. Express gratitude.

But never, ever make explicit demands to be championed.

Third, become a Champion for others. This is the reciprocity principle at work. Not as a quid pro quo, but as a natural expression of how Champions operate in the world.

When you actively champion others - when you make introductions, offer testimonials, speak up in rooms where they aren't present - you demonstrate your understanding of Champion culture.

And culture attracts like-minded people.

Finally, think long-term. Champion relationships aren't transactional. They're transformational. They evolve over years, not meetings.

The businessman who can't help you today might become your strongest Champion five years from now. The employee you mentored might become your industry's rising star.

Plant seeds. Nurture relationships. Think in decades, not quarters.

The Intentional Champion Path

Champions don't materialize by accident.

They're created through intention, cultivation, and design.

The most successful businesses don't hope for Champions - they create Champion pathways. Intentional progressions that transform:

- Customers into advocates

- Partners into promoters
- Employees into ambassadors
- Competitors into collaborators

This isn't manipulation. It's curation.

It's creating experiences so remarkable they demand to be shared. It's solving problems so effectively that they create stories. It's delivering value so unexpected it triggers advocacy.

Most entrepreneurs leave championing to chance. "If I do good work, people will talk about it."

Maybe. Sometimes. Inconsistently.

The entrepreneurial elite leave nothing to chance. They map their Champion pathways:

- How does a stranger become aware of your value?
- How does awareness become experience?
- How does experience become advocacy?
- How does an advocate become a Champion?

Each transition requires deliberate design. Each progression needs intentional touchpoints. Each elevation demands specific nurturing.

This isn't about controlling Champions. It's about creating the conditions where Champions naturally emerge.

Consider the contrast: Random excellence occasionally creates Champions. Systematic excellence consistently creates Champions. Random generosity occasionally activates advocates. Strategic generosity consistently activates advocates.

Championship by design produces more Champions than championship by chance.

The question isn't whether you deserve Champions. The question is: Have you designed the pathways that create them?

Champions in Crisis

You never truly know who your Champions are until everything falls apart.

When our cloud servers crashed during a major product launch, we lost access to our platform, customer data, and our ability to serve clients. Our backup systems would eventually restore most of it, but we needed an immediate solution. Our business was hours from breaching SLAs with our enterprise clients.

I called everyone I knew. Most didn't pick up.

Then my phone rang. It was Tony.

"I heard what happened. I have spare server capacity and engineering resources. They're yours until you get back online."

No contracts. No terms. Just help when it mattered most.

That's when I understood: crisis reveals your true Champions.

Not the people who celebrate your success, but the ones who sustain your survival. Not the people who like being associated with your brand, but the ones who stand by you when your brand is underwater - literally, in my case.

Crisis also creates unexpected allies.

The banker who seemed cold and procedural during good times became our financial advocate during recovery. The customer who constantly complained about minor issues rallied other clients to prepay for services to help our cash flow.

People you wrote off might step up. People you counted on might disappear.

And sometimes, your biggest critics become your strongest Champions.

My client, Regina, lived it. She told me, "The regulator who had previously cited our operation three times, became our fiercest advocate with the Industrial Commission. She fought for emergency permits and expedited our reopening after a wildfire crushed our business."

Why? Because during normal operations, she had seen their commitment to do things right, even when it was harder. They earned her respect before they needed her support.

Crisis doesn't just test your Champions - it creates them.

The Champion Economy

We're entering a new business era where championship is currency.

This isn't a trend. It's a fundamental shift.

Traditional capital - money, equipment, inventory - is becoming commoditized. Anyone can access it. Everyone can leverage it. The playing field is flattening.

But relationship capital? That's becoming the true scarcity. Especially in an AI world.

The willingness of others to stake their reputation on yours. The readiness of others to open doors you couldn't unlock alone. The commitment of others to champion you when you're not in the room.

This is the new economy.

In this economy, the rules have changed:

- The most championed companies grow fastest
- The most advocated-for products scale furthest
- The most vouched-for leaders attract the best talent

This isn't just nice to have. It's survival.

Look at the most disruptive companies of the last decade:

Stripe didn't just have better payment technology. It had Champions in developer communities who evangelized it relentlessly.

Zoom didn't just have better video conferencing. It had Champions in IT departments who fought for its adoption.

Neither could have scaled at their remarkable rates through marketing alone.

Behind the technology, behind the funding, behind the innovation - what do you find? They scaled through Champions. People of influence who decided to stake their reputation on unproven entities. People of connection who opened doors that should have remained closed. People of power who advocated for ideas that shouldn't have worked.

In a world where everyone has access to the same resources, (and AI) the only sustainable advantage is who champions you and how powerfully they do it.

Are you operating in this new economy? Or are you still stuck in the old paradigm where self-promotion trumps Champion-creation? Where marketing budgets matter more than relationship capital? Where what you say about yourself outweighs what others say about you?

If so, you're playing an obsolete game. One with diminishing returns. One where the cost of customer acquisition continually rises. One where trust continues to fall.

The Champion Economy rewards a different approach:

- Less selling, more enabling of Champions to sell for you
- Less promoting, more creating of experiences worth promoting
- Less claiming of greatness, more demonstrating of value that Champions can validate

This is the new competitive landscape. Not winner-take-all, but champion-take-most.

Navigate accordingly.

The Community Connection

Communities have memories.
They remember who gives and who takes.
They remember who shows up and who disappears.

They remember who builds and who extracts.

If you're in any community, you know exactly who is who.
And so does everyone else.
You're thinking of a name right now, right?

Here's the brutal truth:
The business owner who takes more than they give? Rarely championed.
The company that extracts without contributing? Almost never championed.
The entrepreneur who disappears when things get tough? Barely championed.

Communities champion those who champion the community.
They rally around people who show up.

It's not complicated, but it is profound.

I learned this when our software team built an e-commerce site for a nonprofit helping women rescued from trafficking. We weren't doing it for recognition. We had the skills, they had the need.

Six months later, a board member from that nonprofit remembered us and made an introduction. That connection became one of our biggest clients for a decade.

That's how the circuit works.

Championing flows from reputation.
Reputation flows from actions.
Actions flow from values.

Not marketing strategies.
Not networking tactics.
Not calculated giving.

But here's the counterintuitive part: The circuit only completes when you learn to receive help gracefully.

Many entrepreneurs give easily but receive awkwardly.
Help others instinctively, but accept help reluctantly.
This breaks the circuit.

When Billy offered his warehouse space and trucks for a logistically messy office move, my first instinct was to refuse. To preserve my pride at the expense of my project.

Thankfully, I didn't.

I accepted his help with gratitude, not guilt. I allowed him to experience the satisfaction of making a difference. I completed the circuit.

And in doing so, I strengthened our Champion bond rather than severing it.

CAPTAIN TO CAPTAIN:

How many people championed you last month? Not just mentioned you - Actively advocated for you when you weren't there. If your answer is 'I don't know,' you're not paying attention to your most valuable asset.

The Champion Ecosystem

Champions don't exist in isolation.

They form networks. Webs of advocacy. Interconnected systems of reputation and referral.

The single Champion who occasionally mentions you creates linear impact. The Champion network that consistently reinforces your value creates exponential impact.

Most entrepreneurs focus on acquiring individual Champions. The most successful focus on cultivating Champion ecosystems.

These ecosystems have their own dynamics:

- Champion clusters that amplify each other's advocacy
- Champion pathways that create sequential opportunities
- Champion synergies that open doors that no single Champion could access

Think of it like a coral reef. Individual coral polyps create small value. Reef systems create massive value. Neither can exist without the other. The whole becomes vastly greater than the sum of its parts.

Championship works the same way.

THE CHAMPION ECOSYSTEM

Individual Champions create linear value.
Connected Champions create exponential value.

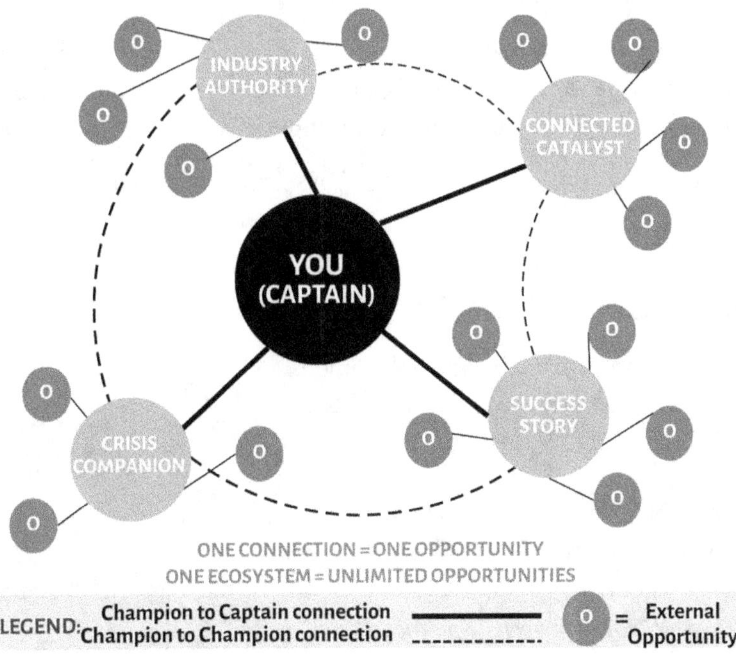

A CTO recommends your software to their team. Linear value.

That CTO recommends you to their professional association. Network value.

The association features your solution at their conference. Ecosystem value.

The conference leads to five Champions in adjacent industries. Exponential value.

The question isn't just "Who are your Champions?"

It's "How are your Champions connected?"

"How do they amplify each other?"

"How does their combined advocacy create opportunities no single Champion could provide?"

Most entrepreneurs never ask these questions. They focus on individual relationships rather than champion ecosystems. They settle for isolated advocacy rather than networked championship.

The result? Limited impact. Constrained opportunities. Slower growth.

Championship at scale requires ecosystem thinking:

- How are you mapping your champion network?
- How are you connecting your Champions to each other?
- How are you transforming isolated advocacy into networked championship?

Build your ecosystem intentionally. Nurture connections between Champions, not just with them. Create opportunities for Champions to collaborate, not just advocate. Develop systems that make Champion relationships self-sustaining, not just sporadic.

The isolated Champion helps your business. The champion ecosystem transforms it.

Becoming a Champion for Others

Here's the counterintuitive truth about Champions: *The fastest way to attract Champions isn't to seek them.*

It's to become one.

Not eventually. Not after you've "made it."
Now. Today. Especially when you think you can't afford to.
Champions aren't something you earn, then practice.
It's something you practice, then earn.
The most championed people I know didn't start by attracting Champions.
They started by being Champions when they had nothing to gain.
Recommended competitors when their solution wasn't the right fit.
Connected peers to opportunities without taking a finder's fee.
Celebrated others' successes as enthusiastically as their own.

And then, almost magically, Champions appeared in their corner.
Not because they asked.
Because they demonstrated.

It really is that simple.
Want to attract Champions? Become one.

Not strategically. Not transactionally. Not with the expectation of return.

Genuinely. Consistently. Generously.

Being a Champion isn't something you do – it's someone you are.
It is someone you become. Intentionally.

It starts with seeing potential in others before they see it in themselves. It continues with connecting people to opportunities they didn't know existed. It culminates in advocating for others when they aren't in the room.

When you champion others, you demonstrate your understanding of how the champion ecosystem works. You show that you value the currency of reputation and relationship. You prove your worthiness to be championed.

This isn't calculated. It's cultural.

The most effective Champions don't keep score. They don't maintain champion balance sheets. They don't expect direct reciprocation.

They advocate and promote others because that's what Champions do.

They introduce because connections create value.
They spotlight because talent deserves recognition.
They support because everyone faces floods.

In the process, they create lasting impact beyond business metrics.

> *The most effective Champions don't keep score.*
> *They don't maintain balance sheets.*
> *They champion because that's what Champions do.*

When I started actively championing three young business owners in our industry, I wasn't thinking about building my Champion network. I was thinking about helping them avoid the dumb mistakes I'd made. (which were many)

Five years later, all three are successful. Two have become Champions for my business in ways I never anticipated. The third moved to a different industry but still refers clients to us.

Was that my plan? No.

Was that the result? Yes.

Being a Champion creates a legacy. It extends your impact beyond your direct business activities. It amplifies your values through others who share them.

And occasionally, it comes back to you multiplied.

Champion Reality Check: Your Personal Assessment

Time for brutal honesty.

Do you have real Champions? Not contacts. Not connections. Not people who say nice things to your face.

Champions.

People who actively advocate for you when you're not present. People who connect you to opportunities without being asked. People who defend your reputation against criticism. People who send business your way without expectation of commission.

If you're not sure, you probably don't.

Real championship is obvious. You see its effects. You hear about it from others. You experience its benefits directly.

Ask yourself:

1. Who has introduced me to a significant opportunity in the last six months without being prompted?
2. Who consistently mentions my business to relevant prospects without my involvement?
3. Who would step up to help if my business faced a serious crisis tomorrow?
4. Who knows enough about my ideal client to effectively champion my business?
5. Whose reputation actively enhances mine through association?

If you struggled to answer these questions, you have Champion gaps.

This isn't failure – it's opportunity.

Every Champion gap represents untapped potential. Every missing Champion represents connections not yet activated. Every advocacy vacuum represents value not yet recognized.

The solution isn't complicated, but it is challenging:

Become more champion-worthy. Clarify who you serve and how you serve them. Make introductions and referrals easy for your Champions by being very specific about who you would like to meet. Focus on delivering exceptional value before seeking exceptional advocacy. Champion others before expecting them to champion you.

Start now. Not with grand gestures, but with immediate actions.

REFLECT: Who have you championed lately when there was nothing in it for you? Who's been championing you when you weren't in the room?

ACT: Make one introduction today that benefits someone else with zero benefit to you or expectation of reciprocity.

Then do it again tomorrow.
And the next day.

Being a Champion is a lifestyle, an identity, not an event.

Who raises your flag when you're not in the room?

There's a world of difference between networkers (who want something FROM you) and Champions (who want something FOR you). One connection with the right Champion creates more opportunities than a thousand cold calls.

I've gathered resources to help you spot Phantom Champions, cultivate Real Champions relationships, and be easy to advocate for. Most importantly, there are resources and opportunities to BE a Champion for someone else in the community.

It's free, my gift to you.

https://TheCaptainsKeys.com/bonus

⚓ NAVIGATE

To Sail the Story/ Full Journey - Continue on to the next page
Study the Maps – Jump ahead to page 349

BERING STEEL

BEYOND THE STORM
Part 8

Jimmy mentally scrolled through the regulars at the bar, the familiar faces that had become fixtures in his new life.

His mind raced. He studied Si's weathered face, searching for any hint, some hidden clue he was overlooking.

A fishery management official he saw weekly?

It made no sense.

Think bigger?

Gray Peterson, who sat in the corner booth nursing the same beer for hours. Mike Donnelly, who talked endlessly about his grandkids in Seattle. Sarah Ling, who ran the harbor supply store and sometimes stopped in for a quick lunch.

No one fit.

"Is it Locklear? The guy with the chess board?" Jimmy ventured.

Si shook his head, amusement dancing in his pale blue eyes.

"Donnelly? He's always reading those government reports. Has to be Donnelly, right?"

"Not even close."

"Sarah from the supply store? Grocery store? Vet? Butcher shop?"

Si's smile widened. "You're overthinking this one, buddy."

Jimmy frowned, frustration gnawing at him like a hook set deep. He wasn't used to feeling this slow, this blind to what was right in front of him. Back in the Keys, he'd known every player, every angle, every secret that mattered.

Here in Kodiak, he was still finding his footing. Still learning to read currents that ran deeper than any ocean.

The silence stretched between them. Outside the wheelhouse, gulls cried their eternal complaints while waves lapped against the hull with metronomic persistence. Jimmy could hear his own heartbeat in his ears.

Who holds that kind of power in a place like this?

"Look," Si said, leaning forward with the deliberate motion of a man about to drop a bombshell. "Who's the person you see the most often outside your crew?"

Jimmy's chest tightened.

"Who knows everything about everyone in this town?"

The pieces began moving in Jimmy's mind, sliding together like tectonic plates before an earthquake.

"Who's been watching you since day one?"

The answer hit him like a rogue wave.

No.

It couldn't be.

"Wait." His voice emerged as barely a whisper. "You don't mean—"

"Your ol' vole buddy." Si's eyes crinkled at the corners, but there was something profound in his expression now. Something that spoke of secrets kept and revelations savored.

Jimmy's world tilted.

The bartender who'd threatened him with a baseball bat named "Mama."

The woman who'd pranked him with live rodents in a gift box.

The person he'd dismissed as just another colorful local character.

She was—

"Carly is a senior member of the North Pacific Fishery Management Council."

Jimmy blinked.

Once.

Twice.

His brain performed the mental equivalent of a ship running aground at full throttle. Every assumption he'd made about power, about influence, about who really ran this corner of Alaska, crumbled like a house of cards in a blizzard.

If it was physically possible for a man's brain to melt and leak out his ears, Jimmy's would have been pooling on the deck by now.

"She's WHAT?"

The words erupted from his throat like a depth charge detonating. They bounced off the steel bulkheads, seeming to echo forever in the confined space.

Si couldn't contain his laughter. The sound rolled through the wheelhouse like distant thunder—rich, unrestrained, and filled with the particular joy of a man who'd just watched someone's entire worldview collapse and rebuild itself in real time.

"You should see your face right now," Si gasped between chuckles. "Absolutely priceless."

Jimmy slumped against the bulkhead, mind reeling. "But she's just a bartender."

The words hung in the air between them, heavy with assumption and ignorance.

"Just a bartender?" Si's laughter doubled down, tears streaming from his eyes. "You guys and your preconceived gender notions. She's been on that board for sixteen years, give or take."

Jimmy felt heat crawl up his neck. "That's not what I meant."

But wasn't it?

Hadn't he made exactly the assumption he'd fought against his entire career in the Keys—that people were only what they appeared to be at first glance? That a woman serving drinks couldn't possibly hold real power?

"She holds a PhD in marine biology from the University of Alaska," Si continued, wiping his eyes. "The bar was her father's legacy. She kept it running while building her reputation in fishery management. Grew up on boats. She's more qualified to run any vessel out here than half the captains, and could probably outfish most of them."

Every interaction with Carly replayed in Jimmy's mind like frames from a film reel.

Her careful observations when he'd first arrived.

Her pointed questions disguised as casual conversation.

The way other captains deferred to her without him even noticing.

The warnings about Walter Mitchell that he'd ignored.

The careful neutral tone when other captains mocked him.

The quiet assessment in her green eyes that first night.

She hadn't just been watching him.

She'd been evaluating him.

Testing him.

Deciding whether he was worth saving.

"She kind of likes you, kid," Si said, his voice softening with something like pride. "And she seriously dislikes most of the captains. You've got the kind of drive and determination she respects."

Si leaned back in his chair. "More importantly, you haven't been lured into pointless feuds with those clowns. She's seen you get knocked down and get back up without losing your integrity."

Jimmy stared out the wheelhouse window, watching gulls wheel against the darkening sky. Their white wings caught the last copper light of day, seemingly suspended between sea and heaven.

"No promises," Si cautioned, "but she told me she'd talk to the rest of the council and do her best to get things straightened out for you. If anyone can do it, it's Carly."

Jimmy's throat tightened with unexpected emotion. All this time, he'd been focused on proving himself to the other captains, to the men who sneered and waited for him to fail. He'd never considered that the real power, the real judgment, the real help might come from an entirely different direction.

"I owe her one," he said quietly. "Actually, several."

The full weight of it crashed over him like the mother of all rogue waves.

His Champion hadn't just been hiding in plain sight.

She'd been pulling strings he didn't even know existed.

"But that's what Champions do, right?" The words came softly, almost to himself. "She's been mine all along and I never even noticed."

Understanding crystallized like ice forming on rigging. "Representing and promoting me to others when I wasn't even in the room. She's signed my letter of consignment, and I get to raise the flag."

Si nodded, satisfaction settling across his weathered features like a familiar coat.

"Now you're getting it. That's the final key, Jimmy." He ticked them off on gnarled fingers, each one a hard-won lesson. "An Anchor keeps you stable when everything else is chaos. A Crew executes the mission when you can't do it alone. A Navigator shows you the way when the path is unclear."

He paused, his pale blue eyes boring into Jimmy's.

"But a Champion? A Champion opens doors you didn't know existed. And sometimes, saves you from enemies you didn't even know you had."

CHAPTER 35

Within forty-eight hours, the official notice arrived - permit and quota approved under a special provision for "vessels of historical significance to the Kodiak fishing community." The bureaucratic language masked the truth of what had happened: someone with influence had intervened directly.

Jimmy tried to catch Carly twice at the bar but missed her both times. Her staff claimed she was "at meetings," which now carried an entirely different meaning. He sent a gift basket instead with a handwritten thank-you note tucked among bottles of small-batch whiskey and artisanal cheeses he could barely afford. Flowers seemed wrong for Carly, but good alcohol and quality food spoke a universal language of appreciation.

That evening, he gathered his crew on the deck of the *Bering Steel*. The men stood in a loose circle - Aidan towering over the others, Richie practically vibrating with eager energy, Old Bob solid and patient, Tom quiet but attentive, and Scott slightly apart, still finding his place.

"Quota's been approved," Jimmy announced without preamble. "We sail on Thursday for a week-long bait run."

The news was met with approving nods rather than celebration. These weren't men given to excessive displays, but Jimmy could read their satisfaction in the slight relaxation of shoulders, the subtle shifting of weight.

"Scott's drawn up our course." Jimmy gestured to the navigator, including him purposefully. "Weather looks favorable through the weekend, then a low-pressure system moving in from the west. Nothing we can't handle."

He paused, looking at each man in turn. "Any questions?"

"Just one." It was Bob who spoke, weathered face serious beneath his salt-and-pepper beard. "When do we get those fancy uniforms with the gold braid?"

The tension broke, laughter rippling through the group. Even Scott's mouth quirked upward at one corner.

"Soon as we catch enough crab to afford them," Jimmy replied, grateful for the moment of lightness.

CHAPTER 36

Bering Steel

Bering Sea, near the Aleutian Islands

Scott was a revelation on the water - a man operating in a different dimension. He could read patterns as they emerged, making predictions about what was coming, what swam beneath them, and where they should go next that left Jimmy speechless with admiration.

His expertise was worth four times what he was making. When Jimmy tried to increase his salary, Scott refused, saying he just wanted his special request at season's end. At the rate they were going the bait run would be finished in half the time.

On their second night out, when Scott pulled out his guitar, and Bob followed suit retrieving his ukelele. The two played together like they had been in a band together for years.

The other guys were amazed. Richie asked, "How do you even know what the other one is going to do?" Jimmy especially enjoyed the music because the combination of instruments reminded him of the Keys.

The next evening, they'd done it again and received some unexpected accompaniment - a low rumble just off the bow had them scrambling into emergency mode, only to discover a massive humpback emerging from the water. The creature regarded them with ancient eyes and called out its own haunting melody before diving back to the depths.

By mid-morning the next day, Jimmy called it. "That's enough bait – we're heading home!" A cheer rose from the deck.

Hours later, the *Bering Steel* slid into port as the afternoon sun slanted low across the harbor. With lines secured and engines finally silent, Jimmy watched his crew congratulating each other on the deck below, their voices carrying the satisfaction of work well done.

Jimmy called the crew on deck. "Well done men. Well done! We're back early. One week from tomorrow we leave for opening day of crab season."

Cheers

"Red Gold!"

More cheers.

"Tonight we celebrate a long and successful partnership! Go home, get cleaned up and we'll meet for dinner. You know the place. Dinner, and drinks, are all on me."

Most cheers.

But as the men began to disperse across the deck, Tom raised his hand. The gesture was subtle - a slight lift of fingers - but it carried the weight of authority.

The crew stopped.

Jimmy felt the shift in the air, the subtle realignment of energies. Something was going on among them, something he hadn't been privy to.

"Captain." Tom's voice was measured, calm. "Before we go, there's something we'd like to put forward."

The others returned to their loose semicircle, facing Jimmy. Not confrontational, not challenging. United.

"What's that?" Jimmy asked, curious more than concerned.

Richie and Aidan exchanged glances. Old Bob stared at his workboots, uncharacteristically solemn. Scott stood a half-step back, not fully part of this yet, but not apart either.

"We've been talking," Tom continued. "About what kind of boat we want this to be."

Old Bob lifted his gaze then, his weathered face catching the afternoon light. Six years sober, Jimmy remembered. Six chips he'd laid on the table during his interview, a declaration of both vulnerability and strength.

"We'd like to make the *Bering Steel* a dry boat, Captain," Tom said. "No alcohol on board. Not for anyone."

"And not in town either," Richie added.

The request hung in the sea air between them, as solid as the steel beneath their feet.

Old Bob's right hand trembled slightly - not from fear, but from the endless battle he fought, minute by minute, day by day. Jimmy had seen the man's daughter's artwork online - her talent was extraordinary, her future bright with possibility. All contingent on her father's continued sobriety, on his ability to provide.

"Bob didn't ask for this," Aidan interjected, his massive frame somehow gentle in that moment. "We decided."

Richie nodded, his young face serious beneath the shock of unruly hair. "We're a team. We stand together."

The sight before Jimmy was worth more than all the crab in the Bering Sea - four men who barely knew each other a month ago, now standing as one. A crew becoming something more.

Jimmy felt something shift in his chest, a tectonic realignment of priorities.

"Done," he said simply. "I'd be honored. I'm in," Jimmy said, meaning every word. "No alcohol on board. For any of us."

He extended his hand, and Tom clasped it firmly - a different kind of contract, more binding than anything written on paper.

"Or in town." Richie added again, the ghost of his usual grin returning. "That includes dinner tonight. We know we're celebrating and all . . . even though you're buying, we'll all be drinking coffee or soda. Together."

"Or in town," Jimmy said, giving a nod to Richie.

Jimmy glanced at Old Bob, saw the relief and gratitude shadowing his eyes. How many crews had rejected him over the years? How many times had his battle been dismissed as weakness rather than the profound strength it truly was?

As they dispersed toward their homes to clean up, Jimmy remained on deck. The wind had picked up, carrying the bite of Arctic chill, but he barely felt it.

His gaze tracked across the harbor to the other vessels - sleek, efficient money-making machines operated by captains who ruled through fear, competition, and solitary authority.

For the first time since the hurricane had wiped away his old life, Jimmy felt something like gratitude for the catastrophe. It had stripped him of everything except what mattered most: the chance to build something true.

Not just a successful fishing venture. This was far more.

A band of brothers.

CHAPTER 37

After spending time with Bella and taking a much-needed shower, he called Lily. Her voice carried across the miles, grounding him just as Si had explained an Anchor should.

They were winding down the conversation when she said something that lit a warm glow in the center of his chest.

"Jimmy? I know neither Dad nor Uncle Rocky was exactly the best with words or with sticking around when we could have used them, but I can tell you that both of them would have been so proud of what you're doing right now. Like bursting-with-pride kind of happiness. You've really accomplished something here. I want you to know that."

He didn't remember the drive to Carl's - his mind was too full of her words, too rich with possibility. Scott had been smart enough to give Captain Si a call, and the old man joined their dinner at a big table they had reserved. Everyone was in high spirits - not just because Jimmy was buying, though that certainly helped.

The first time he saw Carly emerge from the back, he made a beeline to her. She gave him a big smile and thanked him for the gift basket. He thanked her profusely for her role in getting the license and quota sorted out and promised that if he could ever return the favor, she just needed to ask.

While he waited for her to refill his crew's drinks, he finally asked a question that had been on his mind since day one.

"So is Carl your dad or your brother or something? Do I never get to meet this guy?"

The bar seemed to go suddenly, dangerously quiet.

Carly turned toward him with glacial slowness. One eyebrow arched with the precision of a drawn weapon.

"Captain James," she said, venom dripping from each syllable. "Kindly go outside, look up at the sign of this fine establishment, and do not return until you figure out the answer to that question."

He cracked a confused smile, certain this was another of her sarcastic humor bits.

She didn't smile back.

"You serious?"

Her eyes flashed like heat lightning. One hand gestured toward the place behind the bar where she kept the baseball bat.

"Don't make me wake up Mama, James."

Jimmy beat a hasty retreat outdoors, genuinely bewildered. The night air bit through his thin shirt, but embarrassment kept him warm as he stared up at the illuminated sign.

Several people walked past, eyeing him curiously - another drunk tourist trying to read after one too many, their expressions said.

As his fingers began to go numb, comprehension finally dawned.

The sign read:

C A R L _'S

The "Y" wasn't lit.

Not "Carl's."

"Carly's."

It had been her place all along.

Jimmy returned inside, chagrined. Carly waited for him, arms crossed over her chest, weight balanced on one hip.

"Yes, James? Something to say?"

"The 'Y' isn't lit up." He rubbed the back of his neck. "Why don't you get it fixed?"

"Neon doesn't do so great in such cold conditions. I've had it fixed four times already. At some point, it's just not worth it." A smile tugged at the corner of her mouth, relenting. "So, now that you've figured it out where are, welcome to Carly's! Can I take your order?"

CHAPTER 38

Jimmy and his crew sat at their table, at CARLY'S, clear-eyed and alert despite the late hour. Each nursed a coffee or soda - solidarity that hadn't gone unnoticed by the other patrons. The captains and crew a few tables over were another story entirely - faces flushed, voices rising with each round, inhibitions dissolving in direct proportion to their blood alcohol levels.

Jimmy absently traced the rim of his water glass, watching the ice cubes shift and settle. It was strange being the sober one in a bar. He could see things more clearly now - the forced laughter, the desperate bonding, the false courage that came from a bottle.

He'd never realized how much he'd relied on that buffer himself.

Scott leaned toward him, voice low. "You didn't have to do this, you know."

"Do what?" Jimmy met his navigator's eyes.

"Join the pact." Scott glanced at Bob, who was deep in conversation with Richie about his daughter's latest art project. "It's your boat."

Jimmy considered this, rolling the words around in his mind like smooth stones. "That's exactly why I needed to do it. Because it's my boat. My responsibility."

It was more than that, though. The realization struck him with sudden clarity. "This isn't just about supporting Bob. It's about what kind of leader I want to be. The kind of example. The kind of man."

Across the room, Steven Burns and his crew grew louder, their laughter taking on the sharp edge of mockery. Jimmy caught the words "pretty-boy rookie" and "saying the rest of us don't have pride" floating across the room like toxic vapor.

He didn't need advanced deductive reasoning to figure out who was the subject of their conversation.

Tom, sitting with his back to the wall - never comfortable unless he could see all exits - caught Jimmy's eye and gave an almost imperceptible shake of his head. *Not worth it.*

Jimmy nodded once. Burns could talk until his face turned blue. Words were just air.

But when a few of Jimmy's crew prepared to head out, Burns and a pair of his sycophants detached themselves from their table like predators scenting weakness. They materialized behind the departing men, Burns swaying slightly as he found his footing.

The room's atmosphere shifted instantly. Conversations quieted. Eyes darted toward the confrontation, then away - the practiced indifference of those who knew better than to get involved.

"Hey Mayor Flipperhead," Burns called, voice pitched to carry. "You really going to take that piece of junk out crabbing next week?"

Jimmy measured his words carefully, kept his voice neutral. "That's right."

"Pretty-boy Jimmy, Mayor of Crab Island." Pressman joined in on the jabs.

Burns lackeys laughed and parroted the phrase each adding a new pun and insult.

Burns's face contorted, eyes bloodshot and narrow. "With two babies in diapers, two old farts, and Chief Punch Your Nose? You'll be dead in the water faster than that sorry old uncle of yours!"

The mention of Uncle Rocky detonated something primal in Jimmy's chest. A roar of blood filled his ears as he launched from his seat, hands already curling into fists, every cell in his body intent on a single purpose: silencing Burns permanently.

Aidan intercepted him mid-lunge - not roughly, but with the gentle precision of someone who understood exactly how much force was needed. His massive arms locked around Jimmy's chest, lifting him slightly off the ground.

"Not like this, Captain," Aidan murmured, his beard tickling Jimmy's ear. "Not here."

Si stepped between them, placing himself directly in Burns's path. The older captain seemed to expand somehow, his slender frame occupying the space with a presence that belied his physical size.

"Go sleep it off, Burns," Si said, his voice barely above a whisper but carrying the weight of decades at sea. "You don't want this to get rowdy. You might not be comfortable with how few friends you actually have in this bar."

Burns blinked slowly, alcohol-soaked neurons firing just enough to process the veiled threat. His gaze swept the room, taking inventory of potential allies.

No one moved to join him.

The calculation played across his flushed face as clearly as cards on a table. He gave Si a half-hearted shove that barely moved the older man, then turned on his heel, staggering slightly as he headed for the door.

"This isn't over," he slurred over his shoulder.

Jimmy felt the tension drain from his muscles as Aidan released him. He straightened his shirt, acutely aware of how close he'd come to destroying everything they'd built.

"Thanks," he said quietly to Aidan.

The big man shrugged. "Would've done the same for any of us. We're crew."

Those simple words carried a weight that settled deep in Jimmy's soul. *Any of us.* Not "any of them." *Us.* We're crew.

The confrontation had changed the evening's tenor, but as goodbyes began around the table, Jimmy found himself oddly grateful for it. The flash of violence had revealed something he'd needed to see—this crew would protect not just each other, but him as well.

Tom clapped him on the shoulder as he stood to leave. "Hell of a thing, watching Burns try to take you down a peg." His grin was fierce with satisfaction. "Didn't work out like he planned."

As the crew filtered out into the Kodiak night, Jimmy caught fragments of their conversation drifting back through the door. Scott and Richie were already planning their approach for opening day, their voices animated with the kind of anticipation that came before every season.

But it was Bob's words that stopped Jimmy cold.

"Zach's crew knows their business," Bob was saying to Tom. "We were talking about coordinating our fishing strategy. What do you think about partnering up with the *Northern Star*? Pool our intel on the grounds."

Jimmy's pulse quickened. Crew collaboration between boats was rare. Competition usually ruled these waters. But Bob was right—Zach was Si's deck boss. His men were seasoned, and their combined knowledge could give both boats an edge.

"Yeah, let's connect in three days," Tom agreed. "Both crews meet at the docks for final prep. Share what we know about the crab movements."

"I'll set it up with Zach and we'll make it happen", Bob confirmed.

The door swung shut behind them, leaving Jimmy to process what he'd just heard. His crew wasn't just protecting him—they were thinking strategically, building alliances. Of course Si and Jimmy had discussed working together, but the same idea coming from the crews was even better.

Opening day was less than a week away.

Everything was accelerating.

"Jimmy." Si's voice cut through his thoughts. "Stay behind a minute, would you?"

Around them, the activity at Carly's was winding down. Last call. Carly moved between empty tables, her movements efficient but watchful. She glanced toward the windows every few minutes, scanning the parking lot.

"Appreciate the company," she said, catching Jimmy's questioning look. "In case Burns decides to come back with reinforcements."

Jimmy suspected there was more to Si's request, but he settled back into the booth without pressing. The older man's face carried the weight of something unsaid.

Si waited until Carly was out of earshot, wiping down the bar with practiced strokes. The silence stretched between them, comfortable but charged with anticipation.

Finally, Si spoke.

"Burns is trash, but I think you already know that." His voice carried decades of experience with men like Burns—bullies who mistook cruelty for strength. "Focus on the positives here. Play your own game, not his."

The bar's atmosphere had shifted. Gone was the tension of confrontation, replaced by something quieter. The kind of space where hard truths could be spoken.

Si's face softened, years melting away from the lines around his eyes. "You're about to start a process that so many guys try to break into and fail miserably at, repeatedly. You've got an amazing crew, a great boat, and you've grown into quite the leader."

He paused, studying Jimmy with the intensity of someone seeing past surface doubts to deeper potential.

"I wish I had been half the captain you are when I was your age."

The words hit Jimmy like a rogue wave—unexpected, powerful, reshaping everything in their wake. All evening he'd been processing what leadership meant, what his crew expected from him.

Carly appeared with two fresh steaming mugs, the coffee's rich aroma mixing with the bar's familiar scents of salt air and old wood. She set them down without a word, understanding that some conversations required fuel.

Jimmy wrapped his hands around the ceramic warmth, letting Si's words settle into his bones. "Thank you Si, that means a lot. Especially coming from a legend like you."

Si paused, something vulnerable crossing his features. "It's been great getting to know you the past few months. Even better going on this journey with you. I never thought I'd get the opportunity again."

Jimmy tilted his head, puzzled by the last statement. "What do you mean by that, Si?"

The older man's gaze drifted away, focusing on something beyond the room's walls. His shoulders, always so straight and strong, seemed to curve inward under an invisible weight.

"You know the wreck out there past your slip? The one you almost ran into that first morning you took her out?"

"Of course." Jimmy nodded. "You said it was a warning to other sailors. Neglected maintenance caused a broken anchor chain, right?"

"You've got a good memory." Si's voice dropped to nearly a whisper. "Three men died that day. None of them knew what hit them. The chain broke, had no power, and rolled the boat over. Eventually into those rocks where it sits. All three went overboard into that freezing cold water. No survival suits. No hope of rescue."

The old captain's hands, always so steady, trembled slightly as he wrapped them around his coffee mug.

"One was my son Peter. Twenty-three, barely older than Richie. We were too much alike - stubborn, proud. Couldn't work together on the *Northern Star*, so he left for Dutch Harbor. When he came back years later, we tried again. Same result. He joined the crew of Raven's Fortune instead." Si's voice dropped. "Less than a year later, he was gone. Never to return."

The revelation hit Jimmy like a physical blow. He hadn't even known Si had a son.

"Peter was a lot like you Jimmy. Didn't know how strong he could be until he got his feet wet. He's been gone nine years. Still seems like it happened yesterday."

Si continued, his voice thick with emotion, "For years, Rocky was my best friend, and was my anchor during that really rough time. I see him in you too. Over the past months, you have become like a son to me, Jimmy,"

Jimmy reached across the table, covering Si's weathered hand with his own.

"I'm so sorry. And I'm sorry you felt the need to carry that burden while still helping me." Jimmy's throat tightened around the words. "You've been an incredible source of support and a friend when I had almost nothing to offer in return."

He swallowed hard against the lump forming in his throat. "My dad died when I was eight - cancer. Uncle Rocky was his only male relative left alive. He lived far away. Mom and I never really had anyone to help us fill that void. I think I only saw him once or twice since my Dad's funeral. He had his own things going on up here I suppose. I certainly didn't blame him."

Jimmy's gaze shifted from reminiscing around the room to locking eyes with Si.

"But Si, this isn't just a one-way street. I've come to think of you as more than a friend - more like the father I never had but always wanted. I didn't even understand how deep that hole was."

The two men sat in silence for a long moment. When you share that kind of truth, silence can be as warm as a handshake or a hug.

CHAPTER 39

The marina was deserted at this hour, the darkness broken only by the pale pools of light from widely-spaced lamps. The water lapped gently against the hulls, a soothing rhythm that masked the sound of their footsteps on the dock.

Stephen Burns did his best to sober up enough to help Derek Pressman, Johnny Antonelli, and two other deckhands sneak aboard the *Bering Steel*.

The alcohol made his movements clumsy, but it also dulled the voice in his head telling him this was crossing a line. Jimmy had humiliated him tonight. Made him look weak in front of the whole fleet.

That couldn't stand.

"Keep it quiet," Pressman whispered, his voice tight with nervous energy. "Security patrol comes through every two hours."

Burns fumbled with the dock lines, his coordination shot. The whiskey had seemed like courage three hours ago. Now it felt like stupidity.

But Jimmy's face kept flashing in his mind. That calm certainty when he'd faced down the confrontation. The way his crew had rallied around him.

The way the whole bar had watched Burns back down.

"You sure about this?" Antonelli's voice carried doubt. The younger captain kept glancing toward the harbor patrol station, its windows dark but somehow still threatening.

"Shut up and move." Burns hauled himself over the rail, landing harder than he'd intended. The boat rocked slightly, and he froze.

Nothing stirred in the neighboring slips.

Pressman followed with practiced stealth, then helped the others aboard. Four men with four different reasons for being here. Pressman's gambling debts. Antonelli's reliance on Burns for quota and intel. The other two were just deckhand muscle, paid enough to keep their mouths shut.

"Engine room," Burns ordered. "Quick and clean."

They moved across the deck like ghosts, their footsteps muffled by years of experience moving quietly on boats. But this wasn't fishing.

This was something darker.

The engine room hatch opened with a soft creak. Pressman dropped down first, his flashlight beam cutting through the darkness. The massive diesel engine filled most of the space, its bulk intimidating even when silent.

Pressman carried a container full of a foul-smelling concoction that he told Burns would be the perfect revenge on cocky Captain Jimmy Meyer. The liquid caught the flashlight, reflecting an oily rainbow sheen, almost alive in its malevolence.

"This stuff should keep Meyer in port long enough to miss the start of the season," Antonelli whispered, his breath coming in excited puffs of white vapor.

Pressman continued, "By the time he figures out what's wrong and gets this fixed, the season will be done and over."

Burns felt a moment of hesitation. Twenty-three years of honest fishing. Hard work.

And where had it gotten him?

Public humiliation by some kid who'd inherited his uncle's boat.

Burns poured the lumpy liquid himself, watching it disappear into the engine's dark heart. Saltwater, sugar, and several industrial chemicals hastily mixed together in a sinister cocktail.

"Yo ho ho, and a bottle of rum," he muttered.

Let Jimmy call him Blackbeard now.

Antonelli shifted nervously. "What if they trace this back to us?"

"They won't." Burns replaced the oil cap. "This stuff will eat the seals from the inside out. Engine failure. Bad luck for the new captain."

The four men laughed together, shadows among shadows, wishing they could see Meyer's face when he discovered their little "gift".

For a brief moment Antonelli thought Burns was pushing it a little too far, but quickly snuffed that notion.

The end justified the means.

Didn't it?

As they prepared to leave, Burns caught sight of a framed photo mounted near the helm. Jimmy with an older man—his father. Both wearing Chicago Bulls jerseys, both smiling with easy happiness.

The rage flared again, hot and bitter. He grabbed a fire axe from its bracket, raised it toward the photo.

"Boss, no." Antonelli caught his wrist. "That's personal property. This was supposed to be about the boat."

Burns stared at the photo, breathing hard. Jimmy's father looked so much like his son, so much like Rocky. The same steady eyes. The same quiet authority Burns had spent twenty-three years trying to fake.

And failing.

Slowly, he lowered the axe.

"Let's go."

They slipped back onto the dock, four shadows disappearing into the maze of moored vessels. In his drunken haste, Pressman left the empty container behind, rolling forgotten in a corner of the engine room.

Behind them, the *Bering Steel* rocked gently at her moorings, looking peaceful in the lamplight.

But she carried their poison now.

Burns walked away without looking back, whiskey and rage warring in his blood. In a few days, Jimmy would try to take her to sea. From the moment they started it, that engine would begin eating itself alive.

The marina returned to its quiet rhythm. Water lapping against hulls. Rigging singing softly in the wind.

No one had seen them.

No one knew what they'd done.

But the sea would reveal everything soon enough.

CHAPTER 40

Jimmy squinted against the relentless Alaskan sun glinting off Kodiak Harbor's choppy surface. The morning air carried that particular blend of diesel, salt, and possibility that always reminded him he wasn't in Florida anymore. His crew worked with synchronized efficiency on the deck of the *Bering Steel*, their movements carrying the comfortable rhythm of men who had found their place in the world.

"Back in a bit," Jimmy called out. "Going to find Si and talk strategy."

Aidan looked up from securing a crab pot, face weather-reddened but grinning. "Tell the old man we're almost ready for whatever he thinks the Bering Sea can throw at us."

Jimmy nodded, suppressing a smile. The kid's confidence was either his greatest strength or a disaster waiting to happen. Out on these waters, the line between the two was thinner than a spider's web.

He'd promised to bring lunch back for the crew. An easy promise to make - the kind of small gesture that built loyalty without requiring much effort. Unlike the promises that kept him awake at night: delivering a successful season, honoring his uncle's legacy, proving that he was worthy of the trust is uncle had placed on him.

Jimmy found Carly's place sparsely populated - a few solitary fishermen nursing coffees or something stronger, but no sign of Si.

"Haven't seen him all morning," Carly said, wiping down the counter with practiced efficiency. Her eyes held the knowing look of someone who'd watched decades of fishermen come and go. "Not like him to miss coffee. Especially when there's planning to be done."

The faint alarm bell in Jimmy's mind grew louder. Si was reliable to a fault - the kind of man who'd rather suffer in silence than let down his crew.

Jimmy hopped in his truck and unconsciously selected Si's address in his GPS. Like most places in Kodiak he knew where it was - mostly. He'd spent too many years ignoring his instincts, trying to fight the current instead of reading the water. Not anymore.

The small, weathered house sat a couple of miles from the harbor, the kind of practical dwelling that existed solely for sleeping between fishing seasons. Simple, predictable, and steady. No garden. No decorations. Just shelter against the Alaskan elements. The truck in the gravel driveway confirmed Si was home.

Jimmy knocked. Nothing.

He knocked again, harder this time.

Something inside - the muffled sound of a television. He tried the door, found it unlocked. In Kodiak, locks were often considered optional. The threat came from the sea, not from neighbors.

"Hey Si? It's Jimmy."

The living room smelled of coffee and something else - medicinal, almost. The glow of the television cast blue shadows across the small space. "Sea Hunt" played on the screen, deep-sea divers navigating murky waters.

Si sat motionless in a worn recliner, eyes open but unfocused.

"Hey, Si, didn't you hear me knock?" Jimmy moved closer, alarm building in his chest.

Si's eyes slowly tracked to Jimmy's face, recognition dawning, but when he tried to speak, the words emerged slurred and disjointed. "Jim . . .my . . .some . . .thing's . . ."

Cold realization washed over Jimmy like a wave breaking across the deck. He'd seen a stroke once, years ago, on a deep-sea charter seventy miles offshore. The memory flashed vivid and terrifying - the client's suddenly drooping face, the rising panic as they realized how far they were from help.

But they weren't seventy miles offshore now.

Jimmy pulled his phone from his pocket, punched 9-1-1 with a trembling finger. He did his best to control the adrenaline and keep his voice calm. A skill developed from years of maritime emergencies. "I need an ambulance. My friend is having a stroke."

He kept one hand on Si's shoulder, a grounding contact, while giving the dispatcher the address in clipped, precise terms.

"They're coming, Si. Just hold on." Jimmy searched the older man's eyes, looking for the sharp intelligence that usually resided there. "Don't you dare give up on me. Not when we're just getting started."

The next eight minutes stretched like hours. Jimmy filling them with reassurances that sounded hollow even to his own ears. The paramedics arrived with practiced efficiency, their questions rapid-fire, their movements quick but controlled.

They loaded Si onto a stretcher, face partially obscured by an oxygen mask.

"I'm coming with you," Jimmy said, not a question.

The lead paramedic nodded. "You family?"

"Close enough." The lie came easily, necessary.

Jimmy's phone buzzed in his pocket as they loaded Si into the ambulance. He ignored it. Buzzed again. And again. Some emergencies couldn't wait.

The hospital corridor smelled of antiseptic and lingering fear. Jimmy paced outside the room where doctors worked on Si, his footsteps marking time against the polished floor. He couldn't go in – "not family," they'd reminded him curtly. The white lie that had gotten him this far wouldn't get him any closer.

His phone buzzed again. Three missed calls, all from Scott. Finally, Jimmy answered.

"Hey Scott, I'm a little busy right now. Is it an emergency?"

The tension in his Navigator's voice hit Jimmy before the words registered. "I'm afraid so, Boss. We fired up the ship to test that knocking and the whole engine went to crap. Somebody's done something since we went into town yesterday. The boat was a mess. I think someone poured something into the engine. We've been sabotaged."

Silence.

"Sabotaged, Boss. Did you hear me?"

Stunned silence.

"You might want to get down here ASAP. Bob called the police. Whatever this was it weren't no accident. You get me? Deliberate, professional work."

Jimmy's free hand clenched involuntarily, knuckles white. "Burns." The name tasted like bile.

It had to be Burns or one of his men. Or some other crew. The rivalry had simmered for months, but this crossed a line even Jimmy hadn't thought possible. Sabotage days before the start of season opening wasn't just business - it was personal. Calculated to destroy not just their season but their livelihood.

Jimmy sat down, afraid he might fall down if he didn't. The few other faces in the waiting room had no more hope in their eyes than Jimmy.

A doctor emerged from Si's room, walking into the sterile waiting room. His expression carefully neutral. "Are you the one who brought him in?"

Jimmy nodded. "Will he be okay?"

"Too early to say. We're moving him for tests."

Jimmy searched for any hint of a real prognosis but the doctor didn't tip his hand.

"The next twenty-four hours are critical. You did really well getting him here so quickly. Saved his life."

The doctor's pager beeped. "We'll know more soon. Stay strong, son."

Jimmy stood paralyzed between obligations. Si alone in the hospital. His ship crippled at the dock. His crew waiting for direction.

"I'll be back," he promised the empty corridor, then forced himself toward the exit, already dialing Scott back.

His rage built with each step, a familiar but dangerous companion. Rage dragged him under for years after father's death. Rage had fueled foolish choices as a new captain. Rage would make him careless now, when precision mattered most.

Stop. Breathe. Think. Act.

One problem at a time.

CHAPTER 41

The crew had gathered around the *Bering Steel*'s engine, the massive piece of machinery disassembled across the deck. Their faces told the story before Jimmy even arrived - the hard set of Scott's jaw, the smudged grease on Aidan's forearms, the methodical way Bob organized components even as his eyes betrayed their desperation.

"How bad?" Jimmy asked, though he already knew.

Scott straightened, wiping his hands on a rag. "Bad enough. Diesel mechanic most likely, or has spent years around these big engines. Someone knew exactly what they were doing. Whatever it was, the contaminant shredded essential components. We've got parts that need replacing, and the entire system needs cleaning before it'll run right again."

"Timeline?"

"Two weeks for parts, minimum. Another month to clean everything and put it all back together properly." Scott's voice dropped. "We'll miss the entire season at this rate."

The weight of those words settled across Jimmy's shoulders. Missing the season meant financial disaster for his crew. For himself. It meant the saboteur would win without even having to compete.

Jimmy nodded once, processing. "The police find anything helpful?"

Bob shook his head. "By the time they got here, we'd touched everything trying to figure out what was wrong. They didn't even bother trying to find prints. They said they'd check CCTV cameras but said it was a long shot."

"What's going on with Si?" Richie asked, concern etched across his face. "The harbor master called the crew of the *Northern Star*. Said an ambulance went to Si's place?"

"He had a stroke. Doc says it's too early to tell how bad it was. He'll be in the hospital for a while." Jimmy swallowed hard. "He won't be fishing this season."

The silence that followed held the weight of their collective shock. Si was more than a partner captain - he was their touchstone, their connection to these waters and the traditions that defined them.

Jimmy locked himself in his quarters, the small space suddenly suffocating. He pulled out his phone and dialed a number he knew by heart.

"Hey, it's me," he said when Lily's voicemail picked up. His voice broke. "I think it's over, Lil. Someone sabotaged the engine. Si had a stroke. We're dead in the water, literally and figuratively." He paused, hating the defeat in his voice. "I'm sorry. I thought I could do this, but . . ."

He hung up, unable to finish the thought. The phone buzzed almost immediately with a text from Lily:

At doctor with Emily. Can't talk. Be RESOURCEFUL! MAKE A PLAN! I BELIEVE IN YOU! STOP WORRYING and DO WHAT YOU WERE MEANT TO DO!

Jimmy could almost hear her voice - firm, unwavering, the kind of certainty that cut through doubt like a knife through water. Lily had been his Anchor since childhood, the one constant when everything else shifted beneath his feet.

The phone rang again - this time the hospital.

"Mr. Meyer? I'm Dr. Carmen, head of Neurology at Kodiak Mercy Hospital. I wanted to let you know that your friend is stable. As my colleague said, we're still running tests. The stroke was significant, but we're cautiously optimistic." The doctor's voice was professionally compassionate. "He'll need to stay for at least a week or two. We'll know more tomorrow, but with therapy and time, he is likely to make a good recovery."

Jimmy thanked her, relief temporarily overwhelming the other crises demanding his attention. Si was stable. One small victory against the tide of setbacks.

He texted Scott: *Rally the crew at Carly's. We need to talk.*

CHAPTER 42

Carly's place felt different that evening - less a gathering spot and more a war room. The usual background noise of fishermen trading stories had been replaced by the focused energy of the *Bering Steel*'s crew. They'd claimed the corner booth, cups of coffee growing cold as they processed the dual blows of Si's absence and their crippled vessel.

"First things first," Jimmy said after updating them on Si. "We're going to find a way through this. All of us, together."

Richie nodded, though doubt lingered in his eyes. "How exactly do we fix an engine with no parts and the season starting this week?"

"We brainstorm," Jimmy replied, pulling out a notebook. "I want ideas from everyone. No matter how wild they seem. This is our ship, our season, our future. Together."

The hesitation lasted only moments before suggestions began flowing. They worked methodically, creating lists - parts needed, skills required, sequence of repairs. What they had. What they lacked. Potential sources. Alternative solutions.

"We're running out of places to call so source parts," Bob finally said as the evening stretched into night. The number of 'no's' far outweighed the 'maybes.'

Jimmy studied the faces around him - exhausted, worried, but still fighting. "Get some sleep. Tomorrow we call everyone who hasn't hung up on us yet. Meet at the ship at noon with whatever you've found."

Walking back to his quarters that night, Jimmy felt the weight of leadership pressing down. He'd always been responsible for himself, for his dog, occasionally for clients. But now fourteen people - his crew and Si's - were counting on him to salvage not just a season but their livelihoods.

The old Jimmy would have cracked under that pressure. Run away. Found another port, another boat, another life.

But that Jimmy had drowned somewhere between Florida and Alaska.

CHAPTER 43

Morning brought a trickle of parts and possibilities. Not enough - nowhere near enough - but more than they'd had the night before. The crew gathered at noon as instructed, each contribution carefully logged in Jimmy's growing list. Discouragement hung in the air, unacknowledged but palpable.

"Permission to come aboard?" The voice from the dock cut through their planning session.

Jimmy, Bob, and Scott moved to the rail, expressions guarded. Rich Hills, captain of *Red Dawn* stood at the gangway, his posture uncomfortable but determined. Jimmy's jaw tightened at the sight of a "Burns buddy."

"What the hell do you want, Hills?" The words escaped before Jimmy could contain them, sharp with suspicion.

Hills shifted his weight, eyes steady despite the hostility directed at him. "Heard you guys needed parts and labor in a hurry. Thought I might be able to help out. What can I do?"

"You can call up your pal Burns and tell him to go f – " Jimmy's tirade died beneath Scott's heavy hand on his shoulder.

"Another captain is volunteering his time and parts as a gesture of respect and good will," Scott said quietly. "This is when you separate the man you dislike from the captain he is. Si would tell you the same thing."

The reminder of Si - lying in a hospital bed while they stood arguing - snapped Jimmy back to reality. His crew needed solutions, not vendettas.

Bob had already stepped forward, rattling off their critical needs. Hills listened, eyes widening as he grasped the extent of the damage.

"Give me an hour," Hills said, addressing Jimmy directly. "I've got components at my berth that I can loan until replacements arrive. I'll send one of my guys to help." He offered a quick salute and strode purposefully down the pier.

Jimmy watched him go, confusion replacing anger. Hills helping seemed as unlikely as the Bering Sea freezing solid in July.

"You really think he's on the level?" Jimmy asked Scott once Hills was out of earshot.

Scott's weathered face revealed nothing. "Guess we'll find out in about an hour."

Twenty-one minutes later, a truck pulled up at the dock. A familiar face emerged - not Hills, but Rick Webber, captain of the *Alma Jane*, a man Jimmy recognized but had never formally met.

"Permission to come aboard?"

Jimmy waved him on, curiosity outweighing caution.

Webber approached with a box in his hands. "Heard you guys were looking for engine parts. Happen to have an extra crankshaft in my warehouse. Saving it for a rainy day." He grinned, the expression breaking through his weather-beaten face. "Figure this is it."

He passed the part to Jimmy, then clapped him on the shoulder. "Your uncle once hired me when nobody else would take a chance. You seem like a good kid, Meyer. Make it happen."

They came like that all afternoon. Sometimes two at a time, sometimes alone.

Captain after captain.

All people Jimmy had nodded to in passing, but none he knew well. Men and women who'd worked with his uncle. Competitors who should, by all logic, be celebrating his misfortune. Each brought something - a part, advice, an extra set of hands. Each had a story - about Si, about Jimmy's uncle, about the unwritten code that governed their dangerous profession.

By sunset, the *Bering Steel*'s deck was covered with the components they'd need. The problem wasn't parts anymore - it was expertise. The knowledge to rebuild an engine this complex required something beyond good intentions.

"We need someone who really knows what they're doing," Bob admitted as they secured the ship for the night. "I can direct traffic, but putting this all together correctly, quickly? Some of this is really specialized work."

Headlights appeared at the end of the pier as Jimmy was considering their next move. A figure made its way toward them, deliberately, unhurriedly.

Jimmy recognized the silhouette from Carly's place - one of the old-timers who usually sat near Si's regular spot. They met him halfway down the pier.

"Captain Meyer?" The man extended a weathered hand. "Ben Greene, from the *Merlin*. I started my career with Captain Si - seen you in Carly's more than a few times." His grip was firm, calloused from decades on the water. "I just came from the hospital. Si's more awake now. His crew stopped by earlier as well. Trying to get back to whatever passes for normal around here." A ghost of a smile crossed his face. "I told him about what happened to your engine. He sent me out here to lend a hand."

The hope that had been flickering all day suddenly burned brighter.

"We've got the parts," Jimmy said. "What we need now is someone who knows how to put this puzzle back together."

Ben smiled, the expression transforming his serious face. "Then this is the right place for me. I've been a master mechanic for forty-one years." He turned to Bob. "You ready to get after it?"

Bob grinned. "I was born ready."

Ben fist bumped Bob and offered, "We can get start now and we'll have a few more hands to help in the morning."

Bob's hands moved with methodical precision as he broke down the seized hydraulic pump. Jimmy watched, passing tools without being asked.

"You know what the hardest part of getting sober was?" Bob asked suddenly, not looking up from his work. "It wasn't the physical withdrawal or even the cravings. It was admitting I couldn't fix myself alone."

He separated two corroded components with surgical care. "Spent my whole life believing weakness was failure. That asking for help meant I wasn't man enough."

"What changed?" Jimmy asked.

"Rock bottom has a way of clarifying things." Bob set the damaged parts aside. "My sponsor told me something I never forgot: 'Strength isn't about standing alone. It's about knowing when to lock arms with others.'"

He finally looked up at Jimmy, his weathered face serious. "That's what sobriety taught me about leadership. The truly strong captains aren't the ones who never need help – they're the ones who know how to build a system of support around themselves."

Jimmy thought about his own reluctance to lean on others, how it had nearly cost him everything.

A system of support.

A Stability Matrix..

"Like the rigging out there on deck. More connections, more stability."

Bob nodded, a smile crinkling the corners of his eyes. "Exactly. In recovery, we call it a support network. Out here . . ." he gestured to the boat around them ". . . it's what separates the captains that become legends from the ones who wash out or fade away."

With Aidan and Richie as runners, Bob, Ben, and three more local diesel magicians transformed the seemingly insurmountable task into a manageable project."

Six days of round-the-clock meticulous work - testing, cleaning, reassembling. Six days of the crew functioning as a perfectly synchronized unit. Six days of Jimmy's growing realization that he'd found something in Alaska that had eluded him in Florida - not just a crew, but a community.

Each night, he offered quiet thanks in his prayers. For Si's improving condition. For the unexpected generosity of rivals. For the crew that had become something far more than employees. For the second chance he wasn't sure he deserved but was determined to honor.

NAVIGATE

Study the Maps / Full Journey - Continue on to the next page
To Sail the Story – Ride a wave to page 367

THE MATRIX EFFECT
WHEN 2+2=16 IN YOUR LEADERSHIP SYSTEM

"The whole is greater than the sum of its parts."
— ARISTOTLE

The Power of Integration

Here's the thing about leadership support systems: They're not just collections of relationships. They're living ecosystems.

Most leaders collect relationships like baseball cards. A mentor here. An advisor there. A coach, when things get tough. A few key employees. Maybe a business group.

Separate. Disconnected. Fragmented.

Like a ship where the navigator never speaks to the helmsman. Where the lookout doesn't know what the captain is looking for. Where each sailor rows to their own rhythm.

That's not a crew. That's just people on the same boat.

And that's exactly why most businesses hit their ceiling.

The true power of the Stability Matrix isn't in having four different types of relationships. It's in how they interact. How they amplify each other. How they create something greater than the sum of their parts.

I worked with a CEO who had the most impressive roster of advisors I'd ever seen. Former Fortune 500 executives. Industry pioneers. Management gurus.

He was also failing spectacularly.

Why? Because his all-star team never communicated with each other. Each expert optimized their own quadrant without understanding how it affected the others. More alarming was the lack of communication by the same roles within the same quadrant!

His strategy advisor pushed for rapid expansion while his operations team advised caution. His industry connections opened doors that his team wasn't ready to walk through. His personal mentor urged work-life balance while his board demanded 80-hour weeks.

Sound familiar?

Then he did something seemingly small but transformative. He brought key representatives from each quadrant together for a strategy weekend.

For the first time, his Navigator heard from his Anchor. His Crew understood his Champion's perspective. Each relationship gained context from the others.

The result wasn't compromise. It was revelation.

Six months later, his company had doubled revenue and secured major partnership deals. More importantly, he had transformed as a leader – confident, clear, and connected.

What changed? Not the people. Not their advice. Not their support.

What changed was the integration.

This isn't just a nice theory. It's a competitive advantage.

The kind your competitors can't copy, because they're too busy building better products instead of better matrices.

The Price of Matrix Imbalance

Leadership matrices don't fail because they're missing pieces. They fail because they're wildly out of balance.

Like a ship with all its weight on one side. Like an engine with power but no steering. Like a sail with no keel to harness the wind.

When a ship lists, it leans to one side, compromising stability and performance. Sometimes it's subtle - barely noticeable until you try to pour a drink and watch it flow at an angle. Other times, it's dramatic and obvious to everyone.

Your business lists in predictable patterns:

The Growth List - Companies leaning so hard into expansion that they capsize their culture. A software company I worked with grew from 50 to 250 people in sixteen months. Revenue soared. But they listed dangerously toward growth at all costs. Core values eroded. Key employees jumped ship. They were taking on water faster than they could bail.

The Control List - Leaders who lean so far into control that they create a dangerous operational tilt. Their teams become paralyzed, waiting for approval on even minor decisions. Innovation dies. Motivation drowns. The ship stalls in open water.

The Status Quo List - Remember Kodak? They owned the known waters of photography so completely that they became comfortable. They saw the digital wave coming and even owned early digital camera patents, but chose to stay in their familiar harbor. Innovation was a threat to their core business. That didn't end well.

The Work-Life List - Perhaps the most common and destructive list I see is the one where business success comes at the cost of everything else. Leaders justify missing their kids' events, skipping workouts, neglecting relationships - all while telling themselves it's temporary. But like a ship listing in rough seas, if you don't right the ship, you'll eventually roll over.

Your Stability Matrix prevents these dangerous tilts by creating a counterbalance:

Too many Navigators, not enough Anchors? You get brilliant strategy without emotional stability to implement it. Burnout.

Strong Crew, weak Champion? You have the capacity to execute beautifully, but all is quiet because nobody knows about it. Stall out.

Powerful Champion, inadequate Navigator? You attract opportunities you can't strategically evaluate. Then say yes to every project that comes your way because all revenue must be good revenue. Flame out.

Deep Anchor connection, missing Crew? You stay wonderfully centered while your business slowly rolls over and sinks. R.I.P.

Balance isn't just preferred. It's required.

That's why it is called The Stability Matrix.

I've watched brilliant entrepreneurs crumble not because they lacked support, but because their support was dangerously lopsided.

Like Rachel, her industry connections were unparalleled. She cultivated a Champion network that opened every door in Silicon Valley. VCs called her. Partnerships materialized overnight.

But her Navigator quadrant was empty. Her Anchor relationship was superficial. Her Crew was understaffed and overwhelmed.

Those beautifully opened doors? She couldn't walk through them. Couldn't evaluate them. Couldn't capitalize on them.

Eighteen months after raising $40 million, her company imploded. Not from lack of opportunity, but from matrix imbalance.

The harsh truth about capsized ships? They don't sink because they're missing parts. They sink because the weight is wrong.

Are you balanced, Captain? Or just busy building one quadrant while the others fill with water?

Is your ship listing to one side while you keep adding cargo to the heavy end?

Matrix in Motion

The Stability Matrix isn't static. It's dynamic.

Just for a minute, let's go beneath the waves. There is way more going on down there than most people realize. Picture your matrix as a living ocean ecosystem:

Your Anchor is the reef – stable, immovable, providing shelter during storms and a fixed point for navigation.

Your Crew is the current – powerful, directional, creating the movement that propels your vessel forward.

Your Navigator is the instruments - radar, depth finder, and GPS – providing visibility into what's coming, guiding decisions about when to sail and when to shelter.

Your Champion is the tide – lifting all boats when it rises, connecting distant shores, making possible what was unreachable before.

These forces interact constantly.

When they align, progress feels effortless. When they conflict, even simple movement becomes exhausting.

The most powerful dynamics happen at the intersection points. Just like the reef ecosystem, each part affects and benefits the others.

Your Anchor grounds advice from your Navigator, ensuring their strategic guidance doesn't disconnect you from your core values and purpose.

I witnessed this with Victor, whose brilliant strategist pushed him toward aggressive expansion that would have required compromising his core values. Not in an illegal way, it just wasn't in alignment with his goals. His Anchor - his former mentor – didn't tell him what to do. He simply reminded Victor why he started his company in the first place.

That context transformed how he received his Navigator's advice. Not rejecting it, but adapting it to align with his deeper purpose.

MATRIX IN MOTION

Each part supports the Captain and complements the others

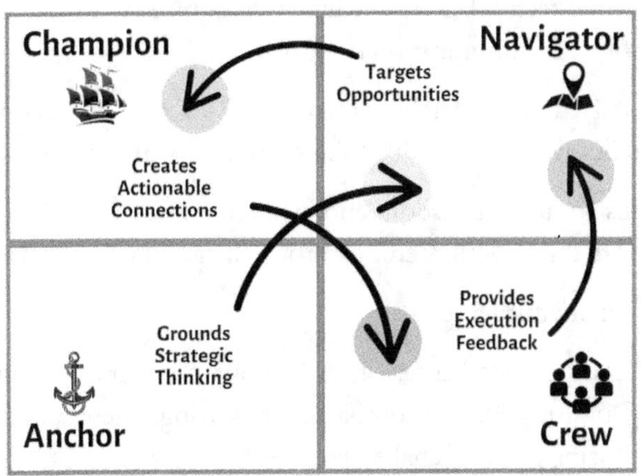

Your Crew executes on your Champion's connections, turning introductions into actual results.

Remember the CTO Martin, my big prospect? It was the advocacy of Alex that opened a door. But it was my VP of Client Success, Sam and her Crew, that walked through it, delivering the implementation that turned opportunity into outcome.

Opportunity without execution is just another form of distraction.

Your Navigator calibrates your Champion's targeting, ensuring they connect you to the right opportunities, not just any opportunities.

When Ryan's Navigator analyzed which partnerships actually aligned with their five-year strategy, his Champion network suddenly became twice as valuable – making half as many introductions that produced three times the results.

These connection points create a self-reinforcing system where each relationship amplifies the others.

But *they don't happen by accident. They happen by design.*

Let me show you what this dynamic integration looks like. Here are three critical real-world scenarios where matrix integration created transformative results:

🚀 Product Failure-to-Launch

When Elena's software company faced a catastrophic bug two days after their major product launch, her matrix activated in a way that transformed potential disaster into unexpected opportunity:

Her Navigator (former tech CEO) immediately recognized the pattern: "This isn't just a technical issue—it's a communication opportunity."

That perspective shifted to her Anchor (mentor of 15 years), who reminded her: "Your reputation isn't built on perfection. It's built on integrity in imperfection."

Her Crew took this combined wisdom and created a transparent communication plan that acknowledged the issue while demonstrating their commitment to quality.

Then something remarkable happened.

Her Champion (industry podcaster) heard about their transparent approach and featured the story, praising Elena's company for "setting a new standard for customer communication" during product challenges.

What could have been a PR nightmare became a brand differentiator—not because any single relationship provided the perfect answer, but because the matrix functioned as an integrated system.

The Unexpected Competitor

When Marcus discovered a new competitor had entered his niche with significant venture funding, his first instinct was panic. But his matrix created something more valuable: perspective in action.

His Crew identified the operational threat: "They're promising delivery timelines we can't match with our current systems."

His Navigator contextualized the challenge: "This is the classic David-Goliath scenario. Their funding is their weakness—they'll be forced to scale before they understand the market."

His Anchor grounded him in identity: "Remember why we built this company: to create craftsmanship at scale, not just growth for growth's sake."

From these integrated perspectives, Marcus formulated a strategy that his Champion then communicated to key clients: "While others are learning the market, we're deepening our expertise in it."

The result wasn't just a defensive response. It was a strategic repositioning that turned their smaller size into a market advantage.

This wasn't coincidence. It was integration.

The Personal Crisis Crossover

The matrix truly proves its power when business and personal challenges collide.

When Sophia's father received a terminal diagnosis the same week her company entered critical acquisition talks, her matrix didn't just support her—it transformed how support itself functioned:

Her Anchor (spouse) created emotional stability while acknowledging she couldn't step away from the business opportunity.

Her Navigator connected her with another CEO who had navigated a similar personal/professional collision, providing priceless, specific guidance.

Her Crew didn't just "handle things"—they restructured responsibilities to create focused blocks where Sophia could be fully present for either family or business without constant switching.

Her Champion spoke directly to the acquisition team, creating understanding without oversharing personal details.

What happened next defied conventional wisdom.

The acquiring company, impressed by how Sophia's team functioned during a personal crisis, increased their offer—specifically citing the "leadership depth" they witnessed.

Sophia was able to be present for her father's final weeks while completing the most significant professional transaction of her career.

Not because she was superhuman. But because her matrix was super-connected.

The Integration Multiplier

Here's what makes matrix integration transformative:

When your Navigator and Anchor communicate directly, strategic decisions get properly grounded in core values.

When your Crew understands your Champion's connections, they prepare specifically for the opportunities most likely to materialize.

When your Anchor has context from your Navigator, they provide emotional support that's connected to business reality, not just general encouragement.

These aren't just nice-to-have interactions. They're force multipliers.

Integrated matrices don't just add value—they multiply it.

They don't just solve problems—they transform them into opportunities. They don't just provide support—they create possibilities that didn't previously exist.

This is why matrix-building isn't just about finding four good relationships. It's about creating an ecosystem where those relationships strengthen each other.

The question isn't whether you have the four key relationships. The question is: Are they talking to each other? Are they functioning as a system rather than isolated connections?

INTEGRATED LIFE WHEEL

Beyond Balance: How work and life elements
integrate with bidirectional influence

PERSONAL LIFE

Interests & Passions

Health & Well Being

Purpose

Spiritual

Meaningful Relationships

**INTEGRATED
SELF**

Career Contribution

Growth & Learning

Impact

Skills & Expertise

Community Connections

PROFESSIONAL LIFE

Purpose energizes relationships. Interests inspire skill development.
Skills enhance personal interests. Community provides growth opportunities.
Learning enriches expertise. Relationships give purpose deeper meaning.
Well-being supports career performance. Career provides resources.

Integration. That's where the real magic happens.
That's when the Stability Matrix truly comes alive.
That's when leadership transforms from burden to breakthrough.

Is your matrix moving, Captain?
Or is it just sitting still?

Crisis Management Through Integration

You never fully appreciate your support system until everything falls apart.

That's when most leadership structures reveal their fragility.

The executive with impressive advisors but no emotional anchors. The entrepreneur with talented employees but no strategic guidance. The founder with strong industry connections but no operational backbone.

These aren't bad support systems. They're incomplete ones.

And incomplete systems shatter under pressure.

Crisis tests completeness.

I watched Annabeth's tech company hit the perfect storm - a major security breach, the same week their biggest client went bankrupt, and their CTO resigned. Triple crisis across three domains.

Most leaders would have collapsed under this weight, focusing on one fire while the others burned uncontrolled.

Anabeth didn't. Her integrated matrix activated instantaneously.

Her Navigator helped her understand the strategic implications and prioritize actions.

Her Crew mobilized to implement the recovery plan while maintaining client commitments.

Her Champion reached out to key stakeholders, maintaining confidence in the company's direction.

Her Anchor kept her centered, reminding her that her value wasn't determined by this temporary crisis.

Each relationship played its role. Each reinforced the others. Each filled gaps the others couldn't.

Would Annabeth have survived with just one or two of these relationships? Maybe.

Would she have emerged stronger, with clients intact and reputation enhanced? Absolutely not.

The integration didn't just prevent collapse. It created resilience that her competitors couldn't match.

Three months later, Annabeth's company had not only recovered but grown. Several competitors had lost significant market share during the same period.

The difference wasn't resources or luck. It was an integrated support system that functioned as a whole rather than disconnected parts.

Crisis doesn't create leadership capabilities. It reveals them. And what it reveals most clearly is the integration of your support system.

Is your matrix ready for the storm that's coming? Not if. When.

Managing Role Overlap

Here's the hard truth about support relationships: You rarely get them in neat, separate packages.

One person, one role. That's the ideal. Reality is messier.

Sometimes your spouse is both Anchor and Crew. Sometimes your mentor serves as both Navigator and Champion. Sometimes your business partner fills three roles at once.

This overlap creates risk.

When one relationship serves multiple functions, a single point of failure emerges. Lose that relationship, and multiple support systems collapse simultaneously.

I've seen entrepreneurs divorce their spouse who was also their business partner, losing their emotional foundation and operational backbone in one devastating blow.

I've watched company founders fall out with mentors who were their primary strategic advisors and industry advocates, creating cascading crises across multiple domains.

These aren't just relationship problems. They're structural vulnerabilities.

The solution isn't artificial separation. It's strategic redundancy.

For critical functions, create intentional overlap. Ensure no essential support role depends entirely on one relationship. Build backup systems.

When Eliza realized her co-founder was serving as Navigator, Champion, and part of her Crew, she didn't force a separation. Instead, she cultivated additional relationships for each function.

She joined a CEO peer group for additional Navigator perspective. She built relationships with industry influencers who could also champion her company. She developed senior team members who could eventually take over her partner's operational roles.

The goal wasn't to replace her partner's input. It was to create a system that could withstand disruption in any single relationship.

Think of it as relationship risk management. Not pessimistic. Prudent.

Because relationships change. People change. Circumstances change. Your support system needs to withstand these changes.

How many critical functions in your matrix depend on a single relationship? That's how many potential catastrophes you're carrying.

Are you building a matrix? Or a house of cards?

> Picture your integrated matrix as a ship's wheel - with you at the center and the spokes extending outward to your key relationships. When any spoke is missing or weak, the wheel becomes harder to turn. When all are strong and properly positioned, navigating even the roughest waters becomes possible. This isn't just a metaphor – it's a visual reminder of what an integrated life looks like in practice.

System Maintenance

Here's the thing about complex systems: They die from neglect, not from failure.

Many leaders treat relationships like emergency services - ignored until a crisis hits. Then they wonder why no one answers when they call.

They're like sailors who hope to get "another season" out of worn parts.
Pilots who never inspect engines until airborne.
Climbers who never examine ropes until they're hanging from the cliff.

Relationship maintenance isn't a cost. It's an investment.

The solution? Quarterly relationship review. One hour, four times a year, five questions:

1. Is this relationship healthy and active?
2. Am I giving as much as receiving?
3. Has anything changed that affects us?
4. What do they need that I haven't provided?
5. Where are the emerging gaps?

These questions catch small issues before they become fatal problems.
They keep relationships active so years don't go by with nothing but a Christmas card or an automated LinkedIn birthday message.

Jason, a manufacturing CEO, discovered during one review that his Navigator was considering retirement within the year. Nine months' notice instead of sudden abandonment.

That's the difference maintenance makes.

Remember: your matrix evolves as your business grows.
Early-stage needs hands-on Crew and practical Navigators.
Growth-stage needs systems builders and scaling experts.
Mature businesses need optimization and innovation leaders.

What supported you yesterday won't tomorrow.

The most successful leaders don't just build their matrix.
They maintain it continuously.
They evolve it intentionally.

Left unattended, support systems degrade, misalign, and eventually fail.
Maintained regularly, they appreciate - growing stronger and more valuable over time.

When was your last maintenance check? If you can't remember, you're already adrift.

Beyond Balance: Integration as Leadership Strategy

Here's the truth about "work-life balance" that nobody wants to admit: It's a myth. A fantasy. A sasquatch that leaders chase but never capture.

Because balance implies equal weight.
Equal time.
Equal attention.

And that's not how life works.

Not for Captains. Not for anyone.

Some days your business needs 14 hours. Some days, your family needs you completely. Every day, your health demands priority - ignore it, and you'll have nothing left for either of the others.

The concept of "balance" creates a false choice - as if work and life were opposing forces that must be perfectly counterweighted.

What if we stopped trying to balance and started integrating instead?

Work-life integration isn't about equal parts. It's about whole systems functioning together.

Just like your Stability Matrix.

The most effective leaders I've worked with don't compartmentalize their lives into neat "work" and "personal" boxes. They create integrated ecosystems where each element strengthens the others:

- The insight gained from a family vacation influences their strategic thinking
- The discipline learned from business challenges improves their parenting
- The perspective gained from personal relationships enhances their leadership

One CEO I worked with struggled for years with the mythical balance. Monday through Friday belonged to the business. Weekends belonged to family. Neither got his best. Both felt shortchanged. He felt like he was failing in both arenas.

Can you relate to that?

Then he shifted to integration. He brought his family into his business world - not just at company picnics, but in meaningful conversations about challenges and victories. He brought business thinking into family life - not by treating his kids like employees, but by applying lessons about growth, communication, and purpose.

Most importantly, he stopped seeing work and life as competing priorities to be balanced and started seeing them as integrated elements of a whole system.

The result? His business thrived. His family connections deepened. His health improved.

This is the ultimate manifestation of your matrix thinking - not just integrating your professional support relationships, but integrating your entire life ecosystem.

When your Anchor knows your Navigator, your business benefits. When your personal values infuse your professional decisions, your leadership strengthens. When your whole life works as an integrated system, you discover what leadership truly means.

Integration isn't just a matrix strategy. It's a life strategy.

And it's what separates struggling leaders from thriving ones.

From Matrix to Crucible

Integration creates possibility. Crisis reveals reality.

Your matrix's true strength isn't visible during calm seas and fair weather. It emerges when storms rage, when resources dwindle, when certainty vanishes.

In the chapter ahead, we'll explore what happens when your leadership - and your matrix - faces its ultimate test. When everything you've built is threatened. When your carefully constructed support system faces challenges it wasn't designed for.

Because here's the uncomfortable truth about leadership:

It's not IF crisis will strike. It's WHEN.

And when it does, your integrated matrix won't just determine whether you survive. It will determine whether you emerge stronger.

The question isn't whether your matrix works when everything's fine. It's whether it holds together when nothing is.

That's the true test of leadership under fire. And it's where we're headed next.

REFLECT: Which relationship in your matrix operates most in isolation from the others? What opportunity are you missing because of these disconnected supporters?

ACT: Create one intentional connection between quadrants this week. Introduce your Navigator to your Champion. Have your Anchor meet your Crew. Watch what happens when your support system starts talking to itself. (and AI bots don't count for this one)

Is your support system integrated or just collected?

Most leaders collect relationships like baseball cards—separate, disconnected, and fragmented. The real power comes when your relationships amplify each other.

I've created visualization tools and reflection exercises to help you see where your matrix might be creating dangerous "lists" and how to balance your support system for maximum stability.

It's free, my gift to you.

https://TheCaptainsKeys.com/bonus

"I had all the right people, just not in the right relationship with each other. My world was completely siloed. These resources helped me create a matrix where every connection strengthens the others."

—CASEY, DIVISION PRESIDENT

⚓ NAVIGATE

To Sail the Story / Full Journey - Continue on to the next page
Study the Maps – Jump ahead to page 407

CAPTAIN'S LOG

Chart your course forward

Reflections

Action Items

NORDIC THRONE

BEYOND THE STORM
Part 9

The boat repairs progressed at a rapid pace, while Si's recovery was more measured. His stumbling speech gave way to recognizable patterns and frustration softening into determination.

From his hospital bed, he coordinated introductions between his crew and Jimmy's, sketching out a partnership strategy on the back of the cafeteria menu. Even in his weakened condition, Si's mind was intent on finding a way to succeed.

"Working jointly," Si explained, voice still shaky but thoughts clear, "will let us secure a fishing area, share information, and catch our quotas faster." His finger tapped the crude map he'd drawn. "Like those whales I showed you. Better together than alone."

The plan made sense, but the only way it worked was as a team. The problem was that this team was down a Captain.

Si wasn't one to just give advice; he lived it. His crew wasn't along for the ride or just for a big paycheck. They were fully committed to the mission and each other.

Over multiple seasons together, every crew member shared knowledge with others so that they developed a broad diversity of skills. No job was siloed, and no task too menial.

All for one, and one for all.

Navigator and relief skipper Zach immediately offered to step in for Si while every other crew member volunteered to step up their roles, including less sleep and more time on wheel watch, so Zach wasn't left alone to run the show solo 24x7.

Repairs were almost complete aboard the *Bering Steel*, and final testing in progress. In six days the crew, captains, volunteer mechanics, and boat crews had created a miracle. With many others lending a hand, every boat was able to adequately prepare for the opening of crab season tomorrow.

"Ready?" Jimmy called down from the wheelhouse to the engine room. "Here we go, in 3...2...1"

Jimmy pressed the final button in the starting sequence. The engine roared to life with a deep-throated rumble that sent a thrill through Jimmy's chest. That sound - powerful, steady, alive - told him everything he needed to know. Around him, the crew and volunteers erupted in cheers. Tom nodded silently, satisfaction in his eyes. Richie pumped his fist in the air, face split with a grin that made him look even younger. Bob clapped him on the shoulder, a gesture worth a thousand words.

Then Aidan surprised everyone. The big deckhand suddenly broke into an elaborate shoulder-popping, arm-swinging routine - part robot, part something completely his own. The crew whooped and laughed as he finished with a dramatic freeze, one massive arm pointed skyward. "Victory dance!" he announced, grinning sheepishly.

For years, Jimmy had celebrated his victories alone. A good catch. A happy customer. A perfect sunset. All experienced in solitude, with only Bella to witness. This was different. This was shared triumph. Five men against the odds. Five men proving something - to themselves, to each other, to the world. To the waiting sea.

The shared trials over the last month had transformed his mismatched crew into something formidable. Jimmy thought back to how far they had come in such a short time. They no longer needed words to communicate - a glance, a gesture, a shift in posture carried messages clearer than shouted orders. When Tom grabbed a wrench, Aidan was already there with the replacement filter. Before Richie could ask, Scott had the manual open to the right page. Old Bob hummed sea shanties as he worked, the melodies becoming their rhythm, their time-keeper in the endless days of preparation.

By night, they gathered in the galley, bent over maps and weather reports. Scott traced potential routes, his finger following currents only he could sense. Tom shared quiet stories of his ancestors who had sailed these waters for thousands of years before any English word named them. Richie shared his dreams of fatherhood, his voice filled with wonder and fear. Aidan, for once, listened more than he spoke, absorbing the wisdom around him like a sponge.

Jimmy had seen it all happen. This strange alchemy transforming five strangers into a single organism with one purpose. They might have come from different worlds – Sun'aq traditions, Colorado mountains, recovery rooms, charter boats - but they were becoming something new. Something unbreakable.

This wasn't just an engine repair.

It was a resurrection.

CHAPTER 45

The final day before launch blurred into a frenzy of preparation. The crew scrambled to check things off their list - load pots, fuel the boat, buy groceries. Divide and conquer.

Jimmy's checklists covered every surface of his cabin - detailed, methodical, repeatedly checked until the paper began disintegrating at the fold lines.

Jimmy's focus narrowed to the weather reports. An Arctic storm warning had been issued - not unusual for the Bering Sea, but the projected intensity raised red flags. He consulted Scott who poured over reports, forecasts, and fishing locations alongside him..

Wind was the real concern. Gusts to fifty, and possibly seventy miles per hour could sweep grown men off the deck. Weather like that could generate waves high enough to capsize smaller vessels, and turn routine tasks into deadly gambles.

Jimmy went outside to get some air and clear his mind. Richie stood near the starboard bow, his gaze shifting from the sea to a paper in his hand.

Richie held up an ultrasound image, his face a mixture of wonder and terror. "She's so small," he whispered.

Jimmy leaned against the rail beside him. The younger man had been uncharacteristically quiet since receiving the envelope that morning.

"Scared?" Jimmy asked.

"Terrified." Richie tucked the image carefully into his jacket pocket. "What if I can't provide for her? What if all this – " he gestured at the boat, the sea " – isn't enough?"

Jimmy watched a seagull glide effortlessly through the wind currents. "My dad used to say that fear makes a poor compass but an excellent teacher."

"What does that even mean?"

"It means you're supposed to learn from your fear, not be guided by it."

Jimmy turned to face him. "You're worried about providing for your daughter. That worry is teaching you something important about responsibility - but if you let it control your decisions, you'll miss opportunities that fear blinds you to."

Richie considered this. "Like taking this job when everyone said I was too young?"

"Exactly." Jimmy smiled. "True leadership isn't fearlessness. It's feeling the fear and finding wisdom in it, then making choices based on that wisdom instead of the fear itself."

"Is that how you do it?" Richie asked. "Make the hard calls when everyone's lives depend on them?"

Jimmy thought about Burns, about the sabotaged engine, about the storm that had nearly claimed them. "Hey buddy, I'm still learning. But I'm starting to understand that the best decisions come when we transform our fears into something stronger."

"Like what?"

"Like purpose." Jimmy nodded toward Richie's pocket where the ultrasound lay. "That little girl isn't just your responsibility. She's your purpose. And purpose outweighs fear every time."

CHAPTER 46

Pots were loaded, bait prepared, fuel tanks filled.

Sleep evaded Jimmy that final night. He lay in his bunk, listening to the sounds of the harbor coming alive around him. Engines warming up. Voices calling across the docks. The familiar symphony of anticipation and anxiety that preceded every season.

All the work. All the pain. All the learning. It all came down to this moment.

The radio crackled to life with an announcement. Crews gathered on deck, activity paused. Hard men stopped dead in their tracks. Hats in hand.

Over the radio, a prayer for the journey . . .

"Father, take this ship inside Thy hands
And protect the souls of these men
Fish with them, and stay with them
Until their journey's end
And to the Captain give guidance
And understanding of the sea
Bless his crew with fair weather
In all that's meant to be
Give peace to their families
That are back on shore
That all will return quite soon
With clear skies above
And inside your love
Beneath a harvest moon
Fill their pots like Peter's nets
On the shores of Galilee
And let them know you love them so
As they fish across the sea
And in their work and in their rest
Teach them to love their fellow man
And to love each other as you have taught
And to try and understand
That peace on earth can surely come
With your blessings and your love

For Captain and Crew of this vessel
Grant safe passage from above"

"May God bless you, keep you, and return you to those of us left behind . . . Be safe out there . . . Good luck."

Activity resumed as if an invisible hand unpaused a movie and played it double-time.

Engines fired up. Crews scrambled to throw lines. Vessels began leaving port, jockeying for position, captains eager to reach their preferred grounds first, ready for the midnight start.

Jimmy picked up the radio and asked Zach, "You ready to get this party started?"

Zach opened the mic, and called out to his crew. "You ready *Northern Star*?"

Jimmy and the crew of the *Bering Steel* didn't need a radio to hear the cheers, whoops, and hollers of their partner boat. The crew echoed back with their own cheer.

Tom called out, "Throw lines."

The *Bering Steel* and *Northern Star* eased out from the pier into the harbor.

"It's about to get real Jimmy," Zach radioed.

Jimmy responded, "Bring it!"

Captain Burns made a deliberate point of crowding the *Bering Steel* and *Northern Star* as they navigated the harbor exit, his *Nordic Throne* modern, sleek, and polished under the dock lights. As he passed, Burns locked eyes with Jimmy and slowly raised his middle finger - a silent promise that their conflict was far from over.

Jimmy turned away, focusing on the wheel beneath his hands. The narrow channel required precision. Burns was a distraction he couldn't afford. Not now. Not with everything at stake.

The combined crews of the *Bering Steel* and *Northern Star* reached their chosen grounds about 3 miles apart and waited.

Less than one hour to go.

The radio crackled to life at exactly midnight, which kicked off a surge of activity. Crab season was officially open.

The first pots splashed over the side, awaiting eight-legged red gold.

Jimmy watched with satisfaction as the crew began the methodical process of baiting and launching pots using the system they'd developed. Everything functioned smoothly. Jimmy's inexperienced crew members had been trained by Si's expert crew and worked alongside them. They put that training to use cod fishing. All the preparation was paying off huge now - way better than Jimmy expected. Following the process produced consistent results.

Jimmy called Zach for an update on the radio. The *Northern Star* was a little more than halfway through setting their crab pots, and the *Bering Steel* was just short of half. An impressive pace for a newer crew.

By late-morning, the weather began shifting. The relatively calm seas gave way to building swells. Wind picked up, driving icy spray across the deck. The storm had accelerated, arriving hours ahead of forecast.

"Change of plans," Jimmy called out over the intercom, voice carrying over the rising wind. "Weather is coming sooner than we'd like. We're setting these pots as fast and as safely possible. Double-time, but no shortcuts."

The urgency served dual purposes - catching crabs, yes, but also lightening the vessel's topside weight. Every pot in the water meant improved stability and reduced risk of capsizing.

Hour after grueling hour, they worked through deteriorating conditions. Waves broke over the rail, drenching men already soaked and chilled to the bone. Hands grew numb despite gloves. Simple tasks became exercises in focused determination.

Zach radioed Jimmy that their pots were set. The *Northern Star* was headed to the back side of St. George Island, about a five hour ride away, until the storm passed.

An hour later at 6 p.m., the last *Bering Steel* pot splashed into the churning sea. Jimmy stood and applauded his exhausted crew. Eighteen hours of hard work in miserable conditions. Zero complaints. "Get food, and try to get some sleep," he ordered. "I'm going to find us some cover while these pots soak. We'll see what we've got tomorrow."

The weather was rough as they too made their way toward St. George where the *Northern Star* had anchored. Scott took the first watch at the wheel for their bumpy ride. Jimmy continued to be amazed by his dedication and insight. Aside from being a relief captain so Jimmy could sleep, Scott was as dedicated and reliable as a clock. Even when he was sleeping, somehow Scott had the uncanny ability to automatically wake every thirty minutes to check radar and weather updates. Then, he could immediately go back to sleep if there was nothing noteworthy, or function normally on virtually no sleep if the weather was rough. His experience proved invaluable as he plotted a course that kept them in the relatively protected area of the storm system.

Other vessels weren't as fortunate. Radio chatter reported alarming conditions across the fishing grounds - fifty-foot waves, hurricane-force winds, near-zero visibility. Several captains had abandoned fishing entirely, focusing solely on survival until the system passed.

Jimmy had just settled into the wheelhouse to relieve Scott when the radio crackled to life, the universal distress call cutting through the white noise of the storm.

CHAPTER 47

Bering Steel

Bering Sea, king crab grounds

207 miles north of Dutch Harbor

"PAN-PAN! PAN-PAN! PAN-PAN! This is *Nordic Throne*! We have lost main engine power and are adrift in heavy seas. Requesting immediate assistance. This is *Nordic Throne*!"

The distress call shattered the rhythm of the *Bering Steel*'s wheelhouse like a gunshot.

Jimmy froze, coffee mug suspended halfway to his lips, a chill crawling up his spine that had nothing to do with the Arctic air howling outside.

He knew that voice.

The Coast Guard response crackled through immediately. "*Nordic Throne, Nordic Throne*, this is Coast Guard Kodiak. We copy your Pan-Pan. What is your current position, and the nature of your engine failure? How many souls on board, and what is your vessel's condition? Coast Guard Kodiak, over."

"Position 56-26 North, 167-54 West. Five souls on board—"

Scott's face hardened as he plotted the coordinates streaming through the static. The rest of the crew had materialized in the wheelhouse doorway, drawn by the unmistakable urgency in the distress call.

No one spoke.

They didn't need to.

The name "*Nordic Throne*" hung in the air between them like a curse.

Burns' voice crackled through again, stripped of its usual arrogance. "A pot got wrapped around the prop. I have a dead boat. Waves pushed us sideways. Taking on water through the engine room. We have no—"

The transmission cut to static.

Jimmy had never heard fear in Burns' voice before. Raw, primal terror that made his own chest tighten with recognition. Every fisherman knew that sound—the moment when the sea stopped being your workplace and became your executioner.

"Lost power to the pumps."

Desperation.

Scott's fingers traced the coordinates on the chart, his expression grim. "Twenty-two miles southeast, Captain. Thirty-foot seas out there, maybe bigger. It's right back into that weather system we've been running from."

Jimmy stared at the chart, his mind calculating distances and timing. Twenty-two miles in these conditions meant an hour and a half, maybe more. The *Nordic Throne* was already taking on water.

"MAYDAY! MAYDAY! MAYDAY! This is *Nordic Throne*! We are taking on water rapidly! Engine room flooding! One man overboard during evacuation attempt! Davis went over! I can't see him! Four souls remaining on board! We are preparing to abandon ship! MAYDAY! This is *Nordic Throne*!"

The words hit Jimmy like physical blows.

One man overboard.

Abandoning ship.

The Coast Guard relayed the mayday, requesting all vessels in the vicinity to assist immediately. Jimmy looked to Scott for guidance, his pulse hammering against his throat.

"What do we do here? Are we too far? Are there other ships closer?"

Scott checked the Automatic Identification System, the green blips on his screen showing nearby vessels. "Jimmy, this thing only goes thirty miles or so. I see the *Nordic Throne* here," he pointed to an icon at the edge of the screen, "but I don't see any other boats that direction."

The moment stretched between them, taut as a mooring line in a gale.

Jimmy felt the weight of his crew's eyes on him. Five men were in jeopardy out there, and he was the only captain close enough to help. And he wasn't even very close.

One of those men was Burns.

The same Burns who'd made his life hell for months. Who'd questioned his right to command, sneered at his inexperience, made him feel like a pretender in his own wheelhouse.

Aidan's face darkened, his massive frame filling the doorway. "That's Burns out there." His voice dropped to a growl. "It's karma if you ask me. Let somebody else deal with it." Tom's jaw tightened, but he said nothing. The others waited, watching.

Jimmy paused in thought. Maybe a little longer than he should have. Every instinct screamed to let Burns face the consequences of his own arrogance. But that wasn't the captain his crew needed him to be

"It doesn't matter what kind of man Burns is." Jimmy met Aidan's glare without flinching. "He's a captain. He's one of us. The crew is in trouble."

The decision felt like stepping off a cliff.

"Plot a course," he ordered Scott.

The navigator nodded once, already moving.

"Richie, get on the radio. Tell the Coast Guard we're responding. Twenty-two miles out, ETA ninety minutes."

An eternity in these frigid waters.

As if summoned by his thoughts, another voice crackled through the radio. "Coast Guard Kodiak, this is the *Alma Jane*. We are responding to the Mayday from *Nordic Throne*, approximately thirty nautical miles from scene."

Relief flooded through Jimmy. They wouldn't be alone out there.

The Coast Guard channel crackled with updates. "*Nordic Throne*, be advised, rescue vessels are being directed to your location. Maintain radio contact..."

But Burns' voice, when it came back, carried nothing but raw terror. "Lost visual on Davis... water's up to the main deck... engine room completely flooded..."

Jimmy's hands tightened on the wheel as he pushed the *Bering Steel* harder through the mounting seas. Behind him, Zach's voice cut through on their private channel.

"Hey Jimmy, don't worry about your pots. We've got your back. And you've got this!"

The encouragement connected deeper than Zach could ever know.

Now five men's lives hung in the balance.

Time to find out what kind of captain he really was.

CHAPTER 48

Bering Steel

30 minutes from last known position of Nordic Throne

The *Bering Steel* carved through waves that seemed determined to drive her back toward safety. Jimmy could feel her straining beneath him, her steel hull groaning as each new swell tried to tear her apart.

Through the wheelhouse windows, he watched Tom and Bob prepare rescue gear on the deck below. Their movements were precise despite the roll and pitch, years of training taking over when instinct mattered most.

His thoughts drifted to the safety videos he'd watched during training. Hypothermia. Core temperature dropping one degree at a time. Confusion setting in. Then the paradoxical undressing as the freezing brain sent false signals.

Then death.

In thirty-two-degree water, a man had maybe twenty minutes before his body shut down completely.

Some calculations didn't require computers.

"Lost all power!" Burns' voice was nearly swallowed by static. "Haven't seen Davis since he went overboard. Hopkins in the water in a survival suit... Miller, Rogers, and I are launching life raft..."

The *Nordic Throne*'s radio gave a long, tortured squeal before Burns' voice returned, fainter now.

"Abandoning ship! All remaining crew in survival suits... launching life raft..."

Jimmy's knuckles were white on the wheel. The *Nordic Throne* was going down. Fifteen miles of storm-tossed ocean still separated the *Bering Steel* from the four men fighting for their lives in a life raft.

And two were already in the frigid water.

"Coast Guard Kodiak, this is Rescue 471," a crisp female voice cut through the static. "Weather is finally stable enough to launch. We are a go for emergency rescue. ETA to scene approximately forty minutes if conditions hold."

A helicopter. Thank God.

But forty minutes was still an eternity.

"Roger, Rescue 471," Jimmy responded. "This is *Bering Steel*. We'll be first on scene. Will coordinate with you on arrival."

"Copy that, *Bering Steel*. Keep us posted on what you're seeing down there."

The professional calm in the pilot's voice was reassuring. Jimmy had heard that tone before—the kind of controlled competence that came from years of pulling people back from the edge.

He was going to need that kind of competence today.

Bering Steel

10 minutes from last known position of Nordic Throne

"I see something!" Aidan's voice cut through the howling wind from his position on the bow. Waving and pointing toward the object, he continued, "It's Orange! Hard to tell, might be a survival suit!"

Jimmy's heart hammered against his ribs.

One suit.

Burns had reported one man overboard initially. This had to be Davis.

"Hold on, buddy," Jimmy said aloud, his voice swallowed by the storm. "We're coming."

The *Bering Steel* was running out of time. The *Nordic Throne*'s crew was running out of time.

And somewhere between the dark sky and darker sea, the line between revenge and redemption had vanished entirely.

"*Bering Steel*, Coast Guard Kodiak," the radio crackled. "The Mayday vessel *Nordic Throne* is no longer on radar. We are receiving an EPIRB signal from the vessel about two miles west of your location. Signal is consistent with water deployment."

The ship had gone down.

Jimmy stared at the churning water ahead, knowing that everything that mattered now was what happened in the next few minutes.

CHAPTER 49

Bering Steel

Last known position of Nordic Throne

The *Bering Steel* lurched violently as another wave crashed over her bow, sweeping across the deck in a frigid torrent. Jimmy braced himself against the helm, muscles burning with the effort of keeping the wheel steady.

Through the spray-lashed windows, he could see the survival suit's reflective tape catching their searchlights, flashing like a desperate beacon in the darkness.

"Range two hundred yards!" Scott called out, his voice tight with tension.

"Coast Guard Kodiak, *Bering Steel* is on scene," Jimmy radioed. "We have visual contact with a survivor. Standing by..."

His hands moved with instinctive precision, years of boat handling experience guiding him as he maneuvered toward the figure in the water. The wrong approach could push the swimmer away—or worse, pull them under the hull.

Every fisherman knew the stories of rescuers who became victims when a desperate maneuver went wrong.

"Coming up on the port side!" Richie shouted toward the wheelhouse, his voice barely carrying over the storm's roar.

The crew moved with the precision born of countless drills. Tom and Bob had already deployed the rescue ladder and lines, the wind whipping the ropes like angry serpents. Aidan stood ready with the grappling hook, his massive frame braced against the rail.

"Survivor coming alongside!" Aidan's voice carried faintly through the screaming wind.

Jimmy watched from the helm as his crew worked in synchronized motion. Tom and Bob, secured by safety lines, reached over the rail. But as they pulled the survival suit closer, Jimmy saw their body language change.

Something was wrong.

"It's empty," Bob's voice came over the radio, disbelief cutting through the static. "The suit's empty."

The words hit Jimmy like a rogue wave.

An empty suit meant one thing—its intended occupant had already been claimed by the sea.

Davis was gone.

A grim silence descended on the wheelhouse. Jimmy stared at the empty orange fabric bobbing in their spotlight, a hollow reminder of how quickly the sea could claim a life.

"Wait!" Scott's voice cut through the despair. "There's another suit in the water. Two hundred yards east."

Jimmy's pulse quickened. "Another survivor?"

"There's a strobe light." Scott's eyes remained fixed to the binoculars. "Could be Hopkins."

Jimmy didn't hesitate. "Tom, Bob—stand ready. Aidan, get the spotlight on that bearing."

No time to mourn Davis.

No time to process what an empty survival suit meant for the others.

Only time to act.

The *Bering Steel* altered course, pitching violently as they turned broadside to the massive swells. The spotlight's beam sliced through the darkness, reflecting off wave tops as Aidan methodically searched the churning sea.

"There!" Aidan's voice carried above the storm. "Survival suit! He's moving!"

The spotlight caught a glimpse of orange—a man weakly swimming, or trying to. His movements were erratic and uncoordinated.

Hypothermia was winning the race.

"He's not going to last another five minutes," Scott murmured, meant for Jimmy alone.

Jimmy knew he was right. Hopkins' body language told the story—sluggish movements, increasingly long pauses between strokes. The man was shutting down, one degree at a time.

"Bring us alongside," Jimmy ordered. "Aidan, get the recovery pole. We're not losing this one."

The *Bering Steel* eased through the waves, Jimmy working the controls with delicate precision despite the treacherous conditions. Too fast or too close, and they'd run Hopkins over. Too slow or too far, and they'd lose him to the darkness.

"Ten yards!" Tom called from the rail.

Hopkins had stopped swimming. His head lolled back in the survival suit, a deep gash visible across his forehead. Blood mixed with seawater on the orange fabric.

He was conscious but fading fast.

"Five yards!"

Aidan extended the recovery pole, its hook aimed for the straps of Hopkins' survival suit. The boat rolled, and the first attempt missed as a wave lifted the swimmer away.

"Come on," Aidan muttered, teeth gritted. "Just... stay... still."

The second attempt connected. The hook caught in the suit's shoulder harness with a solid click that Jimmy could hear even over the storm.

"Got him!" Aidan shouted, immediately bracing against the rail as the boat rolled. "Pulling him in!"

Tom and Bob joined him, three men hauling together against the sea's resistance. Inch by inch, they drew Hopkins toward the hull.

"He's not responding," Bob called out, voice tight with worry.

They managed to secure a rescue strap beneath Hopkins' arms. As they prepared to lift him aboard, a massive wave crashed over the port side, momentarily burying all four men beneath a wall of frigid water.

Jimmy held his breath, counting seconds that felt like hours.

One. Two. Three.

Then the water cleared, revealing all three crewmen still at their posts—and Hopkins still secured to the line.

With a final heave, they pulled him aboard, his body limp as a rag doll.

"Get him below!" Jimmy ordered. "Full treatment protocol!"

As they rushed Hopkins below deck, Scott turned to Jimmy with grim satisfaction in his eyes.

"One down," he said quietly.

Jimmy nodded, already turning back to the storm.

"Three to go."

CHAPTER 50

"Radar showing another contact," Scott reported, his voice deliberately steady. "Larger return, could be the life raft. Half mile southeast."

"Set course," Jimmy ordered, already spinning the wheel. "Richie, get on the radio. Tell the Coast Guard we're tracking the raft."

"*Bering Steel*, Coast Guard Kodiak," the radio crackled. "Be advised, the life raft signal is degrading. Current's pulling it southeast of your position."

Jimmy pushed the throttle forward, feeling his boat shudder under the strain. The *Nordic Throne*'s survivors had reported the raft was damaged during deployment. It was taking on water.

Time was running out.

"How long before we lose any chance of recovery?" Jimmy asked Scott quietly.

"At this drift speed?" Scott calculated quickly, his eyes never leaving the radar. "Twenty minutes if it can stay upright. Maybe less. The sea is a washing machine out there."

Jimmy felt the weight of command settling on his shoulders like a lead blanket. Three men in a sinking raft, drifting away from them with every passing minute.

One of them was Burns.

The man who'd made his life hell was depending on him now.

"Raft, raft, raft!" Aidan's voice carried from the bow. "Life raft, three hundred yards! Port side!"

Through sheets of rain and sea spray, Jimmy caught glimpses of orange fabric. The raft was nearly awash, barely staying afloat as waves crashed over it. He could not see people in the closed raft. He hoped that there were three figures huddled inside, holding on to life itself.

"Too rough for crane recovery," Tom shouted, his voice barely audible over the storm. "We'll have to get lines to them!"

Jimmy studied the sea state, watching the pattern of the waves. The wind was gusting over sixty knots now, turning the surface into chaos—white foam and shifting mountains of water that could crush a boat in seconds.

"Coast Guard Kodiak, this is Rescue 471," the helicopter pilot's voice cut through the static. "We're fighting severe turbulence. ETA now fifteen minutes if conditions hold."

"We can't wait," Jimmy replied, decision made. "We're going in."

"Huge set coming in!" Scott's warning cut through the howling wind. "Get ready to hold on!"

From his vantage point, Jimmy could see it building ahead—a series of waves stacking up, feeding off each other, growing into monsters. They'd have to time this perfectly or lose their one chance.

And maybe their lives in the process.

"Aidan, Tom—get ready with the rescue guns. Soon as we're in range, I want lines on that raft." Jimmy's hands were steady on the wheel despite the adrenaline flooding his system. "Bob, stand by with the life rings."

The raft was being tossed like a toy now, sometimes disappearing completely between waves. Through the spotlight's beam, Jimmy could see Miller frantically bailing while Rogers tried to keep the raft oriented into the seas.

Burns was shouting into his radio, the words lost in the storm's roar.

"Maybe sixty seconds until this set!" Scott called out, his eyes locked on the water. "These are going to be forty-footers at least!"

Jimmy felt time compress around him. Every decision mattered now. Every second counted.

"Now!" he shouted as they crested a wave. "Get those lines out before the big ones hit!"

Aidan and Tom fired the rescue guns simultaneously, compressed air launching the projectiles with sharp hisses. The lines arced out through the rain, trailing their buoyant ropes behind them.

One fell short, swallowed by a wave.

The other...

"They've got it!" Richie shouted from his position by the spotlight. "Burns has the line!"

"Thirty seconds!" Scott's voice was tight with tension. "Captain, we need to turn into these waves!"

Jimmy shook his head. "Not yet. Need to get them closer first."

He'd seen what these seas could do to a rescue line drawn too quickly through the water—it would be like dragging men through a meat grinder.

Scott picked up the intercom, "Hew Crew, big waves coming in twenty seconds. Hold on, hold on, hold on!"

Burns and Miller were pulling themselves along the rope now, fighting against waves that threatened to tear it from their grasp. Twenty yards... fifteen...

Rogers remained in the raft, still fighting to keep it oriented.

"Ten seconds!"

"Almost there..." Jimmy could see their faces now in the spotlight's glare—exhausted, terrified, but moving hand over hand toward safety.

"They're not going to make it before that set hits," Aidan shouted, desperation edging his voice. "We have to pull them in now!"

The first giant wave was already visible—a black wall of water rising behind the raft like judgment itself.

Jimmy made his decision the way he always had—with his gut and his heart.

"Everyone, hold on! Bob—get ready to grab them."

He spun the wheel hard over, bringing the *Bering Steel*'s bow around to face the coming mountains.

"Ten seconds!"

Burns and Miller were almost to the hull. Both had managed to grab the life rings Bob had thrown. Rogers was still in the raft, waving them on, shouting encouragement, lost in the wind's howl.

Shouting to men he thought he hoped to see again.

"NOW!"

Jimmy gunned the engine, using the wave's own power to lift the stern. For a heart-stopping moment, Burns and Miller were suspended in the spotlight's beam, level with the rail.

"GRAB THEM!"

The *Bering Steel*'s crew surged forward as one. Bob and Aidan caught the two men, hauling them bodily over the rail as the wave crested.

The raft, suddenly lightened, flipped completely.

Rogers disappeared beneath the churning foam.

"MAN OVERBOARD!" Tom's voice was lost in the wave's roar as it broke over them. Icy water crashed across the deck, threatening to sweep them all into the abyss.

Jimmy fought the wheel as the boat went nearly vertical, bow pointing toward stars barely visible through the storm. The second wave of the set was already building behind the first.

Even bigger.

"HOLD ON!"

The *Bering Steel* hung suspended between sea and sky for what felt like eternity before crashing down into the trough. Salt water exploded over the wheelhouse windows, momentarily blinding Jimmy.

Warning alarms blared as sensors were overwhelmed.

The third wave hit them broadside before they could fully recover. The boat rolled hard to starboard, rail disappearing under water. Jimmy could hear equipment breaking loose below deck, could feel the engine struggling as the propeller cleared the surface.

For three terrible seconds, he thought they might not come back.

That the *Bering Steel* might roll completely, joining the *Nordic Throne* on the ocean floor.

Then slowly, agonizingly, she righted herself, shaking off the sea's fury like a wounded animal refusing to surrender.

The last thing Jimmy heard from the deck was OVERBOARD. He frantically counted heads. Trying to place each member of his crew and which side the person went over.

Relief washed over him as he counted not only his crew but three extras on the deck.

"Coast Guard Kodiak, *Bering Steel*," Scott managed to transmit with reasonable composure. "Three survivors recovered. One from the water, two from the life raft. Two men still missing. We have three on board. Need immediate medical attention. One has a severe head injury, one a broken arm, and all are hypothermic."

"Copy, *Bering Steel*," came the response. "Rescue 471 is approaching your position."

The Coast Guard helicopter's distinctive thrum finally cut through the storm's howl, its searchlight sweeping across the churning waters like the finger of God.

Jimmy tracked the aircraft's search pattern from his wheelhouse, watching as it methodically covered the area where Rogers had disappeared. The pilot's skill was evident, holding the helicopter steady despite winds that could slam it into the sea in an instant.

"Rescue 471 on scene," the pilot reported. "Visibility one mile and steady. Searching for the remaining survivor."

Below deck, Scott worked frantically over their rescued men. Burns lay on the galley table, his broken arm splinted, skin waxy with hypothermia. Miller sat slumped against the bulkhead, conscious but incoherent.

Hopkins was the worst—still unconscious, the gash on his forehead requiring constant attention to prevent blood loss.

"Life raft debris spotted," came the pilot's voice over the radio. "No visual on survivor."

Jimmy stared at the churning water where Rogers had vanished, carrying with him someone's son, someone's husband, someone's father.

The sea had claimed its price.

Three men saved. Two lost.

The brutal math of the sea written in salt and sorrow.

"Rescue 471, *Bering Steel*, we need a medical evacuation. All three are banged up pretty bad. One has a nasty head wound. One broken arm. All are hypothermic. Need immediate medical attention."

Jimmy checked his instruments. The engine was running rough from being over-revved, and they'd taken on water, but the pumps were keeping up.

"Affirmative, *Bering Steel*. Rescue 471, moving in for extraction."

"Damage report!" Jimmy called out, his voice hoarse from shouting over the storm.

"Port crane's damaged," Richie reported from the deck. "Lost most of the rescue gear. But we're still seaworthy."

More importantly, his crew was intact.

CHAPTER 51

The Coast Guard helicopter hovered thirty feet above the *Bering Steel*'s deck, its rotors slicing through the wind with mechanical precision. Jimmy watched from the wheelhouse as the rescue basket descended through the rotor wash.

"Four minutes in this position," the pilot announced over the radio. "Fuel's getting critical."

Below, Tom and Aidan secured Miller into the basket first. The man had regained consciousness but remained dangerously hypothermic, his skin pale and clammy under the deck lights.

"Hopkins... Davis..." Miller's cracked lips formed the names with effort.

Jimmy leaned closer. "We're still looking."

Some lies were necessary.

The basket began its ascent, spinning slightly in the turbulent air. Burns would be next, then Hopkins on a stretcher for the final evacuation.

As they prepared Burns for extraction, the older captain caught Jimmy's arm with surprising strength.

"Why?"

The single word carried the weight of everything unsaid between them. All the insults. All the sneers. All the times Burns had questioned Jimmy's right to command.

Jimmy met his eyes without flinching. "Because that's what captains do."

Burns stared at him for a long moment, understanding passing between them. Not forgiveness—that might come later, if at all. But recognition.

One captain to another.

Burns was secured and hoisted up to the waiting helicopter. As the basket rose, he caught Jimmy's eye across the distance. No words passed between them, but something did—a look of raw gratitude mixed with something deeper. A reckoning postponed but not forgotten.

Hopkins went up last, still unconscious but breathing. The crew watched the stretcher disappear into the helicopter's belly, carrying with it their silent prayers.

Jimmy raised a hand in acknowledgment as the aircraft banked away, carrying Miller, Hopkins, and Burns toward medical care and the relative safety of Dutch Harbor.

The gesture wasn't friendship.

It was simply what one captain owed another.

As the sound of rotors faded into the storm, Jimmy turned back to his crew. The deck showed the aftermath of their rescue—scattered gear, damaged equipment, evidence of their battle with the sea.

But his men stood tall despite their exhaustion, faces streaked with salt spray and eyes clear with the satisfaction that came only from doing the impossible.

Scott appeared in the wheelhouse doorway, his face etched with fatigue but steady with purpose.

"Current's pushing us southeast," he reported. "Those pots we set yesterday should be right in our path."

Jimmy nodded, keeping his eyes on the horizon where the storm was finally beginning to break. The sky was brightening to the east, painting the clouds in shades of gold and crimson.

Later, there would be time for questions. Time to process what had happened out here, what it meant that he'd risked everything to save the man who'd made his life hell.

For now, there was only the sea, the ship, and the work that defined them.

"Coffee's on," Scott added quietly. "And I'm breaking out those chocolate bars you think we don't know about."

A small smile touched Jimmy's lips as he adjusted their heading. Some secrets weren't worth keeping.

They had work to do and a quota to fill.

The sea waited for no one—not even heroes.

"Let's go pull some pots."

☸ NAVIGATE

Study the Maps / Full Journey - Continue on to the next page
To Sail the Story - Ride a wave to page407

CAPTAIN'S LOG

Chart your course forward

Reflections

____

____

____

____

____

____

Action Items

____

____

____

____

____

____

U.S.
COAST GUA

LEADERSHIP UNDER FIRE
WHEN EVERYTHING BURNS BUT YOU DON'T

"The ultimate measure of a man is not where he stands in moments of comfort and convenience, but where he stands at times of challenge and controversy."
— MARTIN LUTHER KING JR.

When storms hit, Captains don't have time for committees.
They don't have time for uncertainty.
They don't have time for fear.

And neither do you.

The Crucible Moment

Here's the thing about fire: It doesn't care about your resume. It doesn't respect your title. It doesn't negotiate with your ego.

It simply reveals.

That carefully constructed leadership persona? That confident decision-maker image? That unflappable executive your team thinks you are?

Fire melts them all away.

What remains isn't who you claim to be on LinkedIn. It's who you've actually been becoming all along. In the quiet moments. In the small choices. In the habits nobody sees.

I've watched seemingly unshakable CEOs capsize under pressure while unassuming managers navigate the same waters with remarkable steadiness.

The difference wasn't talent, experience, or even temperament. It was preparation. Not crisis plans or contingency documents. Matrix preparation.

Like Dave, whose software company suffered a catastrophic data breach affecting millions of users. His technical team was ready. His PR response was textbook perfect. His legal strategy was sound.

But Dave himself? He folded.

Not publicly. Not obviously. But internally – where the navigation instruments actually matter. His decision-making froze. His communication faltered. His confidence collapsed.

Why? Because his matrix wasn't ready.

He had an impressive Crew – technical experts and crisis responders who executed their roles flawlessly.

He had a solid Navigator – legal and strategic advisors who charted the recovery path.

He even had powerful Champions–industry allies who vouched for his company's integrity during the fallout.

What he lacked was an Anchor.

When reporters questioned his leadership, when customers abandoned the platform, when his board started discussing his replacement – he had nowhere to ground himself. No one who could remind him who he was beneath the CEO title. No one who could separate his worth from his worst moment.

So he drifted. Then he sank.

Six months later, he was gone. The company survived. He didn't.

Not physically. Professionally.

Crisis doesn't just test your strategy or your operations or your messaging. It tests your matrix. It tests integration.

And here's the uncomfortable truth from the US Navy SEAL culture:
You don't rise to the occasion. You fall to the level of your preparation.

Is your leadership matrix ready for the fire? Or will it melt when the temperature rises?

When Everything Burns

The most dangerous storms aren't the ones with the highest waves. They're the ones that hit from multiple directions at once.

The financial shortfall, plus the key employee departure, plus the market shift, plus the competitive threat, plus the personal health challenge.

One problem? You can navigate around it. Two simultaneous crises? You can prioritize. Five simultaneous explosions? That's when most leaders abandon ship.

Not because they lack capability. Because they lack capacity.

Individual strength won't save you when you're surrounded by fire. Only a fully activated, integrated matrix will.

I watched Maria navigate exactly this kind of perfect storm. Her manufacturing company faced:

- A major client bankruptcy instantly vaporized 40% of revenue
- A critical material shortage with no clear alternative source
- A senior executive's unexpected resignation
- A hostile acquisition attempt from a competitor
- Her own diagnosis with a serious health condition requiring immediate treatment

Any one of these would qualify as a company-threatening crisis. Together, they should have been fatal.

But Maria had built her matrix intentionally, with integration at its core.

Her Navigator helped her identify the one thread connecting these crises – the underlying market shift that had contributed to each. Rather than fighting five separate fires, she could address the root cause.

Her Crew mobilized with unprecedented autonomy, making decisions Maria would normally handle, implementing solutions rather than just identifying problems.

Her Champion activated dormant industry connections, opening doors to new clients and alternative suppliers that weren't accessible through normal channels.

Her Anchor – her former mentor – provided perspective that transformed her health diagnosis from a devastating blow to a clarifying moment about what truly mattered.

Most importantly, these relationships worked together – her Navigator briefing her Crew, her Champion connecting with her Anchor, all four creating a support system greater than the sum of its parts.

Like a ship with watertight compartments, Maria's integrated matrix couldn't sink from a single breach. When one section took damage, the others compensated, maintaining buoyancy until repairs could be made.

Maria's company didn't just survive. It transformed.

Within eighteen months, her business had:

- Replaced the lost revenue with higher-margin clients
- Pioneered an innovative alternative to the scarce material
- Promoted internal talent to fill the executive gap
- Fended off the hostile takeover with a more attractive partnership
- Created leadership systems that didn't depend on her daily presence

Was it easy? Of course not. Was it smooth? Never. Was it possible without her integrated matrix? Absolutely not.

The fires will come. The question isn't if. The question is who will be standing with you when they do.

The Isolation Trap (Redux)

Want to know the most dangerous moment in any crisis?

It's not when the bad news arrives. It's not when the threat materializes. It's not even when resources run out.

It's when you decide to captain alone.

Remember the isolation trap? It claims more leaders than any external threat ever could. That's why it keeps emerging.

It starts innocently enough: "I need to figure this out before I involve others."
"I don't want to burden my team until I have a plan."
"No one else can understand what I'm facing."

These aren't just thoughts. They're trapdoors. Each one opens to a deeper level of isolation. Each one harder to escape than the last.

I watched Josh fall through every one of them. When his tech startup's primary technology failed spectacularly during a major client implementation, his first instinct wasn't to activate his matrix.

It was to hide.

From his team: "They'll lose confidence if they see me uncertain."
From his coach: "He's never been through this. Besides, I don't want to disappoint him."
From his investors: "They'll pull funding, or kick me out, if they know how bad it is."
From his family: "Everyone will worry if they understand we could lose everything."

So he carried it alone. Made decisions alone. Developed solutions alone.

And those solutions? They failed. Not because Josh wasn't brilliant. He was. But a crisis doesn't just test your intelligence. It tests your perspective. Your blind spots. Your ability to see around corners when your vision is clouded by fear.

The very relationships Josh was trying to protect by isolating himself were the ones he needed most to navigate the crisis. The very people he was trying to shield from uncertainty held perspectives that could have saved his company.

His Navigator could have spotted the iceberg he missed in the fog. His Crew could have trimmed the sails when he was fighting the wheel. His Champions could have called in rescue vessels he didn't know were nearby. His Anchor could have steadied him when panic clouded his judgment.

Instead, he faced the storm alone. And like most who do, his ship capsized.

Here's the paradox of leadership isolation:
The more responsibility you feel, the more you need your matrix.
The more pressure you face, the more you need multiple perspectives.
The more overwhelmed you become, the more you need others to share the load.

Yet these are precisely the moments when most leaders withdraw. When they mistake self-reliance for strength. When they confuse isolation with leadership.

The strongest response to crisis isn't heroic solitude. It's leaning on your Stability Matrix.

Not after you've figured it out. Not when you have a perfect plan. Now. When everything is still on fire. When you're not sure which way to turn. When the outcome is anything but certain.

That's when your matrix proves its worth. Not just as support, but as salvation.

The Full Matrix Response

Crisis doesn't just test your leadership. It tests your matrix design.

Many leaders don't consciously build a support system at all. They don't even think of it as a system. The ones who do architect something often build their support system for calm seas. For gentle winds. For predictable currents. The normal stuff.

Then they're shocked when it buckles in the storm.

Like building a pleasure yacht, then wondering why it breaks apart in hurricane waters.

A crisis-ready matrix isn't just stronger. It's different.
It supports differently, communicates differently, and functions differently than a fair-weather support system. It's designed to be an all-weather system.

First, it functions simultaneously, not sequentially.

There's no time for one-by-one consultation when waves are crashing over the bow. This is an "all hands" situation. Your entire matrix should function as a unified support system.

I watched Grace handle this brilliantly when her company's primary distribution partner suddenly went bankrupt. Instead of calling advisors individually, she convened an emergency session with key representatives from each quadrant:

- Her Navigator (Business Coach and attorney) for strategic implications
- Her Crew (Leadership Team) for operational response
- Her Champion (Top client and best referral partner) for industry messaging
- Her Anchor (Best friend for 25 years) for personal counsel

Within six hours, she had a comprehensive response plan addressing every dimension of the crisis. Not because she was a genius, but because she accessed the collective intelligence of her entire matrix at once.

Second, it communicates transparently, not selectively.

Crisis amplifies information gaps. What you don't share becomes what others can't solve.

When Mark's company faced a major product safety crisis that affected kids. It was bad. And I mean bad, bad. He made one critical decision: total transparency within his matrix. No sugarcoating the severity. No withholding uncomfortable details. No selective sharing based on "need to know."

The result?

- His Navigator could provide guidance based on complete information.
- His Crew could implement solutions, knowing the full challenge.
- His Champions could advocate with an authentic understanding.
- His Anchor could support him with a clear perspective on the actual stakes.

THE FULL MATRIX RESPONSE
How all four quadrants activate simultaneously during a crisis

Third, it focuses on solutions, not blame.

When the ship is taking on water, there's no time for arguing about who left the porthole open. The only question that matters is "How do we stay afloat?"

Roger embedded this principle in his matrix before the crisis hit. When his company's largest client threatened to leave over an implementation failure, his team's first response wasn't "Who screwed up?" but "How do we make this right?"

This wasn't accidental. It was cultural. Roger had built a matrix where accountability meant owning solutions, not just mistakes. Where every relationship was oriented toward forward movement, not backward blame.

The result? A crisis that could have sunk his company became a transformation that strengthened it. Not just repairing the client relationship, but fundamentally improving how they delivered services.

A crisis-ready matrix isn't just a fair-weather system that tries harder. It's a fundamentally different vessel built for different waters.

Have you designed your Stability Matrix just for sunny days? Or is it built to withstand the storm? How about an arctic hurricane?

And when that storm hits, big or small, how you communicate will determine whether your matrix provides its full strength or merely a fraction of its potential.

Communication Under Pressure

Here's the brutal truth about crisis communication: The story you tell yourself determines the story you tell others.

And the story you tell others determines whether your matrix activates effectively or fails catastrophically.

Most leaders get this exactly wrong.

They filter information to prevent panic. They delay bad news to "get all the facts." They sugarcoat severity to maintain confidence.

And in doing so, they cripple the very support system they need most.

Consider the contrast between two CEOs facing almost identical supply chain collapses:

James communicated partially. Selectively. Optimistically. "We're facing some challenges, but we have it under control." "I just need a little time to sort this out." "Don't worry, we've got this."

His Navigator received insufficient coordinates for effective course plotting. His Crew lacked visibility to navigate through dangerous waters. His Champions advocated based on an incomplete understanding of the storm. His Anchor supported the person James pretended to be, not who he actually was.

The result? Misaligned efforts. Inadequate solutions. Eroding trust.

Then there's Alicia.

When her company's supply chain imploded, she communicated fully. Directly. Honestly. "Here's exactly what we know right now." "These are the critical questions we don't have answers to yet." "This is the potential impact if we don't solve this quickly."

Her Navigator received complete information for meaningful guidance. Her Crew understood the true stakes driving their implementation work. Her Champions advocated with authentic knowledge of the challenge. Her Anchor supported the real Alicia, not a composed facade.

The result? Coordinated response. Innovative solutions. Strengthened trust.

The difference wasn't just communication style. It was communication integrity.

Alicia understood a fundamental truth about how the matrix functions: Your support system can only be as effective as the information you give it.

Half-truths yield half-solutions. Partial information generates partial responses. Artificial calm creates artificial support.

The most powerful phrase in crisis leadership isn't "I have a plan," or "Follow me," or even "Here's what we'll do."

It's simply: "Here's what's really happening."

These five words engage your matrix more effectively than any command or directive. They transform the dynamic instantly - from performance to partnership. From audience to allies.

The raw, unvarnished truth creates something rare in business: authentic alignment.

Your Anchor can't ground you if you're floating on fiction.
Your Crew can't execute without real conditions.

Your Navigator can't chart without accurate coordinates.
Your Champion can't advocate without genuine understanding.

Candor doesn't just build trust. It builds capability.
It turns passengers into crew members.
It transforms observers into problem-solvers.
It converts the tentative into the committed.

Crisis doesn't demand superhuman strength.
It demands superhuman honesty.

First with yourself.
Then with your matrix.
Finally, with the world.

The story you tell yourself in crisis becomes the reality you and your organization live through. Choose your narrative carefully.

Are you telling yourself the truth? Or a comfortable lie that might just cost you everything?

From Defense to Offense

Most captains survive the storm. Few harness its power.

They focus so completely on defense – on protection, preservation, survival – that they miss the hidden opportunities for offense. For transformation. For advantage.

This isn't just a missed opportunity. It's a fundamental misunderstanding of what a crisis actually is.

Crisis isn't just a threat. It's inflection. It's not just danger. It's a possibility in disguise. It's not just something to endure. It's something to harness.

I watched two medical device companies respond to the same FDA regulatory change that suddenly made their flagship products non-compliant. Both had similar resources. Both faced identical threats. Both leaders leaned on their matrix.

But Rick played defense. Elaine played offense.

Rick battened down the hatches. Cut costs. Weathered the storm until conditions normalized.

His Navigator helped him identify where to retrench. His Crew implemented protection measures and efficiency protocols. His Champions reassured stakeholders about stability and continuity. His Anchor reminded him this was temporary, that calm seas would return.

It worked exactly as designed, and Rick's company survived. It emerged largely intact, ready to resume business as usual when the crisis passed. Win!

Then there was Elaine.

While also addressing immediate threats, she asked a different question: "What opportunities has this storm revealed that weren't visible before?"

Her Navigator helped her identify strategic currents that the crisis had changed. Her Crew implemented new sailing techniques that the crisis made necessary. Her Champions connected her to partners seeking similar transformation. Her Anchor helped her see beyond survival to reinvention.

Elaine's company didn't just survive. It transformed.

It emerged fundamentally stronger, with new capabilities, new market positions, and new competitive advantages. Massive WIN!

The difference? Matrix orientation.

Rick's matrix was designed for preservation. Elaine's matrix was designed for transformation.

Both worked as intended. Both delivered exactly what they were designed to deliver.

This isn't about optimism versus pessimism. It's not about positive thinking or seeing silver linings.

It's about matrix design that incorporates offensive capability alongside defensive necessity.

It's about relationships that create possibilities rather than just prevent disasters.

It's about support systems oriented toward where you want to go, not just what you want to avoid.

The strongest matrices don't just help you survive the storm. They help you harness its winds.

Not in a predatory or opportunistic way, but in the sailor's sense – understanding that the same wind that threatens destruction can also power unprecedented forward movement when your sails are properly set.

Is your matrix designed only to weather storms? Or is it designed to harness them?

The difference determines not just how you emerge from a crisis, but who you become through it.

The Crisis Legacy

When the storm has passed, when the seas have calmed, when the immediate danger has receded – that's when most leaders make their biggest mistake.

They exhale. They relax. They return to normal.

And in doing so, they waste the most powerful opportunity crisis creates: The opportunity for permanent transformation.

Crisis changes everything. Not just temporarily. Permanently.

It alters relationship dynamics. It reveals structural weaknesses. It exposes hidden strengths. It clarifies priorities. It establishes new patterns.

These changes don't disappear when the crisis ends. They become your new foundation - if you let them.

I watched Patricia navigate this brilliantly after her company weathered a potential extinction-level event – the loss of their primary technology platform when a key vendor abruptly shut down.

For six weeks, her entire organization operated in emergency mode. New solutions were created on the fly. Decision-making protocols were compressed from days to minutes. Cross-functional collaboration became the norm rather than the exception.

When they finally stabilized with a new platform, Patricia didn't say, "Great job, everyone. Now let's get back to normal."

She said, "What did we just learn about who we can be?"

BRILLIANT!

Together with her matrix, she identified the crisis-forged patterns worth preserving:

- The accelerated decision-making that had eliminated bureaucratic delays

- The cross-functional collaboration that had broken down departmental silos
- The transparent communication that had created unprecedented alignment
- The emphasis on outcomes rather than procedures that had enabled innovation

These weren't just crisis responses. They were crisis advantages. Advantages made possible not by individual quadrants working in isolation, but by the seamless integration of all four - Navigator informing Crew, Champion supporting Navigator, Anchor providing calm in chaos.

The integrated matrix doesn't just perform during a crisis; it transforms through it.

Advantages that would disappear if she allowed her organization to revert to pre-crisis patterns.

So she didn't. She institutionalized them. Made them the new normal. Not through policies or mandates, but through intentional matrix reinforcement.

Her Navigator helped her identify which crisis patterns created a strategic advantage. Her Crew implemented systems to maintain these patterns beyond emergency conditions. Her Champions advocated for these new approaches with key stakeholders. Her Anchor helped her personally embody these changes in her leadership style.

The result? A company that didn't just survive a crisis, but was transformed by it. Not temporarily. Permanently.

This is the crisis legacy: The enduring transformation that outlasts the immediate threat.

It doesn't happen by accident. It happens by intention. It happens through integration. It happens because your matrix doesn't just help you survive the fire – it helps you capture the energy it releases.

Most leaders waste this opportunity. They treat crisis as an aberration to overcome rather than a catalyst to harness. They focus so completely on returning to normal that they miss the chance to establish a better normal.

Don't make this mistake.

When your crisis passes – and it will pass – don't just exhale. Extract.

Extract every lesson. Extract every insight. Extract every advantage.

Then build them into your foundation.

That's how crisis becomes opportunity. Not through wishful thinking or motivational slogans, but through intentional matrix integration that transforms temporary adaptation into permanent evolution.

Is your matrix designed to help you survive a crisis? Or is it designed to help you be transformed by it?

The difference will determine not just what you do in the fire, but who you become through it.

And *who you become is the only crisis outcome that truly matters.*

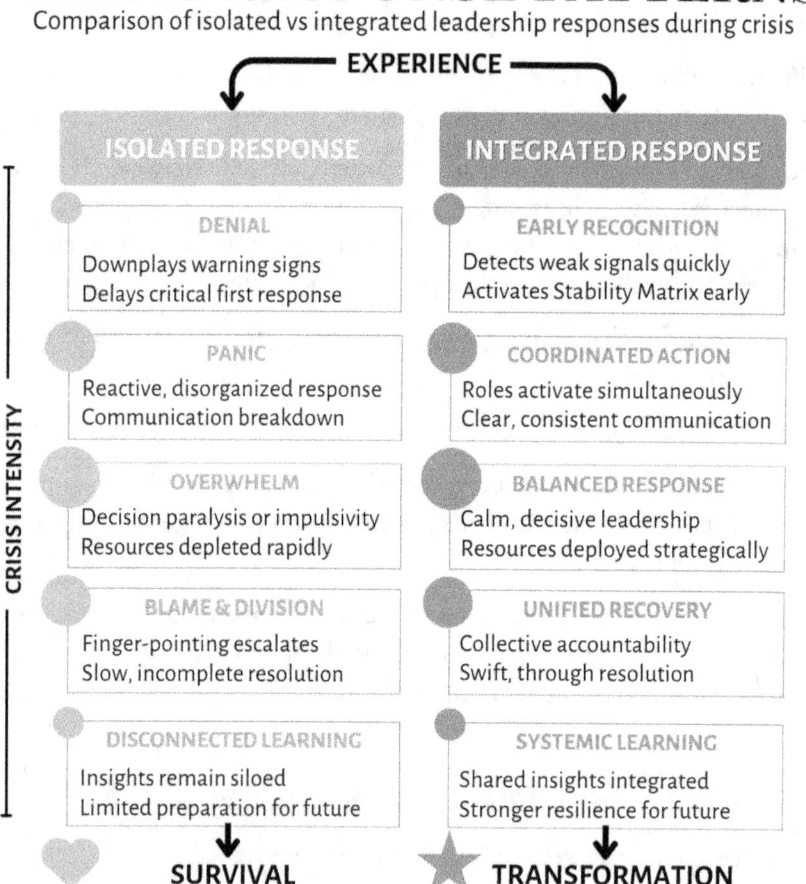

REFLECT: What's your crisis pattern? Do you isolate or activate? Do you freeze or flow?

The next storm will reveal what you've been practicing.

ACT: Run a 3-hour blackout test.

Become completely unreachable to your team. (with warning)

Upon return, don't ask "Did everything go okay?"

Ask, "What decisions did you make without me?"

This reveals your matrix's real-world strength.

Now, ready to go a full day? A week?

Will your support system hold when everything hits the fan?

Crisis doesn't just test your strategy or operations—it tests your entire matrix. And you don't rise to the occasion; you fall to the level of your preparation.

I've gathered crisis response frameworks, communication templates, and stories from leaders who've turned potential disasters into defining moments of transformation.

It's free, my gift to you.

https://TheCaptainsKeys.com/bonus

"When disaster struck, these resources helped me activate my connections in ways that turned potential catastrophe into our defining moment."
—RICK R., FOUNDER

 **NAVIGATE**

To Finish the Story / Full Journey - Continue on to the next page
Study the Maps - Jump ahead to page 421

BEYOND THE STORM
Part 10

Exhaustion settled into Jimmy's bones like wet cement. The adrenaline that had carried them through the rescue crashed hard, leaving behind trembling hands and thousand-yard stares. Every man aboard the *Bering Steel* moved like someone underwater - slow, deliberate, fighting invisible resistance.

No one spoke much. What was there to say? They'd pulled three men from the jaws of death and lost two others to its cold embrace.

Jimmy stared at the red-rimmed horizon, where dawn was breaking through steel-gray clouds. The sea had calmed, as if satisfied with its tribute. Two lives. It could have been more.

"Crew needs rest, Captain," Scott said quietly at his shoulder.

Jimmy nodded. "Four hours. Then we pull our first string."

They had quotas to fill. Time to honor those lost the only way fishermen knew how - by continuing on.

By comparison to that long night, the rest of the trip was almost routine; albeit a routine of frigid conditions, blisters, cuts, scrapes, and vicious competition for the "best spots" on the crab grounds. Within a week, their tanks were stuffed and had already caught slightly more than half their quota.

Teaming up with the *Northern Star* drove exceptional results for both crews. Zach was a tremendous leader, competent and reliable. Just the kind of fishing partner a captain would want.

Both vessels independently headed to port for their first offloads, and more importantly for the crews - their first payday.

When the *Bering Steel* docked at the crab processor in Dutch Harbor, the *Bering Steel* crew gathered on deck. Looking down into the stuffed tanks with anticipation, Tom shook his head and smiled. "You know what the best part is? One more trip like this and we're done!"

The crew cheered.

First boat in meant first boat out, and they were eager to get back to the grounds while the fishing was hot.

CHAPTER 53

Captains Bay

Dutch Harbor, Alaska

The rhythmic whine of the crane filled the pre-dawn air as the processing plant's crew transferred the last of their catch from the *Bering Steel*'s holds. Jimmy watched the numbers climb on the digital display - pounds becoming dollars becoming dreams.

The figures were staggering. Quota was limited and demand was up driving crab prices to a twenty year high. Even split among the crew, it was more money than most of them would see in five years working a normal job on shore. None of this bunch would have been the least bit happy with normal anyway.

The hold was nearly empty and the crew was doing final cleanup when the call came across from the dock, "Permission to come aboard?"

Hoping it was Captain Si come to check their numbers, Jimmy bounded from his chair and rounded the deck to find Captain Burns standing on the gangway, his hat in his hands, one arm in a sling.

He grimaced as he saw Jimmy's expression. He was probably expecting anger or resentment. Compassion obviously wasn't something he got much of.

"Come aboard," Jimmy told him. "How are you and your crew doing?"

Bob appeared and helped Burns on board with his bum arm in a full cast and sling. Burns passed on an offer of coffee and sat down gingerly. "Lost two good men. We're pooling money for their families. Won't last long, but what else can we do?"

Hearing voices, the rest of the crew had stopped to see who it was. Expressions ranged from mild concern to outright hostility. But nobody said anything; they had enough respect for Jimmy to hold their tongues.

"I came by for two reasons," Burns said quietly, his eyes fixed on the deck. "First, to thank you for the rescue. When we started taking on water, I thought we could manage, but . . ." His voice faltered. "Those two men dying is on me. When I heard it was your vessel responding - after how I'd treated you - I couldn't believe it."

He looked up, meeting Jimmy's eyes directly for perhaps the first time. "You could have stayed silent on that radio. No one would have known."

Burns paused, a silent debate visible in the tightening of his jaw. When he continued, each word seemed physically painful to deliver.

"Second reason is harder. For years, I was always second behind your uncle. Always chasing, never catching. When you showed up with his name, his boat . . ." He shook his head. "I thought it was the second act of the Meyer show."

His good hand clenched and unclenched at his side. "Jealousy makes a man crazy." The words fell between them like stones. "I sabotaged your boat, Meyer. Poured chemical sludge straight into your engine's intake. Others helped, but it was my idea."

The confession hung in the frigid air.

Jimmy felt rather than heard the collective gasp from his crew. The deck seemed to tilt beneath his feet as rage surged through him.

Jimmy had suspected, of course. But suspicion was one thing. A full confession was quite another.

"Why?" Jimmy demanded, fists clenched so tight his nails bit into his palms. "You could have killed us all!"

Burns stared past Jimmy toward the horizon, his face carved with unfamiliar lines of shame. "Because I didn't think you belonged here. Young, thinking you could just waltz in alongside men who'd bled into these waters for decades." His voice dropped. "I watched your uncle build something I could never match."

He finally met Jimmy's gaze. "I wanted to drive you away. Make you quit. You hadn't earned it. I hated Rocky. Success came easy for him, while the rest of us had to work ten times harder. And then you show up and get everything handed to you on a silver platter."

Aidan moved with the explosive force of an uncoiling spring. Two steps was all it took for the giant to close the distance, his face contorted with a fury that transformed his usually good-natured features into something primal. Burns didn't flinch - acceptance rather than courage keeping him rooted in place.

"Back off, Aidan! Stand down!" Jimmy's command cut through the charged air.

"Screw that, Captain!" Aidan's voice cracked like a bullwhip. His massive hands clenched and unclenched, veins standing out along his forearms. "He admitted it! He cost us time and money! You know how hard we worked! We should have left him in the water!"

The deck plating seemed to vibrate with his rage. For all his extreme sports bravado, this was the first time Jimmy had seen the real danger in Aidan - a man who could snap an arm like kindling without breaking stride.

"I'm putting him back there for good!"

Jimmy couldn't physically stop Aidan. The young man outweighed him by seventy pounds, all of it muscle. Tom and Richie had shifted subtly, ready to intervene, but even all three of them might not be enough.

Time for a different play.

"You remember whose boat you're on." Jimmy's voice dropped an octave, quiet but carrying the undeniable weight of command. "You remember who the Captain is."

He took a calculated step forward, directly into Aidan's space. Not challenging - claiming. The move of a man absolutely certain of his authority.

The words hit Aidan like a physical force. The big man blinked, the red haze of rage receding from his eyes. He'd spent months pushing his body to impossible limits, mastering fear on mountaintops and in crushing ocean depths. But in all that time, he'd been searching for exactly this - someone worthy of his loyalty. Someone worth following.

His massive shoulders lowered a fraction. Aidan might have wanted to pound Burns' face in, but he respected authority and he hadn't worked so hard to get onto this crew just to throw it away. The threat in his stance receded, though his eyes never left Burns.

Jimmy felt something important shift between them. The final piece of trust clicking into place. In that moment, he knew Aidan would walk through fire for him - and more importantly, would stop at his command.

"I'm truly sorry. I have never done anything so low, so underhanded. It's rock-bottom dirty. I couldn't believe when I saw the other captains supporting you and helping you fix the damage. They're better than me. Even Hills helped you out and he's been my lap dog for years. I'm truly ashamed. If you can't forgive me, I don't blame you one bit."

He reached inside his coat with his good arm. "I can't change the past, but I can help the future. I have crab quota - lots of it - but without a ship I can't use it. Normally I'd lease it to another boat for a percentage, but I'd rather give it to you - free. No percentage, no splits, no strings attached. It's not a bribe to stay quiet about the sabotage either. If you want to call the chief, I'll confess. It doesn't make up for what's done or make us square for saving us, but it's what I have. It's yours if you want it."

The documentation he handed over showed Burns' quota was worth more than half a million dollars in crabs. Jimmy asked Burns to hold tight while they stepped into the galley to talk.

CHAPTER 54

The small galley vibrated with their anger. Aidan paced like a caged animal, veins standing out on his neck. Tom leaned against the bulkhead, arms crossed, his expression unreadable but his eyes cold as Arctic water. Bob and Scott exchanged glances that carried years of seafaring wisdom.

"He sabotaged us," Aidan finally exploded. "Could've killed us all."

Bob's weathered finger traced a coffee ring on the table. "Man's confession took guts. Doesn't make it right."

"His quota is worth half a million," Scott said quietly. "That's not nothing."

Tom hadn't moved. "Where I come from, some debts can't be paid with money."

Jimmy studied these men - his men - feeling the weight of command. Their lives had been risked by Burns' malice. The decision was rightfully theirs as much as his.

"What would you have done," he asked finally, "if you'd heard Burns' distress call knowing what you know now?"

The question hung between them.

""Same damn thing Cap," Richie admitted reluctantly.

Aidan followed, "Yeah, still would've gone after them. It was the right thing to do.""

Nods around the table.

Grudging.

Human.

They filed back onto the deck where Burns waited, tension straightening his spine. Jimmy stepped forward first, extending his hand. Burns' eyes widened, disbelief washing over his features before he grasped it.

"This doesn't make us square," Jimmy said, voice low enough that only Burns could hear. "But everyone deserves a second chance. The feud ends here."

Burns swallowed hard, a muscle working in his jaw.

"What about the police? You've got a right to press charges."

"That could sink us both," Jimmy replied. "You'd lose more than your boat, and I'd lose weeks fighting paperwork instead of catching crab."

He held Burns' gaze. "Consider this your one pass. There won't be another."

Burns nodded, understanding the unspoken terms of their arrangement.

"I don't deserve this."

"No," Jimmy agreed. "You don't."

One by one, the crew followed their captain's lead—Tom with stoic dignity, Scott with professional courtesy, Richie with youthful forgiveness, Bob with the hard-won grace of a man who'd been given his own second chances.

Aidan stepped forward last, towering over Burns. "You pull anything like that again . . ."

He left the threat unfinished, but his massive hand enveloped Burns' in a grip just short of crushing.

Burns' eyes glistened as he descended the gangway, his shoulders straighter than when he'd arrived. He looked lighter, as if he'd set down a weight he'd carried far too long.

Aidan waited until Burns was out of earshot. "Captain - about earlier . . . "

"Don't," Jimmy said. "We all get one moment where we're not our best selves."

A half-smile pulled at Aidan's mouth. "So we're good?"

Jimmy clapped him on the shoulder. "Better than good. We're crew."

CHAPTER 55

Bering Sea

Three Weeks Later

The *Bering Steel*'s holds were near bursting again when Jimmy's phone lit up with a familiar number. He'd been meaning to call Si for days, but between the constant fishing and managing two quotas, time had slipped away like tide water.

"Jimmy? It's Si. I'm back home finally. How's it going over there? You gonna make enough money to get your guys through to next season?"

Jimmy grinned into the phone, watching his crew work with a precision that would have made Si proud. "Si . . . you better sit down for this one. We don't need you having another stroke . . . "

The season consumed them after that, days blurring into nights in an endless cycle of work, eat, sleep - repeat. The bitter cold of the Bering Sea sank into their bones, turned fingers stiff and faces raw despite the best gear money could buy. But the pots came up full. Again and again, the mechanical rhythm of the hydraulics sang the sweetest song in commercial fishing: profit.

They developed a silent language on deck - nods, hand signals, the briefest exchanges carrying the weight of full conversations. No wasted words, no wasted motion. A well-oiled machine that functioned better with each passing day.

At the end of that week, their holds were again stuffed with writhing red crab. The processing plant supervisor's eyes widened when they brought in their final load - numbers climbing on the digital display until they broke past previous *Bering Steel* records.

In a single month, they'd eclipsed what Jimmy would have earned in eight years of Florida charters. But more than money, Jimmy found himself measuring success in other ways: the growing confidence in Richie's stance, the pride in Old Bob's eyes when he called his daughter, Scott's growing peace with memories that once haunted him, Aidan's growing willingness to show vulnerability alongside his strength, and the quiet contentment in Tom's rare but genuine smile.

Numbers on a page were just that - numbers. But the transformation of his crew?

Priceless.

Bob's daughter got her tuition for art school and her dad went from attending AA meetings to leading them.

Richie and his wife Lori welcomed a daughter into the world just four days after the season ended and named her Madelyn Rose for Lori's grandmother and her favorite flower.

Scott finally revealed his mysterious special request to the entire crew a few days after their final offload. They were surprised, and slightly envious they hadn't been savvy enough to come up with the idea. None of them had ever been deep-sea fishing anywhere. The closest they'd been to the Florida Keys was listening to Jimmy Buffett.

Jimmy asked, "What kind of drink do you want, Scotty?"

"I don't care, just as long as it has one of those little umbrellas in it! That was part of the deal."

The entire crew laughed with Scott on that one, pushing each other and making drinking motions with their pinkies extended in the air.

"Just no booze," he added with a sly wink. "All for one."

"And one for all," the crew responded in unison.

CHAPTER 56

Four months after crab season, the crews of the *Bering Steel* and the *Northern Star* boarded a flight from Kodiak to Miami, ready to trade bitter Arctic winds for tropical breezes, king crab for marlin, and survival suits for board shorts. They touched down in the Sunshine State as a unit - minus Captain Si, who claimed medical appointments kept him in Alaska. Lily waited at the terminal, determined to embarrass her baby brother with the longest hug possible before meeting his newfound fishing family.

Jimmy rented a gorgeous beach house in Plantation Key with great views. Unlike their cramped quarters on the boat this place had plenty of space for everyone to live their best island life. The crew made sure Si didn't miss a moment, flooding his inbox with photos of their sun-soaked adventures. His responses were pure Si: 'You all look like tourists,' and 'That's not how you hold a fishing rod, ya morons.' But they could read between the lines – the old salt missed them.

A few days later, Jimmy called in a favor from Mickey Santos, an old friend from his charter days who now ran the biggest party boat in the Keys. The crew piled aboard for some tropical sportfishing and those promised umbrella drinks. They spent the day trying to out-fish and out-joke each other, catching nothing but sunburns and belly laughs. When Aidan swore he saw something the size of a Volkswagen swim under the boat, Tom just smirked and said, "That was probably just your ego, kid."

That evening, they dragged their sunburned selves back to their beach house, still laughing about Aidan's imaginary sea monster and debating where to get dinner. Jimmy paused at the door when he heard a familiar bark of laughter from inside. He froze, then threw open the door to find Captain Si settled in the front room chatting with Lily, and playing peekaboo with her toddler Jesse like he'd been there all along.

'I said I couldn't make the trip - at least not all of it,' Si explained with his newly methodical speech, the stroke's lingering effect still evident but his eyes twinkling. 'But I'll be a vegetarian alligator before I'm going to miss out on a week's vacation in paradise!'

The crew erupted. Hugs and backslaps filled the room, their exhaustion from the day on the water forgotten in the joy of having their old sea dog of a captain back."

Out on the front porch, Jimmy and Si sat in rocking chairs watching the waves roll in on the Gulf shore. Jimmy handed Si another iced tea and settled back into his rocking chair. The Gulf stretched before them, painted in shades of gold and amber by the setting sun

- so different from the steel-gray waters of the Bering Sea, yet somehow the same in its vastness.

"So Si," Jimmy said, watching the waves roll in. "An Anchor, a Crew, a Navigator, and a Champion. Four things I didn't even know I needed, and found them all thanks to you."

Si smiled, the lines around his eyes deepening. His hand still trembled slightly but his gaze was clear and sharp as ever.

"I went through the same quest a lifetime ago," he said, voice measured in the way it hadn't been before his illness. Each word chosen with new care. "Had my share of captains under my wing since then. Most chafed at one part or another."

He took a sip of tea, his gaze drifting to the horizon where the water met the sky.

"Most figured the crew was all they needed - just guys to do what they were told. But confiding in someone? Letting another fight battles they couldn't handle?" Si shook his head. "That's like pouring salt in the wounds of these big-ego guys. They just couldn't stand it."

"What happens to them?" Jimmy asked, though something in him already knew the answer.

"Some still succeed, but they pay for it. Time, energy, health, fractured relationships." Si's voice dropped. "Some fail miserably, quit before they ever sell their first crab. Some go down with their ships and others become a Coast Guard rescue story."

He paused, the silence laden with unspoken grief.

"And some ignore the advice to spite their own father . . . sign on with a crew that has no business on the water . . ." His voice caught. "And it costs them everything."

The weight of Si's loss hung between them like a physical presence. Jimmy thought of all the empty chairs he'd seen in the Fisherman's Bar, all the names mentioned in hushed tones, all the slips standing vacant year after year because no one had the heart to fill them. After a long moment, he covered Si's weathered hand with his own.

"Your son's death wasn't just another cautionary tale, Si," Jimmy said softly. "It changed how you see things, didn't it? Made you understand what really matters out there."

He chose his next words carefully.

"That's why I think there are five keys, not four."

Si wiped his eyes with his free hand. "Five, huh? What's the fifth one then?"

"Friendship," Jimmy said simply.

"It's the glue that holds all those relationships together. Lily is my sister, but we've been best friends our whole lives. The guys on my crew would work great on any boat, but they found something special on the *Bering Steel* that turned them into friends. Carly could have written me off as just another jackass captain, but she saw something worth investing in."

He paused, meeting Si's gaze directly.

"Scott trusted you enough to put aside his grief because you were his friend first. Everything else came after."

Through the screen door, they could hear the crew inside – Aidan's booming laugh, Tom's quiet chuckle, Richie's rapid-fire storytelling, Bob's occasional deadpan comment. The sounds of men who'd faced death together and come out the other side.

"I worked alone for a lot of years," Jimmy continued, watching palm fronds dance in the evening breeze so unlike Alaska's cutting wind. "Just me and Bella. Told myself it was better that way. No one to disappoint, no one to let down."

He shook his head, a rueful smile touching his lips.

"But success tastes like ashes when there's no one to share it with. All that money we made this season? It's worth twice as much because we earned it together."

Si studied him for a long moment, then nodded once. "You figured it all out, son."

The old captain put his feet up and rocked gently, his chair moving in perfect rhythm with the waves rolling up to the beach. His eyes drifted closed, the tension of years seeming to melt from his weathered face.

Through the screen door, Jimmy could see his crew gathered around Lily's dining table. Richie was showing the latest pictures of Madelyn Rose. Tom was teaching Aidan some phrase in his native language. Bob was helping Lily's oldest Emily, with an art project. Scott was assisting Lily in the kitchen, sleeves rolled up and completely absorbed in whatever cooking lesson she was giving him.

The sun dipped lower, painting the sky in brilliant oranges and pinks, just like the ones Jimmy used to watch from his old porch in the Keys. But this sunset was different.

This time, he wasn't alone.

This time, he was surrounded by family - both the kind you're born with and the kind you find along the way.

This wraps up Beyond The Storm - the story section of the book. There are additional tools, resources, and an online community at the link below. It's free, my gift to you.

If you enjoyed this book, and it was valuable, please tell a friend about it. Better yet, send them a copy. That is what a Champion would do. It is guaranteed to start a conversation and deepen a relationship. That is the ultimate goal of this book.

https://TheCaptainsKeys.com/bonus

"When disaster struck, these resources helped me activate my connections in ways that turned potential catastrophe into our defining moment."
—RICK R., FOUNDER

⚙ NAVIGATE

Study the Maps / Full Journey - Continue on to the next page
Start the Story - Go back to page 31

THE LEGACY CAPTAIN
BECOMING SOMEONE'S NORTH STAR

*"The greatest leader is not necessarily the one who does the greatest things.
He is the one that gets people to do the greatest things."*
— RONALD REAGAN

Leadership is a game of giving, not getting.

But most of us play it backward.

We chase Navigators when we should be navigating for others.
We seek Champions when we should be championing someone else.
We hunt for Anchors when we should be anchoring those caught in the storm.

Here's the thing about the sea of leadership:
Those who only take eventually sink.
Those who give eventually become the rising tide.

I call the extraordinary captains who understand this **Full Circle Leaders**.

While everyone else scrambles to build a system to support themselves, they also build to support others.
While everyone else asks, "Who will help me?" they ask, "Who needs my help?"
While everyone else focuses on receiving, they focus on providing.

And that changes everything.

Beyond Support: Creating Support Systems for Others

Think back to the best leader you've ever known. Not the most successful. Not the most powerful. The best.

What made them exceptional wasn't just their vision or their decisions or their results. It was how they made others better. How they created spaces where others could thrive. How they built support systems that extended far beyond themselves.

These leaders intuitively understood what most miss: The highest form of leadership isn't being supported. It's supporting others.

The Ultimate Leadership Evolution: Becoming What You Needed

I've coached thousands of leaders across every industry imaginable. I can tell you exactly where most hit their ceiling.

It's not when they lack vision.
It's not when they lack execution.
It's not even when they lack direct support.

It's when they fail to evolve from matrix-builders to matrix-providers.

The pattern is painfully predictable:

Phase 1: The Captain builds their Stability Matrix. They find their Anchor, assemble their Crew, partner with their Navigator, and attract their Champion. Their leadership capacity expands dramatically.

Phase 2: The Captain hits a new ceiling. Despite having a complete support system, something still feels missing. They've optimized their direct impact, but their indirect impact – their leadership legacy – remains limited.

This is the moment of truth.
The leadership crucible that separates the good from the transformational.

The question isn't whether you need support.
The question is: Who needs your support?

The question isn't who will anchor you.
The question is: Who will you anchor?

The question isn't who will champion your cause.
The question is: Whose cause will you champion?

This shift – from receiver to provider – changes everything about how you lead.

It transforms leadership from consumption to contribution.

From accumulation to multiplication.
From success to significance.

And it starts with a simple, radical choice:
To become for others what you needed most.

How Becoming an Anchor, Crew, Navigator, and a Champion Transforms Your Leadership

Monica runs a $30M software company in Austin. For years, she operated with a solid matrix – supportive spouse as Anchor, a high-functioning leadership team as Crew, a former CEO as Navigator, and powerful industry connections as Champions.

Her business thrived. Her stress decreased. Her impact expanded.

But something still felt missing. A ceiling she couldn't quite break through. A sense that she was built for more than just running a successful company.

The breakthrough came unexpectedly.

"I was having coffee with a first-time founder," she told me. "He was struggling with all the issues I'd faced years earlier – isolation, overwhelm, decision fatigue. Without thinking, I found myself saying, 'You know, I've been there. Let me help you think through this.'"

That conversation became a monthly ritual. The founder began bringing his challenges, and Monica found herself serving as his Navigator – offering perspective, questioning assumptions, identifying patterns, all without taking control.

"Something shifted in me," she explained. "I realized I wasn't just a CEO. I was someone who could help others navigate challenges I'd already overcome. That changed how I saw myself and my purpose."

Monica didn't stop there. She began intentionally serving as:

An Anchor for her rising VP of Product, creating space where he could process leadership challenges without judgment or expectation.

A Crew Member for a nonprofit addressing homelessness, contributing her operational expertise not as CEO but as an implementation partner.

A Navigator for three first-time founders, offering pattern recognition and perspective without taking ownership of their decisions.

A Champion for underrepresented leaders in her industry, opening doors, making introductions, and advocating when they weren't in the room.

The result? Her leadership impact expanded exponentially. Not just through her direct work, but through the ripple effects of those she supported. Her own leadership capacity grew as she practiced different matrix roles. Her network strengthened as she became known not just for what she achieved, but for who she helped.

Most surprisingly, her own business accelerated. The insights she gained from serving in different matrix roles for others brought a fresh perspective to her own challenges.

This isn't just Monica's story. It's the natural evolution of integrated leadership.

When you serve as an Anchor for others, you deepen your own emotional intelligence and perspective-taking.

When you serve as a Crew Member in contexts outside your direct authority, you sharpen your implementation skills and adaptability.

When you serve as a Navigator for emerging leaders, you strengthen your pattern recognition and strategic thinking.

When you serve as a Champion for those with less influence, you expand your network and advocacy skills.

The roles you play for others don't just help them. They transform you.

The matrix connection isn't one-way. It's a loop. A circuit that powers both parties.

What you give comes back multiplied.

Creating Matrix-Building Cultures in Your Organization

The most powerful matrix builders don't just create their own support systems. They create cultures where matrix thinking becomes the oxygen everyone breathes.

I watched Katie transform her healthcare technology company from a political battlefield into a matrix powerhouse in just nine months. Here's exactly how she did it:

First, she stopped talking about "teamwork" in the abstract and started teaching matrix concepts explicitly. In a three-hour workshop, she walked her leadership team through their own matrix assessments, revealing their support gaps in real-time.

The results were uncomfortable but revelatory. Her CTO had strong Navigator support but no emotional Anchors. Her Head of Sales had Champions everywhere but lacked a reliable Crew. Her CFO was everyone's Crew but nobody's Champion.

"For the first time," Katie told me, "they stopped seeing relationships as purely political and started seeing them as structural. As essential to their function as their budgets or their teams."

Then she did something revolutionary: She created "matrix minutes" at the start of every leadership meeting. Two simple questions:

"Who supported you as Anchor, Crew, Navigator, or Champion this week?"

"Who did you support in one of these roles?"

The conversations were awkward at first. Her executives struggled to articulate how they'd been supported or offered support. But within weeks, something shifted.

They began actively noticing these relationship functions.
They began naming them.
They began seeking them intentionally.

By month four, matrix thinking had gone viral. Without being told to, her executives began:

Helping their teams identify their own matrix gaps
Creating cross-functional connections specifically designed to fill those gaps
Celebrating when someone effectively served as Anchor, Navigator, Crew, or Champion

The entire organization evolved from "do your job" to "support each other's success." From vertical hierarchies to dynamic connection networks that solved problems faster, recovered from setbacks quicker, and innovated more consistently.

The numbers tell the story:

- Employee retention improved 34% in 11 months
- Decision velocity increased by 40%
- Innovation metrics doubled
- Crisis recovery time decreased by 60%

This wasn't some kumbaya leadership fantasy or a team-building exercise. It was a fundamental shift in how people connected with each other. Katie didn't dismantle necessary hierarchies or accountability structures - she overlaid them with relationship architectures that made those formal structures more effective.

Want to create your own matrix culture? Start with these three concrete steps:

1. **Make it visible** - Create a physical matrix board where people can map their support relationships and identify gaps. When something's visible, it's discussable.
2. **Make it valued** - Recognize and reward matrix-building behaviors as explicitly as you recognize sales targets or product launches. What gets celebrated gets repeated.
3. **Make it structured** - Dedicate time in every leadership meeting to matrix development. Not as an add-on, but as core infrastructure.

This isn't just another culture initiative. It's not about posters or values statements or team-building exercises.

It's about fundamentally changing how people relate to each other in the context of shared work. It's about creating connection architectures as intentionally as we create organizational charts.

When was the last time your organization invested as much in relationship development as skills development?

The best ones do. Not because they're warm and fuzzy, but because they understand a fundamental truth: In complex, rapidly-changing environments, relationship architecture drives performance more powerfully than skill architecture.

Skills without relationships stay isolated. Relationships without skills stay ineffective. Together, they become exponential.

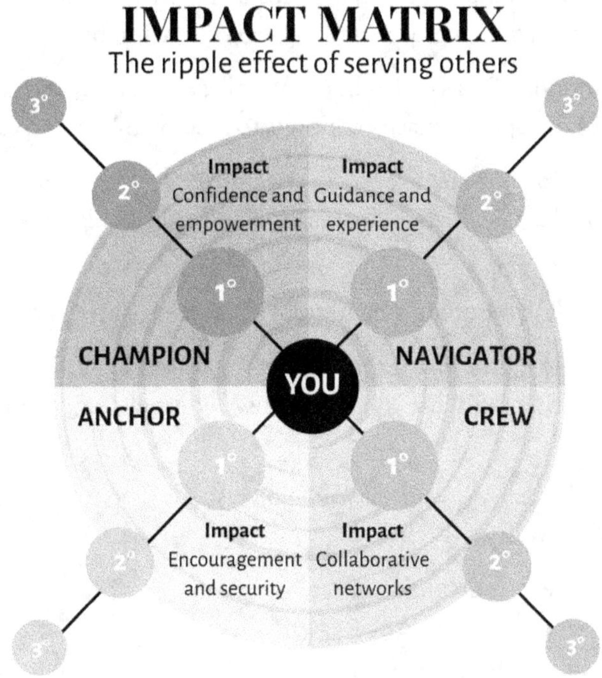

Primary Impact (1°): Direct influence on those you directly support

Secondary Impact (2°): Those you support begin to support others

Tertiary Impact (3°): Ripple continues creating culture of support

The Ripple Effect of Integrated Leadership

Matrix leadership doesn't stop at your organizational boundaries. It creates ripple effects that extend far beyond your direct influence.

I witnessed this in real-time with Eric, a construction CEO who transformed from isolated leader to matrix provider after a near-bankruptcy forced him to rethink everything.

The ripple effects were measurable:

First-Degree Impact: His direct reports built their own matrices, increasing decision quality and execution speed throughout the organization.

Second-Degree Impact: Partners and suppliers who worked closely with his team began adopting similar relationship patterns, creating more integrated industry networks.

Third-Degree Impact: Employees who left his company brought matrix thinking to new organizations, spreading the approach throughout their industry.

Perhaps most profoundly, Eric's high school and college-age kids, watching their father's transformation, began applying matrix concepts to their own lives and careers.

This is how leadership ecosystems evolve – not through programs or initiatives, but through transformed individuals who create transformed relationships that create transformed communities.

It's not fast. It's not flashy. But it's the most powerful leadership legacy you can create.

A single drop creates ripples that reach distant shores. A single leader creates matrix patterns that transform distant organizations. A single transformation creates exponential impact.

Is this the kind of leader you want to be? Not just successful today, but significant forever? The choice is yours.

Individual matrices create individual impact.
But what happens when matrix thinking extends beyond a single leader?
What happens when it permeates teams, organizations, and entire industries?

That's when the real magic begins.

Matrix Leadership at Scale

Individual transformation is just the beginning. The real power emerges when matrix thinking scales beyond single leaders to entire organizations, industries, and communities.

Implementing Matrix Thinking Throughout Organizations

Matrix scaling isn't about mandates. It's about multiplication.

Traditional approaches to organizational transformation rely on top-down implementation – new structures, new policies, new metrics pushed from executive suites to front lines.

Matrix scaling works differently. It spreads through demonstration, invitation, and equipped champions rather than directives.

Consider how David, a regional VP at a global technology company, scaled matrix thinking without formal authority to change company-wide systems:

1. He began by building his own complete matrix, demonstrating the impact on his leadership effectiveness.
2. He introduced the concept to his direct leadership team, helping each member identify their own matrix gaps and strengths.
3. He created "matrix moments" in team meetings – specifically acknowledging when someone was effectively serving as Anchor, Crew, Navigator, or Champion for others.
4. He developed simple tools that made matrix identification easier – relationship maps, support assessments, and gap analyses that any team could use.
5. He equipped willing champions throughout his organization with these tools, inviting them to spread the approach without mandating adoption.

Within two years, matrix thinking had spread to over 70% of his region's leaders – all without a single official program or company-wide initiative.

The results were remarkable:

- Problem-solving velocity increased 43%
- Cross-functional collaboration improved 38%
- Employee engagement scores rose 27%
- Crisis recovery time decreased 52%

Most importantly, when company restructuring eliminated his position, the matrix thinking he'd established continued to flourish without him. He had created something self-sustaining rather than dependent on his presence.

The key insight? Matrix thinking scales through contagion, not command. Through pull, not push. Through voluntary adoption, not mandatory compliance.

This is how emergent behaviors replace rigid commands. It's how leadership expectations evolve without dictates. It's how relationship intelligence becomes part of an organization's DNA rather than its latest program.

The most powerful organizational transformations don't look like transformations at all. They look like wildfire – catching, spreading, transforming through natural connection rather than forced implementation.

You don't mandate matrices. You model them. You don't implement support. You invite it.

Teaching Direct Reports to Build Their Own Matrices

Matrix thinking doesn't just spread. It multiplies.
And it starts with those closest to you.

The most powerful lever for scaling matrix thinking is helping your direct reports build their own complete support systems.

This isn't just delegation. It's multiplication.

The process is simple but profound:

1. Share your own matrix journey, including your struggles and breakthroughs.
2. Help each team member map their current support system, identifying strengths and gaps.
3. Guide them in creating intentional relationship development plans.
4. Create regular check-ins on matrix progress alongside performance discussions.
5. Actively connect them with potential matrix relationships both inside and outside the organization.

The results transform both individual leaders and team dynamics. As each person becomes more supported, they become more supportive. As they experience the value of matrix relationships, they naturally begin creating them for others.

But the biggest impact happens in the relationship between you and your direct reports. When you help someone build their support system, you stop being their only source of guidance and feedback. You become a multiplier of support rather than its sole provider.

It's counterintuitive, but true: The more you help others build diverse support relationships, the stronger your relationship with them becomes.

You shift from being their primary support to being their primary support architect. From the one who answers their questions to the one who connects them to answers. From the pressure of being everything to the freedom of helping them find what they need.

Most leaders think that helping their subordinates build other support relationships diminishes their importance. The opposite happens. You become more valuable, not less. More strategic, not less. More respected, not less.

The real job of leadership isn't providing all the answers. It's connecting people to the answers they need most.

Creating Company-Wide Relationship Resilience

The ultimate outcome of scaled matrix thinking isn't just better-supported individuals. It's an organization with unprecedented relationship resilience.

Traditional corporate resilience focuses on financial buffers, operational redundancies, and risk management protocols. These are essential but incomplete.

True organizational resilience depends equally on relationship structures – the human connections that enable adaptation, innovation, and recovery when formal systems face unprecedented challenges.

I saw this vividly during the pandemic's early days. Organizations with strong matrix cultures adapted three times faster than those with traditional command-and-control structures. Not because their crisis plans were better, but because their relationship architectures enabled faster information flow, more distributed decision-making, and greater emotional stamina.

Matrix-oriented organizations demonstrated:

- Faster identification of emerging threats
- More creative adaptation to supply chain disruptions
- Better employee support during remote transitions
- Higher retention of key talent during uncertainty
- More rapid development of new business models

The difference wasn't resources or strategy. It was relationship architecture.

Organizations with intentional matrix cultures had built internal connection systems that could bend without breaking. That could route around damage like robust neural networks. That could generate solutions from unexpected quarters rather than waiting for top-down direction.

This is what relationship resilience looks like in practice.

It doesn't replace organizational charts or accountability structures. It complements them with dynamic connection patterns that activate when static structures prove insufficient.

Think of it as your organization's immune system. When threats emerge, matrix relationships activate, mobilize resources, and coordinate responses far faster than formal systems can direct.

The organizations that weathered pandemic disruptions most effectively weren't just those with the best crisis plans. They were those with the best crisis relationships – the human connections that enabled improvisation, adaptation, and innovation when playbooks proved insufficient.

Is your organization building this kind of resilience? Or are you still relying solely on plans, processes, and protocols that inevitably fail when unprecedented challenges emerge?

The choice isn't either/or. It's both/and. Build the plans AND build the relationships. Create the protocols AND create the connections. Develop the processes AND develop the people.

That's matrix resilience at scale.

Measuring Support System Effectiveness

Peter Drucker reportedly said, "What gets measured gets managed." If The Stability Matrix, or any support system, is important, we must find ways to measure its effectiveness. But traditional metrics fail us here. Support system effectiveness isn't captured in standard KPIs or performance dashboards.

The most useful measures focus on three dimensions that start from the individual and radiate out in concentric layers. They are:

Relationship Quality:

- Psychological safety scores
- Decision confidence ratings
- Peer support perception
- Cross-functional trust indices

Support System Completeness:

- Matrix gap assessments
- Relationship diversity measurements
- Connection resilience in crisis

- Support redundancy mapping

Organizational Impact:

- Recovery speed from setbacks
- Innovation implementation velocity
- Decision quality under pressure
- Talent retention during disruption

SUPPORT SYSTEM EFFECTIVENESS
Tracking progress and creating visibility

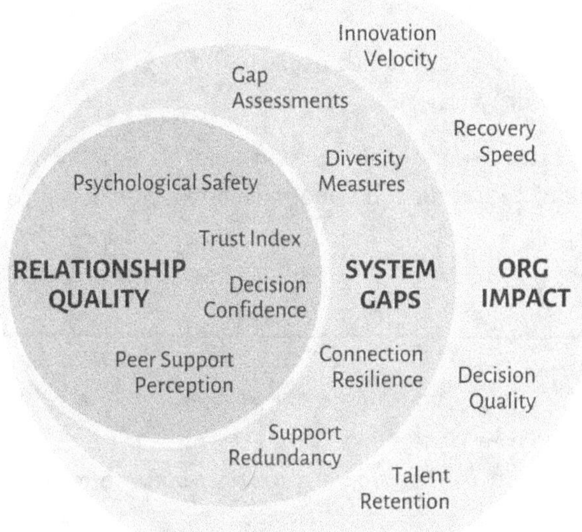

Champion Leadership Group has developed innovative measurement approaches that focus on these key areas:

- **Network Analysis Maps** that visualize relationship patterns across organizational boundaries
- **Support System Inventories** that help leaders identify matrix gaps and redundancies
- **Crisis Response Assessments** that measure how effectively matrices are activated during challenges

- **Matrix Culture Surveys** that track the prevalence of support relationships throughout the organization

These measurements matter not just for tracking progress but for creating visibility. They make the invisible work of relationship-building tangible. They create language for discussing support gaps. They provide evidence for investing in relationship development alongside traditional skill development.

The key insight? *You can't directly measure relationships, but you can measure their effects.*

You can measure how quickly information flows. How effectively resources are mobilized. How rapidly teams adapt to changing conditions. How completely people recover from setbacks.

These indirect measures reveal relationship matrix effectiveness more accurately than any direct attempt to quantify connection.

The question isn't "How strong are our relationships?" It's "What can our relationships accomplish?" It's not about feeling. It's about function. Not about connection quality. But connection impact.

This isn't soft. It's strategic.

The Next Horizon

As you build and scale your leadership matrix, keep one eye on the horizon. The future will demand support systems that are both stronger and more adaptable than today's challenges require.

Future Challenges That Will Require Stronger Matrices

The leadership landscape is shifting beneath our feet. Forces reshaping our world will demand new levels of support:

Accelerating Change – As change cycles compress from years to months to weeks, decision velocity becomes critical. No leader can process fast enough alone. You need multiple perspectives working together to make sense of rapid changes.

Complexity Overload – As systems become more interconnected, cause and effect relationships grow increasingly non-linear. Matrix thinking provides the multiple perspectives needed to navigate complexity that exceeds any individual's cognitive capacity.

Trust Erosion – As institutional trust continues declining, relationship trust becomes the primary currency of influence. Leaders without strong, diverse trust networks will find themselves unable to mobilize resources or create alignment.

Generational Shifts – As younger workers bring dramatically different expectations about authority, purpose, and work structure, leaders must develop more collaborative, less hierarchical support systems to remain effective.

Tech Disruption – As artificial intelligence and automation reshape knowledge work, the uniquely human elements of leadership – emotional intelligence, ethical reasoning, and relationship development – become even more critical.

The successful leaders of the next decade won't be those with the most authority or the most resources. They'll be those with the most robust, diverse relationships.

The stakes couldn't be higher. Those with strong matrix systems will navigate these challenges with adaptivity and resilience. Those without will find themselves increasingly overwhelmed, overworked, and overlooked.

This isn't speculation. It's already happening. The leadership gap between the matrix-supported and the matrix-deficient grows wider every day. Which side are you on?

Evolving Your Relationships for Coming Disruptions

As the landscape shifts, your relationship matrix must evolve. The support system that serves you today may not serve you tomorrow.

Three dimensions of evolution require attention:

Diversity of Perspective – Homogeneous support systems become increasingly dangerous as complexity increases. Future-ready leaders actively build relationships with people who think differently, come from different backgrounds, and challenge their existing mental models.

Dynamic Reconfiguration – Static support systems break under pressure. Future-ready matrices can rapidly reconfigure as challenges shift, activating different relationship combinations for different scenarios.

Cross-Boundary Connections – Traditional support systems limited to industry or function create dangerous blind spots. Future-ready leaders build relationships that cross traditional boundaries – industry, discipline, geography, and generation.

This evolution isn't comfortable. It pushes against our natural tendency to seek confirmation rather than challenge, stability rather than adaptation, similarity rather than difference.

But comfort is overrated. *In rapidly changing environments, comfort becomes risk.*

The leaders who thrive won't be those with the most comfortable matrix relationships. They'll be those with the most challenging ones – relationships that push thinking, question assumptions, and bring genuinely different perspectives.

The question isn't whether your matrix makes you comfortable. It's whether it makes you capable. Not whether it confirms what you believe. But whether it expands what you can see.

Are your relationships evolving as rapidly as your challenges? If not, you're building yesterday's matrix for tomorrow's problems.

Technological Changes and Relationship Constants

As artificial intelligence transforms business, a fascinating paradox emerges: The more technology advances, the more critical human relationships become.

AI will increasingly handle the analytical aspects of leadership – data processing, pattern recognition, scenario modeling, and optimization. These are precisely the domains where human cognition has natural limitations.

But technology cannot replace the uniquely human dimensions of leadership:

- The emotional intelligence to sense unspoken concerns
- The ethical judgment to make values-based decisions
- The creative synthesis that generates novel solutions
- The inspiration that motivates discretionary effort
- The trust-building that enables collective action

These capacities depend on human connection.
On empathy.
On shared experience and mutual vulnerability.

Which means that as technology handles more of the analytical heavy lifting, relationship-based leadership becomes more – not less – important.

Future-ready matrices will integrate technology and human relationships in powerful combinations:

- Digital or AI tools that extend human intelligence
- Virtual platforms that connect distributed matrix members
- AI systems that identify potential matrix relationships
- Analytics that reveal relationship patterns and gaps

The leaders who thrive won't be those who resist technology or those who over-rely on it. They'll be those who use technology to enhance rather than replace human connection – creating matrices that combine the computational power of machines with the wisdom, judgment, and inspiration that only humans can provide.

Here's the urgent question:

Are you developing your uniquely human leadership capacities as rapidly as technology is advancing?

If not, you're preparing for yesterday's leadership challenges, not tomorrow's.

The technical gets automated.
The analytical gets algorithmized or AI'd.

What remains uniquely valuable is the human.

The relational.
The ethical.
The inspirational.

That's where your matrix makes the difference. Not just in what you know or what you do. But in who you connect with and how you connect with them.

Preparing Your Support System for the Unknown

The greatest leadership challenges of the next decade are, by definition, not yet visible.

How do you prepare for what you cannot predict?

Here's the thing about the future: Everyone's trying to predict it. Nobody's preparing for it.

Take artificial intelligence. I've never seen change this fast. What will business look like in five years? That's anyone's guess. The more precisely we try to define it, the more of a guess it becomes.

But here's what's fascinating: We can learn how to prepare from AI itself.

Not by asking ChatGPT about the future. By understanding how it learns.

AI doesn't succeed because it knows what's coming. It succeeds because it adapts to whatever shows up.

Adaptive AI systems don't try to predict every scenario. They build capacity to learn from new information, adjust their responses, and evolve with changing conditions.

That's the model. Not prediction. Adaptation.

The answer lies not in specific preparations but in adaptive capacity – the ability to respond effectively to whatever emerges.

Four practices strengthen matrix adaptivity:

Regular Stress Testing – Scenario planning that explicitly examines how your matrix would respond to different future challenges. Which relationships would activate? Which gaps would become critical? Which connections might break under pressure?

Intentional Diversity – Systematically building relationships with people who bring different perspectives, experiences, and thinking styles. Not as a social exercise, but as a strategic imperative for identifying emerging patterns.

Boundary Spanning – Developing relationships that cross traditional dividing lines – functional, organizational, industry, and cultural. These cross-boundary connections become invaluable when disruption erases existing categories.

Low-Stakes Experimentation – Creating small, safe opportunities to test matrix responsiveness, especially within your Crew, before crisis demands it. Simple exercises like rotating leadership roles, creating artificial constraints, or simulating communication disruptions reveal matrix strengths and vulnerabilities. It's the same reason we have fire drills at office buildings, the military conducts exercises, and pilots fly in simulators.

Remember: The goal isn't to predict or prepare for every possible future.

It's to build a relationship architecture capable of sensing, processing, and responding to whatever emerges.

Most leaders prepare only for the challenges they can see coming. That's necessary but insufficient.

The most dangerous challenges are the ones no one anticipates. The black swans. The unknown unknowns. The emergent complexities.

These can't be prepared for directly. They can only be met with adaptive capacity – the ability to sense, process, and respond to what no one saw coming.

And that capacity doesn't come from plans. It comes from people. Not from processes, but from relationships. Not from protocols, but from connections that activate when protocols fail.

Is your matrix ready not just for the future you can see, but for the one you can't?

The future belongs to those who build relationship architectures.
Not just for themselves.
But for entire systems.

So, where do you begin?

Right where you are.

REFLECT: Whose matrix are you an essential part of?
Who would name you as their Anchor, Navigator, Crew, or Champion?
Where do you see the ripple effect of your impact helping others?

ACT: Today - not tomorrow, not next quarter - identify one person who needs exactly what you needed when you were in their position.

Reach out with a specific offer that serves them, not you.

Ready to become what others need most?

The highest form of leadership isn't being supported—it's supporting others. Your legacy isn't what you leave behind when you're gone; it's what continues through others because you were here.

I've created reflection guides and practical tools to help you serve as an Anchor for those in storms, a Crew member for meaningful missions, a Navigator for those in uncharted waters, and a Champion for those deserving recognition.

It's free, my gift to you.

https://TheCaptainsKeys.com/bonus

"These resources transformed my focus from my own success to becoming what others needed in their journey. That's when my real leadership impact began."
— AVERY T., CEO

CAPTAIN'S LOG

Chart your course forward

441

Reflections

Action Items

LEADERSHIP

EPILOGUE
YOUR JOURNEY BEGINS

The Stability Matrix isn't a destination. It's a journey that evolves throughout your leadership life.

Whether you're just beginning to build your support system or ready to become a Full Circle Leader, serving in roles for others, your next steps matter.

First Steps to Building Your Complete Support System

A perfect Stability Matrix isn't built in a day.
They're built through daily choices.
They expand, grow, change, and uplevel over time.

Start where you are, not where you think you should be. Honest assessment creates the foundation for everything that follows. To assist with this, I created the Leadership Connection Assessment. Access it here: https://TheCaptainsKeys.com/assessment

For the Matrix Beginner:

1. Complete the Leadership Connection Assessment to identify your current relationships and gaps.
2. Select your highest-priority quadrant gap – the relationship type whose absence is most limiting your leadership effectiveness.
3. Identify three potential candidates for this role in your existing network.
4. Schedule intentional conversations with each, focused on exploring mutual support rather than immediate needs.
5. Create a simple relationship development plan for your most promising connection.

For the Partial Matrix Builder:

1. Map your current matrix, noting both strengths and imbalances.
2. Identify quadrant redundancies and dependencies – where are you over-relying on a single relationship to fill multiple roles?
3. Create an action plan for underdeveloped relationships.
4. Schedule monthly matrix reviews to assess relationship health and evolution.
5. Begin by explicitly acknowledging the roles different people play in your leadership effectiveness.

For the Complete Matrix Builder:

1. Identify one person you could serve as an Anchor for in the coming month.
2. Look for opportunities to contribute as Crew outside your direct authority.
3. Offer Navigator perspective to one emerging leader in your network.
4. Actively Champion someone whose voice and contribution deserve greater recognition.
5. Begin teaching matrix concepts to your direct reports, helping them build their own support systems.

The journey begins with a single step – one conversation, one acknowledgment, one invitation to deeper connection.

Don't make this complicated. Don't wait for perfect clarity or perfect timing. Perfection is the enemy of progress when it comes to relationship building. Start small. Start imperfectly. Start today.

The most successful matrix builders aren't those with perfect plans. They're those who take imperfect action consistently. They are the leaders who make small investments daily rather than waiting for some "big moment." The savvy ones who understand that relationship development happens through accumulation, not epiphany.

What's one small step you can take today?

Not tomorrow.

Not next quarter.

Today.

Common Obstacles and How to Overcome Them

Four barriers consistently block matrix development. Recognizing them is the first step to overcoming them.

The Self-Sufficiency Trap – The belief that needing others is weakness rather than wisdom.

>**Symptoms:** Chronic overwork, decision fatigue, limited perspective
>**Solution:** Reframe support-seeking as a leadership strength. Start with small, low-risk requests for input.

The Transactional Mindset – Viewing relationships primarily as exchanges rather than partnerships.

>**Symptoms:** Contact limited to specific needs, resistance to vulnerability, relationship turnover
>**Solution:** Invest in relationship development separate from immediate needs. Create space for genuine connection.

The Homogeneity Bias – Gravitating toward relationships with people who think and act similarly.

>**Symptoms:** Blind spots, groupthink, limited innovation
>**Solution:** Intentionally develop relationships with people who bring different perspectives, backgrounds, and thinking styles.

The Crisis-Only Activation – Engaging support relationships only during difficulties rather than developing them continuously.

>**Symptoms:** Relationships that feel awkward or unreliable when needed most
>**Solution:** Create regular connection rhythms independent of specific needs. Invest before you need to withdraw.

These obstacles aren't just practical barriers. They're mindset limitations that require conscious reframing.

The strongest matrices emerge when we shift from viewing relationships as transactions to seeing them as transformations – ongoing partnerships that change both participants through mutual support and challenge.

Which of these barriers is currently limiting your matrix development? Be honest. Name it. Then take one small action to begin breaking through it today.

The barriers never completely disappear. They're hardwired into how we think about relationships and leadership. The goal isn't to eliminate them but to recognize and navigate them – to continuously choose connection over isolation, partnership over transaction, diversity over similarity.

That's the daily practice of matrix building. Not a one-time event but a continuous commitment to relationship over isolation.

In the online resources, you'll find The 90-Day Matrix Transformation Plan available at TheCaptainsKeys.com. My gift to you.

Significant relationship shifts don't happen overnight, but they can happen faster than you might think. A focused 90-day approach creates momentum that sustains longer-term development.

CAPTAIN TO CAPTAIN:

Ninety days from now, you'll wish you had started today. Unless you start today, then you'll wish you had started sooner. But either way, you'll be grateful you didn't wait until tomorrow.

YOUR LEADERSHIP LEGACY THROUGH RELATIONSHIPS

The greatest leaders aren't remembered primarily for what they achieved. They're remembered for who they developed. Not for the problems they solved, but for the people they transformed. Not for the organizations they built, but for the leaders they created.

Your most enduring impact won't be the products you launched, or the profits you generated, or the innovations you created. It will be the people who became more effective, more fulfilled, and more impactful because of their connection with you.

Think about that. Really think about it.

If your leadership legacy is determined primarily by your impact on others, shouldn't your leadership development focus primarily on relationship capacity rather than just technical skills or strategic thinking?

The Stability Matrix isn't just a framework for personal effectiveness. It's a blueprint for legacy leadership – for creating impact that extends far beyond your direct influence or tenure.

As a Full Circle Leader, you don't just receive support. You create support ecosystems that outlast your involvement. You don't just succeed. You create success conditions for generations of leaders who follow.

Legacy isn't what you leave behind when you're gone. It's what continues through others because you were here. It's not what people say about you. It's how they lead because of you.

What legacy are you creating today? Not years from now when you retire. Today. In how you support others. In how you serve. In how you show up in the four key roles for people who need exactly what you can provide.

Because here's the final truth about leadership matrices:

The strongest ones aren't built. They're grown.

Not through techniques or tactics or tools, though these help. But through consistent investment in others. Through genuine care for their development. Through the courage to both support and challenge. Through the wisdom to know which is needed when.

Full Circle Leaders understand that relationship matrices aren't just something they have. They're something they are.

Look at your calendar from last week.
Where did you serve as a Navigator?
Where did you provide an Anchor?
Where did you offer your strength as Crew?
Where did you open doors as Champion?

Your answer isn't just data.
It's destiny.

Not static structures, but living systems. Not leadership strategies, but leadership identities.

Is this the leader you want to become? Is this the legacy you want to leave?

If so, your journey as a Full Circle Leader begins today. Not with grand gestures or dramatic announcements. But with a single conversation. A single acknowledgment. A single step toward becoming for someone else what you needed most.

The sea ahead is vast. The challenges real. The journey long.

But you don't sail alone, Captain. And neither should anyone else.

The sea is waiting, Captain.
Not just for you to sail it.
But for you to help others navigate it.
Not just for you to survive its storms.
But for you to anchor others through them.

That's the final evolution.
From supported to supporter.
From matrix-builder to matrix-provider.
From successful leader to significant one.

The journey has just begun.

Becoming a Full Circle Leader begins with a single act of service.

What will yours be?

"ENJOY THE JOURNEY!"
— CAPTAIN JEFF

If this book was valuable for you, please tell a friend about it. Better yet, send them a copy. That is what a Champion would do. Letting them know you thought of them is guaranteed to start a conversation and deepen a relationship. Deep, authentic relationships are the ultimate goal of this book. Thank you for partnering with me to eliminate leadership isolation and create healthier, happier, more effective leaders.

https://TheCaptainsKeys.com/bonus

BERING STEEL

CONNECT WITH JEFF

You can connect with and follow Jeff across all social channels using @JeffKMains

Watch Jeff's video training and business scaling content on YouTube @ChampionLeadership

You can learn more about Jeff, plus send questions, comments, speaking, and interview requests at JeffMains.com

Grab a copy of Jeff's first bestselling book *Small Fish Big Pond: Building a World Class Business That Swims Circles Around Competitors.* Available in print, ebook, and audio. All book profits go to charity.

Ready to build a resilient leadership team and futureproof company that outperforms at every level? Visit ChampionLeadership.com

Bring The Stability Matrix™ To Your Organization

Leadership isolation affects teams at every level. Many organizations have found value in providing The Captain's Keys to their entire leadership team, creating a common language and framework for support.

For orders of 100+ books, we offer:

- Custom foreword addressing your organization's specific challenges
- Bulk pricing discounts
- Complimentary resources for implementation
- Optional author Q&A session

> *"Distributing The Captain's Keys across our leadership team created an immediate shift in how we support each other. The common language and framework have been invaluable."*
> —SARAH T., CHIEF PEOPLE OFFICER

Learn more: https://TheCaptainsKeys.com/corporate

Transform Your Leadership Culture

Beyond the book lies a complete leadership development system based on the Stability Matrix™ framework. Organizations worldwide are using these tools to create more resilient, connected leadership teams.

Our programs include:

- Half-day and full-day workshops
- Facilitator certification for internal trainers
- Custom assessment tools
- Ongoing implementation support

Learn more at https://TheCaptainsKeys.com/training

> *"We've tried many leadership frameworks over the years. The Stability Matrix is the only one that's created lasting change in how our leaders actually function, in good times and in unknown waters."*
> —MARK R., CEO

BIBLIOGRAPHY

Tough Convos. (2025, May 9). 2025 leadership insights from top business journals. https://www.toughconvos.com/post/2025-leadership-insights-from-top-business-journals

Hadley, C. N., & Wright, S. L. (2024, November–December). We're still lonely at work. Harvard Business Review. https://hbr.org/2024/11/were-still-lonely-at-work

Boston Consulting Group. (2024, June 11). Four keys to boosting inclusion and beating burnout. https://www.bcg.com/press/11june2024-half-of-workers-around-the-world-struggling-with-burnout

McKinsey & Company. (2024, October 30). The one thing leaders can count on in 2025? More uncertainty. LinkedIn. https://www.linkedin.com/posts/mckinsey_the-one-thing-leaders-can-count-on-in-2025-activity-7257466337034219523-Vrls

Hadley, C. N., & Wright, S. L. (2024, March 22). Fighting loneliness on remote teams. Harvard Business Review. https://hbr.org/2024/03/fighting-loneliness-on-remote-teams

Office presence fails to cure workplace loneliness – HBR study. (2024, October 30). Outsource Accelerator. https://news.outsourceaccelerator.com/office-presence-workplace-loneliness-hbr/

Marketplace Chaplains. (2024, December 9). Beyond the myths: How Marketplace Chaplains tackles workplace loneliness with lessons from Harvard Business Review. https://mchapusa.com/how-marketplace-chaplains-tackles-workplace-loneliness-with-lessons-from-harvard-business-review/

Integrated Benefits Institute. (2024, December 10). Loneliness in the workforce impacts performance, satisfaction, and turnover in the workplace. https://news.ibiweb.org/loneliness-in-the-workforce-impacts-performance-satisfaction-and-turnover-in-the-workplace-according-to-integrated-benefits-institute-analysis

Tingstad, E., Hegge, T. S., & Casoinic, D. (2024). CEOs' perceptions of loneliness in the workplace. Proceedings of the 20th European Conference on Management Leadership and Governance, ECMLG 2024. https://papers.academic-conferences.org/index.php/ecmlg/article/download/3009/2787/11298

Perceptyx. (2024). People leaders under pressure: New data on how to support managers.

Businessolver. (2024). State of workplace empathy study.

Gallup. (2024). State of the global workplace.

Russell Reynolds Associates. (2025). The transformation of the CEO.

Challenger, Gray & Christmas. (2025, April). Q1 sees record CEO turnover; March 2025 slows to 177 exits.

Kelemen, T., Matthews, M., Owens, B., & Matthews, S. (2025, January). Leader humility improves employee mental health. LSE Business Review.

UC San Diego. (2025). People Leader Network.

Knight, R. (2022, January 21). How leaders can build connection in a disconnected workplace. Harvard Business Review. https://hbr.org/2022/01/how-leaders-can-build-connection-in-a-disconnected-workplace

The Conference Board. (2022). CEO tenure and transition 2021.

McKinsey & Company. (2021). Leadership development interventions.

PwC. (2019). 2018 CEO success study. Strategy&.

Cross, R., Grant, A., Rebele, R., & Dillon, K. (2018, November 15). Survey: Remote workers are more disengaged and more likely to quit. Harvard Business Review. https://hbr.org/2018/11/survey-remote-workers-are-more-disengaged-and-more-likely-to-quit

Murthy, V. H. (2017, September). Work and the loneliness epidemic. Harvard Business Review. https://hbr.org/2017/09/work-and-the-loneliness-epidemic

Stanford Graduate School of Business. (2013). Executive coaching survey.

Aarons, G. A., Ehrhart, M. G., Farahnak, L. R., & Sklar, M. (2014). Aligning leadership across systems and organizations to develop a strategic climate for evidence-based practice implementation. Frontiers in Public Health, 2, 46. https://doi.org/10.3389/fpubh.2014.00046

Freeman, M. A., Staudenmaier, P. J., Zisser, M. R., & Andresen, L. A. (2015). Are entrepreneurs touched with fire? Small Business Economics, 45(2), 345–362. https://doi.org/10.1007/s11187-015-9636-z

Gallup. (2014). Wellbeing: The five essential elements. Gallup Press.

RHR International. (2012). CEO snapshot survey. Harvard Business Review.